C# Programmer's Cookbook

Allen Jones

PUBLISHED BY
Microsoft Press
A Division of Microsoft Corporation
One Microsoft Way
Redmond, Washington 98052-6399

Library of Congress Cataloging-in-Publication Data
Jones, Allen
   C# Programmer's Cookbook / Allen Jones.
     p. cm.
      Includes index.
      ISBN 0-7356-1930-1
      1. C# (Computer program language) I. Title.

        QA76.73.C154J64 2003
        005.13'3--dc22   2003058665

Printed and bound in the United States of America.

2 3 4 5 6 7 8 9   QWT   8 7 6 5

Distributed in Canada by H.B. Fenn and Company Ltd.

A CIP catalogue record for this book is available from the British Library.

Microsoft Press books are available through booksellers and distributors worldwide. For further information about international editions, contact your local Microsoft Corporation office or contact Microsoft Press International directly at fax (425) 936-7329. Visit our Web site at www.microsoft.com/mspress. Send comments to *mspinput@microsoft.com*.

Acquisitions Editor: Danielle Bird Voeller
Project Editors: Dick Brown and Denise Bankaitis
Technical Editor: Eric Dettinger
Body Part No. X10-08418

For Brenda

Table of Contents

Introduction

Mastering the development of Microsoft .NET Framework applications in C# is less about knowing the C# language and more about knowing how to use the functionality of the .NET Framework class library most effectively. The *C# Programmer's Cookbook* explores the breadth of the .NET Framework class library and provides specific solutions to common and interesting programming problems. Each solution (or recipe) is presented in a succinct problem/solution format and is accompanied by working code samples.

The *C# Programmer's Cookbook* is not intended to teach you how to program, nor to teach you C#. However, if you have even the most rudimentary experience programming applications built on the .NET Framework using C#, you will find this book to be an invaluable resource.

Ideally, when you are facing a problem, this book will contain a recipe that provides the solution—or at least it will point you in the right direction. Even if you are simply looking to broaden your knowledge of the .NET Framework class library, the *C# Programmer's Cookbook* is the perfect resource to assist you. You cannot become proficient with C# and the classes in the .NET Framework class library merely by reading about them; you must use them and experiment with them by writing programs, programs, and more programs. The structure and content of this book and the real-world applicability of the solutions it provides offer the perfect starting point from which to kick-start your own experimentation.

> **Note** The code in this book has been written for and tested on version 1.1 of the .NET Framework. In many cases, you will find that the sample code will run on version 1.0 of the .NET Framework, but this has not been tested and no guarantees are made.

Code Samples

The code for all recipes in the *C# Programmer's Cookbook* is available online at *http://microsoft.com/mspress/books/6456.asp*. To download the sample files, click the Companion Content link in the More Information menu on the right side of the page. This action loads the Companion Content page, which includes a link for downloading the sample files. To install the sample files, click the Download The Book's Sample Files link and follow the instructions in the setup program. A link to the sample code will be added to your Start menu.

The code is provided as a set of Visual Studio .NET 2003 solutions and projects organized by chapter and recipe number. Each chapter is a separate solution, and each recipe is a separate project within the chapter's solution. Some recipes in Chapter 11 and Chapter 12 that demonstrate network programming include separate projects that contain the client and server elements of the recipe's solution.

Although all samples are provided as Visual Studio .NET projects, most consist of a single source file that you can compile and run independent of Visual Studio .NET. If you are not using Visual Studio .NET 2003 you can locate the code for a particular recipe by navigating through the directory structure of the sample code. For example, to find the code for recipe 4.3, you would look up the code in the directory "Chapter04\Recipe04-03". If you use the command-line compiler, ensure that you include references to all required .NET class library assemblies.

Some of the sample applications require command-line arguments. Where required, the recipe's text will describe the arguments. If you are using Visual Studio .NET, you can enter these arguments in the project properties (under the Debugging node of the Configuration Properties item). Keep in mind that if you need to enter directory or file names that incorporate spaces, you will need to place the full name in quotation marks.

Some additional steps are required to install the two virtual directories used for the examples that accompany Chapter 7, "ASP.NET and Web Forms," and Chapter 12, "XML Web Services and Remoting." These steps are described in a readme.txt file provided with the downloaded code and on the code download page.

System Requirements

To run the sample code accompanying this book, you will need the following software:

- Microsoft .NET Framework SDK version 1.1

- Microsoft Visual Studio .NET 2003 (recommended)

- Microsoft Windows 2000, Windows XP, or Microsoft Windows Server 2003

- Microsoft SQL Server 2000 or MSDE for the recipes in Chapter 10

- Microsoft Internet Information Services (IIS) for some recipes in Chapter 7 and Chapter 12

The minimum hardware specification for development is a 450-MHz Pentium II-class processor, with a minimum of 128 MB of RAM if you're running Microsoft Windows 2000 and 256 MB of RAM if you're running Windows XP, Windows 2000 Server, or Windows Server 2003. You'll need about 5 GB of free hard-disk space to install Visual Studio .NET 2003. These values are minimums, and your development life will be much easier on a system with ample RAM and free disk space.

> **Note**   Although Microsoft's implementation of the .NET Framework for Windows is the focus of the *C# Programmer's Cookbook*, an important goal was to provide a useful resource to all C# programmers regardless of the platform on which they are developing or the tools to which they have access. Apart from specific topics that are not supported on all .NET platforms (such as Windows Forms, ADO.NET, and ASP.NET) many of the samples in this book are valid across all .NET implementations.

Other Books

If you have no programming experience, this book will not teach you how to program. Similarly, if you are a programmer but have little or no C# experience, this book does not provide the structure required to teach you how to program effectively in C#. Depending on your programming background and current level of C# knowledge, the following books can teach you enough about C#

and the .NET Framework to enable you to get the most from the solutions provided in this book:

- *Programming in the Key of C#: A Primer for Aspiring Programmers* (Microsoft Press, 2003) Charles Petzold.

- *Microsoft Visual C# .NET Step by Step Version 2003* (Microsoft Press, 2002) John Sharp and Jon Jagger.

- *Microsoft Visual C# .NET (Core Reference)* (Microsoft Press, 2002) Mickey Williams.

If you want to explore topics discussed in this book in more detail, or you want to understand more about the internal operation of the .NET Framework, I recommend the following books:

- *Inside C#, Second Edition* (Microsoft Press, 2002) Tom Archer and Andrew Whitechapel.

- *Applied Microsoft .NET Framework Programming* (Microsoft Press, 2002) Jeffrey Richter (Wintellect).

- *Essential .NET, Volume 1: The Common Language Runtime* (Addison-Wesley, 2002) Don Box and Chris Sells.

- *Programming Microsoft Windows with C#* (Microsoft Press, 2001) Charles Petzold.

- *Programming .NET Security* (O'Reilly & Associates, 2003) Adam Freeman and Allen Jones.

- *Microsoft ADO.NET (Core Reference)* (Microsoft Press, 2002) David Sceppa.

- *Advanced .NET Remoting* (Apress, 2002) Ingo Rammer.

Microsoft Press Support

Every effort has been made to ensure the accuracy of the book and its companion content. Microsoft also provides corrections for books through the World Wide Web at the following address:

http://www.microsoft.com/mspress/support/

If you have comments, questions, or ideas regarding the presentation or use of this book or the companion content, you can send them to Microsoft using either of the following methods:

Postal Mail:

Microsoft Press
ATTN: *C# Programmer's Cookbook* Editor
One Microsoft Way
Redmond, WA 98052-6399

E-Mail:

mspinput@microsoft.com

Please note that product support isn't offered through the above mail addresses. For support information regarding Visual Studio .NET 2003, go to *http://msdn.microsoft.com/vstudio/*. You can also call Standard Support at (425) 635-7011 weekdays between 6 A.M. and 6 P.M. Pacific time, or you can search Microsoft Product Support Services at *http://support.microsoft.com/support*.

1

Application Development

This chapter covers some of the fundamental activities you will need to perform during the development of your C# solutions. The recipes in this chapter describe how to

- Build Console and Windows Forms applications (recipes 1.1 and 1.2).

- Create and use code modules and libraries (recipes 1.3 and 1.4).

- Access command-line arguments from within your applications (recipe 1.5).

- Use compiler directives and attributes to selectively include code at build time (recipe 1.6).

- Access program elements built in other languages whose names conflict with C# keywords (recipe 1.7).

- Give assemblies strong names and verify strong-named assemblies (recipes 1.8, 1.9, 1.10, and 1.11).

- Sign an assembly with a Microsoft Authenticode digital signature (recipes 1.12 and 1.13).

- Manage the shared assemblies that are stored in the global assembly cache (recipe 1.14).

- Prevent people from decompiling your assembly (recipe 1.15).

> **Note**   All of the tools discussed in this chapter ship with the Microsoft .NET Framework or the .NET Framework SDK. Those tools that are part of the Framework are in the main directory for the version of the Framework that you are running. For example, they are in the directory C:\WINDOWS\Microsoft.NET\Framework\v1.1.4322 if you install version 1.1 of the .NET Framework to the default location. The .NET installation process automatically adds this directory to your environment path.
>
> The tools provided with the SDK are in the Bin subdirectory of the directory in which you install the SDK. This directory is *not* added to your path automatically, so you must manually edit your path in order to have easy access to these tools.
>
> Most of the tools support short and long forms of the command-line switches that control their functionality. This chapter always shows the long form, which is more informative but requires additional typing. For the shortened form of each switch, see the tool's documentation in the .NET Framework SDK.

1.1 Create a Console Application

Problem

You need to build an application that doesn't require a Windows graphical user interface (GUI) but instead displays output to, or reads input from, the Windows command prompt (console).

Solution

Ensure you implement a *static* method named *Main* with one of the following signatures in at least one of your source code files.

```
public static void Main();
public static void Main(string[] args);
public static int Main();
public static int Main(string[] args);
```

Use the */target:exe* switch on the C# compiler (csc.exe) when you compile your assembly.

Discussion

By default, the C# compiler will build a Console application unless you specify otherwise. For this reason, it's not necessary to specify the */target:exe* switch, but doing so makes your intention clearer, which is useful if you are creating build scripts that will be used by others or will be used repeatedly over a period of time. The following example lists a class named *ConsoleUtils* that is defined in a file named ConsoleUtils.cs:

```
using System;

public class ConsoleUtils {

    // A method to display a prompt and read a response from the console
    public static string ReadString(string msg) {

        Console.Write(msg);
        return System.Console.ReadLine();
    }

    // A method to display a message to the console
    public static void WriteString(string msg) {

        System.Console.WriteLine(msg);
    }

    // Main method used for testing ConsoleUtility methods
    public static void Main() {

        // Prompt the reader to enter their name
        string name = ReadString("Please enter your name : ");

        // Welcome the reader to the C# Cookbook
        WriteString("Welcome to the C# Programmer's Cookbook, " + name);
    }
}
```

To build the *ConsoleUtils* class into a Console application named Console-Utils.exe, use the command **csc /target:exe ConsoleUtils.cs**. You can run the resulting executable assembly directly from the command line. When run, the *Main* method of the ConsoleUtils.exe application prompts you for your name and then welcomes you to the *C# Programmer's Cookbook*, as shown here.

```
Please enter your name : Rupert
Welcome to the C# Programmer's Cookbook, Rupert
```

In reality, applications rarely consist of a single source file. As an example, the *HelloWorld* class listed here uses the *ConsoleUtils* class to display the message "Hello, world" to the console. (*HelloWorld* is contained in the HelloWorld.cs file.)

```
public class HelloWorld {

    public static void Main() {

        ConsoleUtils.WriteString("Hello, world");
    }
}
```

To build a Console application consisting of more than one source code file, you must specify all the source files as arguments to the compiler. For example, the following command builds an application named MyFirstApp.exe from the HelloWorld.cs and ConsoleUtils.cs source files.

```
csc /target:exe /main:HelloWorld
/out:MyFirstApp.exe HelloWorld.cs ConsoleUtils.cs
```

The */out* switch allows you to specify the name of the compiled assembly. Otherwise, the assembly is named after the first source file listed—HelloWorld.cs in the example. Because both the *HelloWorld* and *ConsoleUtils* classes contain *Main* methods, the compiler can't automatically determine which method represents the correct entry point for the assembly. You must use the compiler's */main* switch to identify the name of the class that contains the correct entry point for your application.

1.2 Create a Windows-Based Application

Problem

You need to build an application that provides a Windows Forms–based GUI.

Solution

Ensure you implement a *static* method named *Main* in at least one of your source code files. In the *Main* method, create an instance of a class that extends the *System.Windows.Forms.Form* class. (This is your application's main form.) Pass your main form object to the *static* method *Run* of the *System.Windows.Forms.Application* class. Use the */target:winexe* switch on the C# compiler (csc.exe) when you compile your assembly.

Discussion

Building an application that provides a simple Windows GUI is a world away from the development of a full-fledged Windows-based application. However, there are things you must do regardless of whether you are writing the Windows equivalent of Hello World or the next version of Microsoft Word, including the following:

- For each form you need in your application, create a class that extends the *System.Windows.Forms.Form* class.

- In each of your form classes, declare members that represent the controls that will be on that form, for example buttons, labels, lists, and text boxes. These members should be declared *private* or at least *protected* so that other program elements can't access them directly. If you need to expose the methods or properties of these controls, implement the necessary members in your form class, providing indirect and controlled access to the contained controls.

- Declare methods in your form class that will handle events raised by the controls contained by the form, such as button clicks or key presses when a text box is the active control. These methods should be *private* or *protected* and follow the standard .NET *event pattern* (described in recipe 16.10). It's in these methods (or methods called by these methods) where you will define the bulk of your application's functionality.

- Declare a constructor for your form class that instantiates each of the form's controls and configures their initial state (size, color, position, content, and so on). The constructor should also wire up the appropriate event handler methods of your class to the events of each control.

- Declare a *static* method named *Main*—usually as a member of your application's main form class. This method is the entry point for your application, and it can have the same signatures as those mentioned in recipe 1.1. In the *Main* method, create an instance of your application's main form and pass it as an argument to the *static Application.Run* method. The *Run* method makes your main form visible and starts a standard Windows message loop on the current thread, which passes the user input (key presses, mouse clicks, etc.) to your application as events.

The *WelcomeForm* class shown in the following code listing is a simple Windows Forms application that demonstrates the techniques just listed. When run, it prompts a user to enter a name and then displays a message box welcoming the user to the *C# Programmer's Cookbook*.

```csharp
using System.Windows.Forms;

public class WelcomeForm : Form {

    // Private members to hold references to the form's controls.
    private Label label1;
    private TextBox textBox1;
    private Button button1;

    // Constructor used to create an instance of the form and configure
    // the form's controls.
    public WelcomeForm() {

        // Instantiate the controls used on the form.
        this.label1 = new Label();
        this.textBox1 = new TextBox();
        this.button1 = new Button();

        // Suspend the layout logic of the form while we configure and
        // position the controls.
        this.SuspendLayout();

        // Configure label1, which displays the user prompt.
        this.label1.Location = new System.Drawing.Point(16, 36);
        this.label1.Name = "label1";
        this.label1.Size = new System.Drawing.Size(128, 16);
        this.label1.TabIndex = 0;
        this.label1.Text = "Please enter your name:";

        // Configure textBox1, which accepts the user input.
        this.textBox1.Location = new System.Drawing.Point(152, 32);
        this.textBox1.Name = "textBox1";
        this.textBox1.TabIndex = 1;
        this.textBox1.Text = "";

        // Configure button1, which the user presses to enter their name.
        this.button1.Location = new System.Drawing.Point(109, 80);
        this.button1.Name = "button1";
        this.button1.TabIndex = 2;
        this.button1.Text = "Enter";
        this.button1.Click += new System.EventHandler(this.button1_Click);
```

```
    // Configure WelcomeForm and add controls.
    this.ClientSize = new System.Drawing.Size(292, 126);
    this.Controls.Add(this.button1);
    this.Controls.Add(this.textBox1);
    this.Controls.Add(this.label1);
    this.Name = "form1";
    this.Text = "C# Programmer's Cookbook";

    // Resume the layout logic of the form now that all controls are
    // configured.
    this.ResumeLayout(false);
}

// Application entry point, creates an instance of the form, and begins
// running a standard message loop on the current thread. The message
// loop feeds the application with input from the user as events.
public static void Main() {

    Application.Run(new WelcomeForm());
}

// Event handler called when the user clicks the Enter button.
private void button1_Click(object sender, System.EventArgs e) {

    // Write debug message to the console
    System.Console.WriteLine("User entered: " + textBox1.Text);

    // Display welcome as a message box
    MessageBox.Show("Welcome to the C# Programmer's Cookbook, "
        + textBox1.Text, "C# Programmer's Cookbook");
}
}
```

To build the *WelcomeForm* class (contained in a file named Welcome-Form.cs) into an application, use the command **csc /target:winexe Welcome-Form.cs**. The */target:winexe* switch tells the compiler that you are building a Windows-based application. As a result, the compiler builds the executable in such a way that no console is created when you run your application. If you use the */target:exe* switch to build a Windows Forms application instead of */target:winexe*, your application will still work correctly, but you will have a Console window visible while the application is running. Although this is undesirable for production quality software, the Console window is useful if you want to write debug and logging information while you're developing and testing your Windows Forms application. You can write to this console using the *Write* and *WriteLine* methods of the *System.Console* class.

Figure 1-1 shows the WelcomeForm.exe application in operation greeting a user named Rupert. This version of the application is built using the */target:exe* compiler switch, resulting in the visible Console window in which you can see the output from the *Console.WriteLine* statement in the *button1_Click* event handler.

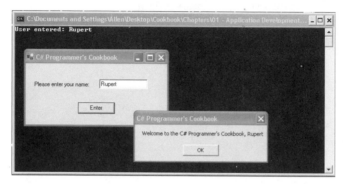

Figure 1-1   A simple Windows Forms application.

> **Note**   Building large GUI-based applications is a time consuming undertaking that involves the correct instantiation, configuration, and wiring up of many forms and controls. Microsoft Visual Studio .NET automates much of the work associated with building graphical applications. Trying to build a large graphical application without the aid of tools like Visual Studio .NET will take you much longer, be extremely tedious, and result in a greater chance of bugs in your code.

1.3 Create and Use a Code Module

Problem

You need to do one or more of the following:

- Improve your application's performance and memory efficiency by ensuring the runtime loads rarely used types only when they are required.

- Compile types written in C# to a form you can build into applications written in other .NET languages.

- Use types developed in another language from within your C# application.

Solution

Build your C# source code into a module using the */target:module* compiler switch. To incorporate existing modules into your assembly, use the */addmodule* compiler switch.

Discussion

Modules are the building blocks of .NET assemblies. Modules consist of a single file that contains the following:

■   Microsoft Intermediate Language (MSIL) code created from your C# source code during compilation

■   Metadata describing the types contained in the module

■   Resources, such as icons and string tables, used by the types in the module

Assemblies consist of one or more modules and an assembly manifest. When there is a single module, the module and assembly manifest are usually built into a single file for convenience. When there is more than one module, the assembly represents a logical grouping of more than one file that you must deploy as a complete unit. In these situations, the assembly manifest is either contained in a separate file or built into one of the modules.

By building an assembly from multiple modules, you complicate the management and deployment of the assembly, but under some circumstances, modules offer significant benefits, including:

■   The runtime will load a module only when the types defined in the module are required. Therefore, where you have a set of types that your application uses rarely, you can partition them into a separate module that the runtime will load only if necessary. This offers the following benefits:

❑   Improved performance, especially if your application is loaded across a network.

❑   Minimizing the use of memory.

■   The ability to use many different languages to write applications that run on the common language runtime (CLR) is a great strength of the .NET Framework. However, the C# compiler can't compile your Microsoft Visual Basic .NET or COBOL .NET code for inclusion in your assembly. You must first use a language-specific compiler to turn your source into MSIL in a structure that the C# compiler can incorporate—a module. Likewise, if you want to allow programmers of other languages to use the types you develop in C#, you must build them into a module.

To compile a source file named ConsoleUtils.cs into a module use the command **csc /target:module ConsoleUtils.cs**. The result is the creation of a file named ConsoleUtils.netmodule. The netmodule extension is the default extension for modules, and the file name is the same as the name of the C# source file.

You can also build modules from multiple source files, which results in a single file (module) containing the MSIL and metadata for all types contained in all the source files. The command **csc /target:module ConsoleUtils.cs WindowsUtils.cs** compiles two source files named ConsoleUtils.cs and Windows-Utils.cs to create the module named ConsoleUtils.netmodule. The module is named after the first source file listed unless you override the name with the */out* compiler switch. For example, the command **csc /target:module /out:Utilities.netmodule ConsoleUtils.cs WindowsUtils.cs** creates a module named Utilities.netmodule.

To build an assembly consisting of multiple modules, you must use the */addmodule* compiler switch. To build an executable named MyFirstApp.exe from two modules named WindowsUtils.netmodule and ConsoleUtils.netmodule and two source files named SourceOne.cs and SourceTwo.cs, use the command **csc /out:MyFirstApp.exe /target:exe /addmodule:WindowsUtils .netmodule,ConsoleUtils.netmodule SourceOne.cs SourceTwo.cs**. This command will result in an assembly consisting of the following files:

- MyFirstApp.exe, which contains the assembly manifest as well as the MSIL for the types declared in the SourceOne.cs and SourceTwo source files.

- ConsoleUtils.netmodule and WindowsUtils.netmodule, which are now integral components of the multi-file assembly but are unchanged by this compilation process. (If you attempt to run MyFirstApp.exe without the netmodules present, a *System.IO.FileNotFoundException* is thrown.)

1.4 Create and Use a Code Library

Problem

You need to build a set of functionality into a reusable code library so that it can be referenced and reused by multiple applications.

Solution

To create the library, use the *target:library* switch on the C# compiler (csc.exe) when you compile your assembly. To reference the library, use the */reference* switch on the C# compiler and specify the names of the required libraries when you compile your application.

Discussion

Recipe 1.1 showed you how to build an application named MyFirstApp.exe from the two source files ConsoleUtils.cs and HelloWorld.cs. The Console-Utils.cs file contains the *ConsoleUtils* class, which provides methods to simplify interaction with the Windows console. If you were to extend the functionality of the *ConsoleUtils* class, it could contain functionality useful to many applications. Instead of including the source code for *ConsoleUtils* in every application, you can build it into a library and deploy it independently, making the functionality accessible to many applications.

To build the ConsoleUtils.cs file into a library, use the command **csc /target:library ConsoleUtils.cs**. This will produce a library file named Console-Utils.dll. To build a library from multiple source files, list the name of each file at the end of the command. You can also specify the name of the library using the */out* compiler switch; otherwise, the library is named after the first source file listed. For example, to build a library named MyFirstLibrary.dll from two source files named ConsoleUtils.cs and WindowsUtils.cs, use the command **csc /out:MyFirstLibrary.dll /target:library ConsoleUtils.cs WindowsUtils.cs**.

Before distributing your library, you might consider strong naming it so that nobody can modify your assembly and pass it off as being the original. Strong naming your library also allows people to install it into the global assembly cache, which makes reuse much easier. (Recipe 1.9 describes how to strong name your assembly and recipe 1.14 describes how to install a strong-named assembly into the global assembly cache.) You might also consider signing your library with an Authenticode signature, which allows users to confirm that you are the publisher of the assembly—see recipe 1.12 for details on signing assemblies with Authenticode.

To compile an assembly that relies on types declared within external libraries, you must tell the compiler which libraries are referenced using the */reference* compiler switch. For example, to compile the HelloWorld.cs source file (from recipe 1.1) if the ConsoleUtils class is contained in the Console-Utils.dll library, use the command **csc /reference:ConsoleUtils.dll HelloWorld.cs**. Three points worth remembering are

- If you reference more than one library, separate each library name with a comma or semicolon, but no spaces. For example, **/reference:ConsoleUtils.dll,WindowsUtils.dll**.

- If the libraries aren't in the same directory as the source code, use the */lib* switch on the compiler to specify the additional directories where the compiler should look for libraries. For example, **/lib:c:\CommonLibraries,c:\Dev\ThirdPartyLibs**.

- If the library you need to reference is a multi-file assembly, reference the file that contains the assembly manifest. (For information about multi-file assemblies, see recipe 1.3.)

1.5 Access Command-Line Arguments

Problem

You need to access the arguments that were specified on the command line when your application was executed.

Solution

Use a signature for your *Main* method that exposes the command-line arguments as a *string* array. Alternatively, access the command-line arguments from anywhere in your code using the *static* members of the *System.Environment* class.

Discussion

Declaring your application's *Main* method with one of the following signatures provides access to the command-line arguments as a *string* array.

```
public static void Main(string[] args) {}
public static int Main(string[] args) {}
```

At run time, the *args* argument will contain a string for each value entered on the command line after your application's name. To demonstrate this, the *Main* method in the following example steps through each of the command-line arguments passed to it and displays them to the console.

```
public class CmdLineArgExample {

    public static void Main(string[] args) {

        // Step through the command-line arguments
        foreach (string s in args) {
            System.Console.WriteLine(s);
        }
    }
}
```

It's important to understand how the arguments are passed to the application. If you execute the *CmdLineArgExample* using the following command:

```
CmdLineArgExample "one \"two\"    three" four 'five    six'
```

the application will generate the following output on the console:

```
one "two"    three
four
'five
six'
```

Notice that unlike C and C++, the application's name is not included in the array of arguments. Also notice that the use of double quotes (") results in more than one word being treated as a single argument, although single quotes (') do not. You can include double quotes in an argument by escaping them with the backslash character (\). Finally, notice that all spaces are stripped from the command line unless they are enclosed in double quotes.

If you need access to the command-line arguments at places in your code other than the *Main* method, you can process the command-line arguments in your *Main* method and store them for later access. Alternatively, you can use the *System.Environment* class, which provides two *static* members that return information about the command line: *CommandLine* and *GetCommandLine-Args*. The *CommandLine* property returns a *string* containing the full command line that launched the current process. Depending on the operating system on which the application is running, path information might precede the application name. Microsoft Windows NT 4.0, Windows 2000, and Windows XP don't include path information, whereas Windows 98 and Windows ME do. The *Get-CommandLineArgs* method returns a *string* array containing the command-line arguments. This array can be processed in the same way as the *string* array passed to the *Main* method, as discussed at the start of this section. Unlike the array passed to the *Main* method, the first element in the array returned by the *GetCommandLineArgs* method is the name of the application.

1.6 Selectively Include Code at Build Time

Problem

You need to selectively include and exclude sections of source code from your compiled assembly.

Solution

Use the *#if*, *#elif*, *#else*, and *#endif* preprocessor directives to identify blocks of code that should be conditionally included in your compiled assembly. Use the *System.Diagnostics.ConditionalAttribute* attribute to define methods that should only be called conditionally. Control the inclusion of the conditional code using the *#define* and *#undef* directives in your code, or use the */define* switch when you run the C# compiler.

Discussion

If you need your application to function differently depending on factors such as the platform or environment on which it runs, you can build run-time checks into the logic of your code that trigger the variations in operation. However, such an approach can bloat your code and affect performance, especially if there are many variations to support or many locations where evaluations need to be made. An alternative approach is to build multiple versions of your application to support the different target platforms and environments. Although this approach overcomes the problems of code bloat and performance degradation, it would be an untenable solution if you had to maintain different source code for each version, so C# provides features that allow you to build customized versions of your application from a single code base.

The *#if*, *#elif*, *#else*, and *#endif* preprocessor directives allow you to identify blocks of code that the compiler should include in your assembly only if specified symbols are defined at compile time. Symbols function as on/off switches; they don't have values—either the symbol is defined, or it is not. To define a symbol you can use either the *#define* directive in your code or use the */define* compiler switch. Symbols defined using *#define* are active until the end of the file in which they are defined. Symbols defined using the */define* compiler switch are active in all source files that are being compiled. To undefine a symbol defined using the */define* compiler switch, C# provides the *#undef* directive, which is useful if you want to ensure a symbol is not defined in specific source files. All *#define* and *#undef* directives must appear at the top of your source file before any code, including any *using* directives. Symbols are case sensitive.

In this example, the code assigns a different value to the local variable *platformName* based on whether the *winXP, win2000, winNT,* or *Win98* symbols are defined. The head of the code defines the symbols *win2000* and *release* (not used in this example) and undefines the *win98* symbol in case it was defined on the compiler command line.

```
#define win2000
#define release
#undef  win98

using System;

public class ConditionalExample {

    public static void Main() {

        // Declare a string to contain the platform name
        string platformName;

        #if winXP        // Compiling for Windows XP
            platformName = "Microsoft Windows XP";
        #elif win2000    // Compiling for Windows 2000
            platformName = "Microsoft Windows 2000";
        #elif winNT      // Compiling for Windows NT
            platformName = "Microsoft Windows NT";
        #elif win98      // Compiling for Windows 98
            platformName = "Microsoft Windows 98";
        #else            // Unknown platform specified
            platformName - "Unknown";
        #endif

        Console.WriteLine(platformName);
    }
}
```

To build the *ConditionalExample* class (contained in a file named ConditionalExample.cs) and define the symbols *winXP* and *DEBUG* (not used in this example), use the command **csc /define:winXP;DEBUG ConditionalExample.cs**.

The *#if .. #endif* construct evaluates *#if* and *#elif* clauses only until it finds one that evaluates to true, meaning that if you define multiple symbols (*winXP* and *win2000,* for example), the order of your clauses is important. The compiler includes only the code in the clause that evaluates to true. If no clause evaluates to true, the compiler includes the code in the *#else* clause.

You can also use logical operators to base conditional compilation on more than one symbol. Table 1-1 summarizes the supported operators.

Table 1-1   Logical Operators Supported by the *#if..#endif* Directive

Operator	Example	Description
==	*#if winXP == true*	Equality. Evaluates to true if the symbol *winXP* is defined. Equivalent to *#if winXP*.
!=	*#if winXP != true*	Inequality. Evaluates to true if the symbol *winXP* is *not* defined. Equivalent to *#if !winXP*.
&&	*#if winXP && release*	Logical AND. Evaluates to true only if the symbols *winXP* AND *release* are defined.
||	*#if winXP || release*	Logical OR. Evaluates to true if either of the symbols *winXP* OR *release* are defined.
()	*#if (winXP || win2000) && release*	Parentheses allow you to group expressions. Evaluates to true if the symbols *winXP* OR *win2000* are defined AND the symbol *release* is defined.

> **Warning**   You must be careful not to overuse conditional compilation directives and not to make your conditional expressions too complex; otherwise, your code can quickly become confusing and unmanageable—especially as your projects become larger.

A less flexible but more elegant alternative to the *#if* preprocessor directive is the attribute *System.Diagnostics.ConditionalAttribute*. If you apply *ConditionalAttribute* to a method, the compiler will ignore any calls to the method if the symbol specified by *ConditionalAttribute* is not defined at the calling point. In the following code, *ConditionalAttribute* specifies that calls to the *DumpState* method should be included in a compiled assembly only if the symbol *DEBUG* is defined during compilation.

```
[System.Diagnostics.Conditional("DEBUG")]
public static void DumpState() {//…}
```

Use of *ConditionalAttribute* centralizes your conditional compilation logic on the method declaration and means that you can freely include calls to conditional methods without the need to litter your code with *#if* directives. However, because the compiler literally removes calls to the conditional method from your code, your code can't have dependencies on return values from the conditional method. This means that you can apply *ConditionalAttribute* only to methods that return *void*.

You can apply multiple *ConditionalAttribute* instances to a method in order to produce logical OR behavior. Calls to the following version of the *DumpState* method will be compiled only if the *DEBUG* OR *TEST* symbols are defined.

```
[System.Diagnostics.Conditional("DEBUG")]
[System.Diagnostics.Conditional("TEST")]
public static void DumpState() {//…}
```

Achieving logical AND behavior is not as clean and involves the use of an intermediate conditional method, quickly leading to overly complex code that is hard to understand and maintain. Here is a quick example that requires definition of both the *DEBUG* AND *TEST* symbols for the *DumpState* functionality (contained in *DumpState2*) to be called.

```
[System.Diagnostics.Conditional("DEBUG")]
public static void DumpState() {
    DumpState2();
}

[System.Diagnostics.Conditional("TEST")]
public static void DumpState2() {//…}
```

> **Note**   The *Debug* and *Trace* classes from the *System.Diagnostics* namespace use *ConditionalAttribute* on many of their methods. The methods of the *Debug* class are conditional on the definition of the symbol *DEBUG*, and the methods of the *Trace* class are conditional on the definition of the symbol *TRACE*.

1.7 Access a Program Element That Has the Same Name as a Keyword

Problem

You need to access a member of a type, but the type or member name is the same as a C# keyword.

Solution

Prefix all instances of the identifier name in your code with the at sign (@).

Discussion

The .Net Framework allows you to use software components developed in other .NET languages from within your C# applications. Each language has its own set of keywords (or reserved words) and imposes different restrictions on the names that programmers can assign to program elements such as types, members, and variables. Therefore, it's possible that a programmer developing a component in another language will inadvertently use a C# keyword as the name of a program element. The symbol @ enables you to use a C# keyword as an identifier and overcome these possible naming conflicts. This code fragment instantiates an object of type *operator* (perhaps a telephone operator) and sets its *volatile* property to *true*—both *operator* and *volatile* are C# key words.

```
// Instantiate an operator object
@operator Operator1 = new @operator();

// Set the operator's volatile property
Operator1.@volatile = true;
```

1.8 Create and Manage Strong-Named Key Pairs

Problem

You need to create public and private keys (a key pair) so that you can assign strong names to your assemblies.

Solution

Use the Strong Name tool (sn.exe) to generate a key pair and store them in a file or cryptographic service provider (CSP) key container.

> **Note**   A cryptographic service provider (CSP) is an element of the Win32 CryptoAPI that provides services such as encryption, decryption, and digital signature generation. CSPs also provide key container facilities, which use strong encryption and operating system security to protect the container's contents. A discussion of CSPs and CryptoAPI is beyond the scope of this book. Refer to the CryptoAPI information in the platform SDK documentation for complete details.

Discussion

To generate a new key pair and store them in the file named MyKeys.snk, execute the command **sn -k MyKeys.snk.** (.snk is the usual extension given to files containing strong name keys.) The generated file contains both your public and private keys. You can view the public key using the command **sn -tp MyKeys.snk**, which will generate output similar to the (abbreviated) listing shown here.

```
Microsoft (R) .NET Framework Strong Name Utility  Version 1.1.4322.573
Copyright (C) Microsoft Corporation 1998-2002. All rights reserved.

Public key is
0702000000240000525341320004000001000100020b4e13c2bbd6470002b64d0dd3f2c7c66uu;<$V
[>
6478802b63cb894a782f3a1adbb46d3ee5ec5577e7dccc818937e964cbe997c12076c19f2d7
ad179f15f7dccca6c6b72a


Public key token is 2a1d3326445fc02a
```

The public key token shown at the end of the listing is the last 8 bytes of a cryptographic hash code computed from the public key. Because the public key is so long, .NET uses the public key token for display purposes and as a compact mechanism for other assemblies to reference your public key. (Chapter 14 includes a general discussion of cryptographic hash codes.)

As the name suggests, you don't need to keep the public key (or public key token) secret. When you strong name your assembly (discussed in recipe 1.9), the compiler uses your private key to generate a digital signature (an encrypted hash code) of the assembly's manifest. The compiler embeds the digital signature and your public key in the assembly so that any consumer of the assembly can verify the digital signature.

Keeping your private key secret is imperative. People with access to your private key can alter your assembly and create a new strong name—leaving your customers unaware that they are using modified code. There's no mechanism to repudiate compromised strong name keys. If your private key is compromised, you must generate new keys and distribute new versions of your assemblies that are strong named using the new keys. You must also notify your customers about the compromised keys and explain to them which versions of your public key to trust—in all, a very costly exercise in terms of both money and credibility. There are many ways to protect your private key; the approach you use will depend on factors such as

- The structure and size of your organization.

- Your development and release process.

- The software and hardware resources you have available.

- The requirements of your customer base.

> **Tip** Commonly, a small group of trusted individuals (the *signing authority*) has responsibility for the security of your company's strong name signing keys and is responsible for signing all assemblies just prior to their final release. The ability to delay sign an assembly (discussed in recipe 1.11) facilitates this model and avoids the need to distribute private keys to all development team members.

One feature provided by the Strong Name tool to simplify the security of strong name keys is the use of CSP key containers. Once you have generated a key pair to a file, you can install the keys into a key container and delete the file. For example, to store the key pair contained in the file MyKeys.snk to a CSP container named StrongNameKeys, use the command **sn -i MyKeys.snk StrongNameKeys**. (Recipe 1.9 explains how to use strong name keys stored in a CSP key container.)

An important aspect of CSP key containers is the fact that there are user-based containers and machine-based containers. Windows security ensures each user can access only their own user-based key containers. However, any user of a machine can access a machine-based container.

By default, the Strong Name tool uses machine-based key containers, meaning that anybody who can log on to your machine and who knows the name of your key container can sign an assembly with your strong name keys. To change the Strong Name tool to use user-based containers, use the command **sn -m n**, and to change back to machine-based stores, use the command **sn -m y**. The command **sn -m** will display whether the Strong Name tool is currently configured to use machine-based or user-based containers.

To delete the strong name keys from the StrongNameKeys container (as well as the container), use the command **sn -d StrongNameKeys**.

1.9 Give an Assembly a Strong Name

Problem

You need to give an assembly a strong name so that it

- Has a unique identity, which allows people to assign specific permissions to the assembly when configuring code access security policy.

- Can't be modified and passed off as your original assembly.

- Supports versioning and version policy.

- Can be shared across multiple applications, and installed in the global assembly cache (GAC).

Solution

Use assembly-level attributes to specify the location of your strong name key pair and optionally a version number and culture for your assembly. The compiler will strong name your assembly as part of the build process.

Discussion

To strong name an assembly using the C# compiler, you need the following:

- A strong name key pair contained either in a file or in a CSP key container. (Recipe 1.8 discusses the creation of strong name key pairs.)

- To use assembly-level attributes to specify the location where the compiler can obtain your strong name key pair.

  - ❑ If your key pair is in a file, apply the attribute *System.Reflection.AssemblyKeyFileAttribute* to your assembly and specify the name of the file that contains the keys.

  - ❑ If your key pair is in a CSP container, apply the attribute *System.Reflection.AssemblyKeyNameAttribute* to your assembly and specify the name of the container in which the keys are stored.

  Optionally, you can also

- Specify the culture that your assembly supports by applying the attribute *System.Reflection.AssemblyCultureAttribute* to the assembly. (You can't specify a culture for executable assemblies because executable assemblies support only the neutral culture.)

- Specify the version of your assembly by applying the attribute *System.Reflection.AssemblyVersionAttribute* to the assembly.

The code that follows (from a file named HelloWorld.cs) shows the use of attributes (shown in boldface text) to specify the keys, the culture, and the version for the assembly.

```
using System;
using System.Reflection;

[assembly:AssemblyKeyName("MyKeys")]
[assembly:AssemblyCulture("")]
[assembly:AssemblyVersion("1.0.0.0")]

public class HelloWorld {

    public static void Main() {

        Console.WriteLine("Hello, world");
    }
}
```

To create a strong-named assembly from the example code, create the strong name keys and store them in a file named MyKeyFile using the command **sn -k MyKeyFile.snk**. Then install the keys into the CSP container named MyKeys using the command **sn -i MyKeyFile.snk MyKeys**. You can now compile the HelloWorld.cs file into a strong-named assembly using the command **csc HelloWorld.cs**.

Note   You can also build strong-named assemblies using the Assembly Linker (al.exe), which allows you to specify the strong name information on the command line instead of using attributes in your code. This is useful when you don't want to embed the strong name attributes in your source file and when you use scripts to build large source trees. Refer to the Assembly Linker information in the .NET Framework SDK documentation for more details.

1.10 Verify That a Strong-Named Assembly Has Not Been Modified

Problem

You need to verify that a strong-named assembly has not been modified after it was built.

Solution

Use the Strong Name tool (sn.exe) to verify the assembly's strong name.

Discussion

Whenever the .NET runtime loads a strong-named assembly, the runtime extracts the encrypted hash code that's embedded in the assembly and decrypts it with the public key, which is also embedded in the assembly. The runtime then calculates the hash code of the assembly manifest and compares it to the decrypted hash code. This verification process will identify if the assembly has changed after compilation.

If an executable assembly fails strong name verification, the runtime will display the dialog box shown in Figure 1-2. If code tries to load an assembly that fails verification, the runtime will throw a *System.IO.FileLoadException* with the message "Strong name validation failed."

Figure 1-2   Error shown when you try to execute a strong-named assembly that has been modified.

As well as the generation and management of strong name keys (discussed in recipe 1.8), the Strong Name tool allows you to verify strong-named assemblies. To verify that the strong-named assembly HelloWorld.exe is unchanged, use the command **sn -vf HelloWorld.exe**. The *-v* switch requests the Strong Name tool to verify the strong name of the specified assembly, and the *-f* switch forces strong name verification even if it has been previously disabled for the specified assembly. (You can disable strong name verification for specific assemblies using the *-Vr* switch, as in **sn -Vr HelloWorld.exe**; see recipe 1.11 for details about why you would disable strong name verification.)

If the assembly passes strong name verification, you will see the following output:

```
Microsoft (R) .NET Framework Strong Name Utility  Version 1.1.4322.573
Copyright (C) Microsoft Corporation 1998-2002. All rights reserved.

Assembly 'HelloWorld.exe' is valid
```

However, if the assembly has been modified, you will see the message

```
Microsoft (R) .NET Framework Strong Name Utility  Version 1.1.4322.573
Copyright (C) Microsoft Corporation 1998-2002. All rights reserved.

Failed to verify assembly -- Unable to format error message 8013141A
```

1.11 Delay Sign an Assembly

Problem

You need to create a strong-named assembly, but you don't want to give all members of your development team access to the private key component of your strong name key pair.

Solution

Extract and distribute the public key component of your strong name key pair. Follow the instructions in recipe 1.9 that describe how to give your assembly a strong name. In addition, apply the attribute *System.Reflection.AssemblyDelay-SignAttribute* to your assembly to identify it as a delay-signed assembly. Disable strong name verification for the assembly using the *-Vr* switch of the Strong Name tool (sn.exe).

Discussion

Assemblies that reference strong-named assemblies contain the public key token of the referenced assemblies. This means that the referenced assembly must be strong named before it can be referenced. In a development environment in which assemblies are regularly rebuilt, this would require every developer and tester to have access to your strong name key pair—a major security risk.

Instead of distributing the private key component of your strong name key pair to all members of the development team, the .NET Framework provides a mechanism named *delay signing* with which you can partially strong name an assembly. The partially strong-named assembly contains the public key and the public key token (required by referencing assemblies), but contains only a placeholder for the signature that would normally be generated using the private key.

After development is complete, the signing authority (who has responsibility for the security and use of your strong name key pair) re-signs the delay-signed assembly to complete its strong name. The signature is calculated using the private key and embedded in the assembly, making the assembly ready for distribution.

To delay sign an assembly, you need access only to the public key component of your strong name key pair. There's no security risk associated with distributing the public key, and the signing authority should make the public key freely available to all developers. To extract the public key component from a strong name key file named MyKeys.snk and write it to a file named MyPublicKey.snk, use the command **sn -p MyKeys.snk MyPublicKey.snk**. If you store your strong name key pair in a CSP key container named MyKeys, extract the public key to a file named MyPublicKey.snk using the command **sn -pc MyKeys MyPublicKey.snk**.

The same attributes discussed in recipe 1.9 are used to declare the version and culture of the assembly, as well as the location of the public key. You must also apply the attribute *AssemblyDelaySign(true)* to your assembly, which tells the compiler that you want to delay sign the assembly. The following code highlights the attributes you would use to delay sign the assembly, in a situation where the public key is in a file named MyPublicKey.snk.

```
using System;
using System.Reflection;

[assembly:AssemblyKeyFile("MyPublicKey.snk")]
[assembly:AssemblyCulture("")]
[assembly:AssemblyVersion("1.0.0.0")]
[assembly:AssemblyDelaySign(true)]

public class HelloWorld {

    public static void Main() {

        Console.WriteLine("Hello, world");
    }
}
```

When the runtime tries to load a delay-signed assembly, the runtime will identify the assembly as strong-named and will attempt to verify the assembly, as discussed in recipe 1.10. Because there's no digital signature, you must disable the runtime from verifying the assembly's strong name using the command **sn -Vr HelloWorld.exe**.

Once development is complete, you need to re-sign the assembly to complete the assembly's strong name. The Strong Name tool allows you to do this without the need to change your source code or to recompile the assembly; however, you must have access to the private key component of the strong name key pair. To re-sign an assembly named HelloWorld.exe with a key pair contained in the file MyKeys.snk, use the command **sn -R HelloWorld.exe MyKeys.snk**. If the keys are stored in a CSP key container named MyKeys, use the command **sn -Rc HelloWorld.exe MyKeys**.

Once you have re-signed the assembly, you should turn strong name verification for that assembly back on using the *–Vu* switch of the Strong Name tool, as in **sn -Vu HelloWorld.exe**. To enable verification for *all* assemblies for which you have disabled strong name verification, use the command **sn -Vx**. You can list the assemblies for which verification is disabled using the command **sn -Vl**.

> **Note**   When using delay-signed assemblies, it's often useful to be able to compare different builds of the same assembly to ensure they differ only by their signatures. This is only possible if a delay-signed assembly has been re-signed using the *-R* switch of the Strong Name tool. To compare the two assemblies, use the command **sn -D assembly1 assembly2**.

1.12 Sign an Assembly with an Authenticode Digital Signature

Problem

You need to sign an assembly with Authenticode so that users of the assembly can be certain that you are its publisher and that the assembly is unchanged after signing.

Solution

Use the File Signing tool (signcode.exe) to sign the assembly with your Software Publisher Certificate (SPC).

Discussion

Strong names provide a unique identity for an assembly as well as proof of the assembly's integrity, but they provide no proof as to the publisher of the assembly. The .NET Framework allows you to use Authenticode technology to sign your assemblies. This enables consumers of your assemblies to confirm that you are the publisher, as well as confirm the integrity of the assembly. Authenticode signatures also act as evidence for the signed assembly, which people can use when configuring code access security policy. (Assembly evidence is discussed in recipes 13.9 and 13.10.)

To sign your assembly with an Authenticode signature, you need an SPC issued by a recognized *certificate authority* (CA). A CA is a company entrusted to issue SPCs (along with many other types of certificates) for use by individuals or companies. Before issuing a certificate, the CA is responsible for confirming that the requesters are who they claim to be and also making sure the requestors sign contracts to ensure they don't misuse the certificates that the CA issues them.

To obtain an SPC, you should view the list of Microsoft Root Certificate Program Members at *http://msdn.microsoft.com/library/default.asp?url=/library /en-us/dnsecure/html/rootcertprog.asp*. Here you will find a list of CAs, many of whom can issue you an SPC. For testing purposes, you can create a test SPC using the process described in recipe 1.13. However, you can't distribute your software signed with this test certificate. Because a test SPC isn't issued by a trusted CA, most responsible users won't trust assemblies signed with it.

Once you have an SPC, you use the File Signing tool to sign your assembly. The File Signing tool creates a digital signature of the assembly using the private key component of your SPC and embeds the signature and the public part of your SPC into your assembly (including your public key). When verifying your assembly, the consumer decrypts the encrypted hash code using your public key, recalculates the hash of the assembly, and compares the two hash codes to ensure they are the same. As long as the two hash codes match, the consumer can be certain that you signed the assembly, and that it has not changed since you signed it.

To Authenticode sign an assembly named MyAssembly.exe with an SPC contained in a file named MyCert.spc and a private key contained in a file named MyPrivateKey.pvk, use the command **signcode -spc MyCert.spc -v MyPrivateKey.pvk MyAssembly.exe**. In this instance, the File Signing tool will display the dialog box shown in Figure 1-3, prompting you for the password used to protect the private key stored in the MyPrivateKey.pvk file.

Figure 1-3   File Signing tool requests a password when accessing file-based private keys.

You can also access keys and certificates contained in key and certificate stores. Table 1-2 lists the most commonly used switches of the File Signing tool. Refer to the .NET Framework SDK documentation for a complete listing.

Table 1-2 Commonly Used Switches of the File Signing Tool

Switch	Description
-k	Specifies the name of the CSP key container where your SPC private key is stored
-s	Specifies the name of the certificate store where your SPC is stored
-spc	Specifies the name of the file that contains your SPC
-v	Specifies the name of the file that contains your SPC private key

If you are signing a multi-file assembly, specify the name of the file that contains the assembly manifest. If you intend to both strong name and Authenticode sign your assembly, you must strong name the assembly first—see recipe 1.9 for details on strong naming assemblies.

To check the validity of a file signed with an Authenticode signature, use the Certificate Verification tool (chktrust.exe). For example, to test MyAssembly.exe, use the command **chktrust MyAssembly.exe**. If you have not already configured your machine to trust the SPC used to sign the assembly, you will see a dialog box similar to that shown in Figure 1-4, which shows you information about the publisher of the assembly, and gives you the opportunity to trust this publisher. (The certificate described in Figure 1-4 is a test certificate created using the process described in recipe 1-10.)

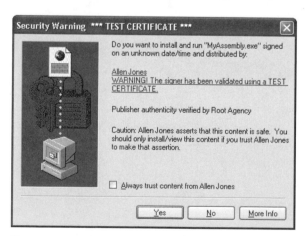

Figure 1-4 Certificate Verification tool.

If you click the Yes button, or you have previously chosen always to trust the SPC, the Certificate Verification tool confirms the validity of the signature and the assembly.

1.13 Create and Trust a Test Software Publisher Certificate

Problem

You need to create an SPC for testing.

Solution

Use the Certificate Creation tool (makecert.exe) to create a test X.509 certificate and the Software Publisher Certificate Test tool (cert2spc.exe) to generate an SPC from this X.509 certificate. Trust the root test certificate using the Set Registry tool (setreg.exe).

Discussion

To create a test SPC for a software publisher named Allen Jones, first create an X.509 certificate using the Certificate Creation tool. The command **makecert -n "CN=Allen Jones" -sk MyKeys TestCertificate.cer** creates a file named Test-Certificate.cer containing an X.509 certificate and stores the associated private key in a CSP key container named MyKeys (which is automatically created if it does not exist). Alternatively, you can write the private key to a file by substituting the -*sk* switch with -*sv*. For example, to write the private key to a file named PrivateKeys.pvk use the command **makecert -n "CN=Allen Jones" -sv PrivateKey.pvk TestCertificate.cer**. If you write your private key to a file, the Certificate Creation tool will prompt you (as shown in Figure 1-5) to provide a password with which to protect the private key file.

Figure 1-5   Certificate Creation tool requests a password when accessing file-based private keys.

The Certificate Creation tool supports many arguments, and Table 1-3 lists some of the more useful ones. You should consult the .NET Framework SDK documentation for full coverage of the Certificate Creation tool.

Table 1-3 Commonly Used Switches of the Certificate Creation Tool

Switch	Description
-e	Specifies the date when the certificate becomes invalid
-m	Specifies the duration—in months—that the certificate remains valid
-n	Specifies an X.500 name to associate with the certificate. This is the name of the software publisher that people will see when they view details of the SPC you create
-sk	Specifies the name of the CSP key store in which to store the private key
-ss	Specifies the name of the certificate store where the Certificate Creation tool should store the generated X.509 certificate
-sv	Specifies the name of the file in which to store the private key

Once you have created your X.509 certificate with the Certificate Creation tool, you need to convert it to an SPC with the Software Publisher Certificate Test tool (cert2spc.exe). To convert the certificate TestCertificate.cer to an SPC, use the command **cert2spc TestCertificate.cer TestCertificate.spc**. The Software Publisher Certificate Test tool doesn't offer any optional switches.

The final step before you can use your test SPC is to trust the root test CA, which is the default issuer of the test certificate. The Set Registry tool (setreg.exe) makes this a simple task with the command **setreg 1 true**. When you have finished using your test SPC, you must remove trust of the root test CA using the command **setreg 1 false**. You can now Authenticode sign assemblies with your test SPC using the process described in recipe 1.12.

1.14 Manage the Global Assembly Cache

Problem

You need to add or remove assemblies from the global assembly cache (GAC).

Solution

Use the Global Assembly Cache tool (gacutil.exe) from the command line to view the contents of the GAC as well as to add and remove assemblies.

Discussion

Before you can install an assembly in the GAC, the assembly must have a strong name; see recipe 1.9 for details on how to strong name your assemblies. To install an assembly named SomeAssembly.dll into the GAC, use the command **gacutil /i SomeAssembly.dll**.

To uninstall the SomeAssembly.dll assembly from the GAC, use the command **gacutil /u SomeAssembly**. Notice that you don't use the .dll extension to refer to the assembly once it's installed in the GAC.

To view the assemblies installed in the GAC, use the command **gacutil /l**. This will produce a long list of all the assemblies installed in the GAC, as well as a listing of assemblies that have been precompiled to binary form and installed in the ngen cache. To avoid searching through this list to determine if a particular assembly is installed in the GAC, use the command **gacutil /l SomeAssembly**.

> **Note**   The .NET Framework uses the GAC only at run time; the C# compiler won't look in the GAC to resolve any external references that your assembly references. During development, the C# compiler must be able to access a local copy of any referenced shared assemblies. You can either copy the shared assembly to the same directory as your source code or use the */lib* switch of the C# compiler to specify the directory where the compiler can find the required assemblies.

1.15 Prevent People from Decompiling Your Code

Problem

You want to ensure people can't decompile your .NET assemblies.

Solution

Build server-based solutions where possible so that people don't have access to your assemblies. If you must distribute assemblies, there's no way to stop people from decompiling them. The best you can do is use obfuscation and components compiled to native code to make your assemblies more difficult to decompile.

Discussion

Because .NET assemblies consist of a standardized, platform-independent set of instruction codes and metadata that describes the types contained in the assembly, they are relatively easy to decompile. This allows decompilers to generate source code that is very close to your original code with ease, which can be problematic if your code contains proprietary information or algorithms that you want to keep secret.

The only way to ensure people can't decompile your assemblies is to stop people from getting your assemblies in the first place. Where possible, implement server-based solutions such as Microsoft ASP.NET applications and XML Web services. With the security correctly configured on your server, nobody will be able to access your assemblies and therefore won't be able to decompile them.

Where building a server solution is not appropriate, you have the following two options:

■   Use an obfuscator to make it difficult to decompile your code. (Visual Studio .NET 2003 includes the Community Edition of an obfuscator named Dotfuscator.) Obfuscators use a variety of techniques to make your assembly difficult to decompile; principal among these techniques are

   ❏   Renaming of *private* methods and fields in such a way that it's difficult to read and understand the purpose of your code.

   ❏   Inserting control flow statements to make the logic of your application difficult to follow.

■   Build the parts of your application that you want to keep secret in native DLLs or COM objects, and then call them from your managed application using P/Invoke or COM interop. (See Chapter 15 for recipes that show you how to call unmanaged code.)

Neither approach will stop a skilled and determined person from reverse engineering your code, but they will make the job significantly more difficult and deter most casual observers.

> **Note**   The risks of application decompilation aren't specific to C# or .NET. A determined person can reverse engineer any software if he has the time and the skill.

2

Working with Data

Most applications need to manipulate some form of data. The Microsoft .NET Framework provides many techniques that simplify or improve the efficiency of common data manipulation tasks. The recipes in this chapter explore some of these techniques and describe how to

- Manipulate strings efficiently (recipe 2.1).

- Represent basic data types using different encoding schemes (recipes 2.2, 2.3, and 2.4).

- Use regular expressions to validate and manipulate strings (recipes 2.5 and 2.6).

- Work with dates and times (recipes 2.7 and 2.8).

- Work with arrays and collections (recipes 2.9, 2.10, and 2.11).

- Serialize object state and persist it to a file (recipe 2.12).

2.1 Manipulate the Contents of a String Efficiently

Problem

You need to manipulate the contents of a *String* object and want to avoid the overhead of automatic *String* creation caused by the immutability of *String* objects.

Solution

Use the *System.Text.StringBuilder* class to perform the manipulations and convert the result to a *String* using the *StringBuilder.ToString* method.

Discussion

String objects in .NET are immutable, meaning that once created they can't be changed. For example, if you build a *String* by concatenating a number of characters or smaller strings, the common language runtime (CLR) will create a completely new *String* object whenever you add a new element to the end of the existing string. This can result in significant overhead if your application performs frequent string manipulation.

The *StringBuilder* class offers a solution by providing a character buffer and allowing you to manipulate its contents without the runtime creating a new object as a result of every change. You can create a new *StringBuilder* object that's empty or initialized with the content of an existing *String* object. You can manipulate the content of the *StringBuilder* object using overloaded methods that allow you to insert and append string representations of different data types. At any time, you can obtain a *String* representation of the current content of the *StringBuilder* by calling *StringBuilder.ToString*.

Two important properties of the *StringBuilder* control its behavior as you append new data: *Capacity* and *Length*. *Capacity* represents the size of the *StringBuilder* buffer, whereas *Length* represents the length of the buffer's current content. If you append new data that results in the number of characters in the *StringBuilder* (*Length*) exceeding the capacity of the *StringBuilder* (*Capacity*), the *StringBuilder* must allocate a new buffer to hold the data. Used carelessly, this buffer reallocation can negate much of the benefit of using the *StringBuilder*. If you know the length of data you need to work with, or know an upper limit, you can avoid unnecessary buffer reallocation by specifying the capacity at creation time or setting the *Capacity* property manually. When setting the *Capacity* and *Length* properties, be aware of the following behavior:

- If you set *Capacity* to a value less than the value of *Length*, the *Capacity* property throws the exception *System.ArgumentOutOfRangeException*.

- If you set *Length* to a value less than the length of the current content, the content is truncated.

- If you set *Length* to a value greater than the length of the current content, the buffer is padded with spaces to the specified length. Setting *Length* to a value greater than *Capacity* automatically adjusts the *Capacity* to the same value as the new *Length*.

The *ReverseString* method shown here demonstrates the use of the *String-Builder* class to reverse a string. If you didn't use the *StringBuilder* class to perform this operation, it would be significantly more expensive in terms of processing power—especially as the input string is made longer. The method creates a *StringBuilder* of the correct capacity to ensure no buffer reallocation is required during the reversal operation.

```
public static string ReverseString(string str) {

    // Make sure we have a reversible string
    if (str == null || str.Length == 1) {
        return str;
    }

    // Create a StringBuilder object with the required capacity
    System.Text.StringBuilder revStr =
        new System.Text.StringBuilder(str.Length);

    // Loop backward through the source string one character at a
    // time and append each character to the StringBuilder
    for (int count = str.Length-1; count > -1; count--) {
        revStr.Append(str[count]);
    }

    // Return the reversed string
    return revStr.ToString();
}
```

2.2 Encode a String Using Alternate Character Encoding

Problem

You need to exchange character data with systems that use character encoding schemes other than UTF-16—the character-encoding scheme used internally by the CLR.

Solution

Use the *System.Text.Encoding* class and its subclasses to convert characters between different encoding schemes.

Discussion

Unicode is not the only character-encoding scheme, nor is UTF-16 the only way to represent Unicode characters. When your application needs to exchange character data with external systems (particularly legacy systems), you must convert the data between UTF-16 and the encoding scheme supported by the other system.

The *abstract* class *Encoding*, and its concrete subclasses, provide the functionality to convert characters to and from a variety of encoding schemes. Each subclass instance supports the conversion of characters between UTF-16 and one other encoding scheme. You obtain instances of the encoding specific classes using the *static* factory method *Encoding.GetEncoding*, which accepts either the name or the code page number of the required encoding scheme.

Table 2-1 lists some commonly used character encoding schemes and the code page number you must pass to the *GetEncoding* method to create an instance of the appropriate encoding class. The table also shows *static* properties of the *Encoding* class that provide shortcuts for obtaining the most commonly used types of encoding object.

Table 2-1   Character Encoding Classes

Encoding Scheme	Class	Create Using
ASCII	*ASCIIEncoding*	*GetEncoding(20127)* or the *ASCII* property
Default (current Microsoft Windows default)	*Encoding*	*GetEncoding(0)* or the *Default* property
UTF-7	*UTF7Encoding*	*GetEncoding(65000)* or the *UTF7* property
UTF-8	*UTF8Encoding*	*GetEncoding(65001)* or the *UTF8* property
UTF-16 (Big Endian)	*UnicodeEncoding*	*GetEncoding(1201)* or the *BigEndianUnicode* property
UTF-16 (Little Endian)	*UnicodeEncoding*	*GetEncoding(1200)* or the *Unicode* property
Windows OS	*Encoding*	*GetEncoding(1252)*

Once you have an *Encoding* object of the appropriate type, you convert a UTF-16 encoded Unicode string to a byte array of encoded characters using the *GetBytes* method and convert a byte array of encoded characters to a string using the *GetString* method. The following code demonstrates the use of some encoding classes.

```
using System;
using System.IO;
using System.Text;

public class CharacterEncodingExample {

    public static void Main() {

        // Create a file to hold the output
        using (StreamWriter output = new StreamWriter("output.txt")) {

            // Create and write a string containing the symbol for Pi
            string srcString = "Area = \u03A0r^2";
            output.WriteLine("Source Text : " + srcString);

            // Write the UTF-16 encoded bytes of the source string
            byte[] utf16String = Encoding.Unicode.GetBytes(srcString);
            output.WriteLine("UTF-16 Bytes: {0}",
                BitConverter.ToString(utf16String));

            // Convert the UTF-16 encoded source string to UTF-8 and ASCII
            byte[] utf8String = Encoding.UTF8.GetBytes(srcString);
            byte[] asciiString = Encoding.ASCII.GetBytes(srcString);

            // Write the UTF-8 and ASCII encoded byte arrays
            output.WriteLine("UTF-8  Bytes: {0}",
                BitConverter.ToString(utf8String));
            output.WriteLine("ASCII  Bytes: {0}",
                BitConverter.ToString(asciiString));

            // Convert UTF-8 and ASCII encoded bytes back to UTF-16
            // encoded string and write
            output.WriteLine("UTF-8  Text : {0}",
                Encoding.UTF8.GetString(utf8String));
            output.WriteLine("ASCII  Text : {0}",
                Encoding.ASCII.GetString(asciiString));

            // Flush and close the output file
            output.Flush();
            output.Close();
        }
    }
}
```

Running *CharacterEncodingExample* will generate a file named output.txt. If you open this file in a text editor that supports Unicode, you will see the following content:

```
Source Text : Area = r^2
UTF-16 Bytes: 41-00-72-00-65-00-61-00-20-00-3D-00-20-00-A0-03-72-00-5E-00-32-00
UTF-8  Bytes: 41-72-65-61-20-3D-20-CE-A0-72-5E-32
ASCII  Bytes: 41-72-65-61-20-3D-20-3F-72-5E-32
UTF-8  Text : Area = r^2
ASCII  Text : Area = ?r^2
```

Notice that using UTF-16 encoding, each character occupies 2 bytes, but because most of the characters are standard characters, the high-order byte is 0. (The use of little-endian byte ordering means that the low-order byte appears first.) This means that most of the characters are encoded using the same numeric values across all three encoding schemes. However, the numeric value for the symbol pi (emphasized in bold in the preceding code) is different in each of the encodings. The value of pi requires more than one byte to represent—UTF-8 encoding uses 2 bytes, but ASCII has no direct equivalent and so replaces pi with the code 3F. As you can see in the text version of the string, 3F is the symbol for an English question mark (?).

> **Warning**   If you convert Unicode characters to ASCII or a specific code page encoding scheme, you risk losing data. Any Unicode character with a character code that can't be represented in the scheme will be ignored.

The *Encoding* class also provides the *static* method *Convert* to simplify the conversion of a byte array from one encoding scheme to another without the need to manually perform an interim conversion to UTF-16. For example, the following statement converts the ASCII encoded bytes contained in the *asciiString* byte array directly from ASCII encoding to UTF-8 encoding:

```
byte[] utf8String = Encoding.Convert(Encoding.ASCII, Encoding.UTF8,
    asciiString);
```

2.3 Convert Basic Value Types to Byte Arrays

Problem

You need to convert basic value types to byte arrays.

Solution

The *static* methods of the *System.BitConverter* class provide a convenient mechanism through which to convert most basic value types—except the *decimal* type—to and from byte arrays. To convert a *decimal* to a byte array, write the *decimal* to a *System.IO.MemoryStream* instance using a *System.IO.BinaryWriter* object and then call the *MemoryStream.ToArray* method. To create a *decimal* from a byte array, create a *MemoryStream* object from the byte array and read the *decimal* from the *MemoryStream* using a *System.IO.BinaryReader* instance.

Discussion

The *static* method *GetBytes* of the *BitConverter* class provides overloads that take most of the standard value types and return the value encoded as an array of bytes. Support is provided for the *bool, char, double, short, int, long, float, ushort, uint,* and *ulong* data types. *BitConverter* also provides a set of *static* methods that support the conversion of byte arrays to each of the standard value types; these are named *ToBoolean, ToUInt32, ToDouble,* and so on. The following code (taken from the sample file ByteConversionExample.cs) demonstrates the use of *BitConverter* to convert a *bool* and an *int* to and from a byte array. The second argument to each of the *ToBoolean* and *ToInt32* methods is a zero-based offset into the byte array where the *BitConverter* should start taking the bytes to create the data value.

```
byte[] b = null;

// Convert a bool to a byte array and display
b = BitConverter.GetBytes(true);
Console.WriteLine(BitConverter.ToString(b));

// Convert a byte array to a bool and display
Console.WriteLine(BitConverter.ToBoolean(b,0));

// Convert an int to a byte array and display
b = BitConverter.GetBytes(3678);
Console.WriteLine(BitConverter.ToString(b));

// Convert a byte array to an int and display
Console.WriteLine(BitConverter.ToInt32(b,0));
```

Unfortunately, *BitConverter* does not provide support for converting the *decimal* type. Instead, the following code shows how to convert a *decimal* to a byte array using a *MemoryStream* and a *BinaryWriter*.

```
// Create a byte array from a decimal
public static byte[] DecimalToByteArray (decimal src) {

    // Create a MemoryStream as a buffer to hold the binary data
    using (MemoryStream stream = new MemoryStream()) {

        // Create a BinaryWriter to write binary data to the stream
        using (BinaryWriter writer = new BinaryWriter(stream)) {

            // Write the decimal to the BinaryWriter/MemoryStream
            writer.Write(src);

            // Return the byte representation of the decimal
            return stream.ToArray();
        }
    }
}
```

To convert a byte array to a *decimal*, use a *BinaryReader* to read from the *MemoryStream*, as shown in this code.

```
// Create a decimal from a byte array
public static decimal ByteArrayToDecimal (byte[] src) {

    // Create a MemoryStream containing the byte array
    using (MemoryStream stream = new MemoryStream(src)) {

        // Create a BinaryReader to read the decimal from the stream
        using (BinaryReader reader = new BinaryReader(stream)) {

            // Read and return the decimal from the
            // BinaryReader/MemoryStream
            return reader.ReadDecimal();
        }
    }
}
```

> **Note**   The *BitConverter.ToString* method provides a convenient mechanism through which to obtain a *String* representation of a byte array. Calling *ToString* and passing a byte array as an argument will return a *String* containing the hexadecimal value of each byte in the array separated by a hyphen, for example "34-A7-2C". Unfortunately, there is no standard method for reversing this process to obtain a byte array from a string with this format.

2.4 Encode Binary Data as Text

Problem

You need to convert binary data into a form that can be stored as part of an ASCII text file (such as an XML file), or sent as part of an e-mail message.

Solution

Use the *static* methods *ToBase64String* and *FromBase64String* of the *System.Convert* class to convert your binary data to and from a Base64-encoded string.

Discussion

Base64 is an encoding scheme that enables you to represent binary data as a series of ASCII characters so that it can be included in text files and e-mail messages in which raw binary data is unacceptable. Base64 encoding works by spreading the contents of 3 bytes of input data across 4 bytes and ensuring each byte uses only the 7 low-order bits to contain data. This means that each byte of Base64-encoded data is equivalent to an ASCII character and can be stored or transmitted anywhere ASCII characters are permitted.

The *ToBase64String* and *FromBase64String* methods of the *Convert* class make it straightforward to Base64 encode and decode data. However, before Base64 encoding, you must convert your data to a byte array. Likewise, after decoding you must convert the byte array back to the appropriate data type; see recipe 2.2 for details on converting string data to and from byte arrays and recipe 2.3 for details on converting basic value types.

The code shown here demonstrates how to Base64 encode and decode a Unicode string, an *int*, and a *decimal* using the *Convert* class. The *DecimalToBase64* and *Base64ToDecimal* methods rely on the *ByteArrayToDecimal* and *DecimalToByteArray* methods listed in recipe 2.3.

```
// Base64 encode a Unicode string
public static string StringToBase64 (string src) {

    // Get a byte representation of the source string
    byte[] b = Encoding.Unicode.GetBytes(src);

    // Return the Base64-encoded string
    return Convert.ToBase64String(b);
}
```

```csharp
// Decode a Base64-encoded Unicode string
public static string Base64ToString (string src) {

    // Decode the Base64-encoded string to a byte array
    byte[] b = Convert.FromBase64String(src);

    // Return the decoded Unicode string
    return Encoding.Unicode.GetString(b);
}

// Base64 encode a decimal
public static string DecimalToBase64 (decimal src) {

    // Get a byte representation of the decimal
    byte[] b = DecimalToByteArray(src);

    // Return the Base64-encoded decimal
    return Convert.ToBase64String(b);
}

// Decode a Base64-encoded decimal
public static decimal Base64ToDecimal (string src) {

    // Decode the Base64-encoded decimal to a byte array
    byte[] b = Convert.FromBase64String(src);

    // Return the decoded decimal
    return ByteArrayToDecimal(b);
}

// Base64 encode an int
public static string IntToBase64 (int src) {

    // Get a byte representation of the int
    byte[] b = BitConverter.GetBytes(src);

    // Return the Base64-encoded int
    return Convert.ToBase64String(b);
}

// Decode a Base64-encoded int
public static int Base64ToInt (string src) {

    // Decode the Base64-encoded int to a byte array
    byte[] b = Convert.FromBase64String(src);

    // Return the decoded int
    return BitConverter.ToInt32(b,0);
}
```

2.5 Validate Input Using Regular Expressions

Problem

You need to validate that user input or data read from a file has the expected structure and content. For example, you want to ensure that a user enters a valid IP address, telephone number, or e-mail address.

Solution

Use regular expressions to ensure that the input data follows the correct structure and contains only valid characters for the expected type of information.

Discussion

When a user inputs data to your application or your application reads data from a file, it's good practice to assume that the data is bad until you have verified its accuracy. One common validation requirement is to ensure that data such as e-mail addresses, telephone numbers, and credit card numbers follow the pattern and content constraints expected of such data. Obviously you can't be sure the data entered is valid until you use it, or compare it against values that are known to be correct, but ensuring the data has the correct structure and content is a good first step to determining whether the input is accurate. Regular expressions provide an excellent mechanism for evaluating strings for the presence of patterns; you can use this to your advantage when validating input data.

The first thing you must do is figure out the regular expression syntax that will correctly match the structure and content of data you are trying to validate. This is by far the most difficult aspect of using regular expressions. Regular expressions are constructed from two types of elements: *literals* and *metacharacters*. Literals represent specific characters that appear in the pattern you want to match. Metacharacters provide support for wildcard matching, ranges, grouping, repetition, conditionals, and other control mechanisms. A full discussion of regular expression syntax is beyond the scope of this book, but Table 2-2 describes some of the more commonly used elements. (Consult the .NET SDK documentation for a full description of regular expressions.)

Table 2-2 **Commonly Used Regular Expression Metacharacter Elements**

Element	Description
.	Specifies any character except a new line (\n)
\d	Specifies any decimal digit
\D	Specifies any nondigit
\s	Specifies any white-space character
\S	Specifies any non-white-space character
\w	Specifies any word character
\W	Specifies any nonword character
^	Specifies the beginning of the string or line
\A	Specifies the beginning of the string
$	Specifies the end of the string or line
\z	Specifies the end of the string
|	Matches one of the expressions separated by the vertical bar; for example AAA|ABA|ABB will match one of AAA, ABA, or ABB. (The expression is evaluated left to right.)
[abc]	Specifies a match with one of the specified characters; for example [AbC] will match A, b, or C but no other character
[^abc]	Specifies a match with any one character except those specified; for example [^AbC] will not match A, b, or C but will match B, F and so on
[a-z]	Specifies a match with any one character in the specified range; for example [A-C] will match A, B, or C
( )	Identifies a subexpression so that it's treated as a single element by the regular expression elements described in this table
?	Specifies one or zero occurrences of the previous character or subexpression; for example A?B matches B, AB, but not AAB
*	Specifies zero or more occurrences of the previous character or subexpression; for example, A*B matches B, AB, AAB, AAAB, and so on
+	Specifies one or more occurrences of the previous character or subexpression; for example, A+B matches AB, AAB, AAAB, and so on, but not B
{n}	Specifies exactly *n* occurrences of the preceding character or sub-expression; for example, A{2} matches *only* AA
{n,}	Specifies a minimum of *n* occurrences of the preceding character or sub-expression; for example, A{2,} matches AA, AAA, AAAA and so on, but not A
{n, m}	Specifies a minimum of *n* and a maximum of *m* occurrences of the preceding character; for example, A{2,4} matches AA, AAA, and AAAA but not A or AAAAA

The more complex the data you are trying to match, the more complex the regular expression syntax becomes. For example, ensuring that input contains only numbers or is of a minimum length is trivial, but ensuring a string contains a valid URL is extremely complex. Table 2-3 shows some example regular expressions that will match against commonly required data types.

Table 2-3   Commonly Used Regular Expressions

Input Type	Description	Regular Expression
Numeric input	The input consists of one or more decimal digits; for example "5", or "5683874674".	^\d+$
PIN	The input consists of four decimal digits; for example "1234".	^\d{4}$
Simple password	The input consists of between 6 through 8 characters; for example "ghtd6f" or "b8c7hogh".	^\w{6,8}$
Credit card number	The input consists of data that matches the pattern of most major credit card numbers, for example "4921835221552042" or "4921 8352 2155-2042".	^\d{4}-?\d{4}-?\d{4}-?\d{4}$
E-mail address	The input consists of an Internet e-mail address. The [\w-]+ expression indicates that each address element must consist of one or more word characters or hyphens; for example some-body@adatum.com.	^[\w-]+@([\w-]+\.)+[\w-]+$
HTTP or HTTPS URL	The input consists of an HTTP-based or HTTPS-based URL, for example *http://www.microsoft.com*.	^https?://([\w-]+\.)+[\w-]+(/[\w- ./?%=]*)?$

Once you know the correct regular expression syntax, create a new *System.Text.RegularExpressions.Regex* object passing a string containing the regular expression to the *Regex* constructor. Then call the *IsMatch* method of the *Regex* object and pass the string that you want to validate; *IsMatch* returns a *bool* indicating whether the *Regex* object found a match in the string. The regular expression syntax determines whether the *Regex* will match only against the full string or whether it will match against patterns contained within the string. (See the ^, \A, $, and \z entries in Table 2-2.)

The *ValidateInput* method shown here tests any input string to see if it matches a specified regular expression.

```
public static bool ValidateInput(string regex, string input) {

    // Create a new Regex based on the specified regular expression.
    Regex r = new Regex(regex);
```

```
        // Test if the specified input matches the regular expression.
        return r.IsMatch(input);
}
```

You can use the *Regex* object repeatedly to test multiple strings, but you can't change the regular expression tested for by a *Regex* object; you must create a new *Regex* object to test for a different pattern. Because the *ValidateInput* method creates a new *Regex* each time it's called, instead you could use a *static* overload of the *IsMatch* method, as shown in the following variant of the *ValidateInput* method.

```
public static bool ValidateInput(string regex, string input) {

        // Test if the specified input matches the regular expression.
        return Regex.IsMatch(input, regex);
}
```

2.6 Use Compiled Regular Expressions

Problem

You need to minimize the impact on application performance that arises from using complex regular expressions frequently.

Solution

When you instantiate the *System.Text.RegularExpressions.Regex* object that represents your regular expression, specify the *Compiled* option of the *System.Text.RegularExpressions.RegexOptions* enumeration to compile the regular expression to Microsoft Intermediate Language (MSIL).

Discussion

By default, when you create a *Regex* object, the regular expression pattern you specify in the constructor is compiled to an intermediate form (not MSIL). Each time you use the *Regex* object, the runtime interprets the pattern's intermediate form and applies it to the target string. With complex regular expressions that are used frequently, this repeated interpretation process can have a detrimental effect on the performance of your application.

By specifying the *RegexOptions.Compiled* option when you create a *Regex* object, you force the .NET runtime to compile the regular expression to MSIL, instead of the interpreted intermediary form. This MSIL is just-in-time (JIT) compiled by the runtime to native machine code on first execution—just like regular assembly code. You use a compiled regular expression in the same way as you use any *Regex* object; compilation simply results in faster execution.

However, there are downsides to offset the performance benefits provided by compiling regular expressions. First, the JIT compiler has to do more work, which will introduce delays during JIT compilation. This is most noticeable if you create your compiled regular expressions as your application starts up. Second, the runtime can't unload a compiled regular expression once you have finished with it. Unlike a normal regular expression, the runtime's garbage collector won't reclaim the memory used by the compiled regular expression. The compiled regular expression will remain in memory until your program terminates or you unload the application domain in which the compiled regular expression is loaded.

This code shows how to create a *Regex* object that's compiled to MSIL instead of the usual intermediate form.

```
Regex reg = new Regex(@"[\w-]+@([\w-]+\.)+[\w-]+", RegexOptions.Compiled);
```

In addition, the *static Regex.CompileToAssembly* method allows you to create a compiled regular expression and write it to an external assembly. This means you can create assemblies containing standard sets of regular expressions that you can use from multiple applications. To compile a regular expression and persist it to an assembly, take the following steps:

1. Create a *System.Text.RegularExpressions.RegexCompilationInfo* array large enough to hold one *RegexCompilationInfo* object for each of the compiled regular expressions you want to create.

2. Create a *RegexCompilationInfo* object for each of the compiled regular expressions, and specify values for its properties as arguments to the object constructor; the most commonly used properties are

    ❏   *IsPublic*, a *bool* that specifies whether the generated regular expression class has *public* visibility.

    ❏   *Name*, a *String* that specifies the class name.

    ❏   *Namespace*, a *String* that specifies the namespace of the class.

    ❏   *Pattern*, a *String* that specifies the pattern that the regular expression will match. (See recipe 2.5 for more details.)

    ❏   *Options*, a *System.Text.RegularExpressions.RegexOptions* value that specifies options for the regular expression.

3. Create a *System.Reflection.AssemblyName* object, and configure it to represent the name of the assembly that the *Regex.CompileToAssembly* method will create.

4. Execute *Regex.CompileToAssembly*, passing the *RegexCompilationInfo* array and the *AssemblyName* object.

This process creates an assembly that contains one class declaration for each compiled regular expression—each class derives from *Regex*. To use the compiled regular expression contained in the assembly, instantiate the regular expression you want to use and call its method as if you had simply created it with the normal *Regex* constructor. (Remember to add a reference to the assembly when you compile the code that uses the compiled regular expression classes.)

The following code shows how to create an assembly named MyRegEx.dll, which contains two regular expressions named *PinRegex* and *CreditCardRegex*.

```
using System.Text.RegularExpressions;
using System.Reflection;

public class CompiledRegexExample {

    public static void Main() {

        // Create the array to hold the Regex info objects
        RegexCompilationInfo[] regexInfo = new RegexCompilationInfo[2];

        // Create the RegexCompilationInfo for PinRegex
        regexInfo[0] = new RegexCompilationInfo(@"^\d{4}$",
            RegexOptions.Compiled, "PinRegex", "", true);

        // Create the RegexCompilationInfo for CreditCardRegex
        regexInfo[1] = new RegexCompilationInfo(
            @"^\d{4}-?\d{4}-?\d{4}-?\d{4}$",
            RegexOptions.Compiled, "CreditCardRegex", "", true);

        // Create the AssemblyName to define the target assembly
        AssemblyName assembly = new AssemblyName();
        assembly.Name = "MyRegEx";

        // Create the compiled regular expression
        Regex.CompileToAssembly(regexInfo, assembly);
    }
}
```

2.7 Create Dates and Times from Strings

Problem

You need to create a *System.DateTime* instance that represents the time and date specified in a string.

Solution

Use the *Parse* or *ParseExact* methods of the *DateTime* class.

Discussion

There are many different ways to represent dates and times as text. For example, 1st June 2003, 1/6/2003, 6/1/2003, and 1-Jun-2003 are all possible representations of the same date, and 16.43 and 4:43pm can both be used to represent the same time. The *static DateTime.Parse* method provides a flexible mechanism by which to create *DateTime* instances from a wide variety of string representations.

The *Parse* method goes to great lengths to generate a *DateTime* from a given string. It will even attempt to generate a *DateTime* from a string containing partial or erroneous information and will substitute defaults for those values it finds missing. Missing date elements default to the current date, and missing time elements default to 12:00:00 am. After all efforts, if *Parse* can't create a *DateTime*, it throws a *System.FormatException*. The following code demonstrates the flexibility of the *Parse* method.

```
// 01/09/2001 00:00:00
DateTime dt1 = DateTime.Parse("Sep 2001");

// 05/09/2001 14:15:33
DateTime dt2 = DateTime.Parse("Wed 5 September 2001 14:15:33");

// 05/09/2001 00:00:00
DateTime dt3 = DateTime.Parse("5,9,01");

// 05/09/2001 14:15:33
DateTime dt4 = DateTime.Parse("5/9/2001 14:15:33");

// 01/07/2003 14:15:00
DateTime dt5 = DateTime.Parse("2:15 PM");
```

The *Parse* method is both flexible and forgiving. However, for many applications this level of flexibility is unnecessary. Often you will want to ensure that

DateTime parses only strings that match a specific format. In these circumstances, use the *ParseExact* method instead of *Parse*. The simplest overload of the *ParseExact* method takes three arguments: the time and date string to parse, a format string that specifies the structure that the time and date string must have, and an *IFormatProvider* reference that provides culture specific information to the *ParseExact* method. If the *IFormatProvider* is *null*, the current thread's culture information is used.

The time and date must meet the requirements specified in the format string or *ParseExact* will throw a *System.FormatException*. You use the same format specifiers for the format string as you use to format a *DateTime* for display as a string. This means you can use both standard and custom format specifiers. The following code demonstrates the use of the *ParseExact* method. Refer to the documentation for the *System.Globalization.DateTimeFormatInfo* class in the .NET Framework SDK document for complete details on all available format specifiers.

```
// Parse only strings containing LongTimePattern
DateTime dt6 = DateTime.ParseExact("2:13:30 PM",
    "h:mm:ss tt", null);

// Parse only strings containing RFC1123Pattern
DateTime dt7 = DateTime.ParseExact(
    "Wed, 05 Sep 2001 14:13:30 GMT",
    "ddd, dd MMM yyyy HH':'mm':'ss 'GMT'", null);

// Parse only strings containing MonthDayPattern
DateTime dt8 = DateTime.ParseExact("September 03",
    "MMMM dd", null);
```

2.8 Add, Subtract, and Compare Dates and Times

Problem

You need to perform basic arithmetic operations or comparisons using dates and times.

Solution

Use the *DateTime* and *TimeSpan* structures, which support standard arithmetic and comparison operators.

Discussion

A *DateTime* instance represents a specific time (such as 4:15 A.M. on September 5, 1970), whereas a *TimeSpan* instance represents a period of time (such as 2 hours, 35 minutes). You will often want to add, subtract, and compare *TimeSpan* and *DateTime* instances.

Internally, both *DateTime* and *TimeSpan* use *ticks* to represent time—a tick is equal to 100 nanoseconds. *TimeSpan* stores its time interval as the number of ticks equal to that interval, and *DateTime* stores time as the number of ticks since 12:00:00 midnight on January 1 in 0001 C.E. (C.E. stands for Common Era and is equivalent to A.D. in the Gregorian Calendar.) This approach and the use of operator overloading makes it easy for *DateTime* and *TimeSpace* to support basic arithmetic and comparison operations. Table 2-4 summarizes the operator support provided by the *DateTime* and *TimeSpan* structures.

Table 2-4   Operators Supported by the *DateTime* and *TimeSpan*

Operator	*TimeSpan*	*DateTime*
Assignment (=)	Because *TimeSpan* is a structure, assignment returns a copy and not a reference.	Because *DateTime* is a structure, assignment returns a copy and not a reference.
Addition (+)	Adds two *TimeSpan* instances.	Adds a *TimeSpan* to a *DateTime*.
Subtraction (-)	Subtracts one *TimeSpan* instance from another.	Subtracts a *TimeSpan* or a *DateTime* from a *DateTime*.
Equality (==)	Compares two *TimeSpan* instances and returns *true* if they are equal.	Compares two *DateTime* instances and returns *true* if they are equal.
Inequality (/=)	Compares two *TimeSpan* instances and returns *true* if they aren't equal.	Compares two *DateTime* instances and returns *true* if they aren't equal.
Greater Than (>)	Determines if one *TimeSpan* is greater than another *TimeSpan*.	Determines if one *DateTime* is greater than another *DateTime*.
Greater Than or Equal (>=)	Determines if one *TimeSpan* is greater than or equal to another *TimeSpan*.	Determines if one *DateTime* is greater than or equal to another *DateTime*.
Less Than (<)	Determines if one *TimeSpan* is less than another *TimeSpan*.	Determines if one *DateTime* is less than another *DateTime*.
Less Than or Equal (<=)	Determines if one *TimeSpan* is less than or equal to another *TimeSpan*.	Determines if one *DateTime* is less than or equal to another *DateTime*.

Table 2-4   Operators Supported by the *DateTime* and *TimeSpan*

Operator	TimeSpan	DateTime
Unary Negation (-)	Returns a *TimeSpan* with a negated value of the specified *TimeSpan*.	Not Supported.
Unary Plus (+)	Returns the *TimeSpan* specified.	Not Supported.

The *DateTime* structure also implements the methods *AddTicks*, *AddMilliseconds*, *AddSeconds*, *AddMinutes*, *AddHours*, *AddDays*, *AddMonths*, and *AddYears*. Each of these methods allows you to add (or subtract using negative values) the appropriate element of time to a *DateTime* instance. These methods and the operators listed in Table 2-4 don't modify the original *DateTime*—instead they create a new instance with the modified value. The following code demonstrates the use of operators to manipulate the *DateTime* and *TimeSpan* structures.

```
// Create a TimeSpan representing 2.5 days
TimeSpan timespan1 = new TimeSpan(2,12,0,0);
// Create a TimeSpan representing 4.5 days
TimeSpan timespan2 = new TimeSpan(4,12,0,0);
// Create a TimeSpan representing 1 week
TimeSpan oneWeek = timespan1 + timespan2;

// Create a DateTime with the current date and time
DateTime now = DateTime.Now;
// Create a DateTime representing 1 week ago
DateTime past = now - oneWeek;
// Create a DateTime representing 1 week in the future
DateTime future = now + oneWeek;
```

2.9 Sort an Array or an *ArrayList*

Problem

You need to sort the elements contained in an array or an *ArrayList*.

Solution

Use the *ArrayList.Sort* method to sort *ArrayList* objects and the *static Array.Sort* method to sort arrays.

Discussion

The simplest *Sort* method overload sorts the objects contained in an array or *ArrayList* as long as the objects implement the *System.IComparable* interface and are of the same type—all of the basic data types implement *IComparable*. The following code excerpt demonstrates how to use the *Sort* method:

```
// Create a new array and populate it.
int[] array = {4, 2, 9, 3};

// Sort the array
Array.Sort(array);

// Display the contents of the sorted array
foreach (int i in array) { Console.WriteLine(i);}

// Create a new ArrayList and populate it.
ArrayList list = new ArrayList(4);
list.Add("Michael");
list.Add("Kate");
list.Add("Andrea");
list.Add("Angus");

// Sort the ArrayList
list.Sort();

// Display the contents of the sorted ArrayList
foreach (string s in list) { Console.WriteLine(s);}
```

To sort objects that don't implement *IComparable*, you must pass the *Sort* method an object that implements the *System.Collections.IComparer* interface. The *IComparer* implementation must be capable of comparing the objects contained within the array or *ArrayList*. (Recipe 16.3 describes how to implement both the *IComparable* and *IComparer* interfaces.)

2.10 Copy a Collection to an Array

Problem

You need to copy the contents of a collection to an array.

Solution

Use the *ICollection.CopyTo* method implemented by all collection classes, or use the *ToArray* method implemented by the *ArrayList*, *Stack*, and *Queue* collections.

Discussion

The *ICollection.CopyTo* method and the *ToArray* method perform roughly the same function—they perform a shallow copy of the elements contained in a collection to an array. The key difference is that *CopyTo* copies the collection's elements to an existing array, whereas *ToArray* creates a new array before copying the collection's elements into it.

The *CopyTo* method takes two arguments: an array and an index. The array is the target of the copy operation and must be of a type appropriate to handle the elements of the collection. If the types don't match or there is no implicit conversion possible from the collection element's type to the array element's type, a *System.InvalidCastException* is thrown. The index is the starting element of the array where the collection's elements will be copied. If the index is equal to or greater than the length of the array, or the number of collection elements exceeds the capacity of the array, a *System.ArgumentException* is thrown. This code excerpt shows how to copy the contents of an *ArrayList* to an array using the *CopyTo* method.

```
// Create a new ArrayList and populate it.
ArrayList list = new ArrayList(5);
list.Add("Brenda");
list.Add("George");
list.Add("Justin");
list.Add("Shaun");
list.Add("Meaghan");

// Create a string[] and use the ICollection.CopyTo method to
// copy the contents of the ArrayList.
string[] array1 = new string[5];
list.CopyTo(array1,0);
```

The *ArrayList*, *Stack*, and *Queue* classes also implement the *ToArray* method, which automatically creates an array of the correct size to accommodate a copy of all the elements of the collection. If you call *ToArray* with no arguments, it returns an *object[]* regardless of the type of objects contained in the collection. However, you can pass a *System.Type* object that specifies the type of array that the *ToArray* method should create. (You must cast the returned strongly typed array to the correct type.) Here is an example of how to use the *ToArray* method on the *ArrayList* created in the previous listing.

```
// Use ArrayList.ToArray to create an object[] from the contents
// of the collection.
object[] array2 = list.ToArray();

// Use ArrayList.ToArray to create a strongly typed string[] from
// the contents of the collection.
string[] array3 =
    (string[])list.ToArray(System.Type.GetType("System.String"));
```

2.11 Create a Strongly Typed Collection

Problem

You need to create a collection that can hold elements only of a specific type.

Solution

Create a class that derives from the *System.Collections.CollectionBase* or *System.Collections.DictionaryBase* classes, and implement type-safe methods for the manipulation of the collection.

Discussion

The *CollectionBase* and *DictionaryBase* classes provide convenient base classes from which to derive type-safe collections without having to implement the standard *IDictionary*, *IList*, *ICollection*, and *IEnumerable* interfaces from scratch.

CollectionBase is for *IList*-based collections (such as *ArrayList*). Internally, *CollectionBase* maintains the collection using a standard *ArrayList* object, which is accessible through the *protected* property *List*. *DictionaryBase* is for *IDictionary*-based collections (such as *Hashtable*). Internally, *DictionaryBase* maintains the collection using a standard *Hashtable* object, which is accessible through the *protected* property *Dictionary*. The following code shows the implementation of a strongly typed collection (based on the *CollectionBase* class) to represent a list of *System.Reflection.AssemblyName* objects.

```
using System.Reflection;
using System.Collections;

public class AssemblyNameList : CollectionBase {
```

```
public int Add(AssemblyName value) {

    return this.List.Add(value);
}

public void Remove(AssemblyName value) {

    this.List.Remove(value);
}

public AssemblyName this[int index] {

    get {
        return (AssemblyName)this.List[index];
    }

    set {
        this.List[index] = value;
    }
}

public bool Contains(AssemblyName value) {

    return this.List.Contains(value);
}

public void Insert(int index, AssemblyName value) {

    this.List.Insert(index, value);
}
}
```

Both the *CollectionBase* and *DictionaryBase* classes implement a set of *protected* methods with the prefix *On**. These methods—such as *OnClear*, *OnClearComplete*, *OnGet*, *OnGetComplete*, and so on—are intended to be over-ridden by a derived class and allow you to implement any custom functionality necessary to manage the strongly typed collection. The *CollectionBase* and *DictionaryBase* classes call the appropriate method before and after modifications are made to the underlying collection through the *List* or *Dictionary* properties.

2.12 Store a Serializable Object to a File

Problem

You need to store a serializable object and its state to a file and then deserialize it later.

Solution

Use a *formatter* to serialize the object and write it to a *System.IO.FileStream*. When you need to retrieve the object, use the same type of formatter to read the serialized data from the file and deserialize the object. The .NET Framework class library includes the following formatter implementations for serializing objects to binary or SOAP format:

- *System.Runtime.Serialization.Formatters.Binary.BinaryFormatter*

- *System.Runtime.Serialization.Formatters.Soap.SoapFormatter*

Discussion

Using the *BinaryFormatter* and *SoapFormatter* classes, you can serialize an instance of any type that's decorated with the attribute *System.SerializableAttribute*. The *BinaryFormatter* produces a binary data stream representing the object and its state, whereas the *SoapFormatter* produces a SOAP document.

Both the *BinaryFormatter* and *SoapFormatter* classes implement the interface *System.Runtime.Serialization.IFormatter*, which defines two methods: *Serialize* and *Deserialize*. The *Serialize* method takes a *System.IO.Stream* reference and a *System.Object* reference as arguments, serializes the *Object*, and writes it to the *Stream*. The *Deserialize* method takes a *Stream* reference as an argument, reads the serialized object data from the *Stream*, and returns an *Object* reference to a deserialized object. You must cast the returned *Object* reference to the correct type.

> **Important**   To call the *Serialize* and *Deserialize* methods of the *BinaryFormatter* class, your code must be granted the *SerializationFormatter* element of the permission *System.Security.Permissions.SecurityPermission*.
>
> To call the *Serialize* and *Deserialize* methods of the *SoapFormatter* class, your code must be granted full trust because the System.Runtime.Serialization.Formatters.Soap.dll assembly in which the *SoapFormatter* class is declared does not allow partially trusted callers. Refer to recipe 13.1 for more information about assemblies and partially trusted callers.

The *BinarySerializationExample* class listed here demonstrates the use of a *BinaryFormatter* to serialize a *System.Collections.ArrayList* containing a list of people to a file. The *ArrayList* is then deserialized from the file and the contents displayed to the console.

```
using System.IO;
using System.Collections;
using System.Runtime.Serialization.Formatters.Binary;

public class BinarySerializationExample {

    public static void Main() {

        // Create and configure the ArrayList to serialize
        ArrayList people = new ArrayList();
        people.Add("Graeme");
        people.Add("Lin");
        people.Add("Andy");

        // Serialize the ArrayList object
        FileStream str = File.Create("people.bin");
        BinaryFormatter bf = new BinaryFormatter();
        bf.Serialize(str, people);
        str.Close();

        // Deserialize the ArrayList object
        str = File.OpenRead("people.bin");
        bf = new BinaryFormatter();
        people = (ArrayList)bf.Deserialize(str);
        str.Close();

        // Display the contents of the deserialized ArrayList object
        foreach (string s in people) {

            System.Console.WriteLine(s);
        }
    }
}
```

You can use a *SoapFormatter* class in exactly the same way as shown in the *BinarySerializationExample* class; all you need to do is replace each instance of *BinaryFormatter* with *SoapFormatter* and change the using directives to import the *System.Runtime.Serialization.Formatters.Soap* namespace. You must also include a reference to the System.Runtime.Serialization.Formatters.Soap.dll assembly when you compile the code. The file SoapSerialization-Example.cs in the sample code for this chapter contains an example of how to use the *SoapFormatter* class.

To illustrate the different results achieved using the *BinaryFormatter* and *SoapFormatter* classes, Figure 2-1 shows the contents of the people.bin file generated using the *BinaryFormatter* class, whereas Figure 2-2 shows the contents of the people.xml file generated using the *SoapFormatter* class.

```
00000000h: 00 01 00 00 00 FF FF FF FF 01 00 00 00 00 00 00 ; .....ÿÿÿ
00000010h: 00 04 01 00 00 00 1C 53 79 73 74 65 6D 2E 43 6F ; .......System.Co
00000020h: 6C 6C 65 63 74 69 6F 6E 73 2E 41 72 72 61 79 4C ; llections.ArrayL
00000030h: 69 73 74 03 00 00 00 06 5F 69 74 65 6D 73 05 5F ; ist....._items._
00000040h: 73 69 7A 65 08 5F 76 65 72 73 69 6F 6E 05 00 00 ; size._ve
00000050h: 08 08 09 02 00 00 00 03 00 00 00 03 00 00 00 10 ; ........
00000060h: 02 00 00 00 10 00 00 00 06 03 00 00 00 06 47 72 ; ........
00000070h: 61 65 6D 65 06 04 00 00 00 03 4C 69 6E 06 05 00 ; aeme....
00000080h: 00 00 04 41 6E 64 79 0D 0D 0B             ; ...Andy.
```

Figure 2-1   Contents of the people.bin file.

```
<SOAP-ENV:Envelope xmlns:xsi="http://www.w3.org/2001/XMLSchema-instance"
xmlns:xsd="http://www.w3.org/2001/XMLSchema" xmlns:SOAP-
ENC="http://schemas.xmlsoap.org/soap/encoding/" xmlns:SOAP-
ENV="http://schemas.xmlsoap.org/soap/envelope/"
xmlns:clr="http://schemas.microsoft.com/soap/encoding/clr/1.0" SOAP-
ENV:encodingStyle="http://schemas.xmlsoap.org/soap/encoding/">
<SOAP-ENV:Body>
<a1:ArrayList id="ref-1"
xmlns:a1="http://schemas.microsoft.com/clr/ns/System.Collections">
<_items href="#ref-2"/>
<_size>3</_size>
<_version>3</_version>
</a1:ArrayList>
<SOAP-ENC:Array id="ref-2" SOAP-ENC:arrayType="xsd:anyType[16]">
<item id="ref-3" xsi:type="SOAP-ENC:string">Graeme</item>
<item id="ref-4" xsi:type="SOAP-ENC:string">Lin</item>
<item id="ref-5" xsi:type="SOAP-ENC:string">Andy</item>
</SOAP-ENC:Array>
</SOAP-ENV:Body>
</SOAP-ENV:Envelope>
```

Figure 2-2   Contents of the people.xml file.

3

Application Domains, Reflection, and Metadata

The power and flexibility of the Microsoft .NET Framework is enhanced by the ability to inspect and manipulate types and metadata at run time. The recipes in this chapter look at some of the more commonly used aspects of application domains, reflection, and metadata, including the following:

- Creating and unloading application domains (recipes 3.1 and 3.9)

- Working with types and objects when using multiple application domains (recipes 3.2, 3.3, 3.4, and 3.8)

- Working with *Type* information (recipes 3.10 and 3.11)

- Dynamically loading assemblies and creating objects at run time (recipes 3.5, 3.6, 3.7, and 3.12)

- Creating and inspecting custom attributes (recipes 3.13 and 3.14)

3.1 Create an Application Domain

Problem

You need to create a new application domain.

Solution

Use the *static* method *CreateDomain* of the *System.AppDomain* class.

Discussion

The simplest overload of the *CreateDomain* method takes a single *string* argument specifying a human-readable name (friendly name) for the new application domain. Other overloads allow you to specify evidence and configuration settings for the new application domain. Evidence is specified using a *System.Security.Policy.Evidence* object; recipe 13.11 discusses the effects of providing evidence when you create an application domain. Configuration settings are specified using a *System.AppDomainSetup* object.

The *AppDomainSetup* class is a container of configuration information for an application domain. Table 3-1 lists some of the properties of the *AppDomainSetup* class that you will use most often when creating application domains. These properties are accessible after creation through members of the *AppDomain* object, and some are modifiable at run time; refer to the .NET Frameworks SDK documentation on the *AppDomain* class for a comprehensive discussion.

Table 3-1   Commonly Used *AppDomainSetup* Properties

Property	Description
ApplicationBase	The directory where the CLR will look during probing to resolve private assemblies. Probing is discussed in recipe 3.5. Effectively, *ApplicationBase* is the root directory for the executing application. By default, this is the directory containing the assembly. Readable after creation using the *AppDomain.BaseDirectory* property.
ConfigurationFile	The name of the configuration file used by code loaded into the application domain. Readable after creation using the *AppDomain.GetData* method with the key *APP_CONFIG_FILE*.
DisallowPublisherPolicy	Controls whether the publisher policy section of the application configuration file is taken into consideration when determining which version of a strong named assembly to bind to. Publisher policy is discussed in recipe 3.5.
PrivateBinPath	A semicolon-separated list of directories that the runtime uses when probing for private assemblies. These directories are relative to the directory specified in *ApplicationBase*. Readable after application domain creation using the *AppDomain.RelativeSearchPath* property. Modifiable at run time using the *AppendPrivatePath* and *ClearPrivatePath* methods.

The following example demonstrates the creation and configuration of an application domain.

```
// Instantiate an AppDomainSetup object.
AppDomainSetup setupInfo = new AppDomainSetup();

// Configure the application domain setup information.
setupInfo.ApplicationBase = @"C:\MyRootDirectory";
setupInfo.ConfigurationFile = "MyApp.config";
setupInfo.PrivateBinPath = "bin;plugins;external";

// Create a new application domain passing null as the evidence
// argument. Remember to save a reference to the new AppDomain as
// this cannot be retrieved any other way.
AppDomain newDomain = AppDomain.CreateDomain(
    "My New AppDomain",
    new System.Security.Policy.Evidence(),
    setupInfo);
```

> **Tip**   You must maintain a reference to the *AppDomain* object when you create it because there's no mechanism to enumerate existing application domains from within managed code.

3.2 Pass Objects Across Application Domain Boundaries

Problem

You need to pass objects across application domain boundaries as arguments or return values.

Solution

Use marshal-by-value or marshal-by-reference objects.

Discussion

The .NET Remoting system (discussed in Chapter 12) makes passing objects across application domain boundaries straightforward. However, to those unfamiliar with .NET Remoting, the results can be very different from those expected. In fact, the most confusing aspect of using multiple application domains stems from the interaction with .NET Remoting and the way objects traverse application domain boundaries.

All types fall into one of three categories: nonremotable, marshal-by-value (MBV), or marshal-by-reference (MBR). Nonremotable types can't cross application domain boundaries and can't be used as arguments or return values in cross-application domain calls. Nonremotable types are discussed in recipe 3.4.

MBV types are serializable types. When you pass an MBV object across an application domain boundary as an argument or return value, the .NET Remoting system serializes the object's current state, passes it to the destination application domain, and creates a new copy of the object with the same state as the original. This results in a copy of the MBV object existing in both application domains. The two instances are initially identical, but they are independent; changes made to one instance are not reflected in the other instance. Here's an example of a serializable type named *Employee* that's passed by value across application domain boundaries. (See recipe 16.1 for details about creating serializable types.)

```
[System.Serializable]
public class Employee {

    // Member implementations
    ⋮
}
```

MBR types are those classes that derive from *System.MarshalByRefObject*. When you pass an MBR object across an application domain boundary as an argument or return value, the .NET Remoting system creates a *proxy* in the destination application domain that represents the remote MBR object. To any class in the destination application domain, the proxy looks and behaves like the remote MBR object that it represents. In reality, when a call is made against the proxy, the .NET Remoting system transparently passes the call and its arguments to the remote application domain and issues the call against the original object. Any results are passed back to the caller via the proxy. Here's a version of the *Employee* class that's passed by reference instead of by value. (See recipe 12.7 for details on how to create MBR types.)

```
public class Employee : System.MarshalByRefObject {

    // Member implementations
    ⋮
}
```

3.3 Avoid Loading Unnecessary Assemblies into Application Domains

Problem

You need to pass an object reference between code running in different application domains; however, you don't want the common language runtime (CLR) to load the object's type metadata into any intermediary application domain.

Solution

Wrap the object reference in a *System.Runtime.Remoting.ObjectHandle* and unwrap the object reference only when you need to access the object.

Discussion

When you pass a marshal by-value (MBV) object across application domain boundaries, the runtime creates a new instance of that object in the destination application domain. This means that the runtime must load the assembly containing that type metadata into the application domain. Passing MBV references across intermediate application domains can result in the runtime loading unnecessary assemblies into application domains. Once loaded, these superfluous assemblies can't be unloaded without unloading the containing application domain. (See recipe 3.9.)

The *ObjectHandle* class allows you to wrap an object reference so that you can pass it between application domains without the runtime loading additional assemblies. When the object reaches the destination application domain, you can unwrap the object reference, causing the runtime to load the required assembly and allowing you to access the object as normal. To wrap an object (such as a *System.Data.DataSet*), use the following statement:

```
// Create a new DataSet.
System.Data.DataSet data1 = new System.Data.DataSet();

// Configure/populate the DataSet.
⋮

// Wrap the DataSet.
System.Runtime.Remoting.ObjectHandle objHandle =
    new System.Runtime.Remoting.ObjectHandle(data1);
```

To unwrap the object, use the *ObjectHandle.Unwrap* method and cast the returned object to the correct type, as shown here.

```
// Unwrap the DataSet
System.Data.DataSet data2 =
    (System.Data.DataSet)objHandle.Unwrap();
```

3.4 Create a Type That Can't Cross Application Domain Boundaries

Problem

You need to create a type such that instances of the type are inaccessible to code in other application domains.

Solution

Ensure the type is nonremotable by making sure it isn't serializable and that it doesn't derive from the *MarshalByRefObject* class.

Discussion

On occasion, you will want to ensure that instances of a type can't transcend application domain boundaries. To create a nonremotable type, ensure that it isn't serializable and that it doesn't derive (directly or indirectly) from the *MarshalByRefObject* class. If you take these steps, you ensure that an object's state can never be accessed from outside the application domain in which the object was instantiated—such objects can't be used as arguments or return values in cross-application domain method calls.

Ensuring that a type isn't serializable is easy because a class doesn't inherit the ability to be serialized from its parent class. To ensure that a type isn't serializable, make sure it doesn't have *System.SerializableAttribute* applied to the type declaration.

Ensuring that a class can't be passed by reference requires a little more attention. Many classes in the .NET class library derive directly or indirectly from *MarshalByRefObject*; you must be careful that you don't inadvertently derive your class from one of these. Commonly used base classes that derive from *MarshalByRefObject* include *System.ComponentModel.Component*, *System.IO.Stream*, *System.IO.TextReader*, *System.IO.TextWriter*, *System.NET.WebRequest*, and *System.Net.WebResponse*. (Check the .NET Framework SDK documentation for a list of classes derived from *MarshalByRefObject*.)

3.5 Load an Assembly into the Current Application Domain

Problem

You need to load an assembly at run time into the current application domain.

Solution

Use the *static Load* or *LoadFrom* methods of the *System.Reflection.Assembly* class.

Discussion

The CLR will automatically load the assemblies identified at build time as being referenced by your assembly. However, you can also explicitly instruct the runtime to load assemblies. The *Load* and *LoadFrom* methods both result in the runtime loading an assembly into the current application domain, and both return an *Assembly* instance that represents the newly loaded assembly. The difference between each method is the arguments that you must provide to identify the assembly to load, and the process that the runtime undertakes to locate the specified assembly.

The *Load* method provides overloads that allow you to specify the assembly to load using one of the following:

- A *string* containing the fully or partially qualified *display name* of the assembly

- A *System.Reflection.AssemblyName* containing details of the assembly

- A *byte* array containing the raw bytes that constitute the assembly

Most often, you will use a display name to load an assembly. A fully qualified display name contains the assembly's text name, version, culture, and public key token, separated by commas (for example, `System.Data, Version=1.0.5000.0, Culture=neutral, PublicKeyToken=b77a5c561934e089`). To specify an assembly that doesn't have a strong name, use `PublicKeyToken=null`. You can also specify a partial display name, but as a minimum, you must specify the assembly name (without the file extension). The following code demonstrates various uses of the *Load* method.

```
// Load the System.Data assembly using a fully
// qualified display name.
string name1 = "System.Data,Version=1.0.5000.0," +
    "Culture=neutral,PublicKeyToken=b77a5c561934e089";
Assembly a1 = Assembly.Load(name1);
```

```
// Load the System.Xml assembly using an AssemblyName.
AssemblyName name2 = new AssemblyName();
name2.Name = "System.Xml";
name2.Version = new Version(1,0,5000,0);
name2.CultureInfo = new CultureInfo("");
name2.SetPublicKeyToken(
    new byte[] {0xb7,0x7a,0x5c,0x56,0x19,0x34,0xe0,0x89});
Assembly a2 = Assembly.Load(name2);

// Load the SomeAssembly assembly using a partial display name
Assembly a3 = Assembly.Load("SomeAssembly");
```

In response to the *Load* call, the runtime undertakes an extensive process to locate and load the specified assembly. Here's a summary; consult the .NET Framework SDK documentation for more details.

1. If you specify a strong-named assembly, the *Load* method will apply version policy and publisher policy to enable requests for one version of an assembly to be satisfied by another version. Version policy is specified in your machine or application configuration file using *<bindingRedirect>* elements. Publisher policy is specified in special resource assemblies installed into the global assembly cache (GAC).

2. Once the runtime has established the correct version of an assembly to use, it attempts to load strong-named assemblies from the GAC.

3. If the assembly isn't strong named or isn't found in the GAC, the runtime looks for applicable *<codeBase>* elements in your machine and application configuration files. A *<codeBase>* element maps an assembly name to a file or a URL. If the assembly is strong named, *<codeBase>* can refer to any location including Internet-based URLs; otherwise, *<codeBase>* must refer to a directory relative to the application directory. If the assembly doesn't exist at the specified location, *Load* throws a *System.IO.FileNotFoundException*.

4. If there are no *<codeBase>* elements relevant to the requested assembly, the runtime will locate the assembly using *probing*. Probing looks for the first file with the assembly's name (with either a .dll or .exe extension) in the following locations:

    ❏   the application root directory

    ❏   directories below the application root that match the assembly's name and culture

    ❏   directories below the application root that are specified in the private *binpath*

The *Load* method is the easiest way to locate and load assemblies, but can also be expensive in terms of processing if the runtime needs to start probing many directories for a weak-named assembly. The *LoadFrom* method allows you to load an assembly from a specific location. If the specified file isn't found, the runtime will throw a *FileNotFoundException*. The runtime won't attempt to locate the assembly in the same way as the *Load* method—*LoadFrom* provides no support for the GAC, policies, *<codebase>* elements, or probing. This code demonstrates use of the *LoadFrom* method to load the assembly named c:\shared\MySharedAssembly.dll. Notice that unlike the *Load* method, *Load-From* requires that you specify the extension of the assembly file.

```
// Load the assembly named c:\shared\MySharedAssembly.dll
Assembly a4 = Assembly.LoadFrom(@"c:\shared\MySharedAssembly.dll");
```

3.6 Execute an Assembly in a Different Application Domain

Problem

You need to execute an assembly in an application domain other than the current one.

Solution

Call the *ExecuteAssembly* method of the *AppDomain* object that represents the application domain, and specify the name of an executable assembly.

Discussion

If you have an executable assembly that you want to load and run in an application domain, the *ExecuteAssembly* method provides the easiest solution. The *ExecuteAssembly* method provides four overloads. The simplest overload takes only a *string* containing the name of the executable assembly to run; you can specify a local file or a URL. Other *ExecuteAssembly* overloads allow you to specify evidence for the assembly (see recipe 13.10) and arguments to pass to the assembly's entry point (equivalent to command-line arguments).

The *ExecuteAssembly* method loads the specified assembly and executes the method defined in metadata as the assembly's entry point (usually the *Main* method). If the specified assembly isn't executable, *ExecuteAssembly* throws a *System.Runtime.InteropServices.COMException*. The CLR doesn't start execution of the assembly in a new thread, so control won't return from the *ExecuteAssembly* method until the newly executed assembly exits. Because the *Execute-Assembly* method loads an assembly using partial information (only the filename), the CLR won't use the GAC or probing to resolve the assembly. (See recipe 3.5 for more information.)

The following example demonstrates the use of the *ExecuteAssembly* method to load and run an assembly. The *ExecuteAssemblyExample* class creates an *AppDomain* and executes itself in that *AppDomain* using the *Execute-Assembly* method. This results in two copies of the *ExecuteAssemblyExample* assembly loaded into two different application domains.

```
using System;

public class ExecuteAssemblyExample {

public static void Main(string[] args) {

        // For the purpose of this example, if this assembly is executing
        // in an AppDomain with the friendly name "NewAppDomain", do not
        // create a new AppDomain. This avoids an infinite loop of
        // AppDomain creation.
        if (AppDomain.CurrentDomain.FriendlyName != "NewAppDomain") {

            // Create a new application domain
            AppDomain domain = AppDomain.CreateDomain("NewAppDomain");

            // Execute this assembly in the new application domain and
            // pass the array of command-line arguments.
            domain.ExecuteAssembly("ExecuteAssemblyExample.exe",
                null, args);
        }

        // Display the command-line arguments to the screen prefixed with
        // the friendly name of the AppDomain.
        foreach (string s in args) {

            Console.WriteLine(AppDomain.CurrentDomain.FriendlyName +
                " : " + s);
        }
    }
}
```

3.7 Instantiate a Type in a Different Application Domain

Problem

You need to instantiate a type in an application domain other than the current one.

Solution

Call the *CreateInstance* or *CreateInstanceFrom* method of the *AppDomain* object that represents the target application domain.

Discussion

The *ExecuteAssembly* method discussed in recipe 3.6 is straightforward to use, but when you are developing sophisticated applications that make use of application domains, you are likely to want more control over the loading of assemblies, instantiation of types, and the invocation of object members within the application domain.

The *CreateInstance* and *CreateInstanceFrom* methods provide a variety of overloads that offer fine-grained control over the process of object instantiation. The simplest overloads assume use of a type's default constructor, but both methods implement overloads that allow you to provide arguments to use any constructor.

The *CreateInstance* method loads a named assembly into the application domain using the process described for the *Assembly.Load* method in recipe 3.5. *CreateInstance* then instantiates a named type and returns a reference to the new object wrapped in an *ObjectHandle* (described in recipe 3.3). The *CreateInstanceFrom* method also instantiates a named type and returns an *ObjectHandle* wrapped object reference; however, *CreateInstanceFrom* loads the specified assembly into the application domain using the process described in recipe 3.5 for the *Assembly.LoadFrom* method.

> **Tip**   *AppDomain* also provides two convenience methods named *CreateInstanceAndUnwrap* and *CreateInstanceFromAndUnwrap* that automatically extract the reference of the instantiated object from the returned *ObjectHandle* object; you must cast the returned *object* to the correct type.

Be aware that if you use *CreateInstance* or *CreateInstanceFrom* to instantiate MBV types in another application domain, the object will be created but the returned *object* reference won't refer to that object. Because of the way MBV objects cross application domain boundaries, the reference will refer to a copy of the object created automatically in the local application domain. Only if you create an MBR type will the returned reference refer to the object in the other application domain. (See recipe 3.2 for more details about MBV and MBR types.)

A common technique to simplify the management of application domains is to use a controller class. A controller class is a custom MBR type. You create an application domain and then instantiate your controller class in the application domain using *CreateInstance*. The controller class implements the functionality required by your application to manipulate the application domain and its contents. This could include the loading of assemblies, creating further application domains, cleaning up prior to the deletion of the application domain, or enumerating program elements (something you can't normally do from outside an application domain).

The following example demonstrates the use of a simplified controller class named *PluginManager*. When instantiated in an application domain, *PluginManager* allows you to instantiate classes that implement the *IPlugin* interface, start and stop those plug-ins, and return a list of currently loaded plug-ins.

```
using System;
using System.Reflection;
using System.Collections;
using System.Collections.Specialized;

// A common interface that all plug-ins must implement.
public interface IPlugin {
    void Start();
    void Stop();
}

// A simple IPlugin implementation to demonstrate the PluginManager
// controller class.
public class SimplePlugin : IPlugin {

    public void Start() {
        Console.WriteLine(AppDomain.CurrentDomain.FriendlyName +
            ": SimplePlugin starting...");
    }

    public void Stop() {
        Console.WriteLine(AppDomain.CurrentDomain.FriendlyName +
            ": SimplePlugin stopping...");
    }
}

// The controller class, which manages the loading and manipulation
// of plug-ins in its application domain.
public class PluginManager : MarshalByRefObject {

    // A ListDictionary to hold keyed references to IPlugin instances.
    private ListDictionary plugins = new ListDictionary();
```

```csharp
// Default constructor.
public PluginManager() {}

// Constructor that loads a set of specified plug-ins on creation.
public PluginManager(ListDictionary pluginList) {

    // Load each of the specified plug-ins.
    foreach (string plugin in pluginList.Keys) {

        this.LoadPlugin((string)pluginList[plugin], plugin);
    }
}

// Load the specified assembly and instantiate the specified
// IPlugin implementation from that assembly.
public bool LoadPlugin(string assemblyName, string pluginName) {

    try {

        // Load the named private assembly.
        Assembly assembly = Assembly.Load(assemblyName);

        // Create the IPlugin instance, ignore case.
        IPlugin plugin =
            (IPlugin)assembly.CreateInstance(pluginName, true);

        if (plugin != null) {

            // Add new IPlugin to ListDictionary
            plugins[pluginName] = plugin;

            return true;

        } else {
            return false;
        }
    } catch {
        return false;
    }
}

public void StartPlugin(string plugin) {

    // Extract the IPlugin from the ListDictionary and call Start.
    ((IPlugin)plugins[plugin]).Start();
}

public void StopPlugin(string plugin) {
```

```
        // Extract the IPLugin from the ListDictionary and call Stop.
        ((IPlugin)plugins[plugin]).Stop();
    }

    public ArrayList GetPluginList() {

        // Return an enumerable list of plug-in names. Take the keys
        // and place them in an ArrayList, which supports marshal-by-value.
        return new ArrayList(plugins.Keys);
    }
}

public class CreateInstanceExample {

    public static void Main() {

        // Create a new application domain.
        AppDomain domain1 = AppDomain.CreateDomain("NewAppDomain1");

        // Create a PluginManager in the new application domain using
        // the default constructor.
        PluginManager manager1 =
            (PluginManager)domain1.CreateInstanceAndUnwrap(
            "CreateInstanceExample", "PluginManager");

        // Load a new plug-in into NewAppDomain1.
        manager1.LoadPlugin("CreateInstanceExample", "SimplePlugin");

        // Start and stop the plug-in in NewAppDomain1.
        manager1.StartPlugin("SimplePlugin");
        manager1.StopPlugin("SimplePlugin");

        // Create a new application domain.
        AppDomain domain2 = AppDomain.CreateDomain("NewAppDomain2");

        // Create a ListDictionary containing a list of plug-ins to create.
        ListDictionary pluginList = new ListDictionary();
        pluginList["SimplePlugin"] = "CreateInstanceExample";

        // Create a PluginManager in the new application domain and
        // specify the default list of plug-ins to create.
        PluginManager manager2 =
            (PluginManager)domain1.CreateInstanceAndUnwrap(
            "CreateInstanceExample", "PluginManager", true, 0,
            null, new object[] {pluginList}, null, null, null);

        // Display the list of plug-ins loaded into NewAppDomain2.
        Console.WriteLine("Plugins in NewAppDomain2:");
```

```
        foreach (string s in manager2.GetPluginList()) {
            Console.WriteLine(" - " + s);
        }

        // Wait to continue
        Console.ReadLine();
    }
}
```

3.8 Pass Data Between Application Domains

Problem

You need a simple mechanism to pass general configuration or state data between application domains.

Solution

Use the *SetData* and *GetData* methods of the *AppDomain* class.

Discussion

You can pass data between application domains as arguments and return values when you invoke the members of objects that exist in other application domains. However, at times it's useful to pass data between application domains in such a way that the data is easily accessible by all code within the application domain.

Every application domain maintains a data cache that contains a set of name/value pairs. Most of the cache content reflects configuration settings of the application domain, such as the values from the *AppDomainSetup* object provided during application domain creation. (See recipe 3.1.) You can also use this data cache as a mechanism to exchange data between application domains or as a simple state storage mechanism for code running within the application domain.

The *SetData* method allows you to associate a string key with an object and store it in the application domain's data cache. The *GetData* method allows you to retrieve an object from the data cache using the key. If code in one application domain calls the *SetData* or *GetData* methods to access the data cache of another application domain, the data object must support marshal-by-value or marshal-by-reference semantics or *System.Runtime.Serialization.SerializationException* is thrown. (See recipe 3.3 for details on the characteristics required to allow objects to transcend application domain boundaries.) This code demonstrates the use of the *SetData* and *GetData* methods by passing a *System.Collections.ArrayList* between two application domains.

```csharp
using System;
using System.Reflection;
using System.Collections;

public class ListModifier {

    public ListModifier () {

        // Get the list from the data cache.
        ArrayList list =
            (ArrayList)AppDomain.CurrentDomain.GetData("Pets");
        // Modify the list.
        list.Add("turtle");
    }
}

public class PassDataExample {

    public static void Main() {

        // Create a new application domain.
        AppDomain domain = AppDomain.CreateDomain("Test");

        // Create an ArrayList and populate with information.
        ArrayList list = new ArrayList();
        list.Add("dog");
        list.Add("cat");
        list.Add("fish");

        // Place the list in the data cache of the new application domain.
        domain.SetData("Pets", list);

        // Instantiate a ListModifier in the new application domain.
        domain.CreateInstance("Recipe03-08", "ListModifier");

        // Get the list and display its contents.
        foreach (string s in (ArrayList)domain.GetData("Pets")) {
            Console.WriteLine(s);
        }

        // Wait to continue
        Console.ReadLine();
    }
}
```

3.9 Unload Assemblies and Application Domains

Problem

You need to unload assemblies or application domains at run time.

Solution

There's no way to unload individual assemblies. You can unload an entire application domain using the *static AppDomain.Unload* method, which has the effect of unloading all assemblies loaded into the application domain.

Discussion

The only way to unload an assembly is to unload the application domain in which the assembly is loaded. Unfortunately, unloading an application domain will unload all of the assemblies that have been loaded into it. This might seem like a heavy-handed and inflexible approach, but with appropriate planning of your application domain and assembly loading structure, it isn't overly restrictive. (This limitation is likely to be resolved in a future version of the .NET Framework.)

You unload an application domain using the *static AppDomain.Unload* method and passing it an *AppDomain* reference to the application domain you wish to unload. You can't unload the default application domain created by the CLR at startup. This code fragment demonstrates the *Unload* method.

```
// Create a new application domain
AppDomain newDomain = AppDomain.CreateDomain("New Domain");

// Load assemblies into the application domain
⋮

// Unload the new application domains
AppDomain.Unload(newDomain);
```

The *Unload* method stops any new threads from entering the specified application domain and calls the *Thread.Abort* method on all threads currently active in the application domain. If the thread calling the *Unload* method is currently running in the specified application domain (making it the target of a *Thread.Abort* call), a new thread is started to carry out the unload operation. If there's a problem unloading an application domain, a *System.CannotUnload-AppDomainException* is thrown by the thread performing the unload operation.

While an application domain is unloading, the CLR calls the finalization method of all objects in the application domain. Depending on the number of objects and nature of their finalization methods, this can take an arbitrary amount of time. The *AppDomain.IsFinalizingForUnload* method returns *true* if the application domain is unloading and the CLR has started to finalize contained objects; otherwise, it returns *false*.

3.10 Retrieve Type Information

Problem

You need to obtain a *System.Type* object that represents a specific type.

Solution

Use one of the following:

- The *typeof* operator
- The *static GetType* method of the *System.Type* class
- The *GetType* method of an existing instance of the type
- The *GetNestedType* or *GetNestedTypes* methods of the *Type* class
- The *GetType* or *GetTypes* methods of the *Assembly* class
- The *GetType*, *GetTypes*, or *FindTypes* methods of the *System.Reflection.Module* class

Discussion

The *Type* object provides a starting point for working with types using reflection. A *Type* object allows you to inspect the metadata of the type, obtain details of the type's members, and create instances of the type. Because of its importance, the .NET Framework provides a variety of mechanisms for obtaining reference to *Type* objects.

The most efficient method of obtaining a *Type* object for a specific type is to use the *typeof* operator shown here.

```
System.Type t1 = typeof(System.Text.StringBuilder);
```

The type name isn't enclosed in quotes and must be resolvable by the compiler. Because the reference is resolved at compile time, the assembly containing the type becomes a static dependency of your assembly and will be listed as such in your assembly's manifest.

An alternative to the *typeof* operator is the *static* method *Type.GetType*, which takes a string containing the type name. Because you use a string to specify the type, you can vary it at run time, which opens the door to a world of dynamic programming opportunities using reflection (see recipe 3.12). If you specify just the type name, the runtime must be able to locate the type in an already loaded assembly. Alternatively, you can specify an assembly-qualified type name. Refer to the .NET Framework SDK documentation for the *Type.Get-Type* method for a complete description of how to structure assembly-qualified type names. The following statements demonstrate the use of the *GetType* method:

```
// Case sensitive, return null if not found
Type t2 = Type.GetType("System.String");
// Case sensitive, throw TypeLoadException if not found
Type t3 = Type.GetType("System.String", true);
// Case insensitive, throw TypeLoadException if not found
Type t4 = Type.GetType("system.string", true, true);
// Assembly qualifed type name
Type t5 = Type.GetType("System.Data.DataSet,System.Data," +
    "Version=1.0.5000.0,Culture=neutral,PublicKeyToken=b77a5c561934e089");
```

To obtain a *Type* object representing the type of an existing object, use the *GetType* method, implemented by *Object* and inherited by all types. Here's an example:

```
System.Text.StringBuilder sb = new System.Text.StringBuilder();
Type t6 = sb.GetType();
```

Table 3-2 summarizes other methods that provide access to *Type* objects.

Table 3-2   Methods That Return Type Objects

Method	Description
Type.GetNestedType	Gets a specified type declared as a nested type within the existing *Type* object
Type.GetNestedTypes	Gets an array of *Type* objects representing the nested types declared within the existing *Type* object
Assembly.GetType	Gets a *Type* object for the specified type declared within the assembly
Assembly.GetTypes	Gets an array of *Type* objects representing the types declared within the assembly
Module.GetType	Gets a *Type* object for the specified type declared within the module

Table 3-2   Methods That Return Type Objects

Method	Description
Module.GetTypes	Gets an array of *Type* objects representing the types declared within the module
Module.FindTypes	Gets a filtered array of *Type* objects representing the types declared within the module—the types are filtered using a delegate that determines if each *Type* should appear in the final array

3.11 Test an Object's Type

Problem

You need to test the type of an object.

Solution

Use the inherited *Object.GetType* method to obtain a *Type* for the object. In some situations, you can also use the *is* and *as* operators to test an object's type.

Discussion

All types inherit the *GetType* method from the *Object* base class. As discussed in recipe 3.10, this method returns a *Type* reference representing the type of the object. The runtime maintains a single instance of *Type* for each type loaded and all references for this type refer to this same object. This means that you can compare two type references efficiently. The *IsStringReader* method shown here demonstrates how to test if an object is a *System.IO.StringReader*.

```
// Create a new StringReader for testing.
Object someObject =
    new StringReader("This is a StringReader");

// Test if someObject is a StringReader by obtaining and
// comparing a Type reference using the typeof operator.
if (typeof(System.IO.StringReader) == someObject.GetType()) {
    // Do something
    ⋮
}
```

C# provides the *is* operator as a quick way to perform the same test as the *IsStringReader* method. In addition, *is* will return *true* if the tested object is derived from the specified class. This code fragment tests if *someObject* is an instance of *System.IO.TextReader*, or a derived class (such as *StringReader*).

```
// Test if someObject is, or is derived from, a TextReader
// using the is operator.
if (someObject is System.IO.TextReader) {
    // Do something
    ⋮
}
```

Both of these approaches require that the type used with the *typeof* and *is* operators be known and resolvable at compile time. A more flexible (but slower) alternative is to use the *Type.GetType* method to return a *Type* reference for a named type. The *Type* reference isn't resolved until run time, which causes the performance hit, but allows you to change the type comparison at run time based on the value of a string. The *IsType* method here returns *true* if an object is of a named type and uses the *Type.IsSubclassOf* method to test if the object is a subclass of the named type.

```
public static bool IsType(object obj, string type) {

    // Get the named type, use case insensitive search, throw
    // an exception if the type is not found.
    Type t = Type.GetType(type, true, true);

    return t == obj.GetType() || obj.GetType().IsSubclassOf(t);
}
```

Finally, you can use the *as* operator to perform a safe cast of any object to a specified type. If the object can't be cast to the specified type, the *as* operator returns *null*. This allows you to perform safe casts that are easy to verify, but the compared type must be resolvable at run time. Here's an example:

```
// Use the "as" operator to perform a safe cast.
StringReader reader = someObject as System.IO.StringReader;
if (reader != null) {
    // Do something with reader
    ⋮
}
```

> **Tip**   The *static* method *GetUnderlyingType* of the *System.Enum* class allows you to retrieve the underlying type of an enumeration.

3.12 Instantiate an Object Using Reflection

Problem

You need to instantiate an object at run time using reflection.

Solution

Obtain a *Type* object representing the type of object you want to instantiate, call its *GetConstructor* method to obtain a *System.Reflection.ConstructorInfo* object representing the constructor you want to use, and execute the *ConstructorInfo.Invoke* method.

Discussion

The first step in creating an object using reflection is to obtain a *Type* object that represents the type you want to instantiate. (See recipe 3.10 for details.) Once you have a *Type* instance, call its *GetConstructor* method to obtain a *ConstructorInfo* representing one of the type's constructors. The most commonly used overload of the *GetConstructor* method takes a *Type* array argument and returns a *ConstructorInfo* representing the constructor that takes the number, order, and type of arguments specified in the *Type* array. To obtain a *ConstructorInfo* representing a parameterless (default) constructor, pass an empty *Type* array (use the *static* field *Type.EmptyTypes*); don't use *null*, or *GetConstructor* will throw a *System.ArgumentNullException*. If *GetConstructor* can't find a constructor with a signature that matches the specified arguments, it will return *null*.

Once you have the desired *ConstructorInfo*, call its *Invoke* method. You must provide an *object* array containing the arguments you want to pass to the constructor. *Invoke* instantiates the new object and returns an *object* reference to it, which you must cast to the appropriate type. The following code demonstrates how to instantiate a *System.Text.StringBuilder* object, specifying the initial content for the *StringBuilder* (a *string*) and its capacity (an *int*).

```
// Obtain the Type for the StringBuilder class.
Type type = typeof(System.Text.StringBuilder);

// Create a Type[] containing Type instances for each
// of the constructor arguments - a string and an int.
Type[] argTypes = new Type[] {typeof(System.String), typeof(System.Int32)};

// Obtain the ConstructorInfo object.
ConstructorInfo cInfo = type.GetConstructor(argTypes);
```

```
// Create an object[] containing the constructor arguments.
object[] argVals = new object[] {"Some string", 30};

// Create the object and cast it to StringBuilder.
StringBuilder sb = (StringBuilder)cInfo.Invoke(argVals);
```

Reflection functionality is commonly used to implement factories in which you use reflection to instantiate concrete classes that either extend a common base class or implement a common interface. Often both an interface and a common base class are used. The abstract base class implements the interface and any common functionality, and then each concrete implementation extends the base class.

There's no mechanism to formally declare that each concrete class must implement constructors with specific signatures. If you intend third parties to implement concrete classes, your documentation must specify the constructor signature called by your factory. A common approach to avoid this problem is to use a default (empty) constructor and configure the object after instantiation using properties and methods. The following code demonstrates a factory to instantiate objects that implement the *IPlugin* interface (first used in recipe 3.7).

```
using System;
using System.Reflection;

// A common interface that all plug-ins must implement.
public interface IPlugin {
    string Description { get; set; }
    void Start();
    void Stop();
}

// An abstract base class from which all plug-ins must derive.
public abstract class AbstractPlugin : IPlugin {

    // Hold a description for the plug-in instance
    private string description = "";

    // Sealed property to get the plug-in description.
    public string Description {
        get { return description; }
        set { description = value; }
    }

    // Declare the members of the IPlugin interface as abstract.
    public abstract void Start();
    public abstract void Stop();
}
```

```
// A simple IPlugin implementation to demonstrate the PluginFactory class.
public class SimplePlugin : AbstractPlugin {

    // Implement Start method.
    public override void Start() {
        Console.WriteLine(Description  + ": Starting...");
    }

    // Implement Stop method.
    public override void Stop() {
        Console.WriteLine(Description + ": Stopping...");
    }
}


// A factory to instantiate instances of IPlugin.
public sealed class PluginFactory {

    public static IPlugin CreatePlugin(string assembly,
        string pluginName, string description) {

        // Obtain the Type for the specified plug-in.
        Type type = Type.GetType(pluginName + ", " + assembly);

        // Obtain the ConstructorInfo object.
        ConstructorInfo cInfo = type.GetConstructor(Type.EmptyTypes);

        // Create the object and cast it to StringBuilder.
        IPlugin plugin = (IPlugin)cInfo.Invoke(null);

        // Configure the new IPlugin
        plugin.Description = description;

        return plugin;
    }
}
```

This statement will create an instance of *SimplePlugin* using the *Plugin-Factory* class.

```
IPlugin plugin = PluginFactory.CreatePlugin(
    "CreateObjectExample",  // Private assembly name
    "SimplePlugin",         // Plug-in class name
    "A Simple Plugin"       // Plug-in instance description
);
```

> **Note** The *System.Activator* class provides two *static* methods named *CreateInstance* and *CreateInstanceFrom* that instantiate objects based on *Type* objects or strings containing type names. See the .NET Framework SDK documentation for more details.

3.13 Create a Custom Attribute

Problem

You need to create a custom attribute.

Solution

Create a class that derives from the *abstract* base class *System.Attribute*. Implement constructors, fields, and properties to allow users to configure the attribute. Use *System.AttributeUsageAttribute* to define the following:

- Which program elements are valid targets of the attribute

- Whether you can apply more than one instance of the attribute to a program element

- Whether the attribute is inherited by derived types

Discussion

Attributes provide a generic mechanism for associating declarative information (metadata) with program elements. This metadata is contained in the compiled assembly allowing programs to retrieve it through reflection at run time. (See recipe 3.14.) Other programs, particularly the CLR, use this information to determine how they should interact with and manage program elements.

To create a custom attribute, derive a class from the *abstract* base class *System.Attribute*. Custom attribute classes must be *public* and by convention should have a name ending in "Attribute". A custom attribute must have at least one *public* constructor. The constructor parameters become the attribute's positional parameters. As with any other class, you can declare more than one constructor, giving users of the attribute the option of using different sets of positional parameters when applying the attribute. Any *public* read/write fields and properties declared by an attribute are automatically exposed as named parameters.

To control how and where a user can apply your attribute, apply the attribute *AttributeUsageAttribute* to your custom attribute. *AttributeUsageAttribute* supports the one positional and two named parameters described in Table 3-3. The default values specify the value that's applied to your custom attribute if you don't apply *AttributeUsageAttribute* or don't specify a value for that particular parameter.

Table 3-3 Members of the *AttributeUsage* Enumeration

Parameter	Type	Description	Default
ValidOn	positional	A member of the *System.AttributeTargets* enumeration that identifies the program elements on which the attribute is valid	*AttributeTargets.All*
AllowMultiple	named	Whether the attribute can be specified more than once for a single element	*false*
Inherited	named	Whether the attribute is inherited by derived classes or overridden members	*true*

The following example shows a custom attribute named *AuthorAttribute*, which you can use to identify the name and company of the person who created an assembly or a class. *AuthorAttribute* declares a single *public* constructor that takes a *string* containing the author's name. This means that users of *AuthorAttribute* must always provide a positional *string* parameter containing the author's name. The *Company* property is *public*, making it an optional named parameter, but the *Name* property is read only—no *set* accessor is declared—meaning that it isn't exposed as a named parameter.

```
using System;

[AttributeUsage(AttributeTargets.Class | AttributeTargets.Assembly,
    AllowMultiple = true, Inherited = false)]
public class AuthorAttribute : System.Attribute {

    private string company; // creator's company
    private string name;    // creator's name

    // Declare a public constructor
    public AuthorAttribute(string name) {
        this.name = name;
        company = "";
    }
```

```
    // Declare a property to get/set the company field
    public string Company {
        get { return company; }
        set { company = value; }
    }

    // Declare a property to get the internal field
    public string Name{
        get { return name;}
    }
}
```

The following example demonstrates some uses of *AuthorAttribute*:

```
// Declare Allen as the assembly author
[assembly:Author("Allen", Company = "Principal Objective Ltd.")]

// Declare a class authored by Allen
[Author("Allen", Company = "Principal Objective Ltd.")]
public class SomeClass {
    ⋮
}

// Declare a class authored by Lena
[Author("Lena")]
public class SomeOtherClass {
    ⋮
}
```

3.14 Inspect the Attributes of a Program Element Using Reflection

Problem

You need to use reflection to inspect the custom attributes applied to a program element.

Solution

Call the *GetCustomAttributes* method on the *System.Reflection.MemberInfo* derived object that represents the program element you need to inspect.

Discussion

All of the classes that represent program elements derive from the *MemberInfo* class. This class includes *Type*, *EventInfo*, *FieldInfo*, *PropertyInfo*, and *Method-Base*. *MethodBase* has two further subclasses: *ConstructorInfo* and *MethodInfo*. If you obtain instances of any of these classes, you can call the inherited method *GetCustomAttributes*, which will return an *object* array containing the custom attributes applied to the program element. The *object* array contains only custom attributes, not those contained in the .NET Framework base class library.

The *GetCustomAttributes* method provides two overloads. The first takes a *bool* that controls whether *GetCustomAttributes* should return attributes inherited from parent classes. The second *GetCustomAttributes* overload takes an additional *Type* argument that acts as a filter, resulting in *GetCustomAttributes* returning only attributes of the specified type.

The following example uses the custom *AuthorAttribute* declared in recipe 3.13 and applies it to the *GetCustomAttributesExample* class. The *Main* method calls the *GetCustomAttributes* method, filtering the attributes so that the method returns only *AuthorAttribute* instances. You can safely cast this set of attributes to *AuthorAttribute* references and access their members without the need to use reflection.

```
using System;

[Author("Lena")]
[Author("Allen", Company = "Principal Objective Ltd.")]
public class GetCustomAttributesExample {

    public static void Main() {

        // Get a Type object for this class.
        Type type = typeof(GetCustomAttributesExample);

        // Get the attributes for the type. Apply a filter so that only
        // instances of AuthorAttribute are returned.
        object[] attrs =
            type.GetCustomAttributes(typeof(AuthorAttribute), true);

        // Enumerate the attributes and display their details.
        foreach (AuthorAttribute a in attrs) {
            Console.WriteLine(a.Name + ", " + a.Company);
        }

        // Wait to continue
        Console.ReadLine();
    }
}
```

4

Threads, Processes, and Synchronization

One of the strengths of the Microsoft Windows operating system is that it allows many programs (processes) to run concurrently and allows each process to perform many tasks concurrently (using multiple threads). This chapter describes how to control processes and threads in your own applications using the features provided by the Microsoft .NET Framework class library. Specifically, the recipes in this chapter describe how to do the following:

■ Use various techniques and features of the .NET Framework to create new threads (recipes 4.1 through 4.5).

■ Control the execution of a thread and know when it has finished (recipes 4.6 and 4.7).

■ Synchronize the execution of multiple threads (recipes 4.8 and 4.9).

■ Start and stop new processes (recipes 4.10 and 4.11).

■ Ensure that only one instance of an application is able to run concurrently (recipe 4.12).

4.1 Execute a Method Using the Thread Pool

Problem

You need to execute a method using a thread from the runtime's thread pool.

Solution

Declare a method containing the code you want to execute; the method must return *void* and take a single *object* argument. Create a *System.Threading.Wait-Callback* delegate instance that references the method. Call the *static* method *QueueUserWorkItem* of the *System.Threading.ThreadPool* class, and pass the delegate instance as an argument. The runtime will queue the delegate instance and execute it when a thread-pool thread becomes available.

Discussion

Applications that use many short-lived threads or maintain large numbers of concurrent threads can suffer performance degradation because of the overhead associated with the creation, operation, and destruction of threads. In addition, it's common in multithreaded systems for threads to sit idle a large portion of the time while they wait for the appropriate conditions to trigger their execution. Use of a thread pool provides a common solution to improve the scalability, efficiency, and performance of multithreaded systems.

The .NET Framework provides a simple thread-pool implementation accessible through the *static* members of the *ThreadPool* class. The *QueueUser-WorkItem* method allows you to execute a method using a thread-pool thread by placing a work item on a queue. The work item is represented by a *Wait-Callback* delegate instance that references the method you want to execute. As a thread from the thread pool becomes available, it takes the next work item from the queue and executes it. The thread carries out the work assigned to it, and when it's finished, instead of terminating, the thread returns to the thread pool and takes the next work item from the work queue.

Use of the runtime's thread pool simplifies multithreaded programming dramatically; however, be aware that the implementation is a simple, general-purpose thread pool. Before deciding to use the thread pool, consider the following points:

- The runtime host determines the maximum number of threads allocated to the thread pool; you can't change this maximum number using configuration parameters or from within managed code. The default limit is 25 threads per CPU in your system. The maximum number of threads in the thread pool does not limit the number of items that can be waiting in the queue.

- As well as allowing you to use the thread pool to execute code directly, the runtime uses the thread pool for many purposes internally. This includes asynchronous method execution (see recipe 4.2) and the execution of timer events (see recipe 4.3). All of these uses can lead to heavy contention for the thread-pool threads, meaning that the work queue can become very long. Although the work queue's maximum length is limited only by the amount of memory available to the runtime's process, an excessively long queue will result in long delays before queued work items are executed.

■ You shouldn't use the thread pool to execute long-running processes. The limited number of threads in the thread pool means that a handful of threads tied up with long-running processes can have a significant effect on the overall performance of the thread pool. Specifically, you should avoid putting thread-pool threads to sleep for any length of time.

■ You have no control over the scheduling of thread-pool threads, nor can you prioritize work items. The thread pool handles each work item in the sequence in which you add it to the work queue.

■ Once a work item is queued, it can't be cancelled or stopped.

The following example demonstrates the use of the *ThreadPool* class to execute a method named *DisplayMessage*. The example passes *DisplayMessage* to the thread pool twice, first with no arguments, and then with a *MessageInfo* object, which allows you to control which message the new thread will display.

```
using System;
using System.Threading;

// A class used to pass data to the DisplayMessage method when it is
// executed using the thread pool.
public class MessageInfo {

    private int iterations;
    private string message;

    // A constructor that takes configuration settings for the thread.
    public MessageInfo(int iterations, string message) {

        this.iterations = iterations;
        this.message = message;
    }

    // Properties to retrieve configuration settings.
    public int Iterations { get { return iterations; } }
    public string Message { get { return message; } }
}
```

```csharp
public class ThreadPoolExample {

    // Displays a message to the console.
    public static void DisplayMessage(object state) {

        // Cast the state argument to a MessageInfo object.
        MessageInfo config = state as MessageInfo;

        // If the config argument is null, no arguments were passed to
        // the ThreadPool.QueueUserWorkItem method, use default values.
        if (config == null) {

            // Display a fixed message to the console 3 times.
            for (int count = 0; count < 3; count++) {

                Console.WriteLine("A thread pool example.");

                // Sleep for the purpose of demonstration. Avoid sleeping
                // on thread-pool threads in real applications.
                Thread.Sleep(1000);
            }

        } else {

            // Display the specified message the specified number of times.
            for (int count = 0; count < config.Iterations; count++) {

                Console.WriteLine(config.Message);

                // Sleep for the purpose of demonstration. Avoid sleeping
                // on thread-pool threads in real applications.
                Thread.Sleep(1000);
            }
        }
    }

    public static void Main() {

        // Create a delegate instance to enable us to pass the
        // DisplayMessage method to the thread pool for execution.
        WaitCallback workMethod =
            new WaitCallback(ThreadPoolExample.DisplayMessage);

        // Execute DisplayMessage using the thread pool and no arguments.
        ThreadPool.QueueUserWorkItem(workMethod);

        // Execute DisplayMessage using the thread pool and providing a
        // MessageInfo object to pass to the DisplayMessage method.
```

```
MessageInfo info =
    new MessageInfo(5, "A thread pool example with arguments.");

ThreadPool.QueueUserWorkItem(workMethod, info);

// Wait to continue.
Console.WriteLine("Main method complete. Press Enter.");
Console.ReadLine();
    }
}
```

4.2 Execute a Method Asynchronously

Problem

You need to start execution of a method and continue with other tasks while the method runs on a separate thread. After the method completes, you need to retrieve its return value.

Solution

Declare a delegate with the same signature as the method you want to execute. Create an instance of the delegate that references the method. Call the *Begin-Invoke* method of the delegate instance to start execution of your method. Use the *EndInvoke* method to determine the method's status as well as obtain the method's return value if complete.

Discussion

Typically, when you invoke a method you do so synchronously, meaning that the calling code blocks until the method is complete. Most of the time, this is the expected and desired behavior because your code requires the operation to complete before it can continue. However, sometimes it's useful to execute a method asynchronously, meaning that you start the method in a separate thread and then continue with other operations.

The .NET Framework implements an asynchronous execution pattern that allows you to call any method asynchronously using a delegate. When you declare and compile a delegate, the compiler automatically generates two methods that support asynchronous execution: *BeginInvoke* and *EndInvoke*. When you call *BeginInvoke* on a delegate instance, the method referenced by the delegate is queued for asynchronous execution. Control returns to the caller immediately, and the referenced method executes in the context of the first available thread-pool thread.

The signature of the *BeginInvoke* method includes the same arguments as those specified by the delegate signature, followed by two additional arguments to support asynchronous completion. These additional arguments are

- A *System.AsyncCallback* delegate instance that references a method that the runtime will call when the asynchronous method completes. The method is executed in the context of a thread-pool thread. Passing *null* means that no method is called and you must use another mechanism (discussed later in this recipe) to determine when the asynchronous method is complete.

- An *object* reference that the runtime associates with the asynchronous operation. The asynchronous method does not use nor have access to this object but it's available to your code when the method completes, allowing you to associate useful state information with an asynchronous operation. For example, this object allows you to map results against initiated operations in situations where you initiate many asynchronous operations that use a common callback method to perform completion.

The *EndInvoke* method allows you to retrieve the return value of a method that was executed asynchronously, but you must first determine when it has finished. Here are the four techniques for determining if an asynchronous method has finished.

- **Blocking**   Blocking stops the execution of the current thread until the asynchronous method completes execution. In effect, this is much the same as synchronous execution. However, you do have the flexibility to decide exactly when your code enters the blocked state, giving you the opportunity to carry out some additional processing before blocking.

- **Polling**   Polling involves repeatedly testing the state of an asynchronous method to determine if it's complete. This is a very simple technique and is not particularly efficient from a processing perspective. You should avoid tight loops that consume processor time; it's best to put the polling thread to sleep for a period using *Thread.Sleep* between completion tests. Because polling involves maintaining a loop, the actions of the waiting thread are limited, but you can easily update some kind of progress indicator.

- **Waiting**   Waiting uses an object derived from the *System.Threading.WaitHandle* class to signal when the asynchronous method completes. Waiting is a more efficient version of polling and in addition allows you to wait for multiple asynchronous methods to complete. You can also specify time-out values to allow your waiting thread to fail if the asynchronous method takes too long, or if you want to periodically update a status indicator.

- ■ **Callbacks**   A callback is a method that the runtime calls when an asynchronous operation completes. The calling code does not have to take any steps to determine when the asynchronous method is complete and is free to continue with other processing. Callbacks provide the greatest flexibility, but also introduce the greatest complexity, especially if you have many asynchronous operations active concurrently that all use the same callback. In such cases, you must use appropriate state objects to match completed methods against those you initiated.

The *AsyncExecutionExample* class in the sample code for this chapter demonstrates use of the asynchronous execution pattern. It uses a delegate named *AsyncExampleDelegate* to execute a method named *LongRunningMethod* asynchronously. *LongRunningMethod* simulates a long-running method using a configurable delay (produced using *Thread.Sleep*). Here is the code for *AsyncExampleDelegate* and *LongRunningMethod*.

```
// A delegate that allows you to perform asynchronous execution of
// AsyncExecutionExample.LongRunningMethod.
public delegate DateTime AsyncExampleDelegate(int delay, string name);

// A simulated long running method.
public static DateTime LongRunningMethod(int delay, string name) {

    Console.WriteLine("{0} : {1} example - thread starting.",
        DateTime.Now.ToString("HH:mm:ss.ffff"), name);

    // Simulate time consuming processing.
    Thread.Sleep(delay);

    Console.WriteLine("{0} : {1} example - thread finishing.",
        DateTime.Now.ToString("HH:mm:ss.ffff"), name);

    // Return the method's completion time.
    return DateTime.Now;
}
```

AsyncExecutionExample contains five methods that demonstrate different approaches for handled asynchronous method completion. A description of these methods and their code is provided here.

The *BlockingExample* method executes *LongRunningMethod* asynchronously and continues with a limited set of processing. Once this processing is complete, *BlockingExample* blocks until *LongRunningMethod* completes. To block, *BlockingExample* calls the *EndInvoke* method of the *AsyncExample-Delegate* delegate instance. If *LongRunningMethod* has already finished, *End-Invoke* returns immediately; otherwise, *BlockingExample* blocks until *LongRunningMethod* completes.

```
public static void BlockingExample() {

    Console.WriteLine(Environment.NewLine +
        "*** Running Blocking Example ***");

    // Invoke LongRunningMethod asynchronously. Pass null for both the
    // callback delegate and the asynchronous state object.
    AsyncExampleDelegate longRunningMethod =
        new AsyncExampleDelegate(LongRunningMethod);

    IAsyncResult asyncResult = longRunningMethod.BeginInvoke(2000,
        "Blocking", null, null);

    // Perform other processing until ready to block.
    for (int count = 0; count < 3; count++) {
        Console.WriteLine("{0} : Continue processing until ready " +
            "to block...", DateTime.Now.ToString("HH:mm:ss.ffff"));
        Thread.Sleep(200);
    }

    // Block until the asynchronous method completes and obtain
    // completion data.
    Console.WriteLine("{0} : Blocking until method is complete...",
        DateTime.Now.ToString("HH:mm:ss.ffff"));
    DateTime completion = longRunningMethod.EndInvoke(asyncResult);

    // Display completion information
    Console.WriteLine("{0} : Blocking example complete.",
        completion.ToString("HH:mm:ss.ffff"));
}
```

The *PollingExample* method executes *LongRunningMethod* asynchronously and then enters a polling loop until *LongRunningMethod* completes. *PollingExample* tests the *IsCompleted* property of the *IAsyncResult* instance returned by *BeginInvoke* to determine if *LongRunningMethod* is complete; otherwise, *PollingExample* calls *Thread.Sleep*.

```
public static void PollingExample() {

    Console.WriteLine(Environment.NewLine +
        "*** Running Polling Example ***");

    // Invoke LongRunningMethod asynchronously. Pass null for both the
    // callback delegate and the asynchronous state object.
    AsyncExampleDelegate longRunningMethod =
        new AsyncExampleDelegate(LongRunningMethod);

    IAsyncResult asyncResult = longRunningMethod.BeginInvoke(2000,
        "Polling", null, null);

    // Poll the asynchronous method to test for completion. If not
    // complete sleep for 300ms before polling again.
    Console.WriteLine("{0} : Poll repeatedly until method is " +
        "complete...", DateTime.Now.ToString("HH:mm:ss.ffff"));
    while(!asyncResult.IsCompleted) {
        Console.WriteLine("{0} : Polling...",
            DateTime.Now.ToString("HH:mm:ss.ffff"));
        Thread.Sleep(300);
    }

    // Obtain the completion data for the asynchronous method.
    DateTime completion = longRunningMethod.EndInvoke(asyncResult);

    // Display completion information
    Console.WriteLine("{0} : Polling example complete.",
        completion.ToString("HH:mm:ss.ffff"));
}
```

The *WaitingExample* method executes *LongRunningMethod* asynchronously and then waits until *LongRunningMethod* completes. *WaitingExample* uses the *AsyncWaitHandle* property of the *IAsyncResult* instance returned by *BeginInvoke* to obtain a *WaitHandle* and then calls its *WaitOne* method. Use of a time-out allows *WaitingExample* to break out of waiting in order to perform other processing or to fail completely if the asynchronous method is taking too long.

```
public static void WaitingExample() {

    Console.WriteLine(Environment.NewLine +
        "*** Running Waiting Example ***");

    // Invoke LongRunningMethod asynchronously. Pass null for both the
    // callback delegate and the asynchronous state object.
    AsyncExampleDelegate longRunningMethod =
```

```
        new AsyncExampleDelegate(LongRunningMethod);

    IAsyncResult asyncResult = longRunningMethod.BeginInvoke(2000,
        "Waiting", null, null);

    // Wait for the asynchronous method to complete. Time out after
    // 300ms and display status to the console before continuing to
    // wait.
    Console.WriteLine("{0} : Waiting until method is complete...",
        DateTime.Now.ToString("HH:mm:ss.ffff"));
    while(!asyncResult.AsyncWaitHandle.WaitOne(300, false)) {
        Console.WriteLine("{0} : Wait timeout...",
            DateTime.Now.ToString("HH:mm:ss.ffff"));
    }

    // Obtain the completion data for the asynchronous method.
    DateTime completion = longRunningMethod.EndInvoke(asyncResult);

    // Display completion information
    Console.WriteLine("{0} : Waiting example complete.",
        completion.ToString("HH:mm:ss.ffff"));
}
```

The *WaitAllExample* method executes *LongRunningMethod* asynchronously multiple times and then uses an array of *WaitHandle* objects to wait efficiently until *all* of the methods are complete.

```
public static void WaitAllExample() {

    Console.WriteLine(Environment.NewLine +
        "*** Running WaitAll Example ***");

    // An ArrayList to hold the IAsyncResult instances for each of the
    // asynchronous methods started.
    ArrayList asyncResults = new ArrayList(3);

    // Invoke three LongRunningMethods asynchronously. Pass null for
    // both the callback delegate and the asynchronous state object.
    // Add the IAsyncResult instance for each method to the ArrayList.
    AsyncExampleDelegate longRunningMethod =
        new AsyncExampleDelegate(LongRunningMethod);

    asyncResults.Add(longRunningMethod.BeginInvoke(3000,
        "WaitAll 1", null, null));

    asyncResults.Add(longRunningMethod.BeginInvoke(2500,
        "WaitAll 2", null, null));
```

```
asyncResults.Add(longRunningMethod.BeginInvoke(1500,
    "WaitAll 3", null, null));

// Create an array of WaitHandle objects that will be used to wait
// for the completion of all of the asynchronous methods.
WaitHandle[] waitHandles = new WaitHandle[3];

for (int count = 0; count < 3; count++) {

    waitHandles[count] =
        ((IAsyncResult)asyncResults[count]).AsyncWaitHandle;
}

// Wait for all three asynchronous method to complete. Time out
// after 300ms and display status to the console before continuing
// to wait.
Console.WriteLine("{0} : Waiting until all 3 methods are " +
    "complete...", DateTime.Now.ToString("HH:mm:ss.ffff"));
while(!WaitHandle.WaitAll(waitHandles, 300, false)) {
    Console.WriteLine("{0} : WaitAll timeout...",
        DateTime.Now.ToString("HH:mm:ss.ffff"));
}

// Inspect the completion data for each method and determine the
// time at which the final method completed.
DateTime completion = DateTime.MinValue;

foreach (IAsyncResult result in asyncResults) {

    DateTime time = longRunningMethod.EndInvoke(result);
    if ( time > completion) completion = time;
}

// Display completion information
Console.WriteLine("{0} : WaitAll example complete.",
    completion.ToString("HH:mm:ss.ffff"));
}
```

The *CallbackExample* method executes *LongRunningMethod* asynchronously and passes an *AsyncCallback* delegate instance (that references the *CallbackHandler* method) to the *BeginInvoke* method. The referenced *CallbackHandler* method is called automatically when the asynchronous *LongRunningMethod* completes, leaving the *CallbackExample* method completely free to continue processing.

```
public static void CallbackExample() {

    Console.WriteLine(Environment.NewLine +
        "*** Running Callback Example ***");
```

```
// Invoke LongRunningMethod asynchronously. Pass an AsyncCallback
// delegate instance referencing the CallbackHandler method which
// will be called automatically when the asynchronous method
// completes. Pass a reference to the AsyncExampleDelegate delegate
// instance as asynchronous state; otherwise, the callback method
// has no access to the delegate instance in order to call
// EndInvoke.
AsyncExampleDelegate longRunningMethod =
    new AsyncExampleDelegate(LongRunningMethod);

IAsyncResult asyncResult = longRunningMethod.BeginInvoke(2000,
    "Callback", new AsyncCallback(CallbackHandler),
    longRunningMethod);

// Continue with other processing.
for (int count = 0; count < 15; count++) {
    Console.WriteLine("{0} : Continue processing...",
        DateTime.Now.ToString("HH:mm:ss.ffff"));
    Thread.Sleep(200);
}
}

// A method to handle asynchronous completion using callbacks.
public static void CallbackHandler(IAsyncResult result) {

    // Extract the reference to the AsyncExampleDelegate instance
    // from the IAsyncResult instance. This allows us to obtain the
    // completion data.
    AsyncExampleDelegate longRunningMethod =
        (AsyncExampleDelegate)result.AsyncState;

    // Obtain the completion data for the asynchronous method.
    DateTime completion = longRunningMethod.EndInvoke(result);

    // Display completion information
    Console.WriteLine("{0} : Callback example complete.",
        completion.ToString("HH:mm:ss.ffff"));
}
```

4.3 Execute a Method Using a Timer

Problem

You need to execute a method in a separate thread either periodically or at a specific time.

Solution

Declare a method that returns *void* and takes a single *object* argument. Create a *System.Threading.TimerCallback* delegate instance that references the method. Create a *System.Threading.Timer* object and pass it the *TimerCallback* delegate instance along with a state *object* that the timer will pass to your method when the timer expires. The runtime will wait until the timer expires and then call your method using a thread from the thread pool.

Discussion

It's often useful to execute a method at a particular time or at regular intervals. For example, you might need to back up data at 1:00 A.M. every day or to clean a data cache every 20 minutes. The *Timer* class makes the timed execution of methods straightforward, allowing you to execute a method referenced by a *TimerCallback* delegate at specified intervals. The referenced method executes in the context of a thread from the thread pool.

When you create a *Timer* object, you specify two time intervals. The first value specifies the millisecond delay until the *Timer* first executes your method. Specify 0 to execute the method immediately, and *System.Threading.Timeout.Infinite* to create the *Timer* in an unstarted state. The second value specifies the interval after which the *Timer* will repeatedly call your method following the initial execution. If you specify a value of 0 or *Timeout.Infinite*, the *Timer* will execute the method only once (as long as the initial delay is not *Timeout.Infinite*). The time intervals can be specified as *int*, *long*, *uint*, or *System.TimeSpan* values.

Once you have created a *Timer* object, you can modify the intervals used by the timer using the *Change* method, but you can't change the method that is called. When you have finished with a *Timer* you should call its *Dispose* method to free system resources held by the timer. Disposing of the *Timer* cancels any method that is scheduled for execution.

The *TimerExample* class shown here demonstrates the use of a *Timer* to call a method named *TimerHandler*. Initially, the *Timer* is configured to call *TimerHandler* after two seconds and then at one-second intervals. The example allows you to enter a new millisecond interval in the console, which is applied using the *Timer.Change* method.

```
using System;
using System.Threading;

public class TimerExample {

    // The method that is executed when the timer expires. Displays
    // a message to the console.
```

```csharp
private static void TimerHandler(object state) {

    Console.WriteLine("{0} : {1}",
        DateTime.Now.ToString("HH:mm:ss.ffff"), state);
}

public static void Main() {

    // Create a new TimerCallback delegate instance that
    // references the static TimerHandler method. TimerHandler
    // will be called when the timer expires.
    TimerCallback handler = new TimerCallback(TimerHandler);

    // Create the state object that is passed to the TimerHandler
    // method when it is triggered. In this case a message to display.
    string state = "Timer expired.";

    Console.WriteLine("{0} : Creating Timer.",
        DateTime.Now.ToString("HH:mm:ss.ffff"));

    // Create a Timer that fires first after 2 seconds and then every
    // second.
    using (Timer timer = new Timer(handler, state, 2000, 1000)) {

        int period;

        // Read the new timer interval from the console until the
        // user enters 0 (zero). Invalid values use a default value
        // of 0, which will stop the example.
        do {

            try {
                period = Int32.Parse(Console.ReadLine());
            } catch {
                period = 0;
            }

            // Change the timer to fire using the new interval starting
            // immediately.
            if (period > 0) timer.Change(0, period);

        } while (period > 0);
    }

    // Wait to continue.
    Console.WriteLine("Main method complete. Press Enter.");
    Console.ReadLine();
}
}
```

Although primarily used for calling methods at regular intervals, the *Timer* also provides the flexibility to call a method at a specific time. You must calculate the difference between the current time and the desired execution time as demonstrated in the *RunAt* method shown here. (The *RunAt* method is a member of the *RunAtExample* class in the sample code for this chapter.)

```
public static void RunAt(DateTime execTime) {

    // Calculate the difference between the specified execution
    // time and the current time.
    TimeSpan waitTime = execTime - DateTime.Now;

    if (waitTime < new TimeSpan(0)) waitTime = new TimeSpan(0);

    // Create a new TimerCallback delegate instance that
    // references the static TimerHandler method. TimerHandler
    // will be called when the timer expires.
    TimerCallback handler = new TimerCallback(TimerHandler);

    // Create a Timer that fires once at the specified time. Specify
    // an interval of -1 to stop the timer executing the method
    // repeatedly.
    new Timer(handler, null, waitTime, new TimeSpan(-1));
}
```

4.4 Execute a Method by Signaling a *WaitHandle* Object

Problem

You need to execute one or more methods automatically when an object derived from *System.Threading.WaitHandle* is signaled.

Solution

Create a *System.Threading.WaitOrTimerCallback* delegate instance that references the method you want to execute. Register the delegate instance and the *WaitHandle* object that will trigger execution with the thread pool using the static *ThreadPool.RegisterWaitForSingleObject* method.

Discussion

You can use classes derived from the *WaitHandle* class (discussed in recipe 4.2) to trigger the execution of a method. Using the *RegisterWaitForSingleObject* method of the *ThreadPool* class, you can register a *WaitOrTimerCallback* delegate instance for execution by a thread-pool thread when a specified *Wait-Handle*-derived object enters a signaled state. You can configure the thread pool to execute the method only once or to automatically reregister the method for execution each time the *WaitHandle* is signaled. If the *WaitHandle* is already signaled when you call *RegisterWaitForSingleObject*, the method will execute immediately. The *Unregister* method of the *System.Threading.RegisteredWaitHandle* object returned by the *RegisterWaitForSingleObject* method is used to cancel a registered wait operation.

The class most commonly used as a trigger is *AutoResetEvent*, which automatically returns to an unsignaled state after it's signaled. However, you can also use the *ManualResetEvent* and *Mutex* classes, which require you to change the signaled state manually. The following example demonstrates the use of an *AutoResetEvent* to trigger the execution of a method named *EventHandler*.

```csharp
using System;
using System.Threading;

public class EventExecutionExample {

    // A method that is executed when the AutoResetEvent is signaled
    // or the wait operation times out.
    private static void EventHandler(object state, bool timedout) {

        // Display appropriate message to the console based on whether
        // the wait timed out or the AutoResetEvent was signaled.
        if (timedout) {

            Console.WriteLine("{0} : Wait timed out.",
                DateTime.Now.ToString("HH:mm:ss.ffff"));
        } else {

            Console.WriteLine("{0} : {1}",
                DateTime.Now.ToString("HH:mm:ss.ffff"), state);
        }
    }

    public static void Main() {

        // Create the new AutoResetEvent in an unsignaled state.
        AutoResetEvent autoEvent = new AutoResetEvent(false);

        // Create a new WaitOrTimerCallback delegate instance that
        // references the static EventHandler method. EventHandler
        // will be called when the AutoResetEvent is signaled or
        // the wait times out.
        WaitOrTimerCallback handler =
```

```
    new WaitOrTimerCallback(EventHandler);

// Create the state object that is passed to the event handler
// method when it is triggered. In this case a message to display.
string state = "AutoResetEvent signaled.";

// Register the delegate instance to wait for the AutoResetEvent to
// be signaled. Set a time-out of 3 seconds, and configure the wait
// operation to reset after activation (last argument).
RegisteredWaitHandle handle =
    ThreadPool.RegisterWaitForSingleObject(autoEvent, handler,
    state, 3000, false);

Console.WriteLine("Press ENTER to signal the AutoResetEvent" +
    " or enter \"Cancel\" to unregister the wait operation.");

while (Console.ReadLine().ToUpper() != "CANCEL") {

    // If "Cancel" has not been entered into the console, signal
    // the AutoResetEvent, which will cause the EventHandler
    // method to execute. The AutoResetEvent will automatically
    // revert to an unsignaled state.
    autoEvent.Set();
}

// Unregister the wait operation.
Console.WriteLine("Unregistering wait operation.");
handle.Unregister(null);

// Wait to continue.
Console.WriteLine("Main method complete. Press Enter.");
Console.ReadLine();
    }
}
```

4.5 Execute a Method Using a New Thread

Problem

You need to execute code in its own thread, and you want complete control over the thread's state and operation.

Solution

Declare a method that returns *void* and takes no arguments. Create a *System.Threading.ThreadStart* delegate instance that references the method. Create a new *System.Threading.Thread* object, and pass the delegate instance as an argument to its constructor. Call the *Thread.Start* method to start the execution of your method.

Discussion

For maximum control and flexibility when creating multithreaded applications, you need to take a direct role in the creation and management of threads. This is the most complex approach to multithreaded programming, but it's the only way to overcome the restrictions and limitations inherent in the approaches using thread-pool threads, as discussed in the four preceding recipes. The *Thread* class provides the mechanism through which you create and control threads. To create and start a new thread, follow this process:

1. Create a *ThreadStart* delegate instance that references the method that contains the code you want the new thread to run. As with any delegate, *ThreadStart* can reference a *static* method or an instance method. The referenced method must take no arguments and return *void*.

2. Create a new *Thread* object, and pass the *ThreadStart* delegate instance as an argument to the *Thread* constructor. The new thread has an initial state of *Unstarted* (a member of the *System.Threading.ThreadState* enumeration).

3. Call *Start* on the *Thread* object, which changes its state to *ThreadState.Running* and begins execution of the method referenced by the *ThreadStart* delegate instance. (If you call *Start* more than once, it will throw a *System.Threading.ThreadStateException*.)

Because the *ThreadStart* delegate declares no arguments, you can't pass data directly to the referenced method. To pass data to a new thread, you must configure the data such that it's accessible to the code running in the new thread. The most common approach is to declare a class that encapsulates both the data required by the thread and the method executed by the thread. When you want to start a new thread, create an instance of the container object, configure its state, and then start the new thread. Here is an example.

```
using System;
using System.Threading;
```

```
public class ThreadExample {

    // Private member variables hold state for use by the new thread.
    private int iterations;
    private string message;
    private int delay;

    public ThreadExample(int iterations, string message, int delay) {

        this.iterations = iterations;
        this.message = message;
        this.delay = delay;
    }

    public void Start() {

        // Create a ThreadStart delegate instance that references
        // DisplayMessage.
        ThreadStart method = new ThreadStart(this.DisplayMessage);

        // Create a new thread object and pass the ThreadStart
        // delegate instance to its constructor.
        Thread thread = new Thread(method);

        Console.WriteLine("{0} : Starting new thread.",
            DateTime.Now.ToString("HH:mm:ss.ffff"));

        // Start the new thread.
        thread.Start();
    }

    private void DisplayMessage() {

        // Display the message to the console the specified number of
        // times, sleeping between each message for the specified duration.
        for (int count = 0; count < iterations; count++) {

            Console.WriteLine("{0} : {1}",
                DateTime.Now.ToString("HH:mm:ss.ffff"), message);

            // Sleep for the specified period.
            Thread.Sleep(delay);
        }
    }

    public static void Main() {
```

```
// Create a new ThreadExample object.
ThreadExample example =
    new ThreadExample(5, "A thread example.", 500);

// Start the ThreadExample object.
example.Start();

// Continue with other processing.
for (int count = 0; count < 13; count++) {
    Console.WriteLine("{0} : Continue processing...",
        DateTime.Now.ToString("HH:mm:ss.ffff"));
    Thread.Sleep(200);
}

// Wait to continue.
Console.WriteLine("Main method complete. Press Enter.");
Console.ReadLine();
        }
    }
```

4.6 Control the Execution of a Thread

Problem

You need to control when a thread starts and stops and be able to pause the execution of a thread.

Solution

Use the *Abort*, *Interrupt*, *Resume*, *Start*, and *Suspend* methods of the *Thread* you need to control.

Discussion

The methods of the *Thread* class summarized in Table 4-1 provide a high degree of control over the execution of a thread. Each of these methods returns to the calling thread immediately. However, the current thread state plays an important role in the result of the method call, and the state of a thread can change rapidly. As a result, you must code defensively to catch and handle the different exceptions that can be thrown when you try to control the execution of a *Thread*.

Table 4-1   Controlling the Execution of a Thread

Method	Description
Abort	Terminates a thread by throwing a *System.Threading.ThreadAbortException* in the code that the thread is running. The aborted thread's code can catch the *ThreadAbortException* to perform cleanup, but the runtime will automatically throw the exception again to ensure that the thread terminates, unless *ResetAbort* is called. *Abort* returns immediately, but the runtime determines exactly when the exception is thrown, so you can't assume the thread has terminated by *Abort* returns. You should use the techniques described in recipe 4.7 if you need to determine when the aborted thread is actually finished. Once you abort a thread, you can't restart it.
Interrupt	Throws a *System.Threading.ThreadInterruptedException* in the code that the thread is running as long as the thread is currently in a *WaitSleepJoin* state. This means that the thread has called *Sleep*, *Join* (recipe 4.7) or is waiting to be signaled by a *WaitHandle* or acquire an object used for thread synchronization (recipe 4.8). If the thread is not in the *WaitSleepJoin* state, *ThreadInterruptedException* is thrown the next time the thread does enter the *WaitSleepJoin* state.
Resume	Resumes the execution of a suspended thread. (See the *Suspend* method.) Calling *Resume* on a thread that isn't suspended generates a *System.Threading.ThreadStateException* in the calling thread.
Start	Starts the execution of a new thread; see recipe 4.5 for a description of how to use the *Start* method.
Suspend	Suspends the execution of a thread until the *Resume* method is called. Suspending an already suspended thread has no effect, but calling *Suspend* on a thread that hasn't started or is already finished will generate a *ThreadStateException* in the calling thread.

The *ThreadControlExample* class shown here demonstrates the use of the *Thread* methods listed in Table 4-1. The example starts a second thread that periodically displays a message to the console and then goes to sleep. By entering commands at the command prompt, you can interrupt, suspend, resume, and abort the secondary thread.

```
using System;
using System.Threading;

public class ThreadControlExample {

    private static void DisplayMessage() {

        // Repeatedly display a message to the console.
        while (true) {
```

```
        try {

            Console.WriteLine("{0} : Second thread running. Enter"
                + " (S)uspend, (R)esume, (I)nterrupt, or (E)xit.",
                DateTime.Now.ToString("HH:mm:ss.ffff"));

            // Sleep for 2 seconds.
            Thread.Sleep(2000);

        } catch (ThreadInterruptedException) {

            // Thread has been interrupted. Catching the
            // ThreadInterruptedException allows the example to
            // take appropriate action and continue execution.
            Console.WriteLine("{0} : Second thread interrupted.",
                DateTime.Now.ToString("HH:mm:ss.ffff"));

        } catch (ThreadAbortException abortEx) {

            // The object in the ThreadAbortException.ExceptionState
            // property is provided by the thread that called
            // Thread.Abort. In this case it contains a string that
            // describes the reason for the abort.
            Console.WriteLine("{0} : Second thread aborted ({1})",
                DateTime.Now.ToString("HH:mm:ss.ffff"),
                abortEx.ExceptionState);

            // Even though ThreadAbortException has been handled, the
            // runtime will throw it again to ensure the thread
            // terminates.
        }
    }
}

public static void Main() {

    // Create a new Thread object and pass it a ThreadStart
    // delegate instance that references DisplayMessage.
    Thread thread = new Thread(new ThreadStart(DisplayMessage));

    Console.WriteLine("{0} : Starting second thread.",
        DateTime.Now.ToString("HH:mm:ss.ffff"));

    // Start the second thread.
    thread.Start();

    // Loop and process the command entered by the user.
    char command = ' ';
```

```
do {

    string input = Console.ReadLine();
    if (input.Length > 0) command = input.ToUpper()[0];
    else command = ' ';

    switch (command) {

        case 'S':
            // Suspend the second thread.
            Console.WriteLine("{0} : Suspending second thread.",
                DateTime.Now.ToString("HH:mm:ss.ffff"));
            thread.Suspend();
            break;

        case 'R':
            // Resume the second thread.
            try {
                Console.WriteLine("{0} : Resuming second thread.",
                    DateTime.Now.ToString("HH:mm:ss.ffff"));
                thread.Resume();
            } catch (ThreadStateException) {
                Console.WriteLine("{0} : Thread wasn't suspended.",
                    DateTime.Now.ToString("HH:mm:ss.ffff"));
            }
            break;

        case 'I':
            // Interrupt the second thread.
            Console.WriteLine("{0} : Interrupting second thread.",
                DateTime.Now.ToString("HH:mm:ss.ffff"));
            thread.Interrupt();
            break;

        case 'E':
            // Abort the second thread and pass a state object to
            // the thread being aborted, in this case a message.
            Console.WriteLine("{0} : Aborting second thread.",
                DateTime.Now.ToString("HH:mm:ss.ffff"));

            thread.Abort("Terminating example.");

            // Wait for the second thread to terminate.
            thread.Join();
            break;
    }
} while (command != 'E');
```

```
                          // Wait to continue.
                          Console.WriteLine("Main method complete. Press Enter.");
                          Console.ReadLine();
                  }
          }
```

4.7 Know When a Thread Finishes

Problem

You need to know when a thread has finished.

Solution

Use the *IsAlive* property or the *Join* method of the *Thread* class.

Discussion

The easiest way to test if a thread has finished executing is to test the *Thread.IsAlive* property. The *IsAlive* property returns *true* if the thread has been started but has not terminated or been aborted.

Commonly, you will need one thread to wait for another thread to complete its processing. Instead of testing *IsAlive* in a loop, you can use the *Thread.Join* method. *Join* causes the calling thread to block until the referenced thread terminates, at which point the calling thread will continue. You can optionally specify an *int* or a *TimeSpan* value that specifies the time after which the *Join* operation will time out and execution of the calling thread will resume. If you specify a time-out value, *Join* returns *true* if the thread terminated, and *false* if *Join* timed out.

The following example executes a second thread and then calls *Join* to wait for the second thread to terminate. Because the second thread takes around five seconds to execute, but the *Join* method specifies a time-out of three seconds, *Join* will always time out and the example will display a message to the console.

```
using System;
using System.Threading;

public class ThreadFinishExample {

    private static void DisplayMessage() {

        // Display a message to the console 5 times.
        for (int count = 0; count < 5; count++) {
```

```
        Console.WriteLine("{0} : Second thread",
            DateTime.Now.ToString("HH:mm:ss.ffff"));

        // Sleep for 1 second.
        Thread.Sleep(1000);
    }
}

public static void Main() {

    // Create a ThreadStart delegate instance that references
    // DisplayMessage.
    ThreadStart method = new ThreadStart(DisplayMessage);

    // Create a new Thread object and pass the ThreadStart
    // delegate instance to its constructor.
    Thread thread = new Thread(method);

    Console.WriteLine("{0} : Starting second thread.",
        DateTime.Now.ToString("HH:mm:ss.ffff"));

    // Start the second thread.
    thread.Start();

    // Block until the second thread finishes, or time out after
    // 3 seconds.
    if (!thread.Join(3000)) {

        Console.WriteLine("{0} : Join timed out !!",
            DateTime.Now.ToString("HH:mm:ss.ffff"));
    }

    // Wait to continue.
    Console.WriteLine("Main method complete. Press Enter.");
    Console.ReadLine();
    }
}
```

4.8 Synchronize the Execution of Multiple Threads

Problem

You need to coordinate the activities of multiple threads to ensure the efficient use of shared resources and that you do not corrupt shared data when a thread context switch occurs during an operation that changes the data.

Solution

Use the *Monitor, AutoResetEvent, ManualResetEvent*, and *Mutex* classes from the *System.Threading* namespace.

Discussion

The greatest challenge in writing a multithreaded application is ensuring that the threads work in concert. This is commonly referred to as thread synchronization and includes

- Ensuring threads access shared objects and data correctly so that they do not cause corruption.

- Ensuring threads execute only when they are meant to and cause minimum overhead when they are idle.

The most commonly used synchronization mechanism is the *Monitor* class. The *Monitor* class allows a single thread to obtain an exclusive lock on an object by calling the *static* method *Monitor.Enter*. By acquiring an exclusive lock prior to accessing a shared resource or data, you ensure that only one thread can access the resource concurrently. Once the thread has finished with the resource, release the lock to allow another thread to access it. A block of code that enforces this behavior is often referred to as a *critical section*.

You can use any object to act as the lock, and it's common to use the keyword *this* in order to obtain a lock on the current object. The key point is that all threads attempting to access a shared resource must try to acquire the *same* lock. Other threads that attempt to acquire a lock on the same object will block (enter a *WaitSleepJoin* state) and are added to the lock's *ready queue* until the thread that owns the lock releases it by calling the *static* method *Monitor.Exit*. When the owning thread calls *Exit*, one of the threads from the ready queue acquires the lock. If the owner of a lock does not release it by calling *Exit*, all other threads will block indefinitely. Therefore, it's important to place the *Exit* call within a *finally* block to ensure that it's called even if an exception occurs.

Because *Monitor* is used so frequently in multithreaded applications, C# provides language-level support through the *lock* statement, which the compiler translates to use of the *Monitor* class. A block of code encapsulated in a *lock* statement is equivalent to calling *Monitor.Enter* when entering the block, and *Monitor.Exit* when exiting the block. In addition, the compiler automatically places the *Monitor.Exit* call in a *finally* block to ensure that the lock is released if an exception is thrown.

The thread that currently owns the lock can call *Monitor.Wait*, which will release the lock and place the calling thread on the lock's *wait queue*. Threads in a wait queue also have a state of *WaitSleepJoin* and will continue to block until a thread that owns the lock calls either of the *Pulse* or *PulseAll* methods of the *Monitor* class. *Pulse* moves one of the waiting threads from the wait queue to the ready queue, whereas *PulseAll* moves all threads. Once a thread has moved from the wait queue to the ready queue, it can acquire the lock next time it's released. It's important to understand that threads on a lock's wait queue *will not* acquire a released lock; they will wait indefinitely until you call *Pulse* or *PulseAll* to move them to the ready queue. The use of *Wait* and *Pulse* is a common approach when a pool of threads is used to process work items from a shared queue.

The *ThreadSyncExample* class shown here demonstrates the use of both the *Monitor* class and the *lock* statement. The example starts three threads that each (in turn) acquire the lock to an object named *consoleGate*. Each thread then calls *Monitor.Wait*. When the user presses the Enter key the first time, *Monitor.Pulse* is called to release one waiting thread. The second time the user presses Enter, *Monitor.PulseAll* is called, releasing all remaining waiting threads.

```
using System;
using System.Threading;

public class ThreadSyncExample {

    // Declare a static object to use for locking in static methods
    // because there is no access to 'this'.
    private static object consoleGate = new Object();

    private static void DisplayMessage() {

        Console.WriteLine("{0} : Thread started, acquiring lock...",
            DateTime.Now.ToString("HH:mm:ss.ffff"));

        // Acquire a lock on the consoleGate object.
        try {

            Monitor.Enter(consoleGate);

            Console.WriteLine("{0} : {1}",
                DateTime.Now.ToString("HH:mm:ss.ffff"),
                "Acquired consoleGate lock, waiting...");

            // Wait until Pulse is called on the consoleGate object.
            Monitor.Wait(consoleGate);
```

```
            Console.WriteLine("{0} : Thread pulsed, terminating.",
                DateTime.Now.ToString("HH:mm:ss.ffff"));

        } finally {

            Monitor.Exit(consoleGate);
        }
    }

    public static void Main() {

        // Acquire a lock on the consoleGate object.
        lock (consoleGate) {

            // Create and start three new threads running the
            // DisplayMesssage method.
            for (int count = 0; count < 3; count++) {

                (new Thread(new ThreadStart(DisplayMessage))).Start();
            }
        }

        Thread.Sleep(1000);

        // Wake up a single waiting thread.
        Console.WriteLine("{0} : {1}",
            DateTime.Now.ToString("HH:mm:ss.ffff"),
            "Press Enter to pulse one waiting thread.");

        Console.ReadLine();

        // Acquire a lock on the consoleGate object.
        lock (consoleGate) {

            // Pulse 1 waiting thread.
            Monitor.Pulse(consoleGate);
        }

        // Wake up all waiting threads.
        Console.WriteLine("{0} : {1}",
            DateTime.Now.ToString("HH:mm:ss.ffff"),
            "Press Enter to pulse all waiting threads.");

        Console.ReadLine();

        // Acquire a lock on the consoleGate object.
        lock (consoleGate) {
```

```
        // Pulse all waiting threads.
        Monitor.PulseAll(consoleGate);
    }

    // Wait to continue.
    Console.WriteLine("Main method complete. Press Enter.");
    Console.ReadLine();
    }
}
```

Other classes commonly used to provide synchronization between threads are the subclasses of the *System.Threading.WaitHandle* class. These include the *AutoResetEvent*, *ManualResetEvent*, and *Mutex*. Instances of these classes can be in either a signaled or unsignaled state. Threads can use the methods of the classes listed in Table 4-2 (inherited from the *WaitHandle* class) to enter a *Wait-SleepJoin* state and wait for the state of one or more *WaitHandle*-derived objects to become signaled.

Table 4-2   *WaitHandle* Methods for Synchronizing Thread Execution

Method	Description
WaitAny	A *static* method that causes the calling thread to enter a *WaitSleepJoin* state and wait for any one of the *WaitHandle* objects in a *WaitHandle* array to be signaled. You can also specify a time-out value.
WaitAll	A *static* method that causes the calling thread to enter a *WaitSleepJoin* state and wait for all the *WaitHandle* objects in a *WaitHandle* array to be signaled. You can also specify a time-out value. The *WaitAllExample* method in recipe 4.2 demonstrates the use of the *WaitAll* method.
WaitOne	Causes the calling thread to enter a *WaitSleepJoin* state and wait for a specific *WaitHandle* object to be signaled. The *WaitingExample* method in recipe 4.2 demonstrates the use of the *WaitOne* method.

The key differences between the *AutoResetEvent*, *ManualResetEvent*, and *Mutex* classes are how they transition from a signaled to an unsignaled state, and their visibility. The *AutoResetEvent* and *ManualResetEvent* classes are local to a process. To signal an *AutoResetEvent*, call its *Set* method, which will release only one thread that is waiting on the event. The *AutoResetEvent* will automatically return to an unsignaled state. The example in recipe 4.4 demonstrates the use of an *AutoResetEvent* class.

The *ManualResetEvent* class must be manually switched back and forth between signaled to unsignaled using its *Set* and *Reset* methods. Calling *Set* on a *ManualResetEvent* will set it to a signaled state, releasing all threads that are waiting on the event. Only by calling *Reset* does the *ManualResetEvent* become unsignaled.

A *Mutex* is signaled when it's not owned by any thread. A thread acquires ownership of the *Mutex* either at construction or by using one of the methods listed in Table 4-2. Ownership of the *Mutex* is released by calling the *Mutex.ReleaseMutex* method, which signals the *Mutex* and allows another thread to gain ownership. The key benefit of a *Mutex* is that you can use them to synchronize threads across process boundaries; recipe 4.12 demonstrates the use of a *Mutex*.

Aside from the functionality already described, a key difference between the *WaitHandle* classes and the *Monitor* class is that *Monitor* is implemented completely in managed code, whereas the *WaitHandle* classes provide wrappers around operating system primitives. This has the following consequences:

- Use of the *Monitor* class means your code is more portable because you are not dependent on the capabilities of the underlying operating system.

- You can use the classes derived from *WaitHandle* to synchronize the execution of both managed and unmanaged threads, whereas *Monitor* can synchronize only managed threads.

4.9 Create a Thread-Safe Collection Instance

Problem

You need multiple threads to be able to safely access the contents of a collection concurrently.

Solution

Use *lock* statements in your code to synchronize thread access to the collection, or access the collection through a thread-safe wrapper.

Discussion

By default, the standard collection classes from the *System.Collections* and *System.Collections.Specialized* namespaces will support multiple threads reading the collection's content concurrently. However, if one or more of these threads tries to modify the collection, you will almost certainly encounter problems. This is because the operating system can interrupt the actions of the thread while modifications to the collection have been only partially applied. This leaves the collection in an indeterminate state, which will almost certainly cause another thread accessing the collection to fail, return incorrect data, or corrupt the collection.

> **Note**   The use of thread synchronization introduces a performance overhead. The decision to make collections non-thread-safe by default provides better performance for the vast majority of situations where multiple threads are not used.

The most commonly used collections all implement a *static* method named *Synchronized*, this includes the *ArrayList*, *Hashtable*, *Queue*, *SortedList*, and *Stack* classes from the *System.Collections* namespace. The *Synchronized* method takes a collection object of the appropriate type as an argument and returns an object that provides a synchronized wrapper around the specified collection object. The wrapper object is returned as the same type as the original collection, but all of the methods and properties that read and write the collection ensure that only a single thread has access to the collection content concurrently. The following code shows how to create a thread-safe *Hashtable*. (You can test if a collection is thread-safe using the *IsSynchronized* property.)

```
// Create a standard Hashtable
Hashtable hUnsync = new Hashtable();

// Create a synchronized wrapper
Hashtable hSync = Hashtable.Synchronized(hUnsync);
```

The collection classes such as *HybridDictionary*, *ListDictionary*, and *StringCollection* from the *System.Collections.Specialized* namespace don't implement a *Synchronized* method. To provide thread-safe access to instances of these classes, you must implement manual synchronization using the *object* returned by their *SyncRoot* property, as shown in the following code:

```
// Create a NameValueCollection.
NameValueCollection nvCollection = new NameValueCollection();

// Obtain a lock on the NameValueCollection before modification.
lock ((((ICollection)nvCollection).SyncRoot) {

    // Modify the NameValueCollection...
}
```

Notice that the *NameValueCollection* class derives from the *NameObject-CollectionBase* class, which uses explicit interface implementation to implement the *ICollection.SyncRoot* property. As shown, you must cast the *NameValue-Collection* to an *ICollection* instance before you can access the *SyncRoot* property. Casting is not necessary with other specialized collection classes such as *HybridDictionary*, *ListDictionary*, and *StringCollection*, which do not use explicit interface implementation to implement *SyncRoot*.

If you need to use the synchronized collection class extensively, you can simplify your code by creating a new class that derives from the collection class you need to use. Override the members of the base class that provide access to the collection's content and perform synchronization before calling the equivalent base class member. You would normally use the *lock* statement to synchronize on the *object* returned by the *SyncRoot* property of the base class as discussed previously. However, by creating a derived class it's also possible to implement more advanced synchronization techniques, such as using the *System.Threading.ReaderWriterLock* to allow multiple reader threads but only a single writer thread.

4.10 Start a New Process

Problem

You need to execute an application in a new process.

Solution

Use a *System.Diagnostics.ProcessStartInfo* object to specify details for the application you want to run, create a *System.Diagnostics.Process* object to represent the new process, assign the *ProcessStartInfo* object to the *StartInfo* property of your *Process* object, and then start the application by calling *Process.Start*.

Discussion

The *Process* class provides a managed representation of an operating system process and provides a simple mechanism through which you can execute both managed and unmanaged applications. The *Process* class implements four overloads of the *Start* method, which you use to start a new process. Two of these overloads are *static* methods that allow you to specify only the name and arguments for the new process. For example, the following statements both execute Notepad in a new process:

```
// Execute notepad.exe with no command-line arguments.
Process.Start("notepad.exe");
```

```
// Execute notepad.exe passing the name of the file to open as a
// command-line argument.
Process.Start("notepad.exe", "SomeFile.txt");
```

The other two *Start* method overloads require you to create a *Process-StartInfo* object configured with the details of the process you want to run; use of the *ProcessStartInfo* object provides greater control over the behavior and configuration of the new process. Table 4-3 summarizes some of the commonly used properties of the *ProcessStartInfo* class.

Table 4-3   Properties of the *ProcessStartInfo* Class

Property	Description
Arguments	The command-line arguments to pass to the new process.
ErrorDialog	If *Process.Start* can't start the specified process, it will throw a *System.ComponentModel.Win32Exception*. If *ErrorDialog* is *true*, *Start* displays an error dialog to the user before throwing the exception.
FileName	The name of the application to start. You can also specify any type of file for which you have configured an application association. For example, you could specify a file with a .doc or .xls extension, which would cause Microsoft Word or Microsoft Excel to run.
WindowStyle	A member of the *System.Diagnostics.ProcessWindowStyle* enumeration, which controls how the window is displayed. Valid values include *Hidden*, *Maximized*, *Minimized*, and *Normal*.
WorkingDirectory	The fully qualified name of the initial directory for the new process.

When finished with a *Process* object, you should dispose of it in order to release system resources—call *Close*, *Dispose*, or create the *Process* object within the scope of a *using* statement. Disposing of a *Process* object has no effect on the underlying system process, which will continue to run.

The following example uses *Process* to execute Notepad in a maximized window and open a file named C:\Temp\file.txt. After creation, the example calls the *Process.WaitForExit* method, which blocks the calling thread until a process terminates or a specified time-out expires.

```
using System;
using System.Diagnostics;

public class StartProcessExample {

    public static void Main () {
```

```csharp
// Create a ProcessStartInfo object and configure it with the
// information required to run the new process.
ProcessStartInfo startInfo = new ProcessStartInfo();

startInfo.FileName = "notepad.exe";
startInfo.Arguments = "file.txt";
startInfo.WorkingDirectory = @"C:\Temp";
startInfo.WindowStyle = ProcessWindowStyle.Maximized;
startInfo.ErrorDialog = true;

// Create a new Process object.
using (Process process = new Process()) {

    // Assign the ProcessStartInfo to the Process.
    process.StartInfo = startInfo;

    try {

        // Start the new process.
        process.Start();

        // Wait for the new process to terminate before exiting.
        Console.WriteLine("Waiting 30 seconds for process to" +
            " finish.");
        process.WaitForExit(30000);

    } catch (Exception ex) {

        Console.WriteLine("Could not start process.");
        Console.WriteLine(ex);
    }
}

// Wait to continue.
Console.WriteLine("Main method complete. Press Enter.");
Console.ReadLine();
    }
}
```

4.11 Terminate a Process

Problem

You need to terminate a process such as an application or a service.

Solution

Obtain a *Process* object representing the operating system process you want to terminate. For Windows-based applications, call *Process.CloseMainWindow* to send a close message to the application's main window. For Windows-based applications that ignore *CloseMainWindow*, or for non-Windows-based applications, call the *Process.Kill* method.

Discussion

If you start a new process from managed code using the *Process* class (discussed in recipe 4.10), you can terminate the process using the *Process* object that represents the new process. You can also obtain *Process* objects that refer to other currently running processes using the *static* methods of the *Process* class summarized in Table 4-4.

Table 4-4   Methods for Obtaining *Process* References

Method	Description
GetCurrentProcess	Returns a *Process* object representing the currently active process.
GetProcessById	Returns a *Process* object representing the process with the specified ID.
GetProcesses	Returns an array of *Process* objects representing all currently active processes.
GetProcessesByName	Returns an array of *Process* objects representing all currently active processes with a specified friendly name. The friendly name is the name of the executable excluding file extension or path; for example, *notepad* or *calc*.

Once you have a *Process* object representing the process that you want to terminate, you need to call either the *CloseMainWindow* method or the *Kill* method. The *CloseMainWindow* method sends a close message to a Windows-based application's main window. This method has the same effect as if the user had closed the main window using the system menu, and it gives the application the opportunity to perform its normal shutdown routine. *CloseMainWindow* won't terminate applications that do not have a main window or applications with a disabled main window—possibly because a modal dialog box is currently displayed. Under such circumstances, *CloseMainWindow* will return *false*.

CloseMainWindow returns *true* if the close message was successfully sent, but doesn't guarantee that the process is actually terminated. For example, applications used to edit data will usually give the user the opportunity to save unsaved data if a close message is received. The user usually has the chance to cancel the close operation under such circumstances. This means that *Close-MainWindow* will return *true*, but the application will still be running once the user cancels. You can use the *Process.WaitForExit* method to signal process termination and the *Process.HasExited* property to test if a process has terminated. Alternatively, you can use the *Kill* method.

The *Kill* method simply terminates a process immediately; the user has no chance to stop the termination, and all unsaved data is lost. *Kill* is the only option for terminating Windows-based applications that do not respond to *CloseMainWindow* and for terminating non-Windows-based applications.

The following example starts a new instance of Notepad, waits five seconds, and then terminates the Notepad process. The example first tries to terminate the process using *CloseMainWindow*. If *CloseMainWindow* returns *false*, or the Notepad process is still running after *CloseMainWindow* is called, the example calls *Kill* and forces the Notepad process to terminate; you can force *Close-MainWindow* to return *false* by leaving the File Open dialog box open.

```csharp
using System;
using System.Threading;
using System.Diagnostics;

public class TerminateProcessExample {

    public static void Main () {

        // Create a new Process and run notepad.exe.
        using (Process process = Process.Start("notepad.exe")) {

            // Wait for 5 seconds and terminate the notepad process.
            Console.WriteLine("Waiting 5 seconds before terminating" +
                " notepad.exe.");
            Thread.Sleep(5000);

            // Terminate notepad process.
            Console.WriteLine("Terminating Notepad with CloseMainWindow.");

            // Try to send a close message to the main window.
            if (!process.CloseMainWindow()) {

                // Close message did not get sent - Kill Notepad.
                Console.WriteLine("CloseMainWindow returned false - " +
                    " terminating Notepad with Kill.");
                process.Kill();
```

```
        } else {

            // Close message sent successfully; wait for 2 seconds
            // for termination confirmation before resorting to Kill.
            if (!process.WaitForExit(2000)) {

                Console.WriteLine("CloseMainWindow failed to" +
                    " terminate - terminating Notepad with Kill.");
                process.Kill();
            }
        }
    }

    // Wait to continue.
    Console.WriteLine("Main method complete. Press Enter.");
    Console.ReadLine();
    }
}
```

4.12 Ensure That Only One Instance of an Application Can Execute Concurrently

Problem

You need to ensure that a user can have only one instance of an application running concurrently.

Solution

Create a named *System.Threading.Mutex* object and have your application try to acquire ownership of it at startup.

Discussion

The *Mutex* provides a mechanism for synchronizing the execution of threads across process boundaries and in addition provides a convenient mechanism through which to ensure that only a single instance of an application is running concurrently. By trying to acquire ownership of a named *Mutex* at startup and exiting if the *Mutex* can't be acquired, you can ensure that only one instance of your application is running. This example uses a *Mutex* named *MutexExample* to ensure that only a single instance of the example can execute.

```
using System;
using System.Threading;
```

```csharp
public class MutexExample {

    public static void Main() {

        // A boolean that indicates whether this application has
        // initial ownership of the Mutex.
        bool ownsMutex;

        // Attempt to create and take ownership of a Mutex named
        // MutexExample.
        using (Mutex mutex =
                    new Mutex(true, "MutexExample", out ownsMutex)) {

            // If the application owns the Mutex it can continue to execute;
            // otherwise, the application should exit.
            if (ownsMutex) {

                Console.WriteLine("This application currently owns the" +
                    " mutex named MutexExample. Additional instances of" +
                    " this application will not run until you release" +
                    " the mutex by pressing Enter.");

                Console.ReadLine();

                // Release the mutex
                mutex.ReleaseMutex();

            } else {

                Console.WriteLine("Another instance of this application " +
                    " already owns the mutex named MutexExample. This" +
                    " instance of the application will terminate.");
            }
        }

        // Wait to continue.
        Console.WriteLine("Main method complete. Press Enter.");
        Console.ReadLine();
    }
}
```

5

XML Processing

One of the most remarkable aspects of the Microsoft .NET Framework is its deep integration with XML. In many .NET applications, you won't even be aware that you're using XML technologies—they'll just be used behind the scenes when you serialize a Microsoft ADO.NET *DataSet*, call an XML Web service, or read application settings in a Web.config configuration file. In other cases, you'll want to work directly with the *System.Xml* namespaces to manipulate XML data. Common XML tasks don't just include parsing an XML file, but also validating it against a schema, applying an XSL transform to create a new document or HTML page, and searching intelligently with XPath. The recipes in this chapter include the following:

- Techniques for reading, parsing, and manipulating XML data (recipes 5.1, 5.2, 5.3, and 5.7).

- Ways to search an XML document for specific nodes, either by name (recipe 5.4), by namespace (recipe 5.5), or using XPath (recipe 5.6).

- How to validate an XML document with an XML schema (recipe 5.8).

- Approaches for serializing an object to XML (recipe 5.9), creating an XML schema for a class (recipe 5.10), and generating the source code for a class based on an XML schema (recipe 5.11).

- How to transform an XML document to another document using an XSLT stylesheet (recipe 5.12).

5.1 Show the Structure of an XML Document in a TreeView

Problem

You need to display the structure and content of an XML document in a Windows-based application.

Solution

Load the XML document using the *System.Xml.XmlDocument* class. Create a re-entrant method that converts a single *XmlNode* into a *System.Windows.Forms.TreeNode*, and call it recursively to walk through the entire document.

Discussion

The .NET Framework provides several different ways to process XML documents. The one you use depends in part upon your programming task. One of the most fully featured classes is *XmlDocument*, which provides an in-memory representation of an XML document that conforms to the W3C Document Object Model (DOM). The *XmlDocument* class allows you to browse through the nodes in any direction, insert and remove nodes, and change the structure on the fly. For details of the DOM specification, go to *http://www.w3c.org*.

To use the *XmlDocument* class, simply create a new instance of the class, and call the *Load* method with a filename, a *Stream*, a *TextReader*, or an *XmlReader* object. You can even supply a URL that points to an XML document. The *XmlDocument* instance will be populated with the tree of elements, or *nodes,* from the source document. The entry point for accessing these nodes is the root element, which is provided through the *XmlDocument.DocumentElement* property. *DocumentElement* is an *XmlElement* object that can contain one or more nested *XmlNode* objects, which in turn can contain more *XmlNode* objects, and so on. An *XmlNode* is the basic ingredient of an XML file. Common XML nodes include elements, attributes, comments, and contained text.

When dealing with an *XmlNode* or a class that derives from it (such as *XmlElement* or *XmlAttribute*), you can use the following basic properties:

- **ChildNodes** is an *XmlNodeList* collection that contains the first level of nested nodes.

- **Name** is the name of the node.

- **NodeType** returns a member of the *System.Xml.XmlNodeType* enumeration that indicates the type of the node (element, attribute, text, and so on).

- ***Value***   is the content of the node, if it's a text or CDATA node.

- ***Attributes***   provides a collection of node objects representing the attributes applied to the element.

- ***InnerText***   retrieves a string with the concatenated value of the node and all nested nodes.

- ***InnerXml***   retrieves a string with the concatenated XML markup for all nested nodes.

- ***OuterXml***   retrieves a string with the concatenated XML markup for the current node and all nested nodes.

The following example walks through every element of an *XmlDocument* using the *ChildNodes* property and a recursive method. Each node is displayed in a *TreeView* control, with descriptive text that either identifies it or shows its content.

```
using System;
using System.Windows.Forms;
using System.Xml;

public class XmlTreeDisplay : System.Windows.Forms.Form{
    private System.Windows.Forms.Button cmdLoad;
    private System.Windows.Forms.Label lblFile;
    private System.Windows.Forms.TextBox txtXmlFile;
    private System.Windows.Forms.TreeView treeXml;

    // (Designer code omitted.)
    private void cmdLoad_Click(object sender, System.EventArgs e) {

        // Clear the tree.
        treeXml.Nodes.Clear();

        // Load the XML Document
        XmlDocument doc = new XmlDocument();
        try {
            doc.Load(txtXmlFile.Text);
        }catch (Exception err) {

            MessageBox.Show(err.Message);
            return;
        }

        // Populate the TreeView.
```

```
        ConvertXmlNodeToTreeNode(doc, treeXml.Nodes);

        // Expand all nodes.
        treeXml.Nodes[0].ExpandAll();
    }

    private void ConvertXmlNodeToTreeNode(XmlNode xmlNode,
      TreeNodeCollection treeNodes) {

        // Add a TreeNode node that represents this XmlNode.
        TreeNode newTreeNode = treeNodes.Add(xmlNode.Name);

        // Customize the TreeNode text based on the XmlNode
        // type and content.
        switch (xmlNode.NodeType) {

            case XmlNodeType.ProcessingInstruction:
            case XmlNodeType.XmlDeclaration:
                newTreeNode.Text = "<?" + xmlNode.Name + " " +
                  xmlNode.Value + "?>";
                break;
            case XmlNodeType.Element:
                newTreeNode.Text = "<" + xmlNode.Name + ">";
                break;
            case XmlNodeType.Attribute:
                newTreeNode.Text = "ATTRIBUTE: " + xmlNode.Name;
                break;
            case XmlNodeType.Text:
            case XmlNodeType.CDATA:
                newTreeNode.Text = xmlNode.Value;
                break;
            case XmlNodeType.Comment:
                newTreeNode.Text = "<!--" + xmlNode.Value + "-->";
                break;
        }

        // Call this routine recursively for each attribute.
        // (XmlAttribute is a subclass of XmlNode.)
        if (xmlNode.Attributes != null) {

            foreach (XmlAttribute attribute in xmlNode.Attributes) {
                ConvertXmlNodeToTreeNode(attribute, newTreeNode.Nodes);
            }
        }

        // Call this routine recursively for each child node.
        // Typically, this child node represents a nested element,
        // or element content.
```

```
        foreach (XmlNode childNode in xmlNode.ChildNodes) {
            ConvertXmlNodeToTreeNode(childNode, newTreeNode.Nodes);
        }
    }
}
```

As an example, consider the following simple XML file (which is included with the sample code as the ProductCatalog.xml file):

```
<?xml version="1.0" ?>
<productCatalog>
    <catalogName>Jones and Jones Unique Catalog 2004</catalogName>
    <expiryDate>2005-01-01</expiryDate>

    <products>
        <product id="1001">
            <productName>Gourmet Coffee</productName>
            <description>The finest beans from rare Chilean
             plantations.</description>
            <productPrice>0.99</productPrice>
            <inStock>true</inStock>
        </product>
        <product id="1002">
            <productName>Blue China Tea Pot</productName>
            <description>A trendy update for tea drinkers.</description>
            <productPrice>102.99</productPrice>
            <inStock>true</inStock>
        </product>
    </products>
</productCatalog>
```

Figure 5-1 shows how this file will be rendered in the *XmlTreeDisplay* form.

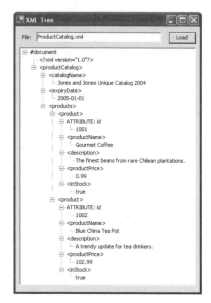

Figure 5-1 The displayed structure of an XML document.

5.2 Insert Nodes in an XML Document

Problem

You need to modify an XML document by inserting new data, or you want to create an entirely new XML document in memory.

Solution

Create the node using the appropriate *XmlDocument* method (such as *CreateElement*, *CreateAttribute*, *CreateNode*, and so on). Then insert it using the appropriate *XmlNode* method (such as *InsertAfter*, *InsertBefore*, or *AppendChild*).

Discussion

Inserting a node into the *XmlDocument* class is a two-step process. You must first create the node, and then you insert it at the appropriate location. Optionally, you can then call *XmlDocument.Save* to persist changes.

To create a node, you use one of the *XmlDocument* methods that start with the word *Create*, depending on the type of node. This ensures that the node will have the same namespace as the rest of the document. (Alternatively, you can supply a namespace as an additional string argument.) Next you must find a suitable related node and use one of its insertion methods to add the new node to the tree.

The following example demonstrates this technique by programmatically creating a new XML document.

```
using System;
using System.Xml;

public class GenerateXml {

    private static void Main() {

        // Create a new, empty document.
        XmlDocument doc = new XmlDocument();
        XmlNode docNode = doc.CreateXmlDeclaration("1.0", "UTF-8", null);
        doc.AppendChild(docNode);

        // Create and insert a new element.
        XmlNode productsNode = doc.CreateElement("products");
        doc.AppendChild(productsNode);

        // Create a nested element (with an attribute).
        XmlNode productNode - doc.CreateElement("product");
        XmlAttribute productAttribute = doc.CreateAttribute("id");
        productAttribute.Value = "1001";
        productNode.Attributes.Append(productAttribute);
        productsNode.AppendChild(productNode);

        // Create and add the sub-elements for this product node
        // (with contained text data).
        XmlNode nameNode = doc.CreateElement("productName");
        nameNode.AppendChild(doc.CreateTextNode("Gourmet Coffee"));
        productNode.AppendChild(nameNode);
        XmlNode priceNode = doc.CreateElement("productPrice");
        priceNode.AppendChild(doc.CreateTextNode("0.99"));
        productNode.AppendChild(priceNode);

        // Create and add another product node.
        productNode = doc.CreateElement("product");
        productAttribute = doc.CreateAttribute("id");
        productAttribute.Value = "1002";
        productNode.Attributes.Append(productAttribute);
        productsNode.AppendChild(productNode);
        nameNode = doc.CreateElement("productName");
        nameNode.AppendChild(doc.CreateTextNode("Blue China Tea Pot"));
        productNode.AppendChild(nameNode);
```

```
            priceNode = doc.CreateElement("productPrice");
            priceNode.AppendChild(doc.CreateTextNode("102.99"));
            productNode.AppendChild(priceNode);

            // Save the document (to the Console window rather than a file).
            doc.Save(Console.Out);
            Console.ReadLine();
        }
}
```

The generated document looks like this:

```
<?xml version="1.0" encoding="UTF-8"?>
<products>
  <product id="1001">
    <productName>Gourmet Coffee</productName>
    <productPrice>0.99</productPrice>
  </product>
  <product id="1002">
    <productName>Blue China Tea Pot</productName>
    <productPrice>102.99</productPrice>
  </product>
</products>
```

5.3 Quickly Append Nodes in an XML Document

Problem

You need to add nodes to an XML document without requiring lengthy, verbose code.

Solution

Create a helper function that accepts a tag name and content and can generate the entire element at once. Alternatively, use the *XmlDocument.CloneNode* method to copy branches of an *XmlDocument*.

Discussion

Inserting a single element into an *XmlDocument* requires several lines of code. There are several ways that you can shorten this code. One approach is to create a dedicated helper class with higher-level methods for adding elements and attributes. For example, you could create an *AddElement* method that generates a new element, inserts it, and adds any contained text—the three operations needed to insert most elements.

Here's an example of one such helper class:

```
using System;
using System.Xml;

public class XmlHelper {

    public static XmlNode AddElement(string tagName,
      string textContent, XmlNode parent) {

        XmlNode node = parent.OwnerDocument.CreateElement(tagName);
        parent.AppendChild(node);

        if (textContent != null) {

            XmlNode content;
            content = parent.OwnerDocument.CreateTextNode(textContent);
            node.AppendChild(content);
        }
        return node;
    }

    public static XmlNode AddAttribute(string attributeName,
      string textContent, XmlNode parent) {

        XmlAttribute attribute;
        attribute = parent.OwnerDocument.CreateAttribute(attributeName);
        attribute.Value = textContent;
        parent.Attributes.Append(attribute);

        return attribute;
    }
}
```

You can now condense the XML-generating code from recipe 5.2 with the simpler syntax shown here:

```
public class GenerateXml {

    private static void Main() {

        // Create the basic document.
        XmlDocument doc = new XmlDocument();
        XmlNode docNode = doc.CreateXmlDeclaration("1.0", "UTF-8", null);
        doc.AppendChild(docNode);
        XmlNode products = doc.CreateElement("products");
        doc.AppendChild(products);

        // Add two products.
```

```
        XmlNode product = XmlHelper.AddElement("product", null, products);
        XmlHelper.AddAttribute("id", "1001", product);
        XmlHelper.AddElement("productName", "Gourmet Coffee", product);
        XmlHelper.AddElement("productPrice", "0.99", product);

        product = XmlHelper.AddElement("product", null, products);
        XmlHelper.AddAttribute("id", "1002", product);
        XmlHelper.AddElement("productName", "Blue China Tea Pot", product);
        XmlHelper.AddElement("productPrice", "102.99", product);

        // Save the document (to the Console window rather than a file).
        doc.Save(Console.Out);
        Console.ReadLine();
    }
}
```

Alternatively, you might want to take the helper methods such as *AddAttribute* and *AddElement* and make them instance methods in a custom class you derive from *XmlDocument*.

Another approach to simplifying writing XML is to duplicate nodes using the *XmlNode.CloneNode* method. *CloneNode* accepts a Boolean *deep* parameter. If you supply *true*, *CloneNode* will duplicate the entire branch, with all nested nodes.

Here's an example that creates a new product node by copying the first node.

```
// (Add first product node.)

// Create a new element based on an existing product.
product = product.CloneNode(true);

// Modify the node data.
product.Attributes[0].Value = "1002";
product.ChildNodes[0].ChildNodes[0].Value = "Blue China Tea Pot";
product.ChildNodes[1].ChildNodes[0].Value = "102.99";

// Add the new element.
products.AppendChild(product);
```

Notice that in this case, certain assumptions are being made about the existing nodes (for example, that the first child in the item node is always the name, and the second child is always the price). If this assumption isn't guaranteed to be true, you might need to examine the node name programmatically.

5.4 Find Specific Elements by Name

Problem

You need to retrieve a specific node from an *XmlDocument*, and you know its name but not its position.

Solution

Use the *XmlDocument.GetElementsByTagName* method, which searches an entire document and returns a *System.Xml.XmlNodeList* containing any matches.

Discussion

The *XmlDocument* class provides a convenient *GetElementsByTagName* method that searches an entire document for nodes that have the indicated element name. It returns the results as a collection of *XmlNode* objects.

This code demonstrates how you could use *GetElementsByTagName* to calculate the total price of items in a catalog by retrieving all elements with the name "*productPrice*":

```
using System;
using System.Xml;

public class FindNodesByName {

    private static void Main() {

        // Load the document.
        XmlDocument doc = new XmlDocument();
        doc.Load("ProductCatalog.xml");

        // Retrieve all prices.
        XmlNodeList prices = doc.GetElementsByTagName("productPrice");

        decimal totalPrice = 0;
        foreach (XmlNode price in prices) {

            // Get the inner text of each matching element.
            totalPrice += Decimal.Parse(price.ChildNodes[0].Value);
        }

        Console.WriteLine("Total catalog value: " + totalPrice.ToString());
        Console.ReadLine();
    }
}
```

You can also search portions of an XML document by using the *XmlElement.GetElementsByTagName* method. It searches all the descendant nodes looking for matches. To use this method, first retrieve an *XmlNode* that corresponds to an element. Then cast this object to an *XmlElement*. The following example demonstrates how to find the *price* node under the first *product* element.

```
// Retrieve a reference to the first product.
XmlNode product = doc.GetElementsByTagName("products")[0];

// Find the price under this product.
XmlNode price = ((XmlElement)product).GetElementsByTagName("productPrice")[0];
Console.WriteLine("Price is " + price.InnerText);
```

If your elements include an attribute of type *ID*, you can also use a method called *GetElementById* to retrieve an element that has a matching *ID* value.

5.5 Get XML Nodes in a Specific XML Namespace

Problem

You need to retrieve nodes from a specific namespace using an *XmlDocument*.

Solution

Use the overload of the *XmlDocument.GetElementsByTagName* method that requires a namespace name as a string argument. Additionally, supply an asterisk (*) for the element name if you wish to match all tags.

Discussion

Many XML documents contain nodes from more than one namespace. For example, an XML document that represents a scientific article might use a separate type of markup for denoting math equations and vector diagrams, or an XML document with information about a purchase order might aggregate client and order information with a shipping record. Similarly, an XML document that represents a business-to-business transaction might include portions from both companies, written in separate markup languages.

A common task in XML programming is to retrieve the elements that are found in a specific namespace. You can perform this task with the overloaded version of the *XmlDocument.GetElementsByTagName* method that requires a namespace name. You can use this method to find tags by name, or to find all the tags in the specified namespace if you supply an asterisk for the tag *name* parameter.

As an example, consider the following compound XML document that includes order and client information, in two different namespaces (*http://mycompany/OrderML* and *http://mycompany/ClientML*).

```
<?xml version="1.0" ?>
<ord:order xmlns:ord="http://mycompany/OrderML"
 xmlns:cli="http://mycompany/ClientML">

  <cli:client>
    <cli:firstName>Sally</cli:firstName>
    <cli:lastName>Sergeyeva</cli:lastName>
  </cli:client>

  <ord:orderItem itemNumber="3211"/>
  <ord:orderItem itemNumber="1155"/>

</ord:order>
```

Here's a simple console application that selects all the tags in the *http://mycompany/OrderML* namespace:

```
using System;
using System.Xml;

public class SelectNodesByNamespace {

    private static void Main() {

        // Load the document.
        XmlDocument doc = new XmlDocument();
        doc.Load("Order.xml");

        // Retrieve all order tags.
        XmlNodeList matches = doc.GetElementsByTagName("*",
          "http://mycompany/OrderML");

        // Display all the information.
        Console.WriteLine("Element \tAttributes");
        Console.WriteLine("******* \t**********");

        foreach (XmlNode node in matches) {

            Console.Write(node.Name + "\t");
            foreach (XmlAttribute attribute in node.Attributes) {
                Console.Write(attribute.Value + "  ");
```

```
        }
        Console.WriteLine();
    }

    Console.ReadLine();
  }
}
```

The output of this program is as follows:

```
Element         Attributes
*******         **********
ord:order       http://mycompany/OrderML  http://mycompany/ClientML
ord:orderItem   3211
ord:orderItem   1155
```

5.6 Find Elements with an XPath Search

Problem

You need to search an XML document for nodes using advanced search criteria. For example, you might want to search a particular branch of an XML document for nodes that have certain attributes or contain a specific number of nested child nodes.

Solution

Execute an XPath expression using the *SelectNodes* or *SelectSingleNode* method of the *XmlDocument* class.

Discussion

The *XmlNode* class defines two methods that perform *XPath* searches: *SelectNodes* and *SelectSingleNode*. These methods operate on all contained child nodes. Because the *XmlDocument* inherits from *XmlNode*, you can call *XmlDocument.SelectNodes* to search an entire document.

For example, consider the following XML document, which represents an order for two items. This document includes text and numeric data, nested elements, and attributes, and so is a good way to test simple XPath expressions.

```
<?xml version="1.0"?>
<Order id="2004-01-30.195496">
  <Client id="ROS-930252034">
    <Name>Remarkable Office Supplies</Name>
  </Client>
```

```
<Items>
  <Item id="1001">
    <Name>Electronic Protractor</Name>
    <Price>42.99</Price>
  </Item>
  <Item id="1002">
    <Name>Invisible Ink</Name>
    <Price>200.25</Price>
  </Item>
</Items>
</Order>
```

Basic XPath syntax uses a path-like notation. For example, the path
/Order/Items/Item indicates an *Item* element that is nested inside an
Items element, which, in turn, in nested in a root *Order* element. This is
an absolute path. The following example uses an XPath absolute path to find
the name of every item in an order.

```
using System;
using System.Xml;

public class XPathSelectNodes {

    private static void Main() {

        // Load the document.
        XmlDocument doc = new XmlDocument();
        doc.Load("orders.xml");

        // Retrieve the name of every item.
        // This could not be accomplished as easily with the
        // GetElementsByTagName() method, because Name elements are
        // used in Item elements and Client elements, and so
        // both types would be returned.
        XmlNodeList nodes = doc.SelectNodes("/Order/Items/Item/Name");

        foreach (XmlNode node in nodes) {
            Console.WriteLine(node.InnerText);
        }

        Console.ReadLine();
    }
}
```

The output of this program is as follows:

```
Electronic Protractor
Invisible Ink
```

XPath provides a rich and powerful search syntax, and it's impossible to explain all the variations you can use in a short recipe. However, Table 5-1 outlines some of the key ingredients in more advanced XPath expressions and includes examples that show how they would work with the order document. For a more detailed reference, refer to the W3C XPath recommendation at *http://www.w3.org/TR/xpath*.

Table 5-1 *XPath* **Expression Syntax**

Expression	Description
/	Starts an absolute path that selects from the root node.
	/Order/Items/Item selects all *Item* elements that are children of an *Items* element, which is itself a child of the root *Order* element.
//	Starts a relative path that selects nodes anywhere.
	//Item/Name selects all the *Name* elements that are children of an *Item* element, regardless of where they appear in the document.
@	Selects an attribute of a node.
	/Order/@id selects the attribute named *id* from the root *Order* element.
*	Selects any element in the path.
	/Order/* selects both *Items* and *Client* nodes because both are contained by a root *Order* element.
|	Combines multiple paths.
	/Order/Items/Item/Name|Order/Client/Name selects the *Name* nodes used to describe a *Client* and the *Name* nodes used to describe an *Item*.
.	Indicates the current (default) node.
	If the current node is an *Order*, the expression ./Items refers to the related items for that order.
..	Indicates the parent node.
	//Name/.. selects any element that is parent to a *Name*, which includes the *Client* and *Item* elements.
[]	Define selection criteria that can test a contained node or attribute value.
	/Order[@id="2004-01-30.195496"] selects the *Order* elements with the indicated attribute value.
	/Order/Items/Item[Price > 50] selects products above $50 in price.
	/Order/Items/Item[Price > 50 and Name="Laser Printer"] selects products that match two criteria.

Table 5-1 *XPath* **Expression Syntax**

Expression	Description
starts-with	This function retrieves elements based on what text a contained element starts with.
	/Order/Items/Item[starts-with(Name, "C")] finds all *Item* elements that have a Name element that starts with the letter *C*.
position	This function retrieves elements based on position.
	/Order/Items/Item[position ()=2] selects the second *Item* element.
count	This function counts elements. You specify the name of the child element to count or an asterisk (*) for all children.
	/Order/Items/Item[count(Price) = 1] retrieves *Item* elements that have exactly one nested *Price* element.

> **Note**   XPath expressions and all element and attribute names that you use inside them are always case sensitive, as XML itself is case sensitive.

5.7 Read and Write XML Without Loading an Entire Document into Memory

Problem

You need to read XML from a stream, or write it to a stream. However, you want to process the information one node at a time, rather than loading it all into memory with an *XmlDocument*.

Solution

To write XML, create an *XmlTextWriter* that wraps a stream and use *Write* methods (such as *WriteStartElement* and *WriteEndElement*). To read XML, create an *XmlTextReader* that wraps a stream and call *Read* to move from node to node.

Discussion

The *XmlTextWriter* and *XmlTextReader* classes read or write XML directly from a stream one node at a time. These classes don't provide the same features for navigating and manipulating your XML as *XmlDocument*, but they do provide higher performance and a smaller memory footprint, particularly if you need to deal with extremely large XML documents.

To write XML to any stream, you can use the streamlined *XmlTextWriter*. It provides *Write* methods that write one node at a time. These include

- *WriteStartDocument*, which writes the document prologue, and *WriteEndDocument*, which closes any open elements at the end of the document.

- *WriteStartElement*, which writes an opening tag for the element you specify. You can then add more elements nested inside this element, or you can call *WriteEndElement* to write the closing tag.

- *WriteElementString*, which writes an entire element, with an opening tag, a closing tag, and text content.

- *WriteAttributeString*, which writes an entire attribute for the nearest open element, with a name and value.

Using these methods usually requires less code than creating an *XmlDocument* by hand, as demonstrated in recipes 5.2 and 5.3.

To read the XML, you use the *Read* method of the *XmlTextReader*. This method advances the reader to the next node, and returns *true*. If no more nodes can be found, it returns *false*. You can retrieve information about the current node through *XmlTextReader* properties, including its *Name*, *Value*, and *NodeType*.

To find out if an element has attributes, you must explicitly test the *HasAttributes* property and then use the *GetAttribute* method to retrieve the attributes by name or index number. The *XmlTextReader* class can access only one node at a time, and it can't move backward or jump to an arbitrary node, which gives much less flexibility than the *XmlDocument* class.

The following console application writes and reads a simple XML document using the *XmlTextWriter* and *XmlTextReader* classes. This is the same XML document created in recipes 5.2 and 5.3 using the *XmlDocument* class.

```csharp
using System;
using System.Xml;
using System.IO;
using System.Text;

public class ReadWriteXml {

    private static void Main() {

        // Create the file and writer.
```

```
FileStream fs = new FileStream("products.xml", FileMode.Create);
XmlTextWriter w = new XmlTextWriter(fs, Encoding.UTF8);

// Start the document.
w.WriteStartDocument();
w.WriteStartElement("products");

// Write a product.
w.WriteStartElement("product");
w.WriteAttributeString("id", "1001");
w.WriteElementString("productName", "Gourmet Coffee");
w.WriteElementString("productPrice", "0.99");
w.WriteEndElement();

// Write another product.
w.WriteStartElement("product");
w.WriteAttributeString("id", "1002");
w.WriteElementString("productName", "Bluc China Tea Pot");
w.WriteElementString("productPrice", "102.99");
w.WriteEndElement();

// End the document.
w.WriteEndElement();
w.WriteEndDocument();
w.Flush();
fs.Close();

Console.WriteLine("Document created. " +
 "Press Enter to read the document.");
Console.ReadLine();

fs = new FileStream("products.xml", FileMode.Open);
XmlTextReader r = new XmlTextReader(fs);

// Read all nodes.
while (r.Read()) {

    if (r.NodeType == XmlNodeType.Element) {

        Console.WriteLine();
        Console.WriteLine("<" + r.Name + ">");

        if (r.HasAttributes) {

            for (int i = 0; i < r.AttributeCount; i++) {
                Console.WriteLine("\tATTRIBUTE: " +
                  r.GetAttribute(i));
            }
```

```
                }
            }else if (r.NodeType == XmlNodeType.Text) {
                Console.WriteLine("\tVALUE: " + r.Value);
            }
        }
        Console.ReadLine();
    }
}
```

5.8 Validate an XML Document Against a Schema

Problem

You need to validate the content of an XML document by ensuring that it conforms to an XML schema.

Solution

Use the *System.Xml.XmlValidatingReader* class. Create an instance, load a schema into the *XmlValidatingReader.Schemas* collection, and then move through the document one node at a time by calling *XmlValidating-Reader.Read*, catching any validation exceptions. To find all the errors in a document without catching exceptions, handle the *ValidationEventHandler* event.

Discussion

An XML schema defines the rules that a given type of XML document must follow. The schema includes rules that define

- the elements and attributes that can appear in a document.

- the data types for elements and attributes.

- the structure of a document, including what elements are children of other elements.

- the order and number of child elements that appear in a document.

- whether elements are empty, can include text, or require fixed values.

XML schema documents are beyond the scope of this chapter, but much can be learned from a simple example. This recipe uses the product catalog first presented in recipe 5.1.

At its most basic level, XML Schema Definition (XSD) is used to define the elements that can occur in an XML document. XSD documents are themselves written in XML, and you use a separate predefined element (named *<element>*) in the XSD document to indicate each element that's required in the target document. The *type* attribute indicates the data type. Here's an example for a product name:

```
<xsd:element name="productName" type="xsd:string" />
```

And here's an example for the product price:

```
<xsd:element name="productPrice" type="xsd:decimal" />
```

The basic schema data types are defined at *http://www.w3.org/TR/ xmlschema-2*. They map closely to .NET data types and include *string*, *int*, *long*, *decimal*, *float*, *dateTime*, *boolean*, and *base64Binary*, to name a few of the most frequently used types.

Both the *productName* and *productPrice* are *simple types* because they contain only character data. Elements that contain nested elements are called *complex types*. You can nest them together using a *<sequence>* tag, if order is important, or an *<all>* tag if it's not. Here's how you might model the *<product>* element in the product catalog. Notice that attributes are always declared after elements, and they aren't grouped with a *<sequence>* or *<all>* tag because order is never important.

```
<xsd:complexType name="product">
  <xsd:sequence>
    <xsd:element name="productName" type="xsd:string"/>
    <xsd:element name="productPrice" type="xsd:decimal"/>
    <xsd:element name="inStock" type="xsd:boolean"/>
  </xsd:sequence>
  <xsd:attribute name="id" type="xsd:integer"/>
</xsd:complexType>
```

By default, a listed element can occur exactly one time in a document. You can configure this behavior by specifying the *maxOccurs* and *minOccurs* attributes. Here's an example that allows an unlimited number of products in the catalog:

```
<xsd:element name="product" type="product" maxOccurs="unbounded" />
```

Here's the complete schema for the product catalog XML:

```
<?xml version="1.0"?>
<xsd:schema xmlns:xsd="http://www.w3.org/2001/XMLSchema">

  <!-- Define the complex type product. -->
  <xsd:complexType name="product">
```

```
    <xsd:sequence>
      <xsd:element name="productName" type="xsd:string"/>
      <xsd:element name="productPrice" type="xsd:decimal"/>
      <xsd:element name="inStock" type="xsd:boolean"/>
    </xsd:sequence>
    <xsd:attribute name="id" type="xsd:integer"/>
  </xsd:complexType>

  <!-- This is the structure the document must match.
       It begins with a productCatalog element that nests other elements. -->
  <xsd:element name="productCatalog">
    <xsd:complexType>
      <xsd:sequence>
        <xsd:element name="catalogName" type="xsd:string"/>
        <xsd:element name="expiryDate" type="xsd:date"/>

        <xsd:element name="products">
          <xsd:complexType>
            <xsd:sequence>
              <xsd:element name="product" type="product"
                maxOccurs="unbounded" />
            </xsd:sequence>
          </xsd:complexType>
        </xsd:element>
      </xsd:sequence>
    </xsd:complexType>
  </xsd:element>

</xsd:schema>
```

The *XmlValidatingReader* class enforces all these schema rules—ensuring the document is *valid*—and it also checks that the XML document is *well formed* (which means there are no illegal characters, all opening tags have a corresponding closing tag, and so on). To check a document, you read through it one node at a time by calling the *XmlValidatingReader.Read* method. If an error is found, *XmlValidatingReader* raises a *ValidationEventHandler* event with information about the error. If you wish, you can handle this event and continue processing the document to find more errors. If you don't handle this event, an *XmlException* will be raised when the first error is encountered and processing will be aborted. To test only if a document is well formed, you can use the *XmlValidatingReader* without a schema.

The next example shows a utility class that displays all errors in an XML document when the *ValidateXml* method is called. Errors are displayed in a console window, and a final Boolean variable is returned to indicate the success or failure of the entire validation operation.

```
using System;
using System.Xml;
using System.Xml.Schema;

public class ConsoleValidator {

    // Set to true if at least one error exists.
    private bool failed;

    public bool Failed {
        get {return failed;}
    }

    public bool ValidateXml(string xmlFilename, string schemaFilename) {

        // Create the validator.
        XmlTextReader r = new XmlTextReader(xmlFilename);
        XmlValidatingReader validator = new XmlValidatingReader(r);
        validator.ValidationType = ValidationType.Schema;

        // Load the schema file into the validator.
        XmlSchemaCollection schemas = new XmlSchemaCollection();
        schemas.Add(null, schemaFilename);
        validator.Schemas.Add(schemas);

        // Set the validation event handler.
        validator.ValidationEventHandler +=
          new ValidationEventHandler(ValidationEventHandler);

        failed = false;
        try {

            // Read all XML data.
            while (validator.Read())
            {}
        }catch (XmlException err) {

            // This happens if the XML document includes illegal characters
            // or tags that aren't properly nested or closed.
            Console.WriteLine("A critical XML error has occurred.");
            Console.WriteLine(err.Message);
            failed = true;
        }finally {
            validator.Close();
        }
```

```
        return !failed;
    }

    private void ValidationEventHandler(object sender,
      ValidationEventArgs args) {

        failed = true;

        // Display the validation error.
        Console.WriteLine("Validation error: " + args.Message);
        Console.WriteLine();
    }
}
```

Here's how you would use the class to validate the product catalog:

```
using System;

public class ValidateXml {

    private static void Main() {

        ConsoleValidator consoleValidator = new ConsoleValidator();
        Console.WriteLine("Validating ProductCatalog.xml.");

        bool success = consoleValidator.ValidateXml("ProductCatalog.xml",
          "ProductCatalog.xsd");
        if (!success) {
            Console.WriteLine("Validation failed.");
        }else {
            Console.WriteLine("Validation succeeded.");
        }

        Console.ReadLine();
    }
}
```

If the document is valid, no messages will appear, and the *success* variable will be set to *true*. But consider what happens if you use a document that breaks schema rules, such as the ProductCatalog_Invalid.xml file shown here:

```
<?xml version="1.0" ?>
<productCatalog>
    <catalogName>Acme Fall 2003 Catalog</catalogName>
    <expiryDate>Jan 1, 2004</expiryDate>

    <products>
        <product id="1001">
            <productName>Magic Ring</productName>
```

```
            <productPrice>$342.10</productPrice>
            <inStock>true</inStock>
        </product>
        <product id="1002">
            <productName>Flying Carpet</productName>
            <productPrice>982.99</productPrice>
            <inStock>Yes</inStock>
        </product>
    </products>
</productCatalog>
```

If you attempt to validate this document, the *success* variable will be set to *false* and the output will indicate each error:

```
Validating ProductCatalog_Invalid.xml.

Validation error: The 'expiryDate' element has an invalid value according to
 its data type. [path information truncated]

Validation error: The 'productPrice' element has an invalid value according to
 its data type. [path information truncated]

Validation error: The 'inStock' element has an invalid value according to its
 data type. [path information truncated]

Validation failed.
```

Finally, if you want to validate an XML document and then process it, you can use *XmlValidatingReader* to scan a document as it's read into an in-memory *XmlDocument*. Here's how it works:

```
XmlDocument doc = new XmlDocument();
XmlTextReader r = new XmlTextReader("ProductCatalog.xml");
XmlValidatingReader validator = new XmlValidatingReader(r);

// Load the schema into the validator.
validator.ValidationType = ValidationType.Schema;
XmlSchemaCollection schemas = new XmlSchemaCollection();
schemas.Add(null, "ProductCatalog.xsd");
validator.Schemas.Add(schemas);

// Load the document and validate it at the same time.
// Don't handle the ValidationEventHandler event. Instead, allow any errors
/// to be thrown as an XmlSchemaException.
try {
    doc.Load(validator);
    // (Validation succeeded if you reach here.)
}catch (XmlSchemaException err) {
    // (Validation failed if you reach here.)
}
```

5.9 Use XML Serialization with Custom Objects

Problem

You need to use XML as a serialization format. However, you don't want to process the XML directly in your code—instead, you want to interact with the data using custom objects.

Solution

Use the *System.Xml.Serialization.XmlSerializer* class to transfer data from your object to XML, and vice versa. You can also mark up your class code with attributes to customize its XML representation.

Discussion

The *XmlSerializer* class allows you to convert objects to XML data, and vice versa. This process is used natively by Web services and provides a customizable serialization mechanism that won't require a single line of custom code. The *XmlSerializer* class is even intelligent enough to correctly create arrays when it finds nested elements.

The only requirements for using *XmlSerializer* are as follows:

- The *XmlSerializer* only serializes properties and *public* variables.

- The classes you want to serialize must include a default zero-argument constructor. The *XmlSerializer* uses this constructor when creating the new object during deserialization.

- All class properties must be readable *and* writable. This is because *XmlSerializer* uses the property *get* accessor to retrieve information, and the property *set* accessor to restore the data after deserialization.

> **Note**   You can also store your objects in an XML-based format using .NET serialization and the *System.Runtime.Serialization.Formatters.Soap.SoapFormatter*. In this case, you simply need to make your class serializable—you don't need to provide a default constructor or ensure all properties are writable. However, this gives you no control over the format of the serialized XML.

To use XML serialization, you must first mark up your data objects with attributes that indicate the desired XML mapping. These attributes are found in the *System.Xml.Serialization* namespace and include the following:

■ ***XmlRoot***   Specifies the name of the root element of the XML file. By default, *XmlSerializer* will use the name of the class. This attribute can be applied to the class declaration.

■ ***XmlElement***   Indicates the element name to use for a property or *public* variable. By default, *XmlSerializer* will use the name of the property or *public* variable.

■ ***XmlAttribute***   Indicates that a property or *public* variable should be serialized as an attribute, not an element, and specifies the attribute name.

■ ***XmlEnum***   Configures the text that should be used when serializing enumerated values. If you don't use *XmlEnum*, the name of the enumerated constant will be used.

■ ***XmlIgnore***   Indicates that a property or *public* variable should not be serialized.

For example, consider the product catalog first shown in recipe 5.1. You can represent this XML document using *ProductCatalog* and *Product* objects. Here's the class code that you might use:

```
using System;
using System.Xml.Serialization;

[XmlRoot("productCatalog")]
public class ProductCatalog {

    [XmlElement("catalogName")]
    public string CatalogName;

    // Use the date data type (and ignore the time portion in the
    // serialized XML).
    [XmlElement(ElementName="expiryDate", DataType="date")]
    public DateTime ExpiryDate;

    // Configure the name of the tag that holds all products,
    // and the name of the product tag itself.
    [XmlArray("products")]
    [XmlArrayItem("product")]
    public Product[] Products;
```

```
        public ProductCatalog() {
            // Default constructor for deserialization.
        }

        public ProductCatalog(string catalogName, DateTime expiryDate) {
            this.CatalogName = catalogName;
            this.ExpiryDate = expiryDate;
        }
    }

    public class Product {

        [XmlElement("productName")]
        public string ProductName;

        [XmlElement("productPrice")]
        public decimal ProductPrice;

        [XmlElement("inStock")]
        public bool InStock;

        [XmlAttributeAttribute(AttributeName="id", DataType="integer")]
        public string Id;

        public Product() {
            // Default constructor for serialization.
        }

        public Product(string productName, decimal productPrice) {
            this.ProductName = productName;
            this.ProductPrice = productPrice;
        }
    }
```

Notice that these classes use the XML serialization attributes to rename element names (using Pascal casing in the class member names, and camel casing in the XML tag names), indicate data types that aren't obvious, and specify how *<product>* elements will be nested in the *<productCatalog>*.

Using these custom classes and the *XmlSerializer* object, you can translate XML into objects and vice versa. Here's the code you would need to create a new *ProductCatalog* object, serialize the results to an XML document, deserialize the document back to an object, and then display the XML document.

```
using System;
using System.Xml;
using System.Xml.Serialization;
using System.IO;
```

```
public class SerializeXml {

    private static void Main() {

        // Create the product catalog.
        ProductCatalog catalog = new ProductCatalog("New Catalog",
          DateTime.Now.AddYears(1));
        Product[] products = new Product[2];
        products[0] = new Product("Product 1", 42.99m);
        products[1] = new Product("Product 2", 202.99m);
        catalog.Products = products;

        // Serialize the order to a file.
        XmlSerializer serializer = new XmlSerializer(typeof(ProductCatalog));
        FileStream fs = new FileStream("ProductCatalog.xml", FileMode.Create);
        serializer.Serialize(fs, catalog);
        fs.Close();

        catalog = null;

        // Deserialize the order from the file.
        fs = new FileStream("ProductCatalog.xml", FileMode.Open);
        catalog = (ProductCatalog)serializer.Deserialize(fs);

        // Serialize the order to the Console window.
        serializer.Serialize(Console.Out, catalog);
        Console.ReadLine();
    }
}
```

5.10 Create a Schema for a .NET Class

Problem

You need to create an XML schema based on one or more C# classes. This will allow you to validate XML documents before deserializing them with the *XmlSerializer.*

Solution

Use the XML Schema Definition Tool (xsd.exe) command-line utility included with the .NET Framework. Specify the name of your assembly as a command-line argument, and add the /t:[TypeName] parameter to indicate the types you want to convert.

Discussion

Recipe 5.9 demonstrated how to use the *XmlSerializer* to serialize .NET objects to XML, and deserialize XML into .NET objects. But if you want to use the XML as a way to interact with other applications, business process, or non-Framework applications, you'll need an easy way to validate the XML before you attempt to deserialize it. You'll also need to define an XML schema document that defines the structure and data types used in your XML format, so that other applications can work with it. One quick solution is to generate an XML schema using the xsd.exe command-line utility.

The xsd.exe utility is included with the .NET Framework. If you've installed Microsoft Visual Studio .NET, you'll find it in a directory like C:\Program Files\Microsoft Visual Studio .NET\FrameworkSDK\Bin. The xsd.exe utility can generate schema documents from compiled assemblies. You simply need to supply the filename and indicate the class that represents the XML document with the /t:[TypeName] parameter.

For example, consider the *ProductCatalog* and *Product* classes shown in recipe 5.9. You could create the XML schema for a product catalog with the following command line:

```
xsd Recipe5-09.exe /t:ProductCatalog
```

You need to specify only the *ProductCatalog* class on the command line because this class represents the actual XML document. The generated schema in this example will represent a complete product catalog, with contained product items. It will be given the default filename schema0.xsd. You can now use the *XmlValidatingReader* shown in recipe 5.8 to test whether the XML document can be successfully validated with the schema.

5.11 Generate a Class from a Schema

Problem

You need to create one or more C# classes based on an XML schema. You can then create an XML document in the appropriate format using these objects and the *XmlSerializer*.

Solution

Use the xsd.exe command-line utility included with the .NET Framework. Specify the name of your schema file as a command-line argument, and add the */c* parameter to indicate that you want to generate class code.

Discussion

Recipe 5.10 introduced the xsd.exe command-line utility, which can be used to generate schemas based on class definitions. The reverse operation—generating C# source code based on an XML schema document—is also possible. This is primarily useful if you want to write a certain format of XML document, but you don't want to manually create the document by writing individual nodes with the *XmlDocument* or *XmlTextWriter* classes. Instead, by using xsd.exe, you can generate a set of full .NET objects. You can then serialize these objects to the required XML representation using the *XmlSerializer*, as described in recipe 5.9.

To generate source code from a schema, you simply need to supply the filename of the schema document and add the */c* parameter to indicate that you want to generate the required classes. For example, consider the schema shown in recipe 5.8. You can generate C# code for this schema with the following command-line:

```
xsd ProductCatalog.xsd /c
```

This will generate one file (ProductCatalog.cs) with two classes: *product* and *productCatalog*. These classes are similar to the ones created in recipe 5.9, except for the fact that the class member names match the XML document exactly.

5.12 Perform an XSL Transform

Problem

You need to transform an XML document into another document using an XSLT stylesheet.

Solution

Use the *System.Xml.Xsl.XslTransform* class. Load the XSLT stylesheet using the *XslTransform.Load* method, and generate the output document by using the *Transform* method and supplying a source document.

Discussion

XSLT (or XSL transforms) is an XML-based language designed to transform one XML document into another document. XSLT can be used to create a new XML document with the same data but arranged in a different structure or to select a subset of the data in a document. It can also be used to create a different type of structured document. XSLT is commonly used in this manner to format an XML document into an HTML page.

XSLT is a rich language, and creating XSL transforms is beyond the scope of this book. However, you can learn how to create simple XSLT documents by looking at a basic example. This recipe transforms the orders.xml document shown in recipe 5.6 into an HTML document with a table and then displays the results. To perform this transformation, you'll need the following XSLT stylesheet:

```
<?xml version="1.0" encoding="UTF-8" ?>
<xsl:stylesheet xmlns:xsl="http://www.w3.org/1999/XSL/Transform"
    version="1.0" >

  <xsl:template match="Order">
    <html><body><p>
    Order <b><xsl:value-of select="Client/@id"/></b>
    for <xsl:value-of select="Client/Name"/></p>
    <table border="1">
    <td>ID</td><td>Name</td><td>Price</td>
    <xsl:apply-templates select="Items/Item"/>
    </table></body></html>
  </xsl:template>

  <xsl:template match="Items/Item">
    <tr>
    <td><xsl:value-of select="@id"/></td>
    <td><xsl:value-of select="Name"/></td>
    <td><xsl:value-of select="Price"/></td>
    </tr>
  </xsl:template>

</xsl:stylesheet>
```

Essentially, every XSL stylesheet consists of a set of templates. Each template matches some set of elements in the source document and then describes the contribution that the matched element will make to the resulting document. To match the template, the XSLT document uses *XPath* expressions, as described in recipe 5.6.

The orders.xslt stylesheet contains two *template* elements (as children of the root *stylesheet* element). The first template matches the root *Order* element. When the XSLT processor finds an *Order* element, it outputs the tags necessary to start an HTML table with appropriate column headings and inserts some data about the client using the **value-of** command, which outputs the text result of an *XPath* expression. In this case, the *XPath* expressions (Client/@id and Client/Name) match the *id* attribute and the *Name* element.

Next the **apply-templates** command is used to branch off and perform processing of any contained *Item* elements. This is required because there might be multiple *Item* elements. Each *Item* element is matched using the *XPath* expression Items/Item. The root *Order* node isn't specified because *Order* is the current node. Finally, the initial template writes the tags necessary to end the HTML document.

If you execute this transform on the sample orders.xml file shown in recipe 5.6, you'll end up with the following HTML document:

```
<html>
  <body>
    <p>
    Order <b>ROS-930252034</b>
    for Remarkable Office Supplies</p>
    <table border="1">
      <td>ID</td>
      <td>Name</td>
      <td>Price</td>
      <tr>
        <td>1001</td>
        <td>Electronic Protractor</td>
        <td>42.99</td>
      </tr>
      <tr>
        <td>1002</td>
        <td>Invisible Ink</td>
        <td>200.25</td>
      </tr>
    </table>
  </body>
</html>
```

To apply an XSLT stylesheet in .NET, you use the *XslTransform* class. The following code shows a Windows-based application that programmatically applies the transformation and then displays the transformed file in a Web browser window. In this example, the code uses the overloaded version of the *Transform* method that saves the result document directly to disk, although you could receive it as a stream and process it inside your application instead.

```
using System;
using System.Windows.Forms;
using System.Xml.Xsl;

public class TransformXml : System.Windows.Forms.Form {

    private AxSHDocVw.AxWebBrowser webBrowser;

    // (Designer code omitted.)

    private void TransformXml_Load(object sender, System.EventArgs e) {
```

```
        XslTransform transform = new XslTransform();

        // Load the XSL stylesheet.
        transform.Load("orders.xslt");

        // Transform orders.xml into orders.html using orders.xslt.
        transform.Transform("orders.xml", "orders.html", null);

        object var = null;
        webBrowser.Navigate(
          "file:///" + Application.StartupPath + @"\orders.html",
          ref var, ref var, ref var, ref var);
    }
}
```

> **Note**   The .NET Framework does not include any controls for render-
> ing HTML content. However, this functionality is available through
> COM interoperability if you use the ActiveX Web browser control pro-
> vided with Microsoft Internet Explorer and the Microsoft Windows
> operating system. This window can show local or remote HTML files,
> and supports JavaScript, VBScript, and all Internet Explorer plug-ins.
> (See recipe 11.4 for details on adding the Web browser control to a
> project.)

The application is shown in Figure 5-2.

Figure 5-2   The stylesheet output for orders.xml.

6

Windows Forms

The Microsoft .NET Framework includes a rich set of classes for creating traditional Microsoft Windows–based applications in the *System.Windows.Forms* namespace. These range from basic ingredients such as the *TextBox*, *Button*, and *MainMenu* classes to specialized controls such as *TreeView*, *LinkLabel*, and *NotifyIcon*. In addition, you'll find all the tools you need to manage Multiple Document Interface (MDI) applications, integrate context-sensitive help, and even create multilingual user interfaces—all without needing to resort to the complexities of the Win32 API.

Most C# developers quickly find themselves at home with the Windows Form programming model. However, there are a number of tips and timesaving techniques that can make Windows programming much more productive. This chapter covers the following topics:

- How to get the most out of controls, including how to add them at runtime (recipe 6.1), link them to arbitrary data (recipe 6.2), and process them generically (recipe 6.3).

- How to work with forms, including tracking them in an application (recipe 6.4), using MDI (recipe 6.5), and storing size and location information (recipe 6.6). You'll also learn how to make multilingual forms (recipe 6.13) and borderless forms (recipe 6.14 and recipe 6.15).

- Tips for working with common controls such as the *ListBox* (recipe 6.7), *TextBox* (recipe 6.8), *ComboBox* (recipe 6.9), *ListView* (recipe 6.10), and *Menu* classes (recipe 6.11 and recipe 6.12).

- How to create an animated system tray icon (recipe 6.16).

- Concepts you can use with multiple control types, including validation (recipe 6.17), drag-and-drop (recipe 6.18), context-sensitive help (recipe 6.19), and Windows XP control styles (recipe 6.20).

> **Note**   Most of the recipes in this chapter use control classes, which
> are always defined in the *System.Windows.Forms* namespace. When
> introducing these classes, the full namespace name is not indicated,
> and *Systems.Windows.Forms* is assumed.

6.1 Add a Control Programmatically

Problem

You need to add a control to a form at runtime, not design time.

Solution

Create an instance of the appropriate control class. Then add the control object
to a form or a container control using the *Add* method of the *ControlCollection*.

Discussion

In a .NET Windows-based application, there's really no difference between creating a control at design time and creating it at runtime. When you create controls at design time (using a tool like Microsoft Visual Studio .NET), the
necessary code is added to your form class, typically in a special method named
InitializeComponent. You can use the same code in your application to create
controls on the fly. Just follow these steps:

1.   Create an instance of the appropriate control class.

2.   Configure the control properties accordingly (particularly the size
     and position coordinates).

3.   Add the control to the form or another container.

4.   In addition, if you need to handle the events for the new control, you
     can wire them up to existing methods.

Every control provides a *Controls* property that references a *ControlCollection* that contains all of its child controls. To add a child control, you invoke
the *ControlCollection.Add* method. The following example demonstrates this
by dynamically creating a list of check boxes. One check box is added for each
item in an array. All the check boxes are added to a panel that has its *AutoScroll*
property set to *true*, which gives basic scrolling support to the check box list.

```
using System;
using System.Windows.Forms;

public class DynamicCheckBox : System.Windows.Forms.Form {

    // (Designer code omitted.)

    private void DynamicCheckBox_Load(object sender, System.EventArgs e) {

        // Create the array.
        string[] foods = {"Grain", "Bread", "Beans", "Eggs",
          "Chicken", "Milk", "Fruit", "Vegetables",
          "Pasta", "Rice", "Fish", "Beef"};

        int topPosition = 10;
        foreach (string food in foods)
        {
            // Create a new check box.
            CheckBox checkBox = new CheckBox();
            checkBox.Left = 10;
            checkBox.Top = topPosition;
            topPosition += 30;
            checkBox.Text = food;

            // Add the check box to the form.
            panel.Controls.Add(checkBox);
        }
    }
}
```

Figure 6-1 shows how the form will look.

Figure 6-1   A dynamically generated check box list.

6.2 Link Data to a Control

Problem

You need to link an object to a specific control (perhaps to store some arbitrary information that relates to a given display item).

Solution

Store a reference to the object in the *Tag* property of the control.

Discussion

Every class that derives from *System.Windows.Forms.Control* provides a *Tag* property that you can use to store a reference to any type of object. The *Tag* property isn't used by the control or the Microsoft .NET Framework. Instead, it's reserved as a convenient storage place for application-specific information. In addition, some other non-*Control*-derived classes provide a *Tag* property. Examples include the *ListViewItem* and *TreeNode* classes (which represent items in a *ListView* or a *TreeView* control). One class that does *not* provide a *Tag* property is *MenuItem*.

The *Tag* property is defined as a generic *Object* type, which means that you can use it to store any value type or reference type, from a simple number or string to a custom object you have defined. When retrieving data from the *Tag* property, you'll need to cast the object to its original type.

The following example adds a list of files to a list view. The corresponding *FileInfo* object for each file is stored in the *Tag* property. When a user double-clicks one of the list items, the code retrieves the *FileInfo* object from the *Tag* property and displays the file size in a *MessageBox* (see Figure 6-2).

```
using System;
using System.Windows.Forms;
using System.IO;

public class TagPropertyExample : System.Windows.Forms.Form (

    // (Designer code omitted.)

    private void TagPropertyExample_Load(object sender, System.EventArgs e) {

        // Get all the files in the directory.
        DirectoryInfo directory = new DirectoryInfo("C:\\");
        FileInfo[] files = directory.GetFiles();
```

```
        // Display all the files in the ListView.
        foreach (FileInfo file in files) {

            ListViewItem item = listView.Items.Add(file.Name);
            item.ImageIndex = 0;
            item.Tag = file;
        }
    }

    private void listView_ItemActivate(object sender, System.EventArgs e) {

        // Get the file's size from the linked FileInfo.
        ListViewItem item = ((ListView)sender).SelectedItems[0];
        FileInfo file = (FileInfo)item.Tag;
        string info = file.FullName + " is " + file.Length + " bytes.";

        // Display the file's size.
        MessageBox.Show(info, "File Information");
    }
}
```

Figure 6-2   Storing data in the *Tag* property.

6.3 Process All the Controls on a Form

Problem

You need to perform a generic task with all the controls on the form (for example, retrieving or clearing their *Text* property, changing their color, or resizing them).

Solution

Iterate recursively through the collection of controls. Interact with each control using the properties and methods of the base *Control* class.

Discussion

You can iterate through the controls on a form using the *Form.Controls* collection, which includes all the controls that are placed directly on the form surface. However, if any of these controls are container controls (such as *GroupBox*, *Panel*, or *TabPage*), they might contain more controls. Thus, it's necessary to use recursive logic that searches the *Controls* collection of every control on the form.

The following example shows a form that performs this recursive logic to find every text box on a form and clears the text they contain. The form tests each control to determine whether it's a text box by using the *typeof* operator.

```csharp
using System;
using System.Windows.Forms;

public class ProcessAllControls : System.Windows.Forms.Form {

    // (Designer code omitted.)

    private void cmdProcessAll_Click(object sender, System.EventArgs e) {
        ProcessControls(this);
    }

    private void ProcessControls(Control ctrl) {

        // Ignore the control unless it's a text box.
        if (ctrl.GetType() == typeof(TextBox)) {
            ctrl.Text = "";
        }

        // Process controls recursively.
        // This is required if controls contain other controls
        // (for example, if you use panels, group boxes, or other
        // container controls).
        foreach (Control ctrlChild in ctrl.Controls) {
            ProcessControls(ctrlChild);
        }
    }
}
```

6.4 Track the Visible Forms in an Application

Problem

You want to keep track of all the forms that are currently being displayed. This is often the case if you want one form to be able to interact with another.

Solution

Create a class that holds the references to *Form* instances. Store the *Form* references using *static* variables.

Discussion

.NET does not provide any way of determining what forms are currently being displayed in an application. (The one exception is MDI applications, as described in recipe 6.5.) If you want to determine what forms are in existence, or what forms are displayed, or you want one form to call the methods or set the properties of another form, you'll need to keep track of form instances on your own.

One useful approach is to create a class consisting of *static* members. This class can track open forms using a collection, or dedicated properties. Here's an example of a class that can track two forms:

```
public class OpenForms {

    public static Form MainForm;
    public static Form SecondaryForm;
}
```

Now when either the main or the secondary form is shown, it can register itself with the *OpenForms* class. A logical place to put this code is in the *Form.Load* event handler.

```
private void MainForm_Load(object sender, EventArgs e) {

    // Register the newly created form instance.
    OpenForms.MainForm = this;
}
```

You can use similar code to remove the reference when the form is closed.

```
private void MainForm_Unload(object sender, EventArgs e) {

    // Remove the form instance.
    OpenForms.MainForm = null;
}
```

Now another form can interact with this form through the *OpenForms* class. For example, here's how the main form would hide the second form:

```
if (OpenForms.SecondaryForm != null) {
    OpenForms.SecondaryForm.Hide();
}
```

In this approach, we assume that every form is created only once. If you have a document-based application where the user can create multiple instances of the same form, you should track these forms using a collection. Here's an example with an *ArrayList* collection:

```
public class OpenForms {

    public static Form MainForm;
    public static ArrayList DocForms = new ArrayList();
}
```

Forms can then add themselves to the document collection as needed, as shown in the following code:

```
private void DocForm_Load(object sender, EventArgs e) {

    // Register the newly created form instance.
    OpenForms.DocForms.Add(this);
}
```

6.5 Find All MDI Child Forms

Problem

You need to find all the forms that are currently being displayed in a Multiple Document Interface application.

Solution

Iterate through the forms in the *MdiChildren* collection of the MDI parent.

Discussion

The .NET Framework includes two convenient shortcuts for managing MDI applications: the *MdiChildren* and the *MdiParent* properties of the *Form* class. You can investigate the *MdiParent* property of any MDI child to find the containing parent window. You can use the *MdiChildren* collection of the parent to find all the MDI child windows.

For example, consider the following example (shown in Figure 6-3), which displays simple child windows. Each child window includes a label with some date information, and a button. When the button is clicked, the event handler walks through all the child windows and displays the label text that each one contains. Each window also exposes the label text through a read-only property.

Here's the form code for the child window:

```
public class MDIChild : System.Windows.Forms.Form {

    private System.Windows.Forms.Button cmdShowAllWindows;
    private System.Windows.Forms.Label label;

    // (Designer code omitted.)

    public string LabelText {

        get {
            return label.Text;
        }
    }

    private void cmdShowAllWindows_Click(object sender, System.EventArgs e) {

        // Walk through the collection of child windows.
        foreach (Form frm in this.MdiParent.MdiChildren) {

            // Cast the generic Form to the expended derived class type.
            MDIChild child = (MDIChild)frm;
            MessageBox.Show(child.LabelText, frm.Text);
        }
    }

    private void MDIChild_Load(object sender, System.EventArgs e){

        label.Text = DateTime.Now.ToString();
    }
}
```

Notice that when the code walks through the collection of child forms, it must convert the generic *Form* reference to the custom derived *MDIChild* form class so that it can use the *LabelText* property.

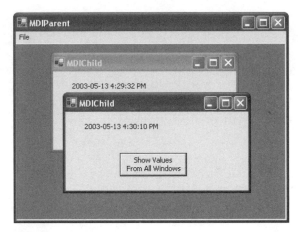

Figure 6-3   Getting information from multiple MDI child windows.

6.6 Save the Size and Location of a Form

Problem

You need to store the size and position of a resizable form and restore it the next time the form is shown.

Solution

Store the *Left*, *Top*, *Width*, and *Height* form properties in the Windows registry.

Discussion

The Windows registry is an ideal place for storing position and size information for a form. Typically, you'll store information about each form in a separate key, perhaps using the class name of the form. These keys will be stored under an application-specific key.

To automate this process, it helps to create a dedicated class that saves and retrieves form settings. The *FormSettingStore* class shown in the following example fills this role. This class provides a *SaveSettings* method that accepts a form and writes its size and position information to the registry, as well as an *ApplySettings* method that accepts a form and applies the settings from the registry. The registry key path and the name of the form subkey are stored as class member variables.

```csharp
using System;
using System.Windows.Forms;
using Microsoft.Win32;

public class FormSettingStore {

    private string regPath;
    private string formName;
    private RegistryKey key;

    public string RegistryPath {
        get {return regPath;}
    }

    public string FormName {
        get {return formName;}
    }

    public FormSettingStore(string registryPath, string formName) {

        this.regPath = registryPath;
        this.formName = formName;

        // Create the key if it doesn't exist.
        key = Registry.LocalMachine.CreateSubKey(registryPath + formName);
    }

    public void SaveSettings(System.Windows.Forms.Form form) {

        key.SetValue("Height", form.Height);
        key.SetValue("Width", form.Width);
        key.SetValue("Left", form.Left);
        key.SetValue("Top", form.Top);
    }

    public void ApplySettings(System.Windows.Forms.Form form) {

        // If form settings are not available, the current form settings
        // are used instead.
        form.Height = (int)key.GetValue("Height", form.Height);
        form.Width = (int)key.GetValue("Width", form.Width);
        form.Left = (int)key.GetValue("Left", form.Left);
        form.Top = (int)key.GetValue("Top", form.Top);
    }
}
```

To use the *FormSettingStore* class, simply add the event-handling code shown here to any form. This code saves the form properties when the form closes and restores them when the form is loaded.

```
private FormSettingStore formSettings;

private void Form1_Load(object sender, System.EventArgs e) {

    formSettings = new FormSettingStore(@"Software\MyApp\", this.Name);
    formSettings.ApplySettings(this);
}

private void Form1_Closed(object sender, System.EventArgs e) {

    formSettings.SaveSettings(this);
}
```

> **Note**   Remember that access to the registry can be limited based on the current Windows user account and code access security policy. When you create an application that requires registry access, it's a good practice to document the fact that the assembly requires access to the registry by using a minimum permission request, as described in recipe 13.7.

6.7 Force a List Box to Scroll

Problem

You need to scroll a list box programmatically so that certain items in the list are visible.

Solution

Set the *ListBox.TopIndex* property, which sets the first visible list item.

Discussion

In some cases, you might have a list box that stores a significant amount of information or one that you add information to periodically. It's often the case that the most recent information, which is added at the end of the list, is more important than the information at the top of the list. One solution is to scroll the list box so that recently added items are visible.

The following example form includes a list box and a button that adds 20 items to the list and then scrolls to the last full page using the *TopIndex* property.

```
using System;
using System.Windows.Forms;

public class ListBoxScrollTest : System.Windows.Forms.Form {

    // (Designer code omitted.)

    int counter = 0;

    private void cmdTest_Click(object sender, System.EventArgs e) {

        for (int i = 0; i < 20; i++) {

            counter++;
            listBox1.Items.Add("Item " + counter.ToString());
        }
        listBox1.TopIndex = listBox1.Items.Count - 1;
    }
}
```

6.8 Restrict a Text Box to Numeric Input

Problem

You need to create a text box that will reject all non-numeric keystrokes.

Solution

Add an event handler for the *TextBox.KeyPress* event. In the event handler, set the *KeyPressEventArgs.Handled* property to *true* to reject an invalid keystroke.

Discussion

The best way to correct invalid input is to prevent it from being entered in the first place. This approach is easy to implement with the text box because it provides a *KeyPress* event that occurs after the keystroke has been received but before it's displayed. You can use the *KeyPressEventArgs* event parameter to effectively "cancel" an invalid keystroke by setting the *Handled* property to *true*.

To allow only numeric input, you must allow a keystroke only if it corresponds to a number (0 through 9) or a special control key (such as delete or the arrow keys). The keystroke character is provided to the *KeyPress* event through the *KeyPressEventArgs.KeyChar* property. You can use two *static* methods of the *System.Char* class—*IsDigit* and *IsControl*—to quickly test the character.

Here's the event handler you would use to prevent non-numeric input:

```
private void textBox1_KeyPress(object sender,
  System.Windows.Forms.KeyPressEventArgs e) {

    if (!Char.IsDigit(e.KeyChar) && !Char.IsControl(e.KeyChar)) {
        e.Handled = true;
    }
}
```

Notice that this code rejects the decimal separator. If you need to allow this character (for example, to permit the user to enter a fractional currency amount), you'll have to modify the code slightly, as shown here:

```
// Get the decimal separator character on this platform
// (typically a "." for US-English).
string decimalString =
  Thread.CurrentThread.CurrentCulture.NumberFormat.CurrencyDecimalSeparator;
char decimalChar = Convert.ToChar(decimalString);

if (Char.IsDigit(e.KeyChar) || Char.IsControl(e.KeyChar)) {}
else if (e.KeyChar == '.' && textBox1.Text.IndexOf(".") == -1) {}
else {
    e.Handled = true;
}
```

This code allows only a single decimal point, but it makes no restriction about how many significant digits can be used. It also doesn't allow the entry of negative numbers. (You could change this behavior by allowing the minus sign (-) provided it's the first character.) Remember that this code also assumes you have imported the *System.Threading* namespace.

6.9 Use an Autocomplete Combo Box

Problem

You want to create a combo box that automatically completes what the user is typing based on the item list.

Solution

You can implement a basic autocomplete combo box by creating a custom control that overrides the *OnKeyPress* and *OnTextChanged* methods.

Discussion

There are many different variations to the autocomplete control. Sometimes, the control fills in values based on a list of recent selections (as Microsoft Excel does when entering cell values) or might display a drop-down list of near matches (as Microsoft Internet Explorer does when typing a URL). You can create a basic autocomplete combo box by handling the *KeyPress* and *TextChanged* events, or by creating a custom class that derives from *ComboBox* and overrides the *OnKeyPress* and *OnTextChanged* methods. This recipe takes the latter approach.

In the *OnKeyPress* method, the combo box determines whether or not an autocomplete replacement should be made. If the user pressed a character key (such as a letter) the replacement can be made, but if the user has pressed a control key (such as the backspace key, the cursor keys, and so on), no action should be taken. The *OnTextChanged* method performs the actual replacement after the key processing is complete. This method looks up the first match for the current text in the list of items, and then adds the rest of the matching text. After the text is added, the combo box selects the characters between the current insertion point and the end of the text. This allows the user to continue typing and replace the autocomplete text if it isn't what the user wants.

Here's the full code for the *AutoCompleteComboBox* class:

```
using System;
using System.Windows.Forms;

public class AutoCompleteComboBox : ComboBox {

    // Track if a special key is pressed
    // (in which case the text replacement operation will be skipped).
    private bool controlKey = false;

    // Determine whether a special key was pressed.
    protected override void OnKeyPress(
      System.Windows.Forms.KeyPressEventArgs e) {

        base.OnKeyPress(e);

        if (e.KeyChar == (int)Keys.Escape) {
```

```
                // Clear the text.
                this.SelectedIndex = -1;
                this.Text = "";
                controlKey = true;
            }
            else if (Char.IsControl(e.KeyChar)) {

                controlKey = true;
            }
            else {

                controlKey = false;
            }
        }


        // Perform the text substitution.
        protected override void OnTextChanged(System.EventArgs e) {

            base.OnTextChanged(e);

            if (this.Text != "" && !controlKey) {

                // Search for a matching entry.
                string matchText = this.Text;
                int match = this.FindString(matchText);

                // If a matching entry is found, insert it now.
                if (match != -1) {

                    this.SelectedIndex = match;

                    // Select the added text so it can be replaced
                    // if the user keeps typing.
                    this.SelectionStart = matchText.Length;
                    this.SelectionLength = this.Text.Length - this.SelectionStart;
                }
            }
        }
    }
}
```

To test the *AutoCompleteComboBox*, you can create a simple Windows client that adds the combo box to a form and fills it with a list of words. In this example, the list of words is retrieved from a text file and the control is added manually. You could also compile the *AutoCompleteComboBox* class to a separate class library assembly and then add it to the Toolbox, so you could add it to a form at design time.

```
using System;
using System.Windows.Forms;
using System.Drawing;
using System.IO;

public class AutoCompleteComboBoxTest : System.Windows.Forms.Form {

    // (Designer code omitted.)

    private void AutoCompleteComboBox_Load(object sender,
      System.EventArgs e) {

        // Add the combo box to the form.
        AutoCompleteComboBox combo = new AutoCompleteComboBox();
        combo.Location = new Point(10,10);
        this.Controls.Add(combo);

        // Add the word list.
        FileStream fs = new FileStream("words.txt", FileMode.Open);
        using (StreamReader r = new StreamReader(fs)) {

            while (r.Peek() > -1) {

                string word = r.ReadLine();
                combo.Items.Add(word);
            }
        }
    }
}
```

Figure 6-4 shows the autocomplete combo box.

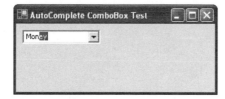

Figure 6-4 An autocomplete combo box.

6.10 Sort a List View by Any Column

Problem

You need to sort a list view, but the built-in *ListView.Sort* method only sorts based on the first column.

Solution

Create a type that implements the *System.Collections.IComparer* interface and can sort *ListViewItem* objects. The *IComparer* type can sort based on any *ListViewItem* criteria you want. Set the *ListView.ListViewItemSorter* property with an instance of the *IComparer* type before calling the *ListView.Sort* method.

Discussion

The *ListView* control provides a *Sort* method that orders items alphabetically based on the text in the first column. If you want to sort based on other column values or order items in any other way, you need to create a custom implementation of the *IComparer* interface that can perform the work.

The *IComparer* interface defines a single method named *Compare*, which takes two objects and determines which one should be ordered first. Here is a custom *ListViewItemComparer* class that implements *IComparer*. It provides two additional properties: *Column* and *Numeric*. *Column* indicates the column that should be used for sorting, and *Numeric* is a Boolean flag that can be set to *true* if you want to perform number-based comparisons instead of alphabetic comparisons.

```
using System;
using System.Collections;
using System.Windows.Forms;

public class ListViewItemComparer : IComparer {

    private int column;
    private bool numeric = false;

    public int Column {

        get {return column;}
        set {column = value;}
    }

    public bool Numeric {
```

```
        get {return numeric;}
        set {numeric = value;}
    }

    public ListViewItemComparer(int columnIndex) {

        Column = columnIndex;
    }

    public int Compare(object x, object y) {

        ListViewItem listX = (ListViewItem)x;
        ListViewItem listY = (ListViewItem)y;

        if (Numeric) {

            // Convert column text to numbers before comparing.
            // If the conversion fails, just use the value 0.
            decimal listXVal, listYVal;
            try {
                listXVal = Decimal.Parse(listX.SubItems[Column].Text);
            }
            catch {
                listXVal = 0;
            }

            try {
                listYVal = Decimal.Parse(listY.SubItems[Column].Text);
            }
            catch {
                listYVal = 0;
            }

            return Decimal.Compare(listXVal, listYVal);
        }
        else {

            // Keep the column text in its native string format
            // and perform an alphabetic comparison.
            string listXText = listX.SubItems[Column].Text;
            string listYText = listY.SubItems[Column].Text;

            return String.Compare(listXText, listYText);
        }
    }
}
```

Now to sort the list view, you simply need to create a *ListViewItemComparer* instance, configure it appropriately, and then set it in the *ListView.ListViewItemSorter* property before you call the *ListView.Sort* method.

The following form demonstrates a simple test of the *ListViewItemComparer*. Every time the user clicks a column header in the list view, a new *ListViewItemComparer* is created and used to sort the list based on the clicked column.

```
using System;
using System.Windows.Forms;

public class ListViewItemSort : System.Windows.Forms.Form {

    // (Designer code omitted.)

    private void ListView1_ColumnClick(object sender,
      System.Windows.Forms.ColumnClickEventArgs e) {

        ListViewItemComparer sorter = new ListViewItemComparer(e.Column);
        ListView1.ListViewItemSorter = sorter;
        ListView1.Sort();
    }
}
```

6.11 Link a Context Menu to a Control

Problem

You need to link a different context menu to each control on a form. However, you don't want to write a separate event handler to show the context menu for each control.

Solution

Write a generic event handler that retrieves the *ContextMenu* instance that's associated with a control and then displays the menu over the appropriate control.

Discussion

You can link a control to a context menu by settings the control's *ContextMenu* property. However, this is only a convenience—to display the context menu you must retrieve the menu and call its *Show* method, supplying both a parent control and a pair of coordinates. Usually, you implement this logic in an event handler for the *MouseDown* event.

The good news is that the logic for showing a context menu is completely generic, no matter what the control is. Every control supports the *ContextMenu* property (which is inherited from the base *Control* class), which means you can easily write a generic event handler that will display context menus for all controls.

For example, consider a form with a label, a picture box, and a text box. You can write a single event handler that responds to the *MouseDown* event for all these objects. Here's how the designer code would look if you connected all these events to an event handler named *Control_MouseDown*:

```
this.label1.MouseDown += new MouseEventHandler(this.Control_MouseDown);
this.pictureBox1.MouseDown += new MouseEventHandler(this.Control_MouseDown);
this.textBox1.MouseDown += new MouseEventHandler(this.Control_MouseDown);
```

The event-handling code is completely generic. It just casts the sender to a *Control*, checks for a linked context menu, and displays it

```
private void Control_MouseDown(object sender,
    System.Windows.Forms.MouseEventArgs e) {

    if (e.Button == MouseButtons.Right) {

        // Get the source control.
        Control ctrl = (Control)sender;

        if (ctrl.ContextMenu != null) {

            // Show the linked menu over the control.
            ctrl.ContextMenu.Show(ctrl, new Point(e.X, e.Y));
        }
    }
}
```

6.12 Use Part of a Main Menu for a Context Menu

Problem

You need to create a context menu that shows the same entries as part of an application's main menu.

Solution

Use the *CloneMenu* method of the *MenuItem* class to duplicate a portion of the main menu.

Discussion

In many applications, a control's context-sensitive menu duplicates a portion of the main menu. However, .NET does not allow you to create a *MenuItem* instance that's contained in more than one menu at a time.

The solution is to make a duplicate copy of a portion of the menu using the *CloneMenu* method. The *CloneMenu* method not only copies the appropriate *MenuItem* items (and any contained submenus), it also registers each *MenuItem* object with the same event handlers. Thus, when a user clicks a cloned menu item in a context menu, the same event handler will be triggered as if the user clicked the duplicate menu item in the main menu.

For example, consider the test application shown in Figure 6-5. In this example, the context menu for the text box shows the same entries that are found in the File menu. Technically, these are duplicate copies of the appropriate *MenuItem* objects. However, if the user clicks on one of these entries, the same event handler is executed.

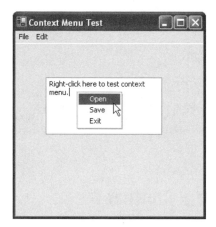

Figure 6-5   Copying part of a main menu to a context menu.

Here's the form code you need to create this example. It duplicates the entries in the main menu when the form first loads. (Unfortunately, it's not possible to perform the same operation at design time.)

```
using System;
using System.Windows.Forms;
using System.Drawing;
```

```csharp
public class ContextMenuCopy : System.Windows.Forms.Form {

    // (Designer code omitted.)

    private void ContextMenuCopy_Load(object sender, System.EventArgs e) {

        ContextMenu mnuContext = new ContextMenu();

        // Copy the menu items from the File menu into a context menu.
        foreach (MenuItem mnuItem in mnuFile.MenuItems) {

            mnuContext.MenuItems.Add(mnuItem.CloneMenu());
        }

        // Attach the context menu to the text box
        TextBox1.ContextMenu = mnuContext;
    }

    private void TextBox1_MouseDown(object sender,
      System.Windows.Forms.MouseEventArgs e) {

        if (e.Button == MouseButtons.Right){

            TextBox1.ContextMenu.Show(TextBox1, new Point(e.X, e.Y));
        }
    }

    private void mnuOpen_Click(object sender, System.EventArgs e) {

        MessageBox.Show("This is the event handler for Open.");
    }

    private void mnuSave_Click(object sender, System.EventArgs e) {

        MessageBox.Show("This is the event handler for Save.");
    }

    private void mnuClick_Click(object sender, System.EventArgs e) {

        MessageBox.Show("This is the event handler for Exit.");
    }
}
```

6.13 Make a Multilingual Form

Problem

You need to create a localizable form that can be deployed in more than one language.

Solution

Store all locale-specific information in resource files, which are compiled into satellite assemblies.

Discussion

The .NET Framework includes built-in support for localization through its use of resource files. The basic idea is to store information that's locale-specific (for example, button text) in a resource file. You can then create multiple resource files for multiple different cultures and compile them into satellite assemblies. When you run the application, .NET will automatically use the correct satellite assembly based on the locale settings of the current computer.

You can read to and write from resource files manually. However, Visual Studio .NET also includes extensive design-time support for localized forms. It works like this:

1.   First set the *Localizable* property of the form to *true* using the Properties window.

2.   Set the *Language* property of the form to the locale for which you would like to enter information. (See Figure 6-6.) Then configure the localizable properties of all the controls on the form. Instead of storing your changes in the designer-generated code for the form, Visual Studio .NET will actually create a new resource file to hold your data.

3.   Repeat step 2 for each language that you want to support. Each time, a new resource file will be generated. If you change the *Language* property to a locale you have already configured, your previous settings will reappear, and you'll be able to modify them.

Figure 6-6   Selecting a language for localizing a form.

You can now compile and test your application on differently localized systems. Visual Studio .NET will create a separate directory and satellite assembly for each resource file in the project. You can select Project | Show All Files from the Visual Studio .NET menu to see how these files are arranged, as shown in Figure 6-7.

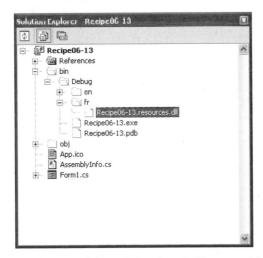

Figure 6-7   A French-locale satellite assembly.

As a testing shortcut, you can also force your application to adopt a specific culture by modifying the *Thread.CurrentUICulture* property of the application thread. However, you must modify this property before the form has loaded.

```
using System;
using System.Windows.Forms;
using System.Threading;
using System.Globalization;

public class MultiLingualForm : System.Windows.Forms.Form {

    private System.Windows.Forms.Label label1;

    // (Designer code omitted.)

    static void Main() {

        Thread.CurrentThread.CurrentUICulture = new CultureInfo("fr");
        Application.Run(new MultiLingualForm());
    }
}
```

> **Note** You can also use a utility called Winres.exe (included with Visual Studio .NET) to edit resource information. It provides a scaled-down form editor that doesn't include the capability to modify code, which is ideal for translators and other nonprogramming professionals who might need to enter locale-specific information.

6.14 Create a Form That Can't Be Moved

Problem

You want to create a form that occupies a fixed location on the screen and can't be moved.

Solution

Make a borderless form by setting the *FormBorderStyle* property of the *Form* class to the value *FormBorderStyle.None*.

Discussion

You can create a borderless form by setting the *FormBorderStyle* property to *None*. Borderless forms can't be moved. However, they also lack any kind of border—if you want the customary blue border, you'll need to add it yourself either with manual drawing code or by using a background image.

There's one other approach to creating an immovable form that provides a basic control-style border. First, set the *ControlBox*, *MinimizeBox*, and *MaximizeBox* properties of the form to *false*. Then set the *Text* property to an empty string. The form will have a raised gray border or black line (depending on the *FormBorderStyle* option you use), similar to a button. Figure 6-8 shows both types of immovable forms.

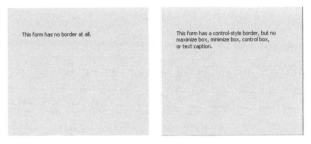

Figure 6-8   Two types of forms that can't be moved.

6.15 Make a Borderless Form Movable

Problem

You need to create a borderless form that can be moved. This might be the case if you are creating a custom window that has a unique look (for example, for a visually rich application such as a game or a media player).

Solution

Create another control that responds to the *MouseDown*, *MouseUp*, and *Mouse-Move* events and programmatically moves the form.

Discussion

Borderless forms omit a title bar, which makes it impossible for a user to move them. You can compensate for this shortcoming by adding a control to the form that serves the same purpose. For example, Figure 6-9 shows a form that includes a label to support dragging. The user can click this label, and then drag the form to a new location on the screen while holding down the mouse button. As the user moves the mouse, the form is automatically moved correspondingly, as though it's "attached" to the mouse pointer.

Figure 6-9   A movable borderless form.

To implement this solution, you need take the following steps:

1.   Create a form-level Boolean variable that tracks whether or not the form is currently being dragged.

2.   When the label is clicked, the code sets the flag to indicate that the form is in drag mode. At the same time, the current mouse position is recorded. You add this logic to the event handler for the *Label.MouseDown* event.

3.   When the user moves the mouse over the label, the form is moved correspondingly so that the position of the mouse over the label is unchanged. You add this logic to the event handler for the *Label.MouseMove* event.

4.   When the user releases the mouse button, the dragging mode is switched off. You add this logic to the event handler for the *Label.MouseUp* event.

Here's the complete form code:

```
using System;
using System.Windows.Forms;
using System.Drawing;

public class DragForm : System.Windows.Forms.Form {

    // (Designer code omitted.)
```

```csharp
// Tracks whether the form is in drag mode. If it is, mouse movements
// over the label will be translated into form movements.
private bool dragging;

// Stores the offset where the label is clicked.
private Point pointClicked;

private void lblDrag_MouseDown(object sender,
    System.Windows.Forms.MouseEventArgs e) {

    if (e.Button == MouseButtons.Left) {

        dragging = true;
        pointClicked = new Point(e.X, e.Y);
    }
    else {

        dragging = false;
    }
}

private void lblDrag_MouseMove(object sender,
    System.Windows.Forms.MouseEventArgs e) {

    if (dragging) {

        Point pointMoveTo;

        // Find the current mouse position in screen coordinates.
        pointMoveTo = this.PointToScreen(new Point(e.X, e.Y));

        // Compensate for the position the control was clicked.
        pointMoveTo.Offset(-pointClicked.X, -pointClicked.Y);

        // Move the form.
        this.Location = pointMoveTo;
    }
}

private void lblDrag_MouseUp(object sender,
    System.Windows.Forms.MouseEventArgs e) {

    dragging = false;
}

private void cmdClose_Click(object sender, System.EventArgs e) {

    this.Close();
}
}
```

6.16 Create an Animated System Tray Icon

Problem

You need to create an animated system tray icon (perhaps to indicate the status of a long-running task).

Solution

Create and show a *NotifyIcon* control. Use a timer that fires periodically (every second or so) and updates the *NotifyIcon.Icon* property.

Discussion

The .NET Framework makes it easy to show a system tray icon with the *Notify-Icon* control. You simply need to add this control to a form, supply an icon by setting the *Icon* property, and, optionally, you can add a linked context menu through the *ContextMenu* property. The *NotifyIcon* control automatically displays its context menu when it's right-clicked, unlike most other controls.

You can animate a system tray icon by simply swapping the icon periodically. For example, the following program uses eight icons, each of which shows a moon graphic in a different stage of fullness. By moving from one image to another, the illusion of animation is created.

```
using System;
using System.Windows.Forms;
using System.Drawing;

public class AnimatedSystemTrayIcon : System.Windows.Forms.Form {

    // (Designer code omitted.)

    Icon[] images;
    int offset = 0;

    private void Form1_Load(object sender, System.EventArgs e) {

        // Load the basic set of eight icons.
        images = new Icon[8];
        images[0] = new Icon("moon01.ico");
        images[1] = new Icon("moon02.ico");
        images[2] = new Icon("moon03.ico");
        images[3] = new Icon("moon04.ico");
        images[4] = new Icon("moon05.ico");
        images[5] = new Icon("moon06.ico");
```

```
      images[6] = new Icon("moon07.ico");
      images[7] = new Icon("moon08.ico");
   }

   private void timer_Elapsed(object sender,
     System.Timers.ElapsedEventArgs e) {

      // Change the icon.
      // This event handler fires once every second (1000 ms).
      notifyIcon.Icon = images[offset];
      offset++;
      if (offset > 7) offset = 0;
   }
}
```

6.17 Validate an Input Control

Problem

You need to alert the user of invalid input in a control, such as a *TextBox*.

Solution

Use the *ErrorProvider* control to display an error icon next to the offending control. Check for errors before allowing the user to continue.

Discussion

There are a number of ways that you can perform validation in a Windows-based application. One approach is to respond to control validation events and prevent users from changing focus from one control to another if an error exists. A less invasive approach is to simply flag the offending control in some way so that the user can review all the errors at once. You can use this approach in .NET with the *ErrorProvider* control.

The *ErrorProvider* is a special provider control that displays error icons next to invalid controls. You show the error icon next to a control by using the *ErrorProvider.SetError* method and specifying the appropriate control and a string error message. The *ErrorProvider* will then show a warning icon automatically to the right of the control. When the user hovers the mouse above the warning icon, the detailed message appears. Figure 6-10 shows how the *Error-Provider* will indicate an input error for a *TextBox* control.

Figure 6-10   A validated form with the *ErrorProvider*.

You only need to add one *ErrorProvider* control to your form, and you can use it to display an error icon next to any control. To add the *ErrorProvider*, drag it into the component tray or create it manually in code. The following form code checks the content of the text box every time a key is pressed. The code validates this text box using a regular expression with checks to see if the value corresponds to a valid e-mail address. If validation fails, the *ErrorProvider* is used to display an error message. If the text is valid, any existing error message is cleared from the *ErrorProvider*. Finally, the *Click* event handler for the OK button steps through all the controls on the form and verifies that none of them have errors before allowing the application to continue.

```
using System;
using System.Windows.Forms;
using System.Text.RegularExpressions;

public class ErrorProviderValidation : System.Windows.Forms.Form {

    // (Designer code omitted.)

    private void txtEmail_TextChanged(object sender, System.EventArgs e) {

        Regex regex;
        regex = new Regex(@"\S+@\S+\.\S+");

        Control ctrl = (Control)sender;
        if (regex.IsMatch(ctrl.Text)) {
            errProvider.SetError(ctrl, "");
        }
        else {
            errProvider.SetError(ctrl, "This is not a valid e-mail address.");
        }
    }

    private void cmdOK_Click(object sender, System.EventArgs e) {

        string errorText = "";
        bool invalidInput = false;
```

```
foreach (Control ctrl in this.Controls) {

    if (errProvider.GetError(ctrl) != "")
    {
        errorText += "   * " + errProvider.GetError(ctrl) + "\n";
        invalidInput = true;
    }
}

if (invalidInput) {

    MessageBox.Show(
      "The form contains the following unresolved errors:\n\n" +
      errorText, "Invalid Input", MessageBoxButtons.OK,
      MessageBoxIcon.Warning);
}
else {
    this.Close();
}
}
}
```

6.18 Use a Drag-and-Drop Operation

Problem

You need to use the drag-and-drop feature to exchange information between two controls (possibly in separate windows or in separate applications).

Solution

Start a drag-and-drop operation using the *DoDragDrop* method of the *Control* class, and then respond to the *DragEnter* and *DragDrop* events.

Discussion

A *drag-and-drop* operation allows the user to transfer information from one place to another by clicking an item and "dragging" it to another location. A drag-and-drop operation consists of the following three basic steps:

1. The user clicks a control, holds the mouse button down, and begins dragging. If the control supports the drag-and-drop feature, it sets aside some information.

2. The user drags the mouse over another control. If this control accepts the dragged type of content, the mouse cursor changes to the special drag-and-drop icon (arrow and page). Otherwise, the mouse cursor becomes a circle with a line drawn through it.

3. When the user releases the mouse button, the data is sent to the control, which can then process it appropriately.

To support drag and drop, you must handle the *DragEnter*, *DragDrop*, and (typically) the *MouseDown* events. This example uses two text boxes. Here's the code needed to attach the event handlers we'll use:

```
this.TextBox2.MouseDown += new MouseEventHandler(this.TextBox_MouseDown);
this.TextBox2.DragDrop += new DragEventHandler(this.TextBox_DragDrop);
this.TextBox2.DragEnter += new DragEventHandler(this.TextBox_DragEnter);

this.TextBox1.MouseDown += new MouseEventHandler(this.TextBox_MouseDown);
this.TextBox1.DragDrop += new DragEventHandler(this.TextBox_DragDrop);
this.TextBox1.DragEnter += new DragEventHandler(this.TextBox_DragEnter);
```

To start a drag-and-drop operation, you call the source control's *DoDrag-Drop* method. At this point you submit the data and specify the type of operations that will be supported (copying, moving, and so on). The following recipe example initiates a drag-and-drop operation when the user clicks a text box:

```
private void TextBox_MouseDown(object sender,
  System.Windows.Forms.MouseEventArgs e) {

    TextBox txt = (TextBox)sender;
    txt.SelectAll();
    txt.DoDragDrop(txt.Text, DragDropEffects.Copy);
}
```

Controls that can receive dragged data must have the *AllowDrop* property set to *true*. These controls will receive a *DragEnter* event when the mouse drags the data over them. At this point, you can examine the data that's being dragged, decide whether the control can accept the drop, and set the *Drag-EventArgs.Effect* property accordingly, as shown here in this code:

```
private void TextBox_DragEnter(object sender,
  System.Windows.Forms.DragEventArgs e) {

    if (e.Data.GetDataPresent(DataFormats.Text)) {
        e.Effect = DragDropEffects.Copy;
    }
    else {
        e.Effect = DragDropEffects.None;
    }
}
```

The final step is to respond to the *DragDrop* event, which occurs when the user releases the mouse button.

```
private void TextBox_DragDrop(object sender,
  System.Windows.Forms.DragEventArgs e) {

    TextBox txt = (TextBox)sender;
    txt.Text = (string)e.Data.GetData(DataFormats.Text);
}
```

Using the code presented so far, you can create a simple drag-and-drop test application (shown in Figure 6-11) that allows text to be dragged from one text box to another. You can also drag text from another application and drop it into either text box.

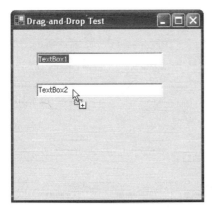

Figure 6-11   A drag-and-drop test application with two text boxes.

6.19 Use Context-Sensitive Help

Problem

You want to display a specific help file topic depending on the currently selected control.

Solution

Use the *System.Windows.Forms.HelpProvider* component, and set the *HelpKeyword* and *HelpNavigator* extender properties for each control.

Discussion

.NET provides support for context-sensitive help through the *HelpProvider* class. The *HelpProvider* class is a special *extender* control. You add it to the component tray of a form, and it extends all the controls on the form with a few additional properties, including *HelpNavigator* and *HelpKeyword*. For example, Figure 6-12 shows a form that has two controls and a *HelpProvider* named *helpProvider1*. The *ListBox* control, which is currently selected, has several help-specific properties that are provided through *HelpProvider*.

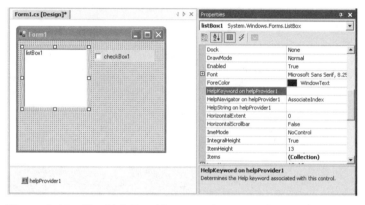

Figure 6-12   The HelpProvider extender properties.

To use context-sensitive help with *HelpProvider*, you simply need to follow these three steps:

1. Set the *HelpProvider.HelpNamespace* property with the name of the help file. (For example, an HTML Help file might be named myhelp.chm.)

2. For every control that requires context-sensitive help, set the *Help-Navigator* extender property to *HelpNavigator.Topic*.

3. For every control that requires context-sensitive help, set the *Help-Keyword* extender property with the name of the topic that should be linked to this control. (The topic names are help-file specific and can be configured in your help authoring tools.)

If the user presses the F1 key while a control has focus, the help file will be launched automatically and the linked topic will be displayed in the help window. If the user presses F1 while positioned on a control that doesn't have a linked help topic, the help settings for the containing control will be used (for example, a group box or a panel). If there are no containing controls or the containing control doesn't have any help settings, the form's help settings will be used. If the form's help settings are also lacking, *HelpProvider* will attempt to launch whatever help file is defined at the project level. You can also use the *HelpProvider* methods to set or modify context-sensitive help mapping at run time.

6.20 Apply Windows XP Control Styles

Problem

You want your controls to have the updated Windows XP appearance on Windows XP systems.

Solution

Set the *FlatStyle* property to *FlatStyle.System* for all controls that support it. In the .NET Framework version 1.0, you must create a manifest file. In .NET Framework version 1.1, you simply need to call the *Application.EnableVisualStyles* method.

Discussion

Windows XP styles are automatically applied to non-client areas of a form (such as the border and the minimize and maximize buttons). However, they won't be applied to controls such as buttons and group boxes unless you take additional steps.

First of all, you must configure all your form's button-style controls (such as buttons, check boxes, and radio buttons). These controls provide a *FlatStyle* property, which must be set to *System*.

The next step depends on the version of .NET that you are using. If you are using the .NET Framework version 1.1, you simply need to call the *Application.EnableVisualStyles* method before you show any forms. For example, you can start your application with the *Main* method shown here:

```
public static void Main() {

    // Enable visual styles.
    Application.EnableVisualStyles();

    // Show the main form for your application.
    Application.Run(new StartForm)
}
```

If you are using the .NET Framework version 1.0, you don't have the convenience of the *Application.EnableVisualStyles* method. However, you can still use visual styles—you simply need to create a manifest file for your application. This manifest file (an ordinary text file with XML content) tells Windows XP that your application requires the new version of the Comctl32.dll file. This file, which defines the new control styles, is included on all Windows XP computers. Windows XP will read and apply the settings from the manifest file automatically, provided you deploy it in the application directory and give it the correct name. The manifest file should have the same name as the executable used for your application, plus the extension .manifest (so TheApp.exe would have the manifest file TheApp.exe.manifest—even though this looks like two extensions).

Following is a sample manifest file. You can copy this file for your own applications—just rename it accordingly. It's also recommended that you modify the name value to use your application name, although this step isn't necessary.

```xml
<?xml version="1.0" encoding="UTF-8" standalone="yes"?>
<assembly xmlns="urn:schemas-microsoft-com:asm.v1" manifestVersion="1.0">
<assemblyIdentity
    version="1.0.0.0"
    processorArchitecture="X86"
    name="TheApp"
    type="win32" />

<dependency>
<dependentAssembly>
<assemblyIdentity
    type="win32"
    name="Microsoft.Windows.Common-Controls"
    version="6.0.0.0"
    processorArchitecture="X86"
    publicKeyToken="6595b64144ccf1df"
    language="*" />

</dependentAssembly>
</dependency>
</assembly>
```

The Windows XP styles won't appear in the Visual Studio .NET design-time environment. To test that this technique is working, run the application. Figure 6-13 shows the difference between the Windows XP and non–Windows XP control styles.

 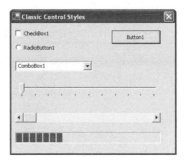

Figure 6-13   Control styles with and without Windows XP.

Note   If you supply a manifest file for an application running on a pre–Windows XP version of Windows, it will simply be ignored, and the classic control styles will be used. For this reason, you might want to test your application both with and without a manifest file.

7

ASP.NET and Web Forms

Microsoft ASP.NET is a platform for developing Web applications, and it's an ambitious part of the Microsoft .NET Framework. ASP.NET allows you to write XML Web services (as described in Chapter 12) and develop rich Web sites (as discussed in this chapter). ASP.NET Web pages use an event-based control model, which makes writing them remarkably similar to crafting ordinary stand-alone Microsoft Windows–based applications. However, this similarity can be deceiving. As most ASP.NET developers will attest, Web applications have their own idiosyncrasies. For example, you'll need to take extra steps to maintain state, transfer information between pages, handle client-side events, perform authentication, and ensure optimal performance when using a database. This chapter considers all these issues.

> **Note** This chapter won't introduce you to ASP.NET if you've never programmed with it before. Instead, it will help intermediate ASP.NET developers solve common problems. For a good introduction to ASP.NET basics, consult one of the many dedicated books and refer to the Microsoft ASP.NET Web site (*http://www.asp.net*).

The recipes you'll find in this chapter cover the following topics:

- How to redirect user requests (recipe 7.1).

- Different ways to maintain state between page requests (recipes 7.2 and 7.3).

- Ways to enhance your interface with client-side features using JavaScript (recipes 7.4, 7.5, and 7.6).

- Ways to allow users to upload files (recipe 7.7).

- Two approaches for authenticating the client: integrated Windows authentication with Internet Information Services (IIS) (recipe 7.8) and custom form-based authentication (recipe 7.9).

- How to validate user input without using ASP.NET validation controls (recipe 7.10).

- Approaches for dynamically generating Web controls (recipe 7.11), graphics (recipe 7.12), and user controls (recipe 7.13).

- Techniques for improving performance with output caching (recipe 7.14) and data caching (recipe 7.15).

- Troubleshooting suggestions to solve the infamous "unable to start debugging on the server" error message (recipe 7.16).

- How to change the Windows account context in which an ASP.NET application runs (recipe 7.17).

This chapter uses the basic Web classes in the *System.Web* namespace and the Web control classes in the *System.Web.UI.WebControls* namespace. When using classes in these core namespaces, the fully qualified class name usually won't be indicated.

> **Note**   Every recipe in this chapter is contained in a separate virtual directory. To create the required virtual directories, refer to the readme.txt included with the sample code that accompanies the book. Alternatively, you can add the Web page files (both the .asmx pages and the .cs code-behind files) to an existing Web project on your computer to use them.

7.1 Redirect the User to Another Page

Problem

You need to transfer execution from one ASP.NET Web page to another, or you want to redirect the user to a completely different site.

Solution

Use the *HttpResponse.Redirect* method to redirect the user to a new URL, or use the *HttpServerUtility.Transfer* method for a faster way to transfer the user to another ASP.NET Web form on the same server.

Discussion

The easiest way to redirect a user from one Web page to another is to use the *HttpResponse.Redirect* method and supply a new URL. You can access the current *HttpResponse* object through the *HttpContext* object or by using the *Reponse* property of a *Page* or a *Control* object. Here's an example of an event handler that redirects the user in response to a button click:

```
private void cmdRedirect_Click(object sender, System.EventArgs e) {

    Response.Redirect("newpage.aspx");
}
```

The *Redirect* method works with relative URLs to resources in the same virtual directory, and with fully qualified URLs. URLs can point to other ASP.NET pages, other types of documents (such as HTML pages or images), and other Web servers.

The *Redirect* method sends a redirect instruction to the browser. The browser then requests the new page. The result is that the browser has to make two roundtrips to the Web server, and the Web server has to handle an extra request. A more efficient option is available through the *HttpServerUtility.Transfer* method, which transfers execution to a different ASP.NET page on the same Web server. Here's an example:

```
private void cmdRedirect_Click(object sender, System.EventArgs e) {

    Server.Transfer("newpage.aspx");
}
```

The *Transfer* method doesn't require an extra trip to the client, but it won't work if you need to transfer execution to another server or another type of resource other than a Web form (including a classic ASP page).

7.2 Store Information Between Requests

Problem

You need to store some user-specific information between page postbacks.

Solution

Use view state, query string arguments, session state, or a cookie, depending on your needs.

Discussion

ASP.NET is a stateless programming model. Every time a postback is triggered, your code loads into memory, executes, and is released from memory. If you want to keep track of information after your code has finished processing, you must use some form of state management.

ASP.NET provides several ways to store information, or state, between requests. The type of state you use determines how long the information will live, where it will be stored, and how secure it will be. Table 7-1 lists the various state options provided by ASP.NET. This table doesn't include the *Cache* object, which provides temporary storage and is described in recipe 7.15. You can also use other, custom, approaches, such as hidden fields or a back-end database.

Table 7-1 **Types of State Management**

Type of State	Allowed Data	Storage Location	Lifetime	Security
View State	All serializable .NET data types.	A hidden field in the current Web page.	Lost when the user navigates to another page.	By default, it's insecure. However, you can use page directives to enforce encryption and hashing to prevent data tampering.
Query String	String data only.	The browser's URL string.	Lost when the user enters a new URL or closes the browser. However, it can be stored in a bookmark.	Clearly visible and easy for the user to modify.
Session State	All serializable .NET data types.	Server memory (can optionally be configured for an external process or database).	Times out after a predefined period (usually 20 minutes, but this period can be altered globally or programmatically).	Secure because data is never transmitted to the client.

Table 7-1   **Types of State Management**

Type of State	Allowed Data	Storage Location	Lifetime	Security
Custom Cookies	String data only.	The client's computer (in memory or a small text file, depending on its lifetime settings).	Set by the programmer. Can be used in multiple pages and can persist between visits.	Insecure, and it can be modified by the user.
Application State	All serializable .NET data types.	Server memory.	The lifetime of the application (typically, until the server is rebooted). Unlike other methods, application data is global to all users.	Secure because data is never transmitted to the client.

The syntax for different data-storing methods is similar. Data is stored in a collection object and indexed using a string name.

Figure 7-1 shows a Web page that performs a test of several different forms of session state. When the user clicks the Store Data button, a new *System.DateTime* object is created and stored in page view state, session state, and a custom cookie. When the user clicks the Get Data button, this information is retrieved and displayed. Finally, the Clear Data button removes information from all types of state.

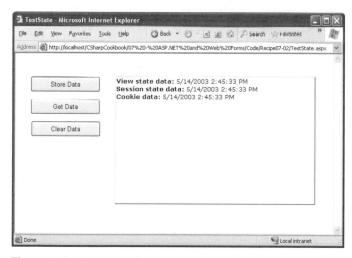

Figure 7-1   Testing different state management approaches.

Here's the page code:

```csharp
using System;
using System.Web;
using System.Web.UI.WebControls;
using System.Web.SessionState;

public class TestState : System.Web.UI.Page {

    protected System.Web.UI.WebControls.Button cmdClear;
    protected System.Web.UI.WebControls.Button cmdStore;
    protected System.Web.UI.WebControls.Button cmdGetData;
    protected System.Web.UI.WebControls.Label lblData;

    // (Designer code omitted.)

    private void cmdStore_Click(object sender, System.EventArgs e) {

        // Create a test object.
        DateTime now = DateTime.Now;

        // Store the object in view state.
        ViewState["TestData"] = now;

        // Store the object in session state.
        Session["TestData"] = now;

        // Store the object in a cookie.
        // Check if the cookie already exists (named Recipe07-02).
        if (Request.Cookies["Recipe07-02"] == null) {

            // Create the cookie.
            HttpCookie cookie = new HttpCookie("Recipe07-02");

            // The cookie can only store string data.
            // It can store multiple values, each with a different key.
            cookie["TestData"] = now.ToString();

            // (You can modify additional Cookie properties to change
            //  the expiry date.)

            // Attach the cookie to the response.
            // It will be submitted with all future requests to this site
            // until it expires.
            Response.Cookies.Add(cookie);
        }
    }
```

```csharp
private void cmdGetData_Click(object sender, System.EventArgs e) {

    lblData.Text = "";

    // Check for information in view state.
    if (ViewState["TestData"] != null) {

        DateTime data = (DateTime)ViewState["TestData"];
        lblData.Text += "<b>View state data:</b> " +
          data.ToString() + "<br>";

    }else {

        lblData.Text += "No view state data found.<br>";
    }

    // Check for information in session state.
    if (Session["TestData"] != null) {

        DateTime data = (DateTime)Session["TestData"];
        lblData.Text += "<b>Session state data:</b> " +
          data.ToString() + "<br>";

    }else {

        lblData.Text += "No session data found.<br>";
    }

    // Check for information in a custom cookie.
    HttpCookie cookie = Request.Cookies["Recipe07-02"];
    if (cookie != null) {

        string cookieData = (string)cookie["TestData"];
        lblData.Text += "<b>Cookie data:</b> " +
        cookieData + "<br>";

    }else {

        lblData.Text += "No cookie data found.<br>";
    }
}

private void cmdClear_Click(object sender, System.EventArgs e) {

    ViewState["TestData"] = null;
    Session["TestData"] = null;
    // (You can also use Session.Abandon to clear all session
    //  information.)
```

```
        // To clear a cookie you must replace it with
        // a cookie that has an expiration date that has already passed.
        HttpCookie cookie = new HttpCookie("Recipe07-02");
        cookie.Expires = DateTime.Now.AddDays(-1);
        Response.Cookies.Add(cookie);
    }
}
```

One type of state that this page doesn't demonstrate is the query string. The query string requires a page redirect and is ideal for transferring information from one page to another. To set information, you must redirect the user to a new page and add the query string arguments to the end of the URL. You can use the *HttpServerUtility.UrlEncode* and *UrlDecode* methods to ensure the string data is URL legal. This method properly escapes any special characters.

```
DateTime now = DateTime.Now;
string data = Server.UrlEncode(now.ToString());
Response.Redirect("newPage.aspx?TestData=" + data);
```

To retrieve this information, you can use the *HttpResponse.QueryString* collection:

```
// Check for information in the query string.
if (Request.QueryString["TestData"] != null) {

    string data = Request.QueryString["TestData"];
    data = Server.UrlDecode(data);
    lblData.Text += "<b>Found query string data:</b> " + data + "<br>";
}
```

7.3 Create Stateful Page Member Variables

Problem

You need to create member variables in your page class and ensure that their values are retained when the page is posted back.

Solution

Respond to the *Page.PreRender* event, and write all the member variables into view state. Respond to the *Page.Load* event, and get all the values of the member variables from view state. The rest of your code can now interact with these variables without worrying about state issues.

Discussion

ASP.NET provides several state mechanisms, as described in recipe 7.2. However, none of these can be used automatically—they all require manual code to serialize and retrieve information. You can add a layer of abstraction by performing this serialization and retrieval once. The rest of your code can then interact directly with the member variables.

In order for this approach to work, you need to read variable values at the start of every postback. The *Page.Load* event is an ideal choice for this code because it always fires before any other control events. You can use a *Page.Load* event handler to pre-initialize all your variables. In addition, you need to store all variables before the page is sent to the user, after all processing is complete. In this case, you can respond to the *Page.PreRender* event, which fires after all event handlers, just before the page is converted to HTML and sent to the client.

The following page shows an example of how you might persist one *Page* member variable (named *memberValue*).

```csharp
using System;
using System.Web;
using System.Web.UI.WebControls;

public class StatefulMembers : System.Web.UI.Page {

    // (Designer code omitted.)

    private int memberValue = 0;

    private void Page_Load(object sender, System.EventArgs e) {

        // Reload all member variables.
        if (ViewState["memberValue"] != null) {
            memberValue = (int)ViewState["memberValue"];
        }
    }

    private void StatefulMembers_PreRender(object sender,
      System.EventArgs e) {

        // Save all member variables.
        ViewState["memberValue"] = memberValue;

        // Display value.
        lblCurrent.Text = memberValue.ToString();
    }

    // (Other event handlers can now work with memberValue directly.)
}
```

7.4 Respond to Client-Side Events with JavaScript

Problem

You need to add client-side JavaScript code to a Web form.

Solution

Define the JavaScript function in a string, and use the *Page.RegisterClientScript-Block* method to add the JavaScript function to the rendered page. You can then add control attributes that call the functions.

Discussion

ASP.NET includes a rich programming model. Unfortunately, once a page is rendered to HTML, you can't execute any more .NET code without first triggering a postback to the server. This limitation greatly reduces the effectiveness of validation code and other niceties that can support polished interactive Web pages.

Of course, there's no reason that you can't mingle client-side JavaScript functionality with your .NET code. Although .NET doesn't include any object interface for creating JavaScript, you can manually inject it into the page. One way to do this is simply to set a control attribute. For example, you can create a text box that displays a message box when it loses focus by including the following JavaScript code:

```
TextBox1.Attributes.Add("onBlur", "alert('The text box has lost focus!');");
```

The *TextBox* tag will be rendered to HTML like this:

```
<input name="TextBox1" type="text" id="TextBox1"
 onBlur="alert('The text box has lost focus!');"  ... />
```

In this case, you're using the built-in JavaScript *alert* function and the JavaScript *onBlur* event, which fires when a control loses focus. Most HTML elements support a small number of events, and some of the most useful include the following:

- ■ ***onFocus***   Occurs when a control receives focus
- ■ ***onBlur***   Occurs when focus leaves a control
- ■ ***onClick***   Occurs when the user clicks a control

■ ***onChange***   Occurs when the user changes the value of certain controls

■ ***onMouseOver***   Occurs when the user moves the mouse pointer over a control

Another approach to adding JavaScript code is to define a JavaScript function in a .NET string variable and then to instruct ASP.NET to insert it into the rendered Web form where it can be used. If you follow this approach, any control can call the function in response to a JavaScript event.

The following example demonstrates this technique with a simple Web page that includes a table and an image (shown in Figure 7-2). As the user moves the mouse over the cells in the table, two custom JavaScript functions are used, one that highlights the current cell and one that removes the highlight from the previous cell. In addition, the highlighting function changes the image URL depending on which table column is currently selected. If the user hovers the mouse over the first column, an animated GIF of a happy face is shown. If the user hovers the mouse over the second or third column, an animated GIF of a book with a flashing question mark is shown instead.

```
using System;
using System.Web;
using System.Web.UI.WebControls;

public class JavaScriptTest : System.Web.UI.Page {

    protected System.Web.UI.WebControls.Table Table1;
    protected System.Web.UI.WebControls.Image Image1;

    // (Designer code omitted.)

    private void Page_Load(object sender, System.EventArgs e) {

        // Define the JavaScript functions.
        string highlightScript =
            "<script language=JavaScript> " +
            "function HighlightCell(cell) {" +
            "cell.bgColor = '#C0C0C0';" +
            "if (cell.cellIndex == 0)"+
            "{document.Form1.Image1.src='happy_animation.gif';}"+
            "else {document.Form1.Image1.src='question_animation.gif';}" +
            ";}" +
            "</script>";

        string unhighlightScript =
            "<script language=JavaScript> " +
```

```
                    "function UnHighlightCell(cell) {" +
                    "cell.bgColor = '#FFFFFF';" +
                    "}" +
                    "</script>";

        // Insert the function into the page (it will appear just after
        // the <form runat=server> tag.
        // Note that each script block is associated with a string name.
        // This allows multiple controls to register the same script block,
        // while ensuring it will only be rendered in the final page once.
        if (!this.IsClientScriptBlockRegistered("Highlight")) {
            Page.RegisterClientScriptBlock("Highlight", highlightScript);
        }

        if (!this.IsClientScriptBlockRegistered("UnHighlight")) {
            Page.RegisterClientScriptBlock("UnHighlight", unhighlightScript);
        }

        // Set the attributes of every cell in the table.
        foreach (TableRow row in Table1.Rows) {

            foreach (TableCell cell in row.Cells) {

            cell.Attributes.Add("onMouseOver", "HighlightCell(this);");
            cell.Attributes.Add("onMouseOut", "UnHighlightCell(this);");
            }
        }
    }
}
```

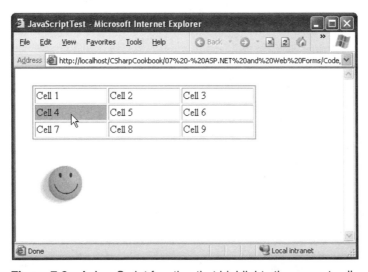

Figure 7-2   A JavaScript function that highlights the current cell.

> **Note** It's important to understand the security implications of Java-Script code. All JavaScript code is rendered directly in the HTML of the page. Therefore, you should assume that the user can examine it, and you should never include any secret algorithms or information in your code. Furthermore, you should use JavaScript validation code as a nicety, not as a way to prevent invalid actions, because users might be able to disable or circumvent JavaScript in their browsers.

You can find numerous sites on the Internet that provide JavaScript tutorials and sample code. In addition, a full JavaScript reference is provided by Netscape at *http://devedge.netscape.com/library/manuals*.

7.5 Show a Pop-Up Window with JavaScript

Problem

You need to show a secondary (pop-up) window, perhaps in response to a user action.

Solution

Register a JavaScript function (or add a control event attribute) that uses the *window.open* JavaScript function.

Discussion

Because all ASP.NET code executes on the server, there is no way to show a new window from your C# page code. You can add URL hyperlinks to a page that will automatically open in a new window by setting the *target* attribute of the *anchor* tag to *_blank*, but this still doesn't give you the ability to control the window size or style.

The solution is to use client-side JavaScript code to open the secondary window. The secondary window itself could be an HTML page, an ASP.NET page, an image file, or any other type of resource that can be opened in the client's browser. To open a secondary window, you use the *window.open* function and specify three parameters. The first parameter is the link for the new page, the second is the frame name of the window, and the third is a comma-separated string of attributes that configure the style and size of the pop-up window. These attributes can include the following:

- The *height* and *width* attributes, which are set to pixel values.

- The *toolbar*, *menuBar*, and *scrollbars* attributes, which can be set to yes or no depending on whether you want to display these elements.

- The *resizable* attribute, which can be set to yes or no depending on whether you want a fixed or resizable window border.

The following example shows how you can configure an ASP.NET *Button* so that it opens a second ASP.NET page in a pop-up window when clicked. Typically, you would add this code to the *Page.Load* event handler.

```
string popupScript = "window.open('PopUp.aspx', " +
  "'CustomPopUp', " +
  "'width=200, height=200, menubar=yes, resizable=no')";

cmdPopUp.Attributes.Add("onClick", popupScript);
```

Here's the code you would use to show a pop-up window automatically when the page is displayed. This code would also go in the *Page.Load* event handler.

```
string popupScript = "<script language='javascript'>" +
  "window.open('PopUp.aspx', " +
  "'CustomPopUp', " +
  "'width=200, height=200, menubar=yes, resizable=no')" +
  "</script>";

Page.RegisterStartupScript("PopupScript", popupScript);
```

7.6 Programmatically Set Control Focus

Problem

You need to specify the control that should be given focus when the page is rendered and sent to the user.

Solution

Create a JavaScript statement that sets the focus, and add it to the page using the *Page.RegisterStartupScript* method.

Discussion

The ASP.NET Web controls don't provide any way to programmatically set control focus. They do provide a *TabIndex* property that allows you to set the tab order, but this property applies only to Microsoft Internet Explorer and can't be used to programmatically set the focus to the control of your choice. To overcome this limitation, you need to add a little snippet of JavaScript code.

The following subroutine generalizes this task. It accepts a reference to any control object, retrieves the associated client ID (which is the ID that the JavaScript code must use to refer to the control), and then builds and registers the startup script for setting the focus.

```
private void SetFocus(Control ctrl) {

    // Define a JavaScript statement that will move focus to
    // the desired control.
    string setFocus = "<script language='javascript'>" +
        "document.getElementById('" + ctrl.ClientID +
        "').focus();</script>";

    // Add the JavaScript code to the page.
    this.RegisterStartupScript("SetFocus", setFocus);
}
```

If you add this subroutine to a Web form, you can call *SetFocus* as needed. Here's an example that sets the focus when the page first loads:

```
private void Page_Load(object sender,
  System.EventArgs e) {

    if (!this.IsPostBack) {
        // Move to a specific text box the first time the page loads.
        SetFocus(TextBox1);
    }
}
```

7.7 Allow the User to Upload a File

Problem

You need to create a page that allows the user to upload a file.

Solution

Use the ASP.NET *HtmlInputFile* control, set the encoding type of the form to *multipart/form-data*, and save the file using the *HtmlInputFile.Posted-File.SaveAs* method.

Discussion

Because ASP.NET executes on the server, there is no way to access any of the resources on the client computer, including files. However, you can use the *System.Web.UI.HtmlControls.HtmlInputFile* control to allow a user to upload a file. This control renders itself as the HTML *<input type="file">* element, which is displayed as a Browse button and a text box that contains a filename. The user clicks the Browse button and chooses a file. This step takes place automatically and doesn't require any custom code. The user must then click another button (which you must create) to start the actual upload process.

Before you can create a working file upload page, you need to take these steps:

■   You must set the encoding type of the form to *multipart/form-data*. To make this change, find the *<form>* tag in your .aspx file and modify it as shown here:

```
<form id="Form1" enctype="multipart/form-data" runat="server">
```

■   You need to add the *HtmlInputFile* control. In Microsoft Visual Studio .NET, you'll find this control under the HTML tab of the Toolbox, with the name File Field. Once you've added this control, you must right-click it and choose Run As Server Control, which creates the required *<input type="file" runat="server">* tag.

■   You must add another button that actually starts the file transfer using the specified file by calling the *HtmlInputFile.Posted-File.SaveAs* method.

Figure 7-3 shows a sample page that allows file uploading. It includes an *HtmlInputFile* control and uses the following code:

```
using System;
using System.Web;
using System.Web.UI.WebControls;
using System.IO;

public class UploadPage : System.Web.UI.Page {
```

```csharp
protected System.Web.UI.WebControls.Label lblInfo;
protected System.Web.UI.WebControls.Button cmdUpload;
protected System.Web.UI.HtmlControls.HtmlInputFile FileInput;

// (Designer code omitted.)

private void cmdUpload_Click(object sender, System.EventArgs e) {

    if (FileInput.PostedFile.FileName == "") {

        // No file was submitted.
        lblInfo.Text = "No file specified.";

    }else {

        try {

            if (FileInput.PostedFile.ContentLength > 1048576) {

                // Forbid files larger than one megabyte.
                lblInfo.Text = "File is too large.";

            }else {

                // The saved file will retain its original filename.
                string fileName =
                  Path.GetFileName(FileInput.PostedFile.FileName);

                // The ASP.NET process must have rights for the location
                // where it is attempting to save the file, or an
                // "access denied" exception will occur.
                FileInput.PostedFile.SaveAs(fileName);
                lblInfo.Text = "File " + fileName + " uploaded.";
            }
        }catch (Exception err) {

            lblInfo.Text = err.Message;
        }
    }
}
```

Figure 7-3 An upload test page.

The code can check various properties of the submitted file, including its size, before saving it, which allows you to prevent a denial of service attack that tricks an ASP.NET application into filling the hard disk with large files. However, this code doesn't prevent a user from submitting the file in the first place, which can still slow down the server and be used to launch a different type of denial of service attack—one that works by tying up all free ASP.NET worker threads. To prevent this type of attack, use the *<httpruntime>* tag in the Web.config file to specify a maximum file size. Specify the maximum, in kilobytes, using the *maxRequestLength* attribute.

```xml
<?xml version="1.0" encoding="utf-8" ?>
<configuration>
  <system.web>

    <httpRuntime maxRequestLength="4096" />
    <!-- Other settings omitted. -->

  </system.web>
</configuration>
```

If you don't specify a maximum length, the default value of 4096 (4 megabytes) will apply. If the user attempts to submit a file that's too large, an exception will be thrown immediately when the page is posted back.

> **Note** There is another way to send files from a client to a Web server: use ASP.NET XML Web services. You simply need to develop a Windows-based application that allows the user to choose a file and then contacts an XML Web service to transmit the information.

7.8 Use IIS Authentication

Problem

You need to prevent users from accessing certain pages unless they have been authenticated against a Windows user account on the server.

Solution

Use IIS Windows authentication. Select the authentication method you'd like to use, and deny anonymous access to the virtual directory using IIS Manager. You can retrieve information about the authenticated user from the page *Page.User* property of the *HttpContext* class.

Discussion

IIS and ASP.NET use a layered security model. When a user requests an ASP.NET Web page over HTTP, the following steps take place:

1. IIS attempts to authenticate the user. If anonymous access is enabled, IIS automatically logs the user on as the anonymous user (typically the IUSR_[ServerName] account). Otherwise, it requests authentication credentials that it will use to log the user on with another Windows account.

2. Provided IIS can authenticate the user successfully, it passes the request to ASP.NET with information about the authenticated user. ASP.NET can then use its own security services based on the settings in the Web.config file (for example, denying specific users or groups access to certain pages or directories). In addition, your code can restrict actions programmatically by checking the user information.

3. If the ASP.NET code accesses any system resources (for example, tries to open a file or connect to a database), the Windows operating system performs its own security checks. Usually, the ASP.NET application code won't actually run under the account of the authenticated user. Thus, these security checks are made against the ASP.NET process account (which is configured using the machine.config file).

The first step to use IIS authentication is to disable anonymous access for the virtual directory. To do so, start IIS Manager (select Settings | Control Panel | Administrative Tools | Internet Information Services from the Start Menu). Then right-click a virtual directory or a subdirectory inside a virtual directory, and choose Properties. Select the Directory Security tab, as shown in Figure 7-4.

Figure 7-4   Directory security settings.

Next, click the Edit button to modify the directory security settings. The window shown in Figure 7-5 will appear. In the bottom half of the window, you can enable one of the Windows authentication methods. However, none of these methods will be used unless you explicitly clear the Anonymous Access check box.

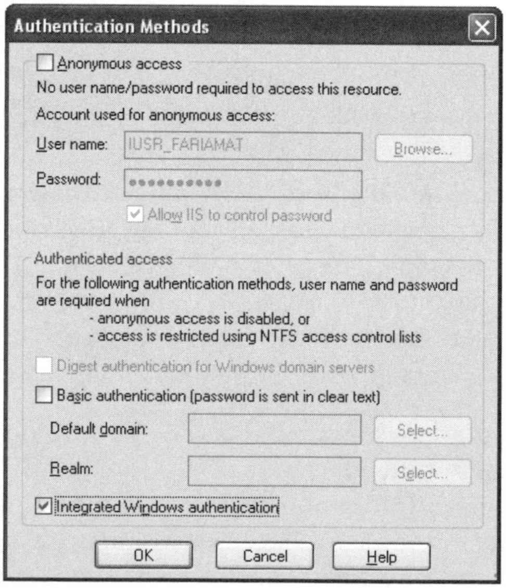

Figure 7-5   Directory authentication.

You can enable more than one authentication method, in which case the client will use the strongest supported method. If anonymous access is enabled, it's always used. The different authentication methods are described in Table 7-2.

Table 7-2 Types of Authentication

Mode	Description
Anonymous	The client is not required to submit any information. Users are logged in using the preset anonymous account (typically IUSR_[ServerName]).
Basic	Basic authentication is a part of the HTTP 1.0 standard, and it is supported by almost all browsers and Web servers. When using basic authentication, the browser presents the user with a login box with a user name and password field. This information is then transmitted to IIS, where it is matched with a local Windows user account. Basic authentication should always be combined with SSL because it doesn't encrypt the logon information before transmitting it.
Digest	Digest authentication sends a digest (also known as a cryptographic hash) over the network. Thus, it's much more secure than Basic authentication because intercepted logon information can't be reused. The primary disadvantage is that Digest authentication is supported only by Internet Explorer 5.0 and later versions. Also, your Web server needs to use Active Directory or have access to an Active Directory server.
Integrated	Integrated Windows authentication is the best choice for most intranet scenarios. When using integrated authentication, Internet Explorer sends the logon token for the current user automatically, provided it is on a trusted domain. Integrated authentication is supported only on Internet Explorer 2.0 and later and can't work over proxy servers.

Once you've enabled the appropriate virtual directory security settings, you should make sure that the Web.config file is set to use Windows authentication. In a Visual Studio .NET project, this is the default setting.

```
<configuration>
  <system.web>
    <!-- Other settings omitted. -->
    <authentication mode="Windows" />
  </system.web>
</configuration>
```

At this point, your virtual directory will require user authentication and your Web application will be able to retrieve the user information. In addition, you can add authorization rules that prevent certain users or groups from accessing Web pages or subdirectories. You do this by adding *<allow>* and *<deny>* tags to the *<authorization>* section of the Web.config file. For example, you can create a subdirectory with the following Web.config file contents:

```
<configuration>
  <system.web>

    <authorization>
      <deny roles="Guest,Associate" />
      <allow users="matthew" />
      <deny users="*" />
    </authorization>

  </system.web>
</configuration>
```

ASP.NET examines rules in the order they appear and stops when it finds a match. In this example, users in the Guest or Associate groups will automatically be denied. The user matthew will be permitted (unless he's a member of one of the previously forbidden groups). All other users will be denied. In this case, these are local groups and user accounts. If you want to refer to a domain account, use the pathlike syntax [DomainName]\[UserName] instead.

Notice that in this example, the Web.config file doesn't contain an *<authentication>* section. This omission is because the authentication is configured in the Web.config file in the Web application directory. Subdirectories can set their own authorization rules, but they can't change the mode of authentication.

Another option is to deny access to specific pages using the *<location>* attribute:

```
<configuration>
  <system.web>
    <!-- Other settings omitted. -->
  </system.web>

  <location path="SecurePage.aspx">
    <system.web>
      <authorization>
        <deny roles="Guest" />
      </authorization>
    </system.web>
  </location>

</configuration>
```

Finally, you can write your own authorization logic by examining the user identity in your Web page code using the *Page.User* property, which provides a *WindowsPrincipal* object. You can retrieve the user name from the *Windows-Principal.Identity.Name* property, and you can test group membership using the *WindowsPrincipal.IsInRole* method. The following Web page code demonstrates these techniques:

```
using System;
using System.Web;
using System.Web.UI.WebControls;
using System.Security.Principal;

public class WindowsSecurityTest : System.Web.UI.Page {

  protected System.Web.UI.WebControls.Label lblMessage;

  // (Designer code omitted.)

  private void Page_Load(object sender, System.EventArgs e) {

    // Get the IIS-authenticated identity.
    WindowsIdentity identity = (WindowsIdentity)User.Identity;

    // Test if it is an Administrator.
    bool isAdmin = User.IsInRole(@"BUILTIN\Administrators");

    // Display some information about the identity.
    lblMessage.Text = "You have reached the secured page, " +
      User.Identity.Name + "." +
      "<br><br>Authentication Type: " +
      identity.AuthenticationType.ToString() +
      "<br>Anonymous: " + identity.IsAnonymous.ToString() +
      "<br>Authenticated: " + identity.IsAuthenticated.ToString() +
      "<br>Guest: " + identity.IsGuest.ToString() +
      "<br>System: " + identity.IsSystem.ToString() +
      "<br>Administrator: " + isAdmin.ToString();
  }
}
```

7.9 Use Forms Authentication

Problem

You need to prevent users from accessing certain pages unless they have first authenticated themselves with a custom logon page.

Solution

Implement forms authentication by configuring the *<authentication>* tag in the application's Web.config file. You must create the logon page, but ASP.NET keeps track of a user's authentication status.

Discussion

Forms authentication is a flexible security model that allows you to prevent unauthenticated users from accessing certain pages. You write the code that performs the authentication, and ASP.NET issues a cookie to authenticated users. Users without the cookie are redirected to a login page when they try to access a secured page.

To implement forms authentication, you must take the following steps:

- Configure forms authentication using the *<authentication>* tag in the application's Web.config file.

- Restrict anonymous users from a specific page or directory using Web.config settings.

- Create the logon page, and add your authentication logic, which leverages the *FormsAuthentication* class from the *System.Web.Security* namespace.

The first step is to configure the Web.config in the root application directory to enable forms authentication, as shown in the following code. You also need to specify your custom login page (where unauthenticated users will be redirected) and a time-out after which the cookie will be removed. The authentication cookie is automatically renewed with each Web request.

```
<configuration>
  <system.web>

    <!-- Other settings omitted. -->

    <authentication mode="Forms">
      <forms loginUrl="login.aspx" timeout="30" />
    </authentication>

  </system.web>
</configuration>
```

Next you need to add an authorization rule denying anonymous users. The easiest way to secure pages is to create a subdirectory with its own Web.config file. The Web.config file should refuse access to anonymous users, as shown here:

```
<configuration>
  <system.web>

    <authorization>
        <deny users="?" />
    </authorization>

    <!-- Other settings omitted. -->
  </system.web>
</configuration>
```

Now ASP.NET will automatically forward unauthenticated requests for pages in this subdirectory to the custom logon page.

Another option is to specifically deny access to specific pages in the current directory by using the *<location>* tag:

```
<configuration>
  <system.web>
    <!-- Other settings omitted. -->
  </system.web>

  <location path="SecurePage.aspx">
    <system.web>
      <authorization>
        <deny users="?" />
      </authorization>
    </system.web>
  </location>

</configuration>
```

You can also deny specific users by entering a comma-separated list of user names instead of the wildcard (?) character, which simply means "all anonymous users."

You need to create the logon page. Your logon page can authenticate the user using a hard-coded password (suitable for simple tests), a server-side database, or any other type of custom authentication logic. Once the user has been successfully authenticated, call the *static FormsAuthentication.RedirectFromLoginPage* method with the username. This method simultaneously sets the forms authentication cookie and redirects the user to the originally requested page.

Here's a rudimentary logon page that simply checks for a specific password when the user clicks a logon button:

```
using System;
using System.Web;
using System.Web.UI.WebControls;
```

```
using System.Web.Security;

public class LoginPage : System.Web.UI.Page {

    protected System.Web.UI.WebControls.Label lblStatus;
    protected System.Web.UI.WebControls.Button cmdLogin;
    protected System.Web.UI.WebControls.TextBox txtPassword;
    protected System.Web.UI.WebControls.TextBox txtName;

    // (Designer code omitted.)

    private void cmdLogin_Click(object sender, System.EventArgs e){
        if (txtPassword.Text.ToLower() == "secret") {
            FormsAuthentication.RedirectFromLoginPage(txtName.Text, false);

        }else {
            lblStatus.Text = "Try again.";
        }
    }
}
```

To test this page with the sample code that accompanies the book, request SecurePage.aspx, which is placed in a secured directory. You'll be redirected to login.aspx, and provided you submit the correct password, you'll be returned to SecurePage.aspx.

7.10 Perform Selective Input Validation

Problem

You need to use ASP.NET validation controls. However, you want to perform validation programmatically so that you can validate only specific controls or sets of controls, or so that you can customize validation error messages based on the invalid input.

Solution

Disable the *EnableClientScript* property of every validation control on your page so that the page can be posted back. Then use the *Page.Validate* method to validate the page or the *BaseValidator.Validate* method to validate individual controls.

Discussion

The ASP.NET validation controls are an ideal solution for quickly validating forms. They work well as long as you want to validate an entire page at a time. If you want to validate only part of a form, or you want to make a programmatic decision about whether to validate a control (perhaps based on the validation success or value of another control), you'll need to use selective validation.

The first step in selective validation is to disable the *EnableClientScript* property of every validation control on your page. Otherwise, validation will be performed at the client through JavaScript, the page won't be posted back if it contains invalid values, and your event handling code won't be executed. Once you've made this change, you can validate the page one control at a time using the *BaseValidator.Validate* method, or you can validate the entire page using the *Page.Validate* method.

The following example uses server-side validation with two validators: a *RangeValidator* and a *RegularExpressionValidator* (which validates an e-mail address). If validation fails, the code steps through the collection of validators on the form using the *Page.Validators* property. Every time the code finds a failed validator, it finds the corresponding control using the *Page.FindControl* method and then displays the offending value (a trick that's not possible with automatic validation).

```
using System;
using System.Web;
using System.Web.UI.WebControls;

public class SelectiveValidation : System.Web.UI.Page {

    protected System.Web.UI.WebControls.TextBox txtNumber;
    protected System.Web.UI.WebControls.TextBox txtEmail;
    protected System.Web.UI.WebControls.Label lblCustomSummary;
    protected System.Web.UI.WebControls.RegularExpressionValidator
      validatorEmail;
    protected System.Web.UI.WebControls.RangeValidator validatorNumber;
    protected System.Web.UI.WebControls.Button cmdValidate;

    // (Designer code omitted.)

    private void cmdValidate_Click(object sender, System.EventArgs e) {

        // Validate the page.
        this.Validate();

        if (!Page.IsValid) {
```

```
            lblCustomSummary.Text = "";
            foreach (BaseValidator validator in this.Validators) {

                if (!validator.IsValid) {

                    TextBox invalidControl = (TextBox)
                        this.FindControl(validator.ControlToValidate);

                    lblCustomSummary.Text +=
                        "The page contains the following error: <b>" +
                        validator.ErrorMessage + "</b>.<br>" +
                        "The invalid input is: <b>" +
                        invalidControl.Text + "</b>." + "<br><br>";
                }
            }

        }else {
            lblCustomSummary.Text = "Validation succeeded.";
        }
    }
}
```

The form is shown, with invalid input, in Figure 7-6.

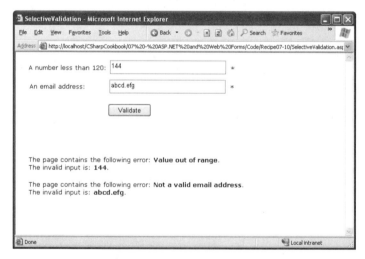

Figure 7-6 Using custom validation.

7.11 Add Controls to a Web Form Dynamically

Problem

You need to add a Web control to a Web page at run time and handle its events.

Solution

Create a control object, add it to the *Controls* collection of a container control, and use the *AddHandler* statement to connect any event handlers. You must create the control after every postback.

Discussion

You can use a technique to add Web controls to a Web page that's similar to the way you would add Windows controls to a form, but there are some differences, including the following:

- Dynamically added controls will exist only until the next postback. If you need them, you must re create them when the page is returned. This requirement doesn't prevent you from writing code that handles their events, however.

- Dynamically added controls aren't as easy to position. Typically, you'll use literal controls containing HTML code (such as the line break *
*) to separate more than one dynamically created control.

- Dynamically created controls should be placed in a container control (such as a *Panel* or a *LiteralControl*) rather than directly on the page itself, which makes it easier to position them.

- If you want to interact with the control later, you should give it a unique ID. You can use this ID to retrieve the control from the *Controls* collection of its container.

The best place to generate new controls is in the *Page.Load* event handler, which ensures that the control will be created each time the page is served. In addition, if you're adding an input control that uses view state, the view state information will be restored to the control after the *Page.Load* event fires. That means a dynamically generated text box will retain its text over multiple postbacks, just like a text box that's defined in the .aspx file. Similarly, because the *Page.Load* event always fires before any other events take place, you can re-create a control that raises server-side events and its event-handling code will be triggered immediately after the *Page.Load* event. For example, this technique allows you to dynamically generate a button that can respond to user clicks.

The following example demonstrates all these concepts. It generates three dynamic server controls (two buttons and a text box) and positions them using literal controls that act as separators. The buttons are connected to distinct event handlers. The text box is given a unique identifier so that its text can be retrieved later, in response to the button clicks. Figure 7-7 shows the page in action.

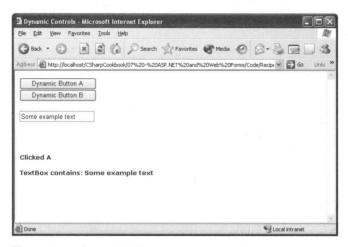

Figure 7-7   Dynamically generated controls.

The full code is shown here:

```
using System;
using System.Web;
using System.Web.UI;
using System.Web.UI.WebControls;
using System.Web.Security;

public class DynamicControls : System.Web.UI.Page {

    protected System.Web.UI.WebControls.Label lblMessage;
    protected System.Web.UI.WebControls.Panel pnl;

    // (Designer code omitted.)

    private void Page_Load(object sender, System.EventArgs e) {

        // Create a dynamic button.
        Button dynamicButton = new Button();
        dynamicButton.Text = "Dynamic Button A";

        // Connect an event handler.
        dynamicButton.Click += new EventHandler(cmdDynamicA_Click);
```

```
        // Add the button to a Panel.
        pnl.Controls.Add(dynamicButton);

        // Add a line break separator.
        pnl.Controls.Add(new LiteralControl("<br>"));

        // Create a second dynamic button.
        dynamicButton = new Button();
        dynamicButton.Text = "Dynamic Button B";
        dynamicButton.Click += new EventHandler(cmdDynamicB_Click);
        pnl.Controls.Add(dynamicButton);

        // Add a line break separator.
        pnl.Controls.Add(new LiteralControl("<br><br>"));

        // Create a dynamic textbox.
        TextBox dynamicText = new TextBox();
        pnl.Controls.Add(dynamicText);

        // Assign a unique ID so the textbox can be retrieved
        // from the control collection later.
        dynamicText.ID = "DynamicText";
    }

private void cmdDynamicA_Click(object sender, System.EventArgs e) {

        lblMessage.Text = "Clicked A";
        GetText();
    }

private void cmdDynamicB_Click(object sender, System.EventArgs e) {

        lblMessage.Text = "Clicked B";
        GetText();
    }

private void GetText(){
        lblMessage.Text += "<br><br>";

        foreach (Control ctrl in pnl.Controls){
            if (ctrl.ID == "DynamicText"){
                lblMessage.Text += "TextBox contains: " +
                    ((TextBox)ctrl).Text;
            }
        }
    }
}
```

If you need to dynamically create complex layouts that include some pre-built control "groups," you might prefer to use user controls and load them dynamically into a page. This technique is demonstrated in recipe 7.13.

7.12 Dynamically Render an Image

Problem

You need to render dynamic graphics (perhaps to build the output for a chart or graph control).

Solution

Build the graphic using GDI+ and an in-memory *System.Drawing.Bitmap* object. Then you can write it to the page output stream, or you can save it to the server's hard drive and display it with an *Image* Web control.

Discussion

You can draw dynamic graphics using the same GDI+ code in a Web application that you'd use in a Windows-based application. The only difference is how you render the final graphic. There are basically two approaches that you can use.

■   You can stream the binary contents of the image directly to the *Out-putStream* property of the *HttpResponse* object. This is a good approach if you need to generate a wide range of images and don't want to clutter the server hard drive with image files that won't be used again. It's also the best choice if you need to create dynamic images that are tailored to match user input.

■   You can save the image to the Web server's file system and use an HTML *<img>* tag to display the created image. This is a good choice if you need to create a graphic that will be reused because it will avoid the overhead of continuously re-creating the graphic.

This recipe explores both approaches. First we'll consider how to dynamically create an image without saving it to a file. In this example, the goal is to create a simple banner (as shown in Figure 7-8).

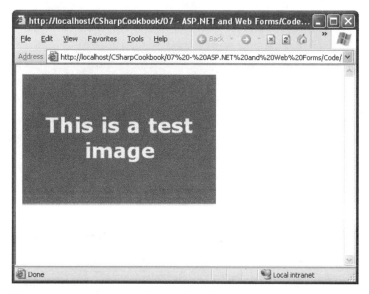

Figure 7-8   A dynamically generated banner.

You'll notice that the only user-supplied value in this example is the banner text itself, which is supplied through the query string. The font, colors, and dimensions are hard-coded (although they could easily be set based on other query string parameters or Web.config defaults).

Here's the full page code:

```
using System;
using System.Web;
using System.Web.UI.WebControls;
using System.Drawing;
using System.Drawing.Drawing2D;

public class DynamicGraphic : System.Web.UI.Page {

    // (Designer code omitted.)

    private void Page_Load(object sender, System.EventArgs e) {

        // Get the text from the query string.
        // If no text is supplied, choose a default.
        string text = "";
        if (Request.QueryString["image"] == null) {

            Response.Redirect(Request.Url + "?image=" +
            Server.UrlEncode("This is a test image"));
        }
```

```
            else {
                text = Server.UrlDecode(Request.QueryString["image"]);
            }

    // Create an in-memory bitmap where you will draw the image.
            // The Bitmap is 300 pixels wide and 200 pixels high.
            int width = 300, height = 200;
            Bitmap bitmap = new Bitmap(width, height);

            // Get the graphics context for the bitmap.
            Graphics graphics = Graphics.FromImage(bitmap);

            // Set the background color and rendering quality.
            // This color will become the border
            graphics.Clear(Color.OrangeRed);
            graphics.SmoothingMode = SmoothingMode.AntiAlias;

            // Paint a rectangle.
            graphics.FillRectangle(new SolidBrush(Color.Olive), 5, 5,
              width - 10, height - 10);

            // Choose a font and alignment for the text.
            Font fontBanner = new Font("Verdana", 24, FontStyle.Bold);
            StringFormat stringFormat = new StringFormat();
            stringFormat.Alignment = StringAlignment.Center;
            stringFormat.LineAlignment = StringAlignment.Center;

            // Paint the text.
            graphics.DrawString(text, fontBanner, new
            SolidBrush(Color.LightYellow), new Rectangle(0, 0, width, height),
              stringFormat);

            // Render the image to the HTML output stream.
            bitmap.Save(Response.OutputStream,
              System.Drawing.Imaging.ImageFormat.Gif);

            graphics.Dispose();
            bitmap.Dispose();
        }
    }
}
```

When you save an image to the response stream, you replace any other output. Therefore, you can't use this technique with a page that also includes Web controls or static HTML content. Thus, if you want to use a page that combines dynamically generated images and Web controls, you need to wrap the dynamically generated image in a control or write the image to the hard drive before displaying it.

If you want to save the file to the hard drive, you move the image generation code into a separate method, which we'll call *GenerateBanner*. Then, in the *Page.Load* event handler, you begin by checking to see whether the file already exists by using the *static File.Exists* method. If the file doesn't exist, you generate it in memory by calling *GenerateBanner* and save it using the *Bitmap.Save* method. Otherwise, you simply load the image directly.

The following code shows the basic approach you must take:

```
using System;
using System.IO;
using System.Web;
using System.Web.UI.WebControls;
using System.Drawing;
using System.Drawing.Drawing2D;

public class DynamicGraphic : System.Web.UI.Page {

    protected System.Web.UI.WebControls.Image imageControl;

    // (Designer code omitted.)

    private Bitmap GenerateBanner() {

        // Create the image using the same code as in the previous example.
        // (Code omitted.)
    }

    private void Page_Load(object sender, System.EventArgs e) {

        // Set the filename based on the image text.
        // We assume this only includes characters that are
        // legal for a filename.
        string fileName = Request.QueryString["image"] + ".gif";

        Bitmap bitmap = null;

        // Check if an image with this text already exists.
        if (File.Exists(fileName)) {

            // Load the existing image.
            try {
                bitmap = new Bitmap(fileName);
            }catch {
                bitmap = GenerateBanner();
            }
        }
    }
}
```

```
        else {
            bitmap = GenerateBanner();

            // Save the image.
            bitmap.Save(fileName, System.Drawing.Imaging.ImageFormat.Gif);
        }

        // Display the image by setting an Image property.
        imageControl.ImageUrl = fileName;
    }
}
```

7.13 Load User Controls Programmatically

Problem

You need to dynamically build the user interface of a page out of one or more user controls.

Solution

Use the *Page.LoadControl* method to instantiate the control object from its .ascx file, and then add it to the *Controls* collection of a container control.

Discussion

User controls are self-contained groups of controls. Like Web forms, user controls consist of a layout portion that defines the contained controls (.ascx file) and a code-behind portion with the event-handling logic (.cs file). User controls allow you to reuse common interface elements on multiple pages and build complex interfaces out of smaller building blocks. One useful characteristic of user controls is that they can be loaded programmatically, which allows you to create a highly configurable interface that you can tailor dynamically according to the user. You simply load the control, configure its properties, and then add it to another container control.

For example, consider the page that generated dynamic graphics in recipe 7.12. The same basic solution could be implemented in a more object-oriented way by creating a custom user control that encapsulates the dynamic graphic. The user control could allow the page to set the text, font, colors, and so on through various properties. Here's an example of what the custom control would look like:

```csharp
using System;
using System.Web;
using System.Web.UI.WebControls;
using System.Drawing;
using System.Drawing.Drawing2D;

public class DynamicGraphicControl : System.Web.UI.UserControl {

    // (Designer code omitted.)

    private string imageText = "";
    public string ImageText {
        get {
            return imageText;
        }
        set {
            imageText = value;
        }
    }

    private Font textFont;
    public Font TextFont {
        get {
            return textFont;
        }
        set {
            textFont = value;
        }
    }

    private Size imageSize;
    public Size ImageSize {
        get {
            return imageSize;
        }
        set {
            imageSize = value;
        }
    }

    private Color foreColor;
    public Color ForeColor {
        get {
            return foreColor;
        }
        set {
            foreColor = value;
        }
```

```csharp
        }

        private Color backColor;
        public Color BackColor {
            get {
                return backColor;
            }
            set {
                backColor = value;
            }
        }

        private Color borderColor;
        public Color BorderColor {
            get {
                return borderColor;
            }
            set {
                borderColor = value;
            }
        }

        private void Page_Load(object sender, System.EventArgs e) {

            if (ImageText == "")
                return;

            // Create an in-memory bitmap where you will draw the image.
            Bitmap bitmap = new Bitmap(ImageSize.Width, ImageSize.Height);

            // Get the graphics context for the bitmap.
            Graphics graphics = Graphics.FromImage(bitmap);

            // Set the background color and rendering quality.
            // This color will become the border
            graphics.Clear(BorderColor);
            graphics.SmoothingMode = SmoothingMode.AntiAlias;

            // Paint a rectangle.
            graphics.FillRectangle(new SolidBrush(BackColor), 5, 5,
              ImageSize.Width - 10, ImageSize.Height - 10);

            // Set the alignment for the text.
            StringFormat stringFormat = new StringFormat();
            stringFormat.Alignment = StringAlignment.Center;
            stringFormat.LineAlignment = StringAlignment.Center;

            // Paint the text.
```

```
    graphics.DrawString(ImageText, TextFont, new SolidBrush(ForeColor),
      new Rectangle(0, 0, ImageSize.Width, ImageSize.Height),
      stringFormat);

    // Render the image to the HTML output stream.
    bitmap.Save(Response.OutputStream,
    System.Drawing.Imaging.ImageFormat.Gif);

    graphics.Dispose();
    bitmap.Dispose();
  }
}
```

The Web form loads this user control in the *Page.Load* event handler. The user control is placed in a *Panel* control container. The *LoadControl* method returns a generic *Control* object, which the code casts to the appropriate user control class.

```
using System;
using System.Web;
using System.Web.UI.WebControls;
using System.Drawing;

public class DynamicControlTest : System.Web.UI.Page {

    protected System.Web.UI.WebControls.Panel pnl;

    // (Designer code omitted.)

    private void Page_Load(object sender, System.EventArgs e) {

        // Load the control.
        DynamicGraphicControl ctrl;
        ctrl = (DynamicGraphicControl)
          Page.LoadControl("DynamicGraphicControl.ascx");

        // Configure the control properties.
        ctrl.ImageText = "This is a new banner test";
        ctrl.ImageSize = new Size(300, 200);
        ctrl.TextFont = new Font("Verdana", 24, FontStyle.Bold);
        ctrl.BackColor = Color.Olive;
        ctrl.ForeColor = Color.LightYellow;
        ctrl.BorderColor = Color.OrangeRed;

        // Add the control to the page.
        pnl.Controls.Add(ctrl);
    }
}
```

In Visual Studio .NET, the user control class is always available because classes are compiled into a single .dll assembly. If the user control is not a part of the project, however, you won't have the required user control class and you won't be able to access any of the user control's properties or methods. To remedy this problem, you can define a base class or an interface that defines the basic functionality you need to be able to access in any of your custom user controls.

Note   For an excellent full-scale demonstration of this technique, download the IBuySpy portal case study from *http://www.asp.net /IBS_Portal*. It demonstrates a highly customizable layout that's built entirely out of dynamically loaded user controls.

7.14 Use Page and Fragment Caching

Problem

You need to increase performance by caching completely rendered pages.

Solution

Add the *OutputCache* directive to a page or a user control, and specify how long (in seconds) the page should be kept in the cache.

Discussion

A modest use of caching can reduce bottlenecks such as database access and dramatically increase a Web site's overall performance. Caching has the greatest effect in a highly trafficked site. For example, consider what happens if you cache a page that displays the results of a database query. If you cache this page for one minute, and 10 requests are received for the page over that one-minute period, you'll reduce the database overhead by a factor of 10.

Implementing caching is easy. You simply add an *OutputCache* directive to the Web page. This directive must be added to the .aspx markup file, not to the .cs code-behind file. Here's an example that caches a page for 20 seconds:

```
<%@ OutputCache Duration="20" VaryByParam="None" %>
```

And here's an example that caches a page for 20 seconds but maintains separate cached copies depending on the value of query string arguments:

```
<%@ OutputCache Duration="20" VaryByParam="*" %>
```

You can test caching by using a page that displays the server date and time. You'll notice that subsequent requests for such a page won't cause it to be regenerated. Thus, the old time will be shown until the page expires.

Output caching is not effective in the following situations:

- Your page needs to customize itself according to user-specific settings, such as user authentication information (the built-in *User* object) or state (the *Session* object). In this case, it doesn't make sense to reuse the same page for all users.

- Your page includes controls that post back and raise server-side events.

- Your page needs to perform another action (such as write to a log, enter some information in a database, or change an application variable). A cached page reuses the fully rendered HTML; all page code is bypassed.

- Your page includes data that must be generated with the most current data. This might be the case for a stock lookup, but it probably won't be the case for a product catalog.

In these cases, you might still be able to use a more flexible form of caching. You can use data caching, as described in recipe 7.15, to store a specific object. Or you can use fragment caching to cache a portion of a page. To use fragment caching, create a user control that includes all the content that can be cached and add the *OutputCache* directive to the user control. You can then use the user control in a Web page. The Web page code will still run, but the embedded user control can be cached.

7.15 Reuse Data with the ASP.NET Cache

Problem

You need to use caching, but you can't cache an entire page because it includes some code that must run or some content that must be generated dynamically.

Solution

Use the *Cache.Insert* method to store any object with a sliding or absolute expiration policy.

Discussion

The *Cache* object allows you to store almost any .NET object using a string key with the expiration policy you define. ASP.NET maintains the cache automatically, removing objects when they expire or when memory becomes scarce.

There are two types of expiration policies that you can use when storing data in the cache. Absolute expiration invalidates cached items after a fixed period of time, much like output caching. Absolute expiration is the best approach if you need to store information that needs to be periodically refreshed (such as a product catalog).

```
// Store ObjectToCache under the key "Catalog" for 10 minutes.
// TimeSpan.Zero indicates that we won't use sliding expiration.
Cache.Insert("Catalog", ObjectToCache, null,
  DateTime.Now.AddMinutes(10), TimeSpan.Zero);
```

ASP.NET also supports a sliding expiration policy, which removes objects after a period of disuse. In this case, every time the object is accessed, its lifetime is reset. Sliding expiration works well when you have information that is always valid but is not always being used (such as historical data). This information doesn't need to be refreshed, but it shouldn't be kept in the cache if it isn't being used.

```
// Store ObjectToCache under the key "Catalog" as long as it is being used
// at least once every ten minutes.
// DateTime.MaxValue indicates that we won't use absolute expiration.
Cache.Insert("Catalog", ObjectToCache, null,
  DateTime.MaxValue, TimeSpan.FromMinutes(10));
```

You can retrieve items from the cache by key name. However, you must always first check to see whether the item exists and then cast it to the desired type.

When adding objects to the cache, the best design pattern is to create a separate function that can re-create the object as needed. For example, if you're storing a *DataSet*, create a function that checks the cache and requeries the database only if the *DataSet* can't be found. This allows you to avoid the most time-consuming part of the page processing—querying the database—while still allowing your code to tailor the display (for example, apply a user-requested sort order) or perform other actions.

The next example demonstrates this pattern. It displays a table with customer information drawn from a *DataSet*. The key ingredient is the *Customer-Database* class, which encapsulates the functionality needed to fill the *DataSet* and manage the cache. Because this class doesn't inherit from *Page*, it needs to use the *static HttpContext.Current* property to retrieve a reference to the *Cache* object.

```
using System;
using System.Data;
using System.Web;
using System.Configuration;
using System.Diagnostics;
using System.Web.Caching;
using System.Data.SqlClient;

public class CustomerDatabase {

    private string connectionString;

    // Retrieve the reference to the Cache object.
    private Cache cache = HttpContext.Current.Cache;

    public CustomerDatabase() {

        // Get the connection string from the Web.config file.
        connectionString = ConfigurationSettings.AppSettings["NorthwindCon"];
    }

    public DataSet GetCustomers() {

        DataSet customersDS;

        // Check for cached item.
        if (cache["Customers"] == null) {

            // Get DataSet from database.
            customersDS = GetCustomersFromDatabase();

            // Store the item in the cache
            // with a sliding expiration policy of 60 seconds.
            cache.Insert("Customers", customersDS, null,
              DateTime.MaxValue, TimeSpan.FromSeconds(60));

            // Show a debug message.
            Debug.WriteLine("DataSet created from data source.");

        }else {

            // Show a debug message.
```

```
            Debug.WriteLine("DataSet retrieved from cache.");

            // Retrieve the item.
            customersDS = (DataSet)cache["Customers"];
        }

        // Return the DataSet.
        return customersDS;
    }

    private DataSet GetCustomersFromDatabase() {

        // Create the DataSet.
        DataSet customersDS = new DataSet();

        // Fill the DataSet (from a file).
        SqlConnection con = new SqlConnection(connectionString);
        SqlCommand cmd = new SqlCommand("SELECT * FROM Customers", con);
        SqlDataAdapter adapter = new SqlDataAdapter(cmd);

        try {

            con.Open();
            adapter.Fill(customersDS, "Customers");
        }catch {

            customersDS = null;
        }
        finally {
            con.Close();
        }
```

The next step is to create a Web page that uses the *CustomerDatabase* class. The following example shows a page with a *DataGrid* and a single *Button*. Every time the user clicks the *Button*, the page calls the *CustomerDatabase.GetCustomers* method. The information is retrieved from the cache if available or requeried if the 60-second time period has elapsed. You can determine whether the *DataSet* was retrieved from the cache by looking at the output in the Debug window.

```
using System;
using System.Web;
using System.Web.UI.WebControls;
```

```
public class LoginPage : System.Web.UI.Page {

    protected System.Web.UI.WebControls.DataGrid DataGrid1;
    protected System.Web.UI.WebControls.Button cmdGetData;

    // (Designer code omitted.)

    private void cmdGetData_Click(object sender, System.EventArgs e){
        CustomerDatabase custDB = new CustomerDatabase();
        DataGrid1.DataSource = custDB.GetCustomers();
        DataGrid1.DataBind();
    }
}
```

7.16 Enable Web Site Debugging

Problem

When attempting to debug a Web application with Visual Studio .NET, you receive an "unable to start debugging on the Web server" error.

Solution

Ensure that Internet Information Services (IIS) is installed correctly, that IIS was installed before the Microsoft .NET Framework, and that Integrated Windows authentication is enabled for the Web application directory.

Discussion

The "unable to start debugging" error signals that Visual Studio .NET was able to compile the Web application but can't execute it in debug mode. Unfortunately, this problem can arise for different reasons, including the following:

■ IIS, the Windows component that hosts Web applications, is not installed or is installed incorrectly.

■ The user running Visual Studio .NET is not a member of the Debugger Users group for the Web server.

■ The user running Visual Studio .NET doesn't have permissions to debug the ASP.NET process. For example, if the ASP.NET process is running under the local system account, the user must have Administrator privileges to debug it.

■ The Web server is running a version of Windows that doesn't support debugging, such as Microsoft Windows NT and Windows XP Home Edition. (Windows 2000, Windows XP Professional, Windows XP Server, and Windows Server 2003 all support debugging.)

■ The Web application doesn't have a Web.config file, or the Web.config file doesn't enable debugging.

■ You're running Visual Studio .NET, and you haven't enabled Integrated Windows authentication for the virtual directory.

The first step that you should take when diagnosing why you can't debug a Web application is to check that IIS is installed on the Web server. To do so, open *http://localhost/localstart.asp* in your browser. (localhost is an alias for the current computer.) If the test page doesn't appear, IIS is not installed or is not enabled. You can also attempt to start your Web application without debugging by selecting Debug | Start Without Debugging from the Visual Studio .NET main menu. If this test is successful, IIS is correctly installed.

If you installed IIS after you installed Visual Studio .NET or the .NET Framework, you might need to "repair" the .NET Framework by using the original setup CD or DVD. To start this process, type the following command at the command line (or in the Run window), using the Visual Studio .NET DVD. (It's split into two lines below because of page constraints, but it should be entered on a single line.)

```
<DVD Drive>:\wcu\dotNetFramework\dotnetfx.exe /t:c:\temp
  /c:"msiexec.exe /fvecms c:\temp\netfx.msi"
```

If you're using the CD version of Visual Studio .NET, use the following command line with the Windows Component Update disc:

```
<CD Drive>:\dotNetFramework\dotnetfx.exe /t:c:\temp
  /c:"msiexec.exe /fvecms c:\temp\netfx.msi"
```

If IIS is properly installed, the next step is to validate your Web application's Web.config file. The Web.config file should follow the structure shown here:

```
<configuration>
  <system.web>
    <compilation defaultLanguage="c#"
      debug="true" >

  <!-- Other settings omitted. -->

  </system.web>
</configuration>
```

By default, Visual Studio .NET adds the *compilation* tag to the automatically generated Web.config file with the *debug* attribute set to *true*.

The next step is to verify the IIS configuration. Problems will occur if you fail to create the required virtual application directory or if you try to run a Web application after you've removed or modified the virtual directory. To correct these problems, modify the virtual directory settings in IIS Manager by selecting Control Panel | Administrative Tools | Internet Information Services from the Start menu. Verify that the virtual application directory exists and that it's configured as a Web application. (You can see virtual directory settings by right-clicking the directory and choosing Properties.) For example, in the screen shot shown in Figure 7-9, the virtual directory exists but is not configured as a Web application. To resolve this problem, you simply need to click the Create button in the Application Settings section.

Figure 7-9   A virtual directory that is not a Web application.

One other IIS configuration problem that can occur in Visual Studio .NET is a failure to authenticate. Visual Studio .NET attempts to access the local Web server using Integrated Windows authentication, even if you have anonymous authentication enabled for the virtual directory. This means that your virtual directory must allow both anonymous and Integrated Windows authentication. To allow both authentication methods, follow these steps:

1. In IIS Manager, right-click the virtual directory for your application and choose Properties. (Alternatively, you can configure authentication for all directories if you right-click the Web Sites folder and choose Properties.)

2. Select the Directory Security tab.

3. In the Anonymous access and authentication control section, click the Edit button.

4. In the Authentication Methods dialog box, under Authenticated access, select Integrated Windows authentication, as shown in Figure 7-10.

5. Click OK to apply your changes.

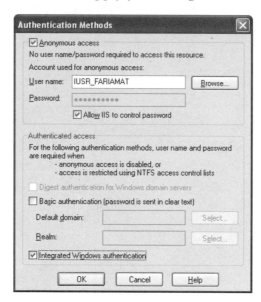

Figure 7-10   Enabling Integrated Windows authentication for debugging.

Note   Microsoft describes these steps and some other troubleshooting steps for remote servers in a white paper at *http://msdn.microsoft.com/library/default.asp?url=/library/en-us/vsdebug/html/vxtbshttpservererrors.asp.*

7.17 Change the Permissions Given to ASP.NET Code

Problem

You need to give your Web page or Web service code more Windows privileges (such as rights to files, registry settings, databases, and other resources), or you need to restrict the existing privileges.

Solution

You can assign privileges directly to the local ASPNET account, or you can configure your ASP.NET code to use a completely different account by modifying the *<processModel>* tag in the machine.config file. Alternatively, you can use impersonation so that some code executes with the rights of the IIS-authenticated user.

Discussion

ASP.NET code doesn't run under the IIS authenticated user or the anonymous IUSR_[ServerName] account. Part of the reason is that this account usually won't have sufficient privileges for ASP.NET code, which needs to be able to create and delete temporary files to manage the Web page compilation process.

By default, ASP.NET pages run using the local ASPNET account, which has a carefully limited set of privileges. If you need your ASP.NET code to perform something that is not allowed by default for the local account (writing to the server hard drive or the event log, for example), you can explicitly grant these rights to the ASPNET process. You can also change the setting by editing the machine.config file and modifying the *<processModel>* tag. You can set the *userName* and *password* attributes to any arbitrary user, or you can make use of the built-in local ASPNET process (set *userName* to Machine and *password* to AutoGenerate) or local system account (set *userName* to System and *password* to AutoGenerate). Because the local system has full rights to the computer, using this account is never recommended except for testing purposes. The ASP.NET account settings are global, and all Web applications will share the account that you specify.

You can also change the account used to execute certain applications or specific code by using impersonation. For example, to configure a single Web application to run under a different user account, add the *<identity>* tag to the Web.config file, as shown here:

```
<configuration>
  <system.web>
```

```
<!-- Other settings omitted. -->

<identity impersonate="true" name="domain\user" password="pwd"/>

   </system.web>
</configuration>
```

You can also instruct the Web application to use the identity that was authenticated by IIS, which will be the anonymous IUSR_[ServerName] account if you aren't using Windows authentication (discussed in recipe 7.8). Simply add the *<identity>* tag without supplying any user credentials:

```
<identity impersonate="true"/>
```

Remember, for this type of impersonation to work, the user account will require read/write access to the Temporary ASP.NET Files directory where the compiled ASP.NET files are stored. This directory is located under the path C:\[WindowsDirectory]\Microsoft.NET\Framework\[version]\Temporary ASP.NET Files.

Finally, you can also use impersonation programmatically, to change the account used to execute a particular section of code. This topic is described in more detail in recipe 16.15. However, the following code snippet shows a brief example that works in conjunction with Windows authentication. Provided IIS has authenticated the user (as described in recipe 7.8), that user identity will be assumed when the *WindowsIdentity.Impersonate* method is used. To use this code, you must import the *System.Security.Principal* namespace.

```
if (User.GetType() == typeof(WindowsPrincipal)) {

    WindowsIdentity id = (WindowsIdentity)User.Identity;
    WindowsImpersonationContext impersonate = id.Impersonate();

    // (Now perform tasks under the impersonated ID.)

    // Revert to the original ID as shown below.
    impersonate.Undo();
} else {

    // User is not Windows authenticated.
    // Throw an error to or take other steps.
}
```

8

Graphics, Multimedia, and Printing

Graphics, video, sound, and printing are the hallmarks of a traditional rich client on the Microsoft Windows operating system. When it comes to multimedia, the Microsoft .NET Framework delivers a compromise, providing support for some of these features, while ignoring others. For example, you'll find a sophisticated set of tools for two-dimensional drawing and event-based printing with GDI+ and the types in the *System.Drawing* namespaces. These classes wrap the native Graphics Device Interface (GDI) functions in the Windows API, and they make it much easier to draw complex shapes, work with coordinates and transforms, and process images. On the other hand, if you want to play a sound recording, show a video file, or get information about the current print jobs, you'll need to look beyond the .NET Framework.

This chapter presents recipes that show you how to use built-in .NET features and, where necessary, native Win32 libraries via P/Invoke or COM interop. Some of the techniques you'll see include

- Recipes to find and use installed fonts (recipe 8.1), draw scrollable images (recipe 8.5) and thumbnails (recipe 8.8), as well as perform a screen capture using the Win32 API (recipe 8.6).

- Approaches for working with owner-drawn custom controls (recipes 8.3 and 8.4) and manipulating graphical objects on the screen (recipes 8.2 and 8.7).

- Playing audio and video, including WAV, MP3, and MPEG files, using the Quartz type library included with Windows Media Player (recipes 8.9, 8.10, and 8.11).

■ Printing both simple and complex documents (recipes 8.13 and 8.14), wrapping text (recipe 8.15), creating a print preview (recipe 8.16), and retrieving information about printers (recipe 8.12) and print queues using WMI (recipe 8.17).

8.1 Find All Installed Fonts

Problem

You need to retrieve a list of all the fonts that are installed on the current computer.

Solution

Create a new instance of the *System.Drawing.Text.InstalledFontCollection* class, which contains a collection of *FontFamily* objects representing all the installed fonts.

Discussion

The *InstalledFontCollection* class allows you to retrieve information about currently installed fonts. The following code shows a form that iterates through the font collection when it's first created. Every time it finds a font, it creates a new label that will display the font name in the given font face (at a size of 14 point). The label is added to a scrollable panel, allowing the user to scroll through the list of available fonts.

```
using System;
using System.Windows.Forms;
using System.Drawing;
using System.Drawing.Text;

public class ListFonts : System.Windows.Forms.Form {

    private System.Windows.Forms.Panel pnlFonts;

    // (Designer code omitted.)

    private void ListFonts_Load(object sender, System.EventArgs e) {

        // Create the font collection.
        InstalledFontCollection fontFamilies = new InstalledFontCollection();

        // Iterate through all font families.
        int offset = 10;
```

```
foreach (FontFamily family in fontFamilies.Families) {

    try {

        // Create a label that will display text in this font.
        Label fontLabel = new Label();
        fontLabel.Text = family.Name;
        fontLabel.Font = new Font(family, 14);
        fontLabel.Left = 10;
        fontLabel.Width = pnlFonts.Width;
        fontLabel.Top = offset;

        // Add the label to a scrollable panel.
        pnlFonts.Controls.Add(fontLabel);
        offset += 30;

    }catch {

        // An error will occur if the selected font does
        // not support normal style (the default used when
        // creating a Font object). This problem can be
        // harmlessly ignored.
    }
  }
 }
}
```

Figure 8-1 shows a screen shot of this simple test application.

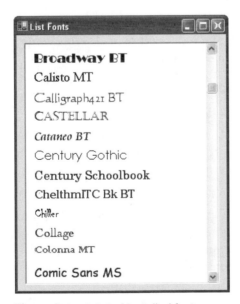

Figure 8-1   A list of installed fonts.

8.2 Perform Hit Testing with Shapes

Problem

You need to detect if a user clicks inside a shape.

Solution

Test the point where the user clicked with methods such as *Rectangle.Contains* and *Region.IsVisible* (in the *System.Drawing* namespace), or *Graphics-Path.IsVisible* (in the *System.Drawing.Drawing2D* namespace), depending on the type of shape.

Discussion

Often, if you use GDI+ to draw shapes on a form, you need to be able to determine when a user clicks inside a given shape. The .NET Framework provides three methods that can help with this task:

- The *Rectangle.Contains* method, which takes a point and returns *true* if the point is inside a given rectangle. In many cases, you can retrieve a rectangle for another type of shape. For example, you can use *Image.GetBounds* to retrieve the invisible rectangle that represents the image boundaries. The *Rectangle* struct is a member of the *System.Drawing* namespace.

- The *GraphicsPath.IsVisible* method, which takes a point and returns *true* if the point is inside the area defined by a closed *GraphicsPath*. Because a *GraphicsPath* can contain multiple lines, shapes, and figures, this approach is useful if you want to test if a point is contained inside a nonrectangular region. The *GraphicsPath* class is a member of the *System.Drawing.Drawing2D* namespace.

- The *Region.IsVisible* method, which takes a point and returns *true* if the point is inside the area defined by a *Region*. A *Region*, like the *GraphicsPath*, can represent a complex nonrectangular shape. *Region* is a member of the *System.Drawing* namespace.

The following example shows a form that creates a *Rectangle* and a *GraphicsPath*. By default, these two shapes are given light blue backgrounds. However, an event handler responds to the *Form.MouseMove* event, checks to see if the mouse pointer is in one of these shapes, and updates the background to bright pink if the pointer is there.

```
using System;
using System.Windows.Forms;
using System.Drawing;
using System.Drawing.Drawing2D;

public class HitTesting : System.Windows.Forms.Form {

    // (Designer code omitted.)

    // Define the shapes used on this form.
    private GraphicsPath path;
    private Rectangle rectangle;

    // Define the flags that track where the mouse pointer is.
    private bool inPath = false;
    private bool inRectangle = false;

    // Define the brushes used for painting the shapes.
    Brush highlightBrush = Brushes.HotPink;
    Brush defaultBrush = Brushes.LightBlue;

    private void HitTesting_Load(object sender, System.EventArgs e) {

        // Create the shapes that will be displayed.
        path = new GraphicsPath();
        path.AddEllipse(10, 10, 100, 60);
        path.AddCurve(new Point[] {new Point(50, 50),
                    new Point(10,33), new Point(80,43)});
        path.AddLine(50, 120, 250, 80);
        path.AddLine(120, 40, 110, 50);
        path.CloseFigure();

        rectangle = new Rectangle(100, 170, 220, 120);
    }

    private void HitTesting_Paint(object sender,
      System.Windows.Forms.PaintEventArgs e) {

        Graphics g = e.Graphics;

        // Paint the shapes according to the current selection.
        if (inPath) {

            g.FillPath(highlightBrush, path);
            g.FillRectangle(defaultBrush, rectangle);

        }else if (inRectangle) {
```

```
            g.FillRectangle(highlightBrush, rectangle);
            g.FillPath(defaultBrush, path);

        }else {

            g.FillPath(defaultBrush, path);
            g.FillRectangle(defaultBrush, rectangle);
        }
        g.DrawPath(Pens.Black, path);
        g.DrawRectangle(Pens.Black, rectangle);
    }

    private void HitTesting_MouseMove(object sender,
      System.Windows.Forms.MouseEventArgs e) {

        Graphics g = this.CreateGraphics();

        // Perform hit testing with rectangle.
        if (rectangle.Contains(e.X, e.Y)) {

            if (!inRectangle) {

                inRectangle = true;

                // Highlight the rectangle.
                g.FillRectangle(highlightBrush, rectangle);
                g.DrawRectangle(Pens.Black, rectangle);
            }

        }else if (inRectangle) {

            inRectangle = false;

            // Restore the unhighlighted rectangle.
            g.FillRectangle(defaultBrush, rectangle);
            g.DrawRectangle(Pens.Black, rectangle);
        }

        // Perform hit testing with path.
        if (path.IsVisible(e.X, e.Y)) {

            if (!inPath) {

                inPath = true;

                // Highlight the path.
                g.FillPath(highlightBrush, path);
                g.DrawPath(Pens.Black, path);
            }
```

```
    }else if (inPath) {

        inPath = false;

        // Restore the unhighlighted path.
        g.FillPath(defaultBrush, path);
        g.DrawPath(Pens.Black, path);
    }

    g.Dispose();
    }
}
```

Notice that this highlighting operation takes place directly inside the *MouseMove* event handler. The painting is only performed if the current selection has changed. For simpler code, you could invalidate the entire form every time the mouse pointer moves in or out of a region and handle all the drawing in the *Form.Paint* event handler, but this would lead to more drawing and generate additional flicker as the entire form is repainted.

Figure 8-2 shows the application in action.

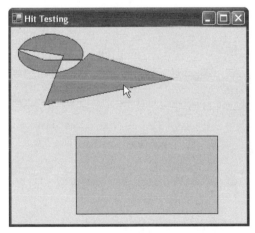

Figure 8-2   Hit testing with a *Rectangle* and a *GraphicsPath* object.

8.3 Create an Irregularly Shaped Control

Problem

You need to create a nonrectangular form or control.

Solution

Create a new *System.Drawing.Region* object that has the shape you want for the form, and assign it to the *Form.Region* or the *Control.Region* property.

Discussion

To create a nonrectangular form or control, you first need to define the shape you want. The easiest approach is to use the *System.Drawing.Drawing2D.GraphicsPath* object, which can accommodate any combination of ellipses, rectangles, and closed curves. You can add shapes to a *GraphicsPath* instance using methods such as *AddEllipse*, *AddRectangle*, and *AddClosedCurve*. Once you are finished defining the shape you want, you can create a *Region* object from this *GraphicsPath*—just submit the *GraphicsPath* in the *Region* class constructor. Finally, you can assign the *Region* to the *Form.Region* or *Control.Region* property.

In the example that follows, an irregularly shaped form (shown in Figure 8-3) is created using two curves made of multiple points, which are converted into a closed figure using the *GraphicsPath.CloseAllFigures* method.

```
using System;
using System.Windows.Forms;
using System.Drawing;
using System.Drawing.Drawing2D;

public class IrregularForm : System.Windows.Forms.Form {

    private System.Windows.Forms.Button cmdClose;
    private System.Windows.Forms.Label label1;

    // (Designer code omitted.)

    private void IrregularForm_Load(object sender, System.EventArgs e) {

        GraphicsPath path = new GraphicsPath();
        Point[] pointsA = new Point[] {new Point(0, 0),
          new Point(40, 60), new Point(this.Width - 100, 10)};
        path.AddCurve(pointsA);

        Point[] pointsB = new Point[]
          {new Point(this.Width - 40, this.Height - 60),
           new Point(this.Width, this.Height),
           new Point(10, this.Height)};
        path.AddCurve(pointsB);
```

```
        path.CloseAllFigures();
        this.Region = new Region(path);
    }

    private void cmdClose_Click(object sender, System.EventArgs e) {

        this.Close();
    }
}
```

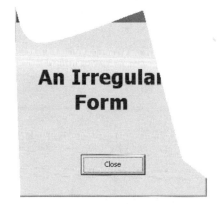

Figure 8-3   A nonrectangular form.

For an example that demonstrates a nonrectangular control, refer to recipe 8.4.

8.4 Create a Movable Sprite

Problem

You need to create a shape that the user can manipulate on a form, perhaps by dragging it, resizing, or otherwise interacting with it.

Solution

Create a custom control, and override the painting logic to draw a shape. Assign your shape to the *Control.Region* property. You can then use this *Region* to perform hit testing.

Discussion

If you need to create a complex user interface that incorporates many custom-drawn elements, you need a way to track these elements and allow the user to interact with them. The easiest approach in .NET is to create a dedicated control by deriving a class from *System.Windows.Forms.Control*. You can then customize the way this control is painted in the way its basic set of events is raised.

The following example shows a control that represents a simple ellipse shape on a form. All controls are associated with a rectangular region on a form, so the *EllipseShape* control generates an ellipse that fills these boundaries (provided through the *Control.ClientRectangle* property). Once the shape has been generated, the *Control.Region* property is set according to the bounds on the ellipse. This ensures that events such as *MouseMove, MouseDown, Click*, and so on will occur only if the mouse is over the ellipse, not the entire client rectangle.

The full *EllipseShape* code is shown in the following code:

```
using System;
using System.Windows.Forms;
using System.Drawing;
using System.Drawing.Drawing2D;

public class EllipseShape : System.Windows.Forms.Control {

    private GraphicsPath path = null;

    private void RefreshPath() {

        // Create the GraphicsPath for the shape (in this case
        // an ellipse that fits inside the full control area)
        // and apply it to the control by setting
        // the Region property.
        path = new GraphicsPath();
        path.AddEllipse(this.ClientRectangle);
        this.Region = new Region(path);
    }

    protected override void OnResize(System.EventArgs e) {

        base.OnResize(e);
        RefreshPath();
        this.Invalidate();
    }

    protected override void OnPaint(System.Windows.Forms.PaintEventArgs e) {
```

```
        base.OnPaint(e);
        if (path != null) {

            e.Graphics.SmoothingMode = SmoothingMode.AntiAlias;
            e.Graphics.FillPath(new SolidBrush(this.BackColor), path);
            e.Graphics.DrawPath(new Pen(this.ForeColor, 4), path);
        }
    }
}
```

You could define the *EllipseShape* control in a separate class library assembly so that it could be added to the Microsoft Visual Studio .NET Toolbox and used at design time. However, even without taking this step, it's easy to create a simple test application. The following Windows form creates two ellipses and allows the user to drag both of them around the form, simply by holding the mouse down and moving the pointer.

```
public class SpriteTest : System.Windows.Forms.Form {

    // (Designer code omitted.)

    // Tracks when drag mode is on.
    private bool isDraggingA = false;
    private bool isDraggingB = false;

    // The ellipse shape controls.
    private EllipseShape ellipseA, ellipseB;

    private void SpriteTest_Load(object sender, System.EventArgs e) {

        // Create and configure both ellipses.
        ellipseA = new EllipseShape();
        ellipseA.Width = ellipseA.Height = 100;
        ellipseA.Top = ellipseA.Left = 30;
        ellipseA.BackColor = Color.Red;
        this.Controls.Add(ellipseA);

        ellipseB = new EllipseShape();
        ellipseB.Width = ellipseB.Height = 100;
        ellipseB.Top = ellipseB.Left = 130;
        ellipseB.BackColor = Color.Azure;
        this.Controls.Add(ellipseB);

        // Attach both ellipses to the same set of event handlers.
        ellipseA.MouseDown += new MouseEventHandler(Ellipse_MouseDown);
        ellipseA.MouseUp += new MouseEventHandler(Ellipse_MouseUp);
        ellipseA.MouseMove += new MouseEventHandler(Ellipse_MouseMove);
```

```
        ellipseB.MouseDown += new MouseEventHandler(Ellipse_MouseDown);
        ellipseB.MouseUp += new MouseEventHandler(Ellipse_MouseUp);
        ellipseB.MouseMove += new MouseEventHandler(Ellipse_MouseMove);
    }

    private void Ellipse_MouseDown(object sender, MouseEventArgs e) {

        // Get the ellipse that triggered this event.
        Control control = (Control)sender;

        if (e.Button == MouseButtons.Left) {

            control.Tag = new Point(e.X, e.Y);
            if (control == ellipseA) {
                isDraggingA = true;

            }else {
                isDraggingB = true;
            }
        }
    }

    private void Ellipse_MouseUp(object sender, MouseEventArgs e) {

        isDraggingA = false;
        isDraggingB = false;
    }

    private void Ellipse_MouseMove(object sender, MouseEventArgs e) {

        // Get the ellipse that triggered this event.
        Control control = (Control)sender;

        if ((isDraggingA && control == ellipseA) ||
          (isDraggingB && control == ellipseB)) {

            // Get the offset.
            Point point = (Point)control.Tag;

            // Move the control.
            control.Left = e.X + control.Left - point.X;
            control.Top = e.Y + control.Top - point.Y;
        }
    }
}
```

Figure 8-4 shows the user about to drag an ellipse.

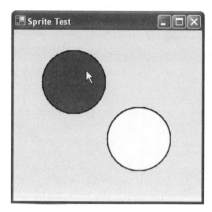

Figure 8-4 Dragging custom shape controls on a form.

8.5 Create a Scrollable Image

Problem

You need to create a scrollable picture with dynamic content.

Solution

Leverage the automatic scroll capabilities of the *System.Windows.Forms.Panel* control by setting *Panel.AutoScroll* to *true* and placing a *System.Windows.Forms.PictureBox* with the image content inside the *Panel*

Discussion

The *Panel* control has built-in scrolling support. If you place any controls in it that extend beyond its bounds, and you set *Panel.AutoScroll* to *true*, the panel will show scroll bars that allow the user to move through the content. This works particularly well with large images. You can load or create the image in memory, assign it to a picture box (which has no intrinsic support for scrolling), and then show the picture box inside the panel. The only consideration you need to remember is to make sure you set the picture box dimensions equal to the full size of the image you want to show.

The following example creates an image the represents a document. The image is generated as an in-memory bitmap, and several lines of text are added using the *Graphics.DrawString* method. The image is then bound to a picture box, which is shown in a scrollable panel, as shown in Figure 8-5.

```csharp
using System;
using System.Windows.Forms;
using System.Drawing;

public class PictureScroll : System.Windows.Forms.Form {

    private System.Windows.Forms.PictureBox pictureBox1;
    private System.Windows.Forms.Panel panel1;

    // (Designer code omitted.)

    private void PictureScroll_Load(object sender, System.EventArgs e) {

        string text = "The quick brown fox jumps over the lazy dog.";
        Font font = new Font("Tahoma", 20);

        // Create an in-memory bitmap.
        Bitmap b = new Bitmap(600, 600);
        Graphics g = Graphics.FromImage(b);
        g.FillRectangle(Brushes.White, new Rectangle(0, 0, b.Width,
          b.Height));

        // Draw several lines of text on the bitmap.
        for (int i=0; i < 10; i++) {
            g.DrawString(text, font, Brushes.Black, 50, 50 + i*60);
        }

        // Display the bitmap in the picture box.
        pictureBox1.BackgroundImage = b;
        pictureBox1.Size = b.Size;
    }
}
```

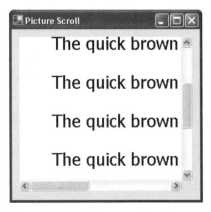

Figure 8-5 Adding scrolling support to custom content.

8.6 Perform a Screen Capture

Problem

You need to take a snapshot of the current desktop.

Solution

Use the Win32 API calls *GetDesktopWindow*, *GetDC*, and *ReleaseDC* from the user32.dll. In addition, use *GetCurrentObject* from gdi32.dll.

Discussion

The .NET Framework doesn't expose any classes for capturing the full screen (often referred to as the *desktop window*). However, you can access these features by using P/Invoke with the Win32 API.

The first step is to create a class that encapsulates the Win32 API functions you need to use. The following example shows a class that declares these functions and uses them in a *public Capture* method to return a .NET *Image* object with the desktop window.

```
using System;
using System.Drawing;
using System.Runtime.InteropServices;
using System.Windows.Forms;

public class DesktopCapture {

    [DllImport("user32.dll")]
    private extern static IntPtr GetDesktopWindow();

    [DllImport("user32.dll")]
    private extern static IntPtr GetDC(IntPtr windowHandle);

    [DllImport("gdi32.dll")]
    private extern static IntPtr GetCurrentObject(IntPtr hdc,
        ushort objectType);

    [DllImport("user32.dll")]
    private extern static void ReleaseDC( IntPtr hdc );

    const int OBJ_BITMAP = 7;

    public static Bitmap Capture() {

        // Get the device context for the desktop window.
        IntPtr desktopWindow = GetDesktopWindow();
        IntPtr desktopDC = GetDC( desktopWindow );
```

```
        // Get a GDI handle to the image.
        IntPtr desktopBitmap = GetCurrentObject(desktopDC, OBJ_BITMAP);

        // Use the handle to create a .NET Image object.
        Bitmap desktopImage = Image.FromHbitmap( desktopBitmap );

        // Release the device context and return the image.
        ReleaseDC(desktopDC);
        return desktopImage;
    }
}
```

The next step is to create a client that can use this functionality. The following code creates a form (shown in Figure 8-6) that displays the captured image in a picture box (which is inside a scrollable panel, as described in recipe 8.5).

```
public class ScreenCapture : System.Windows.Forms.Form {

    private System.Windows.Forms.PictureBox pictureBox1;
    private System.Windows.Forms.Panel panel1;

    // (Designer code omitted.)
    private void cmdCapture_Click(object sender, System.EventArgs e) {

        pictureBox1.Image = DesktopCapture.Capture();
        pictureBox1.Size = pictureBox1.Image.Size;
    }
}
```

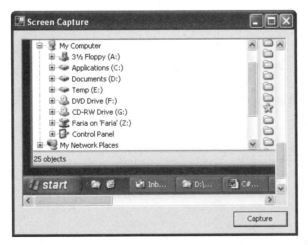

Figure 8-6 Capturing the screen contents.

8.7 Use Double Buffering to Increase Redraw Speed

Problem

You need to optimize drawing for a form that is frequently refreshed, and you want to reduce flicker.

Solution

Render the graphics to an in-memory bitmap, and then copy the finalized bitmap to the form.

Discussion

In some applications you need to repaint a form or control frequently. This is commonly the case when performing animation. For example, you might use a timer to invalidate your form every second. Your painting code could then redraw an image at a new location, creating the illusion of motion. The problem with this approach is that every time you invalidate the form, Windows repaints the window background (clearing the form) and then runs your painting code, which draws the graphic element by element. This can cause substantial on-screen flicker.

Double buffering is a technique you can implement to reduce this flicker. With double buffering, your drawing logic writes to an in-memory bitmap, which is copied to the form at the end of the drawing operation in a single, seamless repaint operation. Flickering is reduced dramatically.

The first step when implementing double buffering is to ensure that the form background isn't repainted automatically when the form is invalidated. This automatic clearing is the most significant cause of flicker because it replaces your image with a blank frame (if only for a fraction of a second). To prevent background painting, override the form's *OnPaintBackground* method so that it takes no action. The second step is to change the painting code so that it draws the image to an in-memory bitmap. When complete, the bitmap is copied to the form. This approach ensures that the refresh is a single repaint operation, and that time-consuming drawing logic won't cause additional flicker.

The following example shows an animation of an image (in this case, the Windows logo) alternately growing and shrinking on the page. The drawing logic is performed in the *Form.Paint* event handler, and a timer is used to invalidate the form every 10 milliseconds so that the image can be redrawn. The user can choose whether to enable double buffering through a check box on the form. Without double buffering, the form flickers noticeably. When double buffering is enabled, however, the image grows and shrinks with smooth, flicker-free animation.

```csharp
using System;
using System.Drawing;
using System.Drawing.Drawing2D;
using System.Windows.Forms;

public class DoubleBuffering : System.Windows.Forms.Form {

    private System.Windows.Forms.CheckBox chkUseDoubleBuffering;
    private System.Windows.Forms.Timer tmrRefresh;

    // (Designer code omitted.)

    // Track the image size, and the type of animation
    // (expanding or shrinking).
    private bool isShrinking = false;
    private int imageSize = 0;

    // Store the logo that will be painted on the form.
    private Image image;

    private void DoubleBuffering_Load(object sender, System.EventArgs e) {

        // Load the logo image from the file.
        image = Image.FromFile("image.bmp");

        // Start the timer that invalidates the form.
        tmrRefresh.Start();
    }

    private void tmrRefresh_Tick(object sender, System.EventArgs e) {

        // Change the desired image size according to the animation mode.
        if (isShrinking) {
            imageSize--;

        }else {
            imageSize++;
        }

        // Change the sizing direction if it nears the form border.
        if (imageSize > (this.Width - 150)) {
            isShrinking = true;

        }else if (imageSize < 1) {
            isShrinking = false;
        }
```

```
        // Repaint the form.
        this.Invalidate();
    }

    private void DoubleBuffering_Paint(object sender,
      System.Windows.Forms.PaintEventArgs e) {

        Graphics g;
        Bitmap drawing = null;

        if (chkUseDoubleBuffering.Checked) {

            // Double buffering is being used.
            // Create a new in-memory bitmap that represents the
            // form's surface.
            drawing = new Bitmap(this.Width, this.Height, e.Graphics);
            g = Graphics.FromImage(drawing);

        }else {

            // Double buffering is not being used.
            // Draw directly to the form.
            g = e.Graphics;
        }

        g.SmoothingMode = SmoothingMode.HighQuality;

        // Draw the background.
        g.FillRectangle(Brushes.Yellow, new Rectangle(new Point(0, 0),
        this.ClientSize));

        // Draw the logo image.
        g.DrawImage(image, 50, 50, 50 + imageSize, 50 + imageSize);

        // If using double buffering, copy the completed in-memory
        // bitmap to the form.
        if (chkUseDoubleBuffering.Checked) {

            e.Graphics.DrawImageUnscaled(drawing, 0, 0);
            g.Dispose();
        }
    }

    protected override void OnPaintBackground(
      System.Windows.Forms.PaintEventArgs pevent) {

        // Do nothing.
    }
}
```

8.8 Show a Thumbnail for an Image

Problem

You need to show *thumbnails* (small representations of a picture) for the images in a directory.

Solution

Read the image from the file using the *static FromFile* method of the *System.Drawing.Image* class. You can then retrieve a thumbnail using the *Image.GetThumbnailImage* method.

Discussion

The *Image* class provides the functionality for generating thumbnails through the *GetThumbnailImage* method. You simply need to pass the width and height of the thumbnail you want (in pixels), and the *Image* class will create a new *Image* object that fits these criteria. Antialiasing is used when reducing the image to ensure the best possible image quality, although some blurriness and loss of detail is inevitable. (*Antialiasing* is the process of removing jagged edges, often in resized graphics, by adding shading with an intermediate color.) In addition, you can supply a notification callback, allowing you to create thumbnails asynchronously.

When generating a thumbnail, it's important to ensure that the aspect ratio remains constant. For example, if you reduce a 200 × 100 picture to a 50 × 50 thumbnail, the width will be compressed to one quarter and the height will be compressed to one half, distorting the image. To ensure that the aspect ratio remains constant, you can change either the width or the height to a fixed size, and then adjust the other dimension proportionately.

The following example reads a bitmap file and generates a thumbnail that is not greater than 50 × 50 pixels, while preserving the original aspect ratio.

```
using System;
using System.Drawing;
using System.Windows.Forms;

public class Thumbnails : System.Windows.Forms.Form {

    // (Designer code omitted.)

    Image thumbnail;

    private void Thumbnails_Load(object sender, System.EventArgs e) {
```

```
Image img = Image.FromFile("test.jpg");
int thumbnailWidth = 0, thumbnailHeight = 0;

// Adjust the largest dimension to 50 pixels.
// This ensures that a thumbnail will not be larger than 50x50 pixels.
// If you are showing multiple thumbnails, you would reserve a 50x50
// pixel square for each one.
if (img.Width > img.Height) {

    thumbnailWidth = 50;
    thumbnailHeight = Convert.ToInt32(((50F / img.Width) *
        img.Height));

}else {

    thumbnailHeight = 50;
    thumbnailWidth = Convert.ToInt32(((50F / img.Height) *
        img.Width));
}

thumbnail = img.GetThumbnailImage(thumbnailWidth, thumbnailHeight,
    null, IntPtr.Zero);
}

private void Thumbnails_Paint(object sender,
  System.Windows.Forms.PaintEventArgs e) {

    e.Graphics.DrawImage(thumbnail, 10, 10);
}
}
```

8.9 Play a Simple Beep

Problem

You need to play a simple sound, such as the system-defined beep.

Solution

Use an unmanaged Win32 API function such as *Beep* or *sndPlaySound*, or call
the Microsoft Visual Basic .NET *Beep* function.

Discussion

The .NET Framework does not include any managed classes for playing audio files or even for playing the system beep sound. However, you can easily bridge this gap using the Win32 API or Visual Basic .NET, which provides a legacy *Beep* function that's exposed through the *Microsoft.VisualBasic.Interaction* class. In the latter case, you must add a reference to the Microsoft.VisualBasic.dll assembly (which is included with all versions of the .NET Framework).

The following example uses both the *Beep* API function and the Visual Basic *Beep* function. Notice that the API function actually uses the computer's internal speaker and plays a tone with the indicated frequency (in hertz, ranging from 37 to 32,767) and duration (in milliseconds). This won't produce any sound if the computer does not have an internal speaker. The Visual Basic *Beep* function, on the other hand, plays the standard system-defined beep sound event (which is a WAV audio file). This won't produce any sound if the computer doesn't have a sound card, if the sound card is not connected to external speakers, or if Windows is configured (via the Sounds and Audio Devices section of the Control Panel) to not play sounds.

```
using System;
using System.Runtime.InteropServices;
using Microsoft.VisualBasic;

public class BeepTest {

    [DllImport("kernel32.dll")]
    private static extern bool Beep(int freq, int dur);

    [STAThread]
    private static void Main(string[] args) {

        // Play a 440 Hz tone for 100 milliseconds on the internal speaker.
        Console.WriteLine("Win32 API beep test.");
        Beep(440, 100);
        Console.ReadLine();

        // Play the default beep system sound (a WAV audio file).
        Console.WriteLine("VB beep test.");
        Interaction.Beep();
        Console.ReadLine();
    }
}
```

You can also use Win32 API functions to play an audio file of your choosing. This technique is described in recipe 8.10.

8.10 Play a WAV or an MP3 File

Problem

You need to play a WAV or MP3 audio file.

Solution

Use the unmanaged *sndPlaySound* API function for basic WAV file support, or use the ActiveMovie COM component included with Windows Media Player, which supports WAV and MP3 audio.

Discussion

To play any sound in a .NET application, you need to enlist the help of an outside library or system call. Fortunately, two easy options are readily available.

- The winmm.dll included with Windows includes a function named *sndPlaySound* that accepts the name of a WAV file and a parameter indicating how to play it. You can choose to play a sound synchronously (interrupting the execution of the program until the sound is complete), asynchronously, or in a continuous background loop.

- The Quartz type library provides a COM component that can play various types of audio files, including the WAV and MP3 formats. The Quartz type library is provided through quartz.dll and is included as a part of Microsoft DirectX with Windows Media Player and the Windows operating system.

In this example, we'll use the latter approach. The first step is to generate an interop class that can manage the interaction between your .NET application and the unmanaged Quartz library. You can generate a C# class with this interop code using the Type Library Importer utility (tlbimp.exe) and the following command line, where [WindowsDir] is the path for your installation of Windows:

```
tlbimp [WindowsDir]\system32\quartz.dll /out:QuartzTypeLib.dll
```

Alternatively, you can generate the interop class using Visual Studio .NET by adding a reference. Simply right-click your project in the Solution Explorer, and choose Add Reference from the context menu. Then select the COM tab, and scroll down to select ActiveMovie control type library.

Once the interop class is generated, you can work with the *IMediaControl* interface. You can specify the file you want to play using *RenderFile*, and you can control playback using methods such as *Run*, *Stop*, and *Pause*. The actual playback takes place on a separate thread, so it won't block your code.

The following example shows a simple Console utility that plays the audio file that's specified as the first command-line argument.

```
using System;

class PlayAudio {

    public static void Main(string[] args) {

        // Get the filename specified in the first parameter.
        string filename = args[0];

        // Access the IMediaControl interface.
        QuartzTypeLib.FilgraphManager graphManager =
          new QuartzTypeLib.FilgraphManager();
        QuartzTypeLib.IMediaControl mc =
          (QuartzTypeLib.IMediaControl)graphManager;

        // Specify the file.
        mc.RenderFile(filename);

        // Start playing the audio asynchronously.
        mc.Run();

        Console.WriteLine("Press Enter to continue.");
        Console.ReadLine();
        mc.Stop();
    }
}
```

You can also use the Quartz library to show movie files, as demonstrated in recipe 8.11.

8.11 Show an Animation with DirectShow

Problem

You need to play a video file (such as an MPEG, an AVI, or a WMV file) in a Windows form.

Solution

Use the ActiveMovie COM component included with Media Player. Bind the video output to a picture box on your form by setting the *IVideoWindow.Owner* property to the *PictureBox.Handle* property.

Discussion

Although the .NET Framework does not include any managed classes for interacting with video files, you can leverage the functionality of DirectShow using the COM-based Quartz library included with Windows Media Player and the Windows operating system. For information about creating an interop assembly for the Quartz type library, refer to the instructions in recipe 8.10.

Once you have created the interop assembly, you can use the *IMediaControl* interface to load and play a movie. This is essentially the same technique demonstrated in recipe 8.10 with audio files. However, if you want to show the video window inside your application interface (rather than in a separate stand-alone window), you must also use the *IVideoWindow* interface. The core *FilgraphManager* object can be cast to both the *IMediaControl* and the *IVideoWindow* interface—and several other interfaces are also supported, such as *IBasicAudio* (which allows you to configure balance and volume settings). With the *IVideoWindow* interface, you can bind the video output to an object on your form, such as a panel or a picture box. To do so, set the *IVideoWindow.Owner* property to the handle for the control, which you can retrieve using the *Control.Handle* property. Then, call *IVideoWindow.SetWindowPosition* to set the window size and location. This method can be called to change the video size changes during playback (for example, if the form is resized).

The following example shows a simple form that allows users to open any video file and play it back in the provided picture box. The picture box is anchored to all sides of the form, so it changes size as the form is resized. The code responds to the *PictureBox.SizeChanged* event to change the size of the corresponding video window.

```
using System;
using QuartzTypeLib;
using System.Windows.Forms;

public class ShowMovie : System.Windows.Forms.Form {

    private System.Windows.Forms.PictureBox pictureBox1;
    private System.Windows.Forms.Button cmdOpen;

    // (Designer code omitted.)

    // Define constants used for specifying the window style.
    private const int WM_APP = 0x8000;
    private const int WM_GRAPHNOTIFY = WM_APP + 1;
    private const int EC_COMPLETE = 0x01;
    private const int WS_CHILD = 0x40000000;
    private const int WS_CLIPCHILDREN = 0x2000000;
```

```csharp
// Hold a form-level reference to the media control interface,
// so the code can control playback of the currently loaded
// movie.
private IMediaControl mc = null;

// Hold a form-level reference to the video window in case it
// needs to be resized.
private IVideoWindow videoWindow = null;

private void cmdOpen_Click(object sender, System.EventArgs e) {

    // Allow the user to choose a file.
    OpenFileDialog openFileDialog = new OpenFileDialog();
    openFileDialog.Filter =
    "Media Files|*.mpg;*.avi;*.wma;*.mov;*.wav;*.mp2;*.mp3|All Files|*.*";

    if (DialogResult.OK == openFileDialog.ShowDialog()) {

        // Stop the playback for the current movie, if it exists.
        if (mc != null) mc.Stop();

        // Load the movie file.
        FilgraphManager graphManager = new FilgraphManager();
        graphManager.RenderFile(openFileDialog.FileName);

        // Attach the view to a picture box on the form.
        try {

            videoWindow = (IVideoWindow)graphManager;
            videoWindow.Owner = (int) pictureBox1.Handle;
            videoWindow.WindowStyle = WS_CHILD | WS_CLIPCHILDREN;
            videoWindow.SetWindowPosition(
              pictureBox1.ClientRectangle.Left,
              pictureBox1.ClientRectangle.Top,
              pictureBox1.ClientRectangle.Width,
              pictureBox1.ClientRectangle.Height);

        }catch {

            // An error can occur if the file does not have a video
            // source (for example, an MP3 file.)
            // You can ignore this error and still allow playback to
            // continue (without any visualization).
        }

        // Start the playback (asynchronously).
        mc = (IMediaControl)graphManager;
```

```
            mc.Run();
        }
    }

    private void pictureBox1_SizeChanged(object sender, System.EventArgs e) {

        if (videoWindow != null) {

            try {

                videoWindow.SetWindowPosition(
                    pictureBox1.ClientRectangle.Left,
                    pictureBox1.ClientRectangle.Top,
                    pictureBox1.ClientRectangle.Width,
                    pictureBox1.ClientRectangle.Height);

            }catch {

                // Ignore the exception thrown when resizing the form
                // when the file does not have a video source.
            }
        }
    }

    private void ShowMovie_Closing(object sender,
      System.ComponentModel.CancelEventArgs e) {

        if (mc != null) mc.Stop();
    }
}
```

An example of the output you'll see is shown in Figure 8-7.

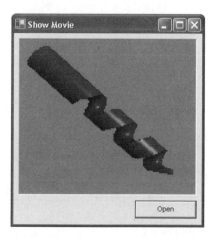

Figure 8-7   Playing a video file.

8.12 Retrieve Information About the Installed Printers

Problem

You need to retrieve a list of available printers.

Solution

Read the names in the *InstalledPrinters* collection of the *System.Drawing.Printing.PrinterSettings* class.

Discussion

The *PrinterSettings* class encapsulates the settings for a printer and information about the printer. For example, you can use the *PrinterSettings* class to determine supported paper sizes, paper sources, and resolutions and check for the ability to print color or double-sided (or *duplexed*) pages. In addition, you can retrieve default page settings for margins, page orientation, and so on.

The *PrinterSettings* class provides a *static InstalledPrinters* collection, which includes the name of every printer that's installed on the computer. If you want to find out more information about the settings for a specific printer, you simply need to create a *PrinterSettings* instance and set the *PrinterName* property accordingly.

The following code shows a Console application that finds all the printers that are installed on a computer and displays information about the paper sizes and the resolutions supported by each one.

```csharp
using System;
using System.Drawing.Printing;

public class ListPrinters {

    private static void Main(string[] args) {

        foreach (string printerName in PrinterSettings.InstalledPrinters) {

            // Display the printer name.
            Console.WriteLine("Printer: {0}", printerName);

            // Retrieve the printer settings.
            PrinterSettings printer = new PrinterSettings();
            printer.PrinterName = printerName;

            // Check that this is a valid printer.
```

```
            // (This step might be required if you read the printer name
            // from a user-supplied value or a registry or configuration file
            // setting.)
            if (printer.IsValid) {

                // Display the list of valid resolutions.
                Console.WriteLine("Supported Resolutions:");

                foreach (PrinterResolution resolution in
                  printer.PrinterResolutions) {
                    Console.WriteLine("  {0}", resolution);
                }
                Console.WriteLine();

                // Display the list of valid paper sizes.
                Console.WriteLine("Supported Paper Sizes:");

                foreach (PaperSize size in printer.PaperSizes) {

                    if (Enum.IsDefined(size.Kind.GetType(), size.Kind)) {
                        Console.WriteLine("  {0}", size);
                    }
                }
                Console.WriteLine();
            }
        }
        Console.ReadLine();
    }
}
```

Here's the type of output this utility displays:

```
Printer: HP LaserJet 5L
Supported Resolutions:
  [PrinterResolution High]
  [PrinterResolution Medium]
  [PrinterResolution Low]
  [PrinterResolution Draft]
  [PrinterResolution X=600 Y=600]
  [PrinterResolution X=300 Y=300]

Supported Paper Sizes:
  [PaperSize Letter Kind=Letter Height=1100 Width=850]
  [PaperSize Legal Kind=Legal Height=1400 Width=850]
  [PaperSize Executive Kind=Executive Height=1050 Width=725]
  [PaperSize A4 Kind=A4 Height=1169 Width=827]
  [PaperSize Envelope #10 Kind=Number10Envelope Height=950 Width=412]
  [PaperSize Envelope DL Kind=DLEnvelope Height=866 Width=433]
  [PaperSize Envelope C5 Kind=C5Envelope Height=902 Width=638]
```

```
[PaperSize Envelope B5 Kind=B5Envelope Height=984 Width=693]
[PaperSize Envelope Monarch Kind=MonarchEnvelope Height=750 Width=387]

Printer: Generic PostScript Printer
. . .
```

You don't need to take this approach when creating an application that provides printing features. As you'll see in recipe 8.13, you can use *PrintDialog* to prompt the user to choose a printer and its settings. The *PrintDialog* class can automatically apply its settings to the appropriate *PrintDocument* without any additional code.

> **Note**   You can print a document in almost any type of application. However, your application must include a reference to the System.Drawing.dll assembly. If you are using a project type in Visual Studio .NET that wouldn't normally have this reference (such as a Console application), you must add it.

8.13 Print a Simple Document

Problem

You need to print text or images.

Solution

Handle the *PrintDocument.PrintPage* event, and use the *DrawString* and *DrawImage* methods of the *Graphics* class to print data to the page.

Discussion

.NET uses an asynchronous event-based printing model. To print a document, you create a *System.Drawing.Printing.PrintDocument* instance, configure its properties, and then call its *Print* method, which schedules the print job. The common language runtime will then fire the *BeginPrint*, *PrintPage*, and *End-Print* events of the *PrintDocument* class on a new thread. You handle these events and use the provided *System.Drawing.Graphics* object to output data to the page. Graphics and text are written to a page in exactly the same way as you draw to a window using GDI+. However, you might need to track your position on a page, because every *Graphics* class method requires explicit coordinates that indicate where to draw.

Printer settings are configured through the *PrintDocument.PrinterSettings* and *PrintDocument.DefaultPageSettings* properties. The *PrinterSettings* property returns a full *PrinterSettings* object (as described in recipe 8.12), which identifies the printer that will be used. The *DefaultPageSettings* property provides a full *PageSettings* object that specifies printer resolution, margins, orientation, and so on. You can configure these properties in code, or you can use the *System.Windows.Forms.PrintDialog* class to let the user make the changes using the standard Windows print dialog (shown in Figure 8-8). In the print dialog box, the user can select a printer and choose a number of copies. The user can also click the Properties button to configure advanced settings such as page layout and printer resolution. Finally, the user can either accept or cancel the print operation by clicking OK or Cancel.

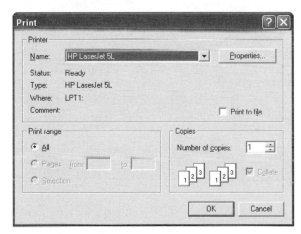

Figure 8-8   The *PrintDialog*.

Before using the *PrintDialog* class, you must explicitly attach it to a *Print-Document* object by setting the *PrintDialog.Document* property. Then any changes the user makes in the print dialog will be automatically applied to the *PrintDocument* object.

The following example provides a form with a single button. When the user clicks the button, the application creates a new *PrintDocument*, allows the user to configure print settings, and then starts an asynchronous print operation (provided the user clicks OK). An event handler responds to the *PrintPage* event and writes several lines of text and an image.

```
using System;
using System.Windows.Forms;
```

```csharp
using System.Drawing;
using System.Drawing.Printing;

public class SimplePrint : System.Windows.Forms.Form {

    private System.Windows.Forms.Button cmdPrint;

    // (Designer code omitted.)

    private void cmdPrint_Click(object sender, System.EventArgs e) {

        // Create the document and attach an event handler.
        PrintDocument doc = new PrintDocument();
        doc.PrintPage += new PrintPageEventHandler(this.Doc_PrintPage);

        // Allow the user to choose a printer and specify other settings.
        PrintDialog dlgSettings = new PrintDialog();
        dlgSettings.Document = doc;

        // If the user clicked OK, print the document.
        if (dlgSettings.ShowDialog() == DialogResult.OK) {

            // This method returns immediately, before the print job starts.
            // The PrintPage event will fire asynchronously.
            doc.Print();
        }
    }

    private void Doc_PrintPage(object sender, PrintPageEventArgs e) {

        // Define the font.
        Font font = new Font("Arial", 30);

        // Determine the position on the page.
        // In this case, we read the margin settings
        // (although there is nothing that prevents your code
        // from going outside the margin bounds.)
        float x = e.MarginBounds.Left;
        float y = e.MarginBounds.Top;

        // Determine the height of a line (based on the font used).
        float lineHeight = font.GetHeight(e.Graphics);

        // Print five lines of text.
        for (int i=0; i < 5; i++) {

            // Draw the text with a black brush,
            // using the font and coordinates we have determined.
```

```
        e.Graphics.DrawString("This is line " + i.ToString(),
          font, Brushes.Black, x, y);

        // Move down the equivalent spacing of one line.
        y += lineHeight;
      }
      y += lineHeight;

      // Draw an image.
      e.Graphics.DrawImage(Image.FromFile(Application.StartupPath +
        "\\test.bmp"), x, y);
    }
}
```

This example has one limitation: it can only print a single page. To print more complex documents and span multiple pages, you will probably want to create a specialized class that encapsulates the document information, the current page, and so on. This technique is demonstrated in recipe 8.14.

8.14 Print a Multipage Document

Problem

You need to print complex documents with multiple pages and possibly print several different documents at once.

Solution

Place the information you want to print into a custom class that derives from *PrintDocument*, and set the *PrintPageEventArgs.HasMorePages* property to *true* as long as there are pages remaining.

Discussion

The *PrintDocument.PrintPage* event allows you to print only a single page. If you need to print more pages, you need to set the *PrintPageEventArgs.Has-MorePages* property to *true* in the *PrintPage* event handler. As long as *Has-MorePages* is *true*, the *PrintDocument* class will continue firing *PrintPage* events, one for each page. However, it's up to you to track what page you are on, what data should be placed on each page, and so on. To facilitate this tracking, it's a good idea to create a custom class.

The following example shows a class called *TextDocument*. This class inherits from *PrintDocument* and adds three properties. *Text* stores an array of text lines, *PageNumber* reflects the last printed page, and *Offset* indicates the last line that was printed from the *Text* array.

```
public class TextDocument : PrintDocument {

    private string[] text;
    private int pageNumber;
    private int offset;

    public string[] Text {
        get {return text;}
        set {text = value;}
    }

    public int PageNumber {
        get {return pageNumber;}
        set {pageNumber = value;}
    }

    public int Offset {
        get {return offset;}
        set {offset = value;}
    }

    public TextDocument(string[] text) {
        this.Text = text;
    }
}
```

Depending on the type of material you are printing, you might want to modify this class. For example, you could store an array of image data, some content that should be used as a header or footer on each page, font information, or even the name of a file from which you want to read the information. Encapsulating the information in a single class makes it easier to print more than one document at the same time.

The code that initiates printing is the same as in recipe 8.13, only now it creates a *TextDocument* instance instead of a *PrintDocument* instance. The *PrintPage* event handler keeps track of the current line and checks if there is space on the page before attempting to print the next line. If a new page is needed, the *HasMorePages* property is set to *true* and the *PrintPage* event fires again for the next page. If not, the print operation is deemed complete.

The full form code is shown here:

```
using System;
using System.Windows.Forms;
using System.Drawing;
```

```
using System.Drawing.Printing;

public class MultiPagePrint : System.Windows.Forms.Form {

    private System.Windows.Forms.Button cmdPrint;

    // (Designer code omitted.)

    private void cmdPrint_Click(object sender, System.EventArgs e) {

        // Create a document with 100 lines.
        string[] printText = new string[101];
        for (int i=0; i < 101; i++) {

            printText[i] = i.ToString();
            printText[i] += ": The quick brown fox jumps over the lazy dog.";
        }

        PrintDocument doc = new TextDocument(printText);
        doc.PrintPage += new PrintPageEventHandler(this.Doc_PrintPage);

        PrintDialog dlgSettings = new PrintDialog();
        dlgSettings.Document = doc;

        // If the user clicked OK, print the document.
        if (dlgSettings.ShowDialog() == DialogResult.OK) {
            doc.Print();
        }
    }

    private void Doc_PrintPage(object sender, PrintPageEventArgs e) {

        // Retrieve the document that sent this event.
        TextDocument doc = (TextDocument)sender;

        // Define the font and determine the line height.
        Font font = new Font("Arial", 10);
        float lineHeight = font.GetHeight(e.Graphics);

        // Create variables to hold position on page.
        float x = e.MarginBounds.Left;
        float y = e.MarginBounds.Top;

        // Increment the page counter (to reflect the page that is about to be
        // printed).
        doc.PageNumber += 1;

        // Print all the information that can fit on the page.
```

```
// This loop ends when the next line would go over the margin bounds,
// or there are no more lines to print.

while ((y + lineHeight) < e.MarginBounds.Bottom &&
    doc.Offset <= doc.Text.GetUpperBound(0)) {

    e.Graphics.DrawString(doc.Text[doc.Offset], font,
        Brushes.Black, x, y);

    // Move to the next line of data.
    doc.Offset += 1;

    // Move the equivalent of one line down the page.
    y += lineHeight;
}

if (doc.Offset < doc.Text.GetUpperBound(0)) {

    // There is still at least one more page.
    // Signal this event to fire again.
    e.HasMorePages = true;

}else {

    // Printing is complete.
    doc.Offset = 0;
}
}
}
```

8.15 Print Wrapped Text

Problem

You need to parse a large block of text into distinct lines that fit on a page.

Solution

Use the *Graphics.DrawString* method overload that accepts a bounding rectangle.

Discussion

Often, you'll need to break a large block of text into separate lines that can be printed individually on a page. The .NET Framework can perform this task automatically, provided you use a version of the *Graphics.DrawString* method that accepts a bounding rectangle. You specify a rectangle that represents where you want the text to be displayed. The text is then wrapped automatically to fit within those confines.

The following code demonstrates this approach, using the bounding rectangle that represents the printable portion of the page. It prints a large block of text from a text box on the form.

```csharp
using System;
using System.Windows.Forms;
using System.Drawing;
using System.Drawing.Printing;

public class WrappedPrint : System.Windows.Forms.Form {

    private System.Windows.Forms.Button cmdPrint;

    // (Designer code omitted.)

    private void cmdPrint_Click(object sender, System.EventArgs e) {

        // Create the document and attach an event handler.
        string text = "Windows Server 2003 builds on the core strengths " +
          "of the Windows family of operating systems--security, " +
          "manageability, reliability, availability, and scalability. " +
          "Windows Server 2003 provides an application environment to " +
          "build, deploy, manage, and run XML Web services. " +
          "Additionally, advances in Windows Server 2003 provide many " +
          "benefits for developing applications.";
        PrintDocument doc = new ParagraphDocument(text);
        doc.PrintPage += new PrintPageEventHandler(this.Doc_PrintPage);

        // Allow the user to choose a printer and specify other settings.
        PrintDialog dlgSettings = new PrintDialog();
        dlgSettings.Document = doc;

        // If the user clicked OK, print the document.
        if (dlgSettings.ShowDialog() == DialogResult.OK) {
            doc.Print();
        }
    }

    private void Doc_PrintPage(object sender, PrintPageEventArgs e) {

        // Retrieve the document that sent this event.
        ParagraphDocument doc = (ParagraphDocument)sender;
```

```
            // Define the font and text.
            Font font = new Font("Arial", 15);

            e.Graphics.DrawString(doc.Text, font, Brushes.Black,
                e.MarginBounds, StringFormat.GenericDefault);
        }
    }

    public class ParagraphDocument : PrintDocument {

        private string text;

        public string Text {
            get {return text;}
            set {text = value;}
        }

        public ParagraphDocument(string text) {
            this.Text = text;
        }
    }
}
```

The wrapped text is shown in Figure 8-9.

Windows Server 2003 builds on the core strengths of the Windows
family of operating systems--security, manageability, reliability,
availability, and scalability. Windows Server 2003 provides an
application environment to build, deploy, manage, and run XML
Web services. Additionally, advances in Windows Server 2003
provide many benefits for developing applications.

Figure 8-9   The printed document with wrapping.

8.16 Show a Dynamic Print Preview

Problem

You need to use an on-screen preview that shows how a printed document will
look.

Solution

Use *PrintPreviewDialog* or *PrintPreviewControl* (both of which are found in the
System.Windows.Forms namespace).

Discussion

.NET provides two controls that can take a *PrintDocument* instance, run your printing code, and use it to generate a graphical on-screen preview. These controls are

- The *PrintPreviewDialog*, which shows a preview in a standalone window.

- The *PrintPreviewControl*, which shows a preview in one of your own custom forms.

To use a standalone print preview, you simply create a *PrintPrevewDialog* object, assign the document, and call the *PrintPreviewDialog.Show* method.

```
PrintPreviewDialog dlgPreview = new PrintPreviewDialog();
dlgPreview.Document = doc;
dlgPreview.Show();
```

The print preview window (shown in Figure 8-10) provides all the controls the user needs to move from page to page, zoom in, and so on. The window even provides a print button that allows the user to send the document directly to the printer. You can tailor the window to some extent by modifying the *PrintPreviewDialog* properties.

Figure 8-10   The *PrintPreviewDialog*.

You can also add *PrintPreviewControl* to any of your forms to show a preview alongside other information. In this case, you don't need to call the *Show* method. As soon as you set the *PrintPreviewControl.Document* property, the preview is generated. To clear the preview, set the *Document* property to *null*, and to refresh the preview, simply reassign the *Document* property. *PrintPreviewControl* only shows the preview pages, not any additional controls. However, you can add your own controls for zooming, tiling multiple pages, and so on. You simply need to adjust the *PrintPreviewControl* properties accordingly.

For example, consider the form shown in Figure 8-11. It incorporates a *PrintPreviewControl* and allows the user to select a zoom setting.

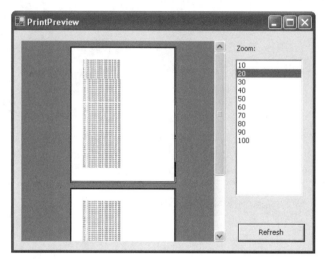

Figure 8-11 The *PrintPreviewControl* in a custom window.

Here's the complete form code:

```
using System;
using System.Windows.Forms;
using System.Drawing;
using System.Drawing.Printing;

public class PrintPreview : System.Windows.Forms.Form {

    private System.Windows.Forms.PrintPreviewControl printPreviewControl;
    private System.Windows.Forms.Button cmdPreview;
    private System.Windows.Forms.ListBox lstZoom;
    private System.Windows.Forms.Label label1;

    // (Designer code omitted.)

    private PrintDocument doc;
```

```
// (PrintDocument.PrintPage event handler code omitted.
// See code in recipe 8.14.)

private void PrintPreview_Load(object sender, System.EventArgs e) {

    // Set the allowed zoom settings.
    for (int i=1; i <= 10; i++) {
        lstZoom.Items.Add((i * 10).ToString());
    }

    // Create a document with 100 lines.
    string[] printText = new string[100];
    for (int i=0; i < 100; i++) {
        printText[i] = i.ToString();
        printText[i] += ": The quick brown fox jumps over the lazy dog.";
    }

    doc = new TextDocument(printText);
    doc.PrintPage += new PrintPageEventHandler(this.Doc_PrintPage);

    lstZoom.Text = "100";
    printPreviewControl.Zoom = 1;
    printPreviewControl.Document = doc;
    printPreviewControl.Rows = 2;
}

private void cmdPreview_Click(object sender, System.EventArgs e) {

    // Set the zoom.
    printPreviewControl.Zoom = Single.Parse(lstZoom.Text) / 100;

    // Show the full two pages, one above the other.
    printPreviewControl.Rows = 2;

    // Rebind the PrintDocument to refresh the preview.
    printPreviewControl.Document = doc;
}
}

// (TextDocument class code omitted. See recipe 8.14.)
```

8.17 Manage Print Jobs

Problem

You need to pause or resume a print job or a print queue.

Solution

Use Windows Management Instrumentation. You can retrieve information from the print queue using a query with the *Win32_PrintJob* class, and you can use the *Pause* and *Resume* methods of the WMI *Win32_PrintJob* and *Win32_Printer* classes to manage the queue.

Discussion

Windows Management Instrumentation allows you to retrieve a vast amount of system information using a query-like syntax. One of the tasks you can perform with WMI is to retrieve a list of outstanding print jobs, along with information about each one. You can also perform operations such as printing and resuming a job or all the jobs for a printer. In order to use WMI, you need to add a reference to the System.Management.dll assembly.

The following code shows a Windows-based application that interacts with the print queue. It performs a WMI query to get a list of all the outstanding jobs on the computer and displays the job ID for each one in a list box. When the user selects the item, a more complete WMI query is performed, and additional details about the print job are displayed in a text box. Finally, the user can click the Pause and Resume button after selecting a job to change its status.

```
using System;
using System.Windows.Forms;
using System.Management;
using System.Collections;

public class PrintQueueTest : System.Windows.Forms.Form {

    private System.Windows.Forms.ListBox lstJobs;
    private System.Windows.Forms.Button cmdRefresh;
    private System.Windows.Forms.TextBox txtJobInfo;
    private System.Windows.Forms.Button cmdPause;
    private System.Windows.Forms.Button cmdResume;
    private System.Windows.Forms.Label label1;
    private System.Windows.Forms.Label label2;

    // (Designer code omitted.)
    private void PrintQueueTest_Load(object sender, System.EventArgs e) {

        cmdRefresh_Click(null, null);
    }

    private void cmdRefresh_Click(object sender, System.EventArgs e) {
```

```csharp
    // Select all the outstanding print jobs.
    string query = "SELECT * FROM Win32_PrintJob";
    ManagementObjectSearcher jobQuery =
      new ManagementObjectSearcher(query);
    ManagementObjectCollection jobs = jobQuery.Get();

    // Add the jobs in the queue to the list box.
    lstJobs.Items.Clear();
    txtJobInfo.Text = "";
    foreach (ManagementObject job in jobs) {
        lstJobs.Items.Add(job["JobID"]);
    }
}

// This helper method performs a WMI query and returns the
// WMI job for the currently selected list box item.
private ManagementObject GetSelectedJob() {

    try {

        // Select the matching print job.
        string query = "SELECT * FROM Win32_PrintJob " +
          "WHERE JobID='" + lstJobs.Text + "'";
        ManagementObjectSearcher jobQuery =
          new ManagementObjectSearcher(query);
        ManagementObjectCollection jobs = jobQuery.Get();
        IEnumerator enumerator = jobs.GetEnumerator();
        enumerator.MoveNext();
        return (ManagementObject)enumerator.Current;

    }catch (InvalidOperationException){

        // the Current property of the enumerator is invalid
        return null;
    }
}

private void lstJobs_SelectedIndexChanged(object sender,
  System.EventArgs e) {

    ManagementObject job = GetSelectedJob();
    if (job == null) {
        txtJobInfo.Text = "";
        return;
    }

    // Display job information.
    string jobInfo = "Document: " + job["Document"].ToString();
```

```csharp
            jobInfo += Environment.NewLine;
            jobInfo += "DriverName: " + job["DriverName"].ToString();
            jobInfo += Environment.NewLine;
            jobInfo += "Status: " + job["Status"].ToString();
            jobInfo += Environment.NewLine;
            jobInfo += "Owner: " + job["Owner"].ToString();

            jobInfo += Environment.NewLine;
            jobInfo += "PagesPrinted: " +
            job["PagesPrinted"].ToString();
            jobInfo += Environment.NewLine;
            jobInfo += "TotalPages: " + job["TotalPages"].ToString();

            if (job["JobStatus"] != null) {
                txtJobInfo.Text += Environment.NewLine;
                txtJobInfo.Text += "JobStatus: " + job["JobStatus"].ToString();
            }
            if (job["StartTime"] != null) {
                jobInfo += Environment.NewLine;
                jobInfo += "StartTime: " + job["StartTime"].ToString();
            }

            txtJobInfo.Text = jobInfo;
        }

        private void cmdPause_Click(object sender, System.EventArgs e) {

            if (lstJobs.SelectedIndex == -1) return;
            ManagementObject job = GetSelectedJob();
            if (job == null) return;

            // Attempt to pause the job.
            int returnValue = Int32.Parse(
              job.InvokeMethod("Pause", null).ToString());

            // Display information about the return value.
            if (returnValue == 0) {
                MessageBox.Show("Successfully paused job.");

            }else {
                MessageBox.Show("Unrecognized return value when pausing job.");
            }
        }

        private void cmdResume_Click(object sender, System.EventArgs e) {

            if (lstJobs.SelectedIndex == -1) return;
            ManagementObject job = GetSelectedJob();
```

```
    if (job == null) return;

    if ((Int32.Parse(job["StatusMask"].ToString()) & 1) == 1) {

        // Attempt to resume the job.
        int returnValue = Int32.Parse(
          job.InvokeMethod("Resume", null).ToString());

        // Display information about the return value.
        if (returnValue == 0) {
            MessageBox.Show("Successfully resumed job.");

        }else if (returnValue == 5) {
            MessageBox.Show("Access denied.");

        }else {
            MessageBox.Show(
                "Unrecognized return value when resuming job.");
        }
    }
  }
}
```

The window for this application is shown in Figure 8-12.

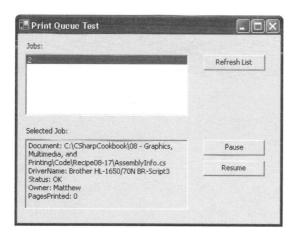

Figure 8-12   Retrieving information from the print queue.

Remember that Windows permissions might prevent you from pausing or removing a print job created by another user. In fact, permissions might even prevent you from retrieving status information and could cause an exception to be thrown.

> **Note** Other WMI methods that you might use in a printing scenario include *AddPrinterConnection*, *SetDefaultPrinter*, *CancelAllJobs*, and *PrintTestPage*, all of which work with the *Win32_Printer* class. For more information about using WMI to retrieve information about Windows hardware, refer to the Microsoft Developer Network (MSDN) documentation at *http://msdn.microsoft.com/library/en-us/wmisdk/ wmi/computer_system_hardware_classes.asp*.

9

Files, Directories, and I/O

The Microsoft .NET I/O classes fall into two basic categories. First are the classes that retrieve information from the file system and allow you to perform file system operations such as copying files and moving directories. Two examples include the *FileInfo* and the *DirectoryInfo* classes. Second, and possibly more important, are a broad range of classes that allow you to write and read data from all types of *streams*. Streams can correspond to binary or text files, a file in an isolated store, a network connection, or even a memory buffer. In all cases, the way you interact with a stream is the same. In this chapter, we'll look at the file system classes and a wide range of stream-based classes.

The recipes you'll find in this chapter cover the following topics.

- How to retrieve or modify information about a file or a directory (recipes 9.1, 9.2, 9.4, 9.5, and 9.16).

- How to copy, move, and delete files and directories (recipe 9.3).

- How to display a directory tree dynamically in a Microsoft Windows–based application (recipe 9.6) and use the common file dialog boxes (recipe 9.17).

- How to read and write text (recipe 9.7) and binary (recipe 9.8) files, as well as how to create temporary files (recipe 9.15) and files in a user-specific isolated store (recipe 9.18).

- How to read files asynchronously (recipe 9.9).

- How to search for specific files (recipe 9.10) and test files for equality (recipe 9.11).

- How to work with strings that contain path information (recipes 9.12 to 9.14).

■   How to monitor the file system for changes (recipe 9.19).

■   How to write to a COM port (recipe 9.20).

9.1 Retrieving Information About a File or Directory

Problem

You need to retrieve information about a file or directory, such as its attributes or creation date.

Solution

Create a *System.IO.FileInfo* object for a file or a *System.IO.DirectoryInfo* object for a directory, supplying the path in the constructor. You can then retrieve information through the properties of the object.

Discussion

To create a *FileInfo* or a *DirectoryInfo* object, you simply supply a relative or fully qualified path in the constructor. You can retrieve information about the file or directory through the corresponding object properties. Table 9-1 lists the members that are declared in *FileInfo* or *DirectoryInfo* classes.

Table 9-1   Members for Files and Directories

Member	Applies To	Description
Exists	*FileInfo* and *DirectoryInfo*	Returns *true* or *false*, depending on whether a file or a directory exists at the specified location.
Attributes	*FileInfo* and *DirectoryInfo*	Returns one or more values from the *System.IO.FileAttributes* enumeration, which represents the attributes of the file or the directory.
CreationTime, *LastAccessTime*, and *LastWriteTime*	*FileInfo* and *DirectoryInfo*	Return *System.DateTime* instances that describe when a file or a directory was created, last accessed, and last updated, respectively.
FullName, Name, and *Extension*	*FileInfo* and *DirectoryInfo*	Returns a *string* that represents the fully qualified name, the directory or the file name (with extension), and the extension on its own.

Table 9-1   Members for Files and Directories *(continued)*

Member	Applies To	Description
Length	*FileInfo*	Returns the file size as a number of bytes.
DirectoryName and *Directory*	*FileInfo*	*DirectoryName* returns the name of the parent directory as a *string*, whereas *Directory* returns a full *DirectoryInfo* object that represents the parent directory and allows you to retrieve more information about it.
Parent and *Root*	*DirectoryInfo*	Returns a *DirectoryInfo* object that represents the parent or root directory.
CreateSubdirectory	*DirectoryInfo*	Creates a directory with the specified name in the directory represented by the *DirectoryInfo* object. It also returns a new *DirectoryInfo* object that represents the subdirectory.
GetDirectories	*DirectoryInfo*	Returns an array of *DirectoryInfo* objects, with one element for each subdirectory contained in this directory.
GetFiles	*DirectoryInfo*	Returns an array of *FileInfo* objects, with one element for each file contained in this directory.

There are two important considerations for working with *FileInfo* and *DirectoryInfo* objects:

- The full set of *FileInfo* or *DirectoryInfo* object properties is read the first time you interrogate any property. If the file changes after this point, you must call the *Refresh* method to update the properties.

- You won't encounter an error if you specify a path that doesn't correspond to an actual, existing file or directory when creating a *FileInfo* or *DirectoryInfo* object. Instead, you'll receive an object that represents a file or directory that doesn't exist—its *Exists* property will be *false*. You can use this object to create the file or directory using the *Create* method. If you attempt to read most other properties, however, a *FileNotFoundException* or *DirectoryNotFoundException* is thrown.

The following Console application takes a file path from a command-line argument and then displays information about the file and the containing directory.

```csharp
using System;
using System.IO;

public class FileInformation {

    private static void Main(string[] args) {

        if (args.Length == 0) {

            Console.WriteLine("Please supply a file name.");
            return;
        }

        FileInfo file = new FileInfo(args[0]);

        // Display file information.
        Console.WriteLine("Checking file: " + file.Name);
        Console.WriteLine("File exists: " + file.Exists.ToString());

        if (file.Exists) {

            Console.Write("File created: ");
            Console.WriteLine(file.CreationTime.ToString());
            Console.Write("File last updated: ");
            Console.WriteLine(file.LastWriteTime.ToString());
            Console.Write("File last accessed: ");
            Console.WriteLine(file.LastAccessTime.ToString());
            Console.Write("File size (bytes): ");
            Console.WriteLine(file.Length.ToString());
            Console.Write("File attribute list: ");
            Console.WriteLine(file.Attributes.ToString());

        }
        Console.WriteLine();

        // Display directory information.
        DirectoryInfo dir = file.Directory;

        Console.WriteLine("Checking directory: " + dir.Name);
        Console.WriteLine("In directory: " + dir.Parent.Name);
        Console.Write("Directory exists: ");
        Console.WriteLine(dir.Exists.ToString());

        if (dir.Exists) {
            Console.Write("Directory created: ");
            Console.WriteLine(dir.CreationTime.ToString());
```

```
        Console.Write("Directory last updated: ");
        Console.WriteLine(dir.LastWriteTime.ToString());
        Console.Write("Directory last accessed: ");
        Console.WriteLine(dir.LastAccessTime.ToString());
        Console.Write("Directory attribute list: ");
        Console.WriteLine(dir.Attributes.ToString());
        Console.WriteLine("Directory contains: " +
            dir.GetFiles().Length.ToString() + " files");
    }

    Console.ReadLine();
}
}
```

If you execute the command **FileInformation c:\windows\win.ini**
here is the output you might expect:

```
Checking file: win.ini
File exists: True
File created: 2001 00 23 8:00:00 AM
File last updated: 2003-03-22 9:55:16 AM
File last accessed: 2003-05-26 2:21:53 PM
File size (bytes): 2128
File attribute list: Archive

Checking directory: windows
In directory: c:\
Directory exists: True
Directory created: 2000-01-01 8:03:33 AM
Directory last updated: 2003-05-26 2:25:25 PM
Directory last accessed: 2003-05-26 2:25:25 PM
Directory attribute list: Directory
Directory contains: 147 files
```

> **Note**   Instead of using the instance methods of the *FileInfo* and *DirectoryInfo* classes, you can use the *static File* and *Directory* classes. The *File* and *Directory* methods expose most of the same functionality, but they require you to submit the file name or path with every method invocation. In cases where you have to perform multiple operations with the same file or directory, using the *FileInfo* and *DirectoryInfo* classes will be faster, because they will perform security checks only once.

9.2 Set File and Directory Attributes

Problem

You need to test or modify file or directory attributes.

Solution

Create a *System.IO.FileInfo* object for a file or a *System.IO.DirectoryInfo* object for a directory and use the bitwise AND (*&*) and OR (*|*) arithmetic operators to modify the value of the *Attributes* property.

Discussion

The *FileInfo.Attributes* and *DirectoryInfo.Attributes* properties represent file attributes such as archive, system, hidden, read-only, compressed, and encrypted. (Refer to the MSDN reference for the full list.) Because a file can possess any combination of attributes, the *Attributes* property accepts a combination of enumerated values. To individually test for a single attribute or change a single attribute, you need to use bitwise arithmetic.

For example, consider the following code, which takes a read-only test file and checks for the read-only attribute.

```
using System;
using System.IO;

public class Attributes {

    private static void Main() {

        // This file has the archive and read-only attributes.
        FileInfo file = new FileInfo("data.txt");

        // This displays the string "ReadOnly, Archive "
        Console.WriteLine(file.Attributes.ToString());

        // This test fails, because other attributes are set.
        if (file.Attributes == FileAttributes.ReadOnly) {
            Console.WriteLine("File is read-only (faulty test).");
        }

        // This test succeeds, because it filters out just the
        // read-only attribute.
        if ((file.Attributes & FileAttributes.ReadOnly) ==
```

```
        FileAttributes.ReadOnly) {
          Console.WriteLine("File is read-only (correct test).");
        }

      Console.ReadLine();
    }
}
```

> **Note**   To understand how the preceding code works, you need to realize that the *Attributes* setting is made up (in binary) of a series of ones and zeros, such as 00010011. Each *1* represents an attribute that is present, while each *0* represents an attribute that is not. When you use a bitwise AND (&) operation, it compares each individual digit against each digit in the enumerated value. For example, if you bitwise AND a value of 00100001 (representing an individual file's archive and read only attributes) with the enumerated value 00000001 (which represents the read-only flag), the resulting value will be 00000001—it will have a 1 only where it can be matched in both values.

When setting an attribute, you must also use bitwise arithmetic. In this case, it's needed to ensure that you don't inadvertently wipe out the other attributes.

```
// This adds just the read only attribute.
file.Attributes = file.Attributes | FileAttributes.ReadOnly;

// This removes just the read-only attribute.
file.Attributes = file.Attributes & ~FileAttributes.ReadOnly;
```

9.3 Copy, Move, or Delete a File or a Directory

Problem

You need to copy, move, or delete a file or directory.

Solution

Create a *System.IO.FileInfo* object for a file or a *System.IO.DirectoryInfo* object for a directory, supplying the path in the constructor. You can then use the object's methods to copy, move, and delete.

Discussion

The *FileInfo* and *DirectoryInfo* classes include a host of valuable methods for manipulating files and directories. Table 9-2 shows methods for the *FileInfo* class, while Table 9-3 shows methods for the *DirectoryInfo* class.

Table 9-2 Methods for Manipulating a *FileInfo* Object

Member	Description
CopyTo	Copies a file to the new path and file name specified as a parameter. It also returns a new *FileInfo* object that represents the new (copied) file. You can supply an optional additional parameter of *true* to allow overwriting.
Create and *CreateText*	*Create* creates the specified file and returns a *FileStream* object that you can use to write to it. *CreateText* performs the same task, but returns a *StreamWriter* object that wraps the stream. For more information about writing files, see recipes 9.7 and 9.8.
Open, *OpenRead*, *Open-Text*, and *OpenWrite*	Open a file (provided it exists). *OpenRead* and *OpenText* open a file in read-only mode, returning a *FileStream* or a *StreamReader* object. *OpenWrite* opens a file in write-only mode, returning a *FileStream*. For more information about reading files, see recipes 9.7 and 9.8.
Delete	Removes the file, if it exists.
MoveTo	Moves the file to the new path and file name specified as a parameter. *MoveTo* can also be used to rename a file without changing its location.

Table 9-3 Methods for Manipulating a *DirectoryInfo* Object

Member	Description
Create	Creates the specified directory. If the path specifies multiple directories that don't exist, they will all be created at once.
CreateSubdirectory	Creates a directory with the specified name in the directory represented by the *DirectoryInfo* object. It also returns a new *DirectoryInfo* object that represents the subdirectory.
Delete	Removes the directory, if it exists. If you want to delete a directory that contains other directories, you must use the overloaded *Delete* method that accepts a parameter named *recursive* and set it to *true*.
MoveTo	Moves the directory (contents and all) to a new path. *MoveTo* can also be used to rename a directory without changing its location.

One useful feature that's missing from the *DirectoryInfo* class is a copy method. Fortunately, you can write this logic easily enough by relying on recursive logic and the *FileInfo* object. Here's a helper function that can copy any directory, and its contents:

```
using System;
using System.IO;

public class FileSystemUtil {

    public static void CopyDirectory(DirectoryInfo source,
        DirectoryInfo destination) {

        if (!destination.Exists) {
            destination.Create();
        }

        // Copy all files.
        FileInfo[] files = source.GetFiles();
        foreach (FileInfo file in files) {

            file.CopyTo(Path.Combine(destination.FullName, file.Name));
        }

        // Process sub-directories.
        DirectoryInfo[] dirs = sourceDir.GetDirectories();
        foreach (DirectoryInfo dir in dirs) {

            // Get destination directory.
            string destinationDir = Path.Combine(destination.FullName,
                dir.Name);

            // Call CopyDirectory() recursively.
            CopyDirectory(dir, new DirectoryInfo(destinationDir));
        }
    }
}
```

Here's a simple test application that copies directories based on the supplied command-line arguments:

```
public class CopyDir {

    private static void Main(string[] args) {

        if (args.Length != 2) {

            Console.WriteLine("usage:  " +
                "CopyDir [sourcePath] [destinationPath]");
```

```
        return;
    }

    DirectoryInfo sourceDir = new DirectoryInfo(args[0]);
    DirectoryInfo destinationDir = new DirectoryInfo(args[1]);

    FileSystemUtil.CopyDirectory(new DirectoryInfo(sourceDir),
      new DirectoryInfo(destinationDir));

    Console.WriteLine("Copy complete.");
    Console.ReadLine();
    }
}
```

9.4 Calculate the Size of a Directory

Problem

You need to calculate the size of all files contained in a directory (and option-ally, its subdirectories).

Solution

Examine all the files in a directory, and add together their *FileInfo.Length* prop-erties. Use recursive logic to include the size of files in contained subdirectories.

Discussion

The *DirectoryInfo* class does not provide any property that returns size infor-mation. However, you can easily calculate the size of all files contained in a directory using the *FileInfo.Length* property.

Here's a method that uses this technique and optionally examines con-tained directories recursively:

```
using System;
using System.IO;

public class FileSystemUtil {

    public static long CalculateDirectorySize(DirectoryInfo directory,
      bool includeSubdirectories) {

        long totalSize = 0;
```

```
        // Examine all contained files.
        FileInfo[] files = directory.GetFiles();
        foreach (FileInfo file in files) {
            totalSize += file.Length;
        }

        // Examine all contained directories.
        if (includeSubdirectories) {

            DirectoryInfo[] dirs = directory.GetDirectories();
            foreach (DirectoryInfo dir in dirs) {
                totalSize += CalculateDirectorySize(dir, true);
            }
        }

        return totalSize;
    }
}
```

Here's a simple test application:

```
using System;
using System.IO;

public class CalculateDirSize {

    private static void Main(string[] args) {

        if (args.Length == 0) {

            Console.WriteLine("Please supply a directory path.");
            return;
        }

        DirectoryInfo dir = new DirectoryInfo(args[0]);
        Console.WriteLine("Total size: " +
          FileSystemUtil.CalculateDirectorySize(dir, true).ToString() +
          " bytes.");
        Console.ReadLine();
    }
}
```

9.5 Retrieve Version Information for a File

Problem

You want to retrieve file version information such as the publisher of a file, its revision number, associated comments, and so on.

Solution

Use the *static GetVersionInfo* method of the *System.Diagnostics.FileVersionInfo* class.

Discussion

The .NET Framework allows you to retrieve file information without resorting to the Windows API. Instead, you simply need to use the *FileVersionInfo* class and call the *GetVersionInfo* method with the file name as a parameter. You can then retrieve extensive information through the *FileVersionInfo* properties.

The *FileVersionInfo* properties are too numerous to list here, but the following code snippet shows an example of what you might retrieve:

```
using System;
using System.Diagnostics;

public class VersionInfo {

    private static void Main(string[] args) {

        if (args.Length == 0) {

            Console.WriteLine("Please supply a  file name.");
            return;
        }

        FileVersionInfo info = FileVersionInfo.GetVersionInfo(args[0]);

        // Display version information.
        Console.WriteLine("Checking File: " + info. file name);
        Console.WriteLine("Product Name: " + info.ProductName);
        Console.WriteLine("Product Version: " + info.ProductVersion);
        Console.WriteLine("Company Name: " + info.CompanyName);
        Console.WriteLine("File Version: " + info.FileVersion);
        Console.WriteLine("File Description: " + info.FileDescription);
        Console.WriteLine("Original  file name: " + info.Original file name);
        Console.WriteLine("Legal Copyright: " + info.LegalCopyright);
        Console.WriteLine("InternalName: " + info.InternalName);
        Console.WriteLine("IsDebug: " + info.IsDebug);
        Console.WriteLine("IsPatched: " + info.IsPatched);
        Console.WriteLine("IsPreRelease: " + info.IsPreRelease);
        Console.WriteLine("IsPrivateBuild: " + info.IsPrivateBuild);
        Console.WriteLine("IsSpecialBuild: " + info.IsSpecialBuild);

        Console.ReadLine();
    }
}
```

Here's the output this code produces if you run the command **Version-Info c:\windows\explorer.exe**:

```
Checking File: c:\windows\explorer.exe
Product Name: Microsoftr Windowsr Operating System
Product Version: 6.00.2600.0000
Company Name: Microsoft Corporation
File Version: 6.00.2600.0000 (xpclient.010817-1148)
File Description: Windows Explorer
Original  file name: EXPLORER.EXE
Legal Copyright: c Microsoft Corporation. All rights reserved.
InternalName: explorer
IsDebug: False
IsPatched; False
IsPreRelease: False
IsPrivateBuild: False
IsSpecialBuild: False
```

9.6 Show a Just-in-Time Directory Tree in the *TreeView* Control

Problem

You need to display a directory tree in the *TreeView* control. However, filling the directory tree structure at startup is too time consuming.

Solution

Fill the first level of directories in the *TreeView* control, and add a hidden dummy node to each directory branch. React to the *TreeView.BeforeExpand* event to fill in subdirectories in a branch just before it's displayed.

Discussion

You can use recursion to build an entire directory tree. However, scanning the file system in this way can be slow, particularly for large drives. For this reason, professional file management software programs (including Windows Explorer) use a different technique—querying the necessary directory information when the user requests it.

The *TreeView* control is particularly well suited to this approach because it provides a *BeforeExpand* event that fires before a new level of nodes is displayed. You can use a placeholder (such as an asterisk or empty *TreeNode*) in all the directory branches that aren't filled in. This allows you to fill in parts of the directory tree as they are displayed.

To use this type of solution, you need the following three ingredients:

- A *Fill* method that adds a single level of directory nodes based on a single directory. You'll use this method to fill directory levels as they are expanded.

- A basic *Form.Load* event handler that uses the *Fill* method to add the first level of directories for the drive.

- A *TreeView.BeforeExpand* event handler that reacts when the user expands a node and calls the *Fill* method if this directory information has not yet been added.

Here's the full form code for this solution:

```csharp
using System;
using System.IO;
using System.Drawing;
using System.Windows.Forms;

public class DirectoryTree : System.Windows.Forms.Form {

    private System.Windows.Forms.TreeView treeDirectory;

    // (Designer code omitted.)

    private void Fill(TreeNode dirNode) {

        DirectoryInfo dir = new DirectoryInfo(dirNode.FullPath);

        // An exception could be thrown in this code if you don't
        // have sufficient security permissions for a file or directory.
        // You can catch and then ignore this exception.
        foreach (DirectoryInfo dirItem in dir.GetDirectories()) {

            // Add node for the directory.
            TreeNode newNode = new TreeNode(dirItem.Name);
            dirNode.Nodes.Add(newNode);
            newNode.Nodes.Add("*");
        }
    }

    private void DirectoryTree_Load(object sender, System.EventArgs e) {

        // Set the first node.
        TreeNode rootNode = new TreeNode("C:\\");
        treeDirectory.Nodes.Add(rootNode);
```

```
        // Fill the first level and expand it.
        Fill(rootNode);
        treeDirectory.Nodes[0].Expand();
    }

    private void treeDirectory_BeforeExpand(object sender,
        System.Windows.Forms.TreeViewCancelEventArgs e) {

        // If a dummy node is found, remove it and read the
        // real directory list.
        if (e.Node.Nodes[0].Text == "*") {

            e.Node.Nodes.Clear();
            Fill(e.Node);
        }
    }
}
```

Figure 9-1 shows the directory tree in action.

Figure 9-1   A directory tree with the TreeView.

9.7 Read and Write a Text File

Problem

You need to write data to a sequential text file using ASCII, Unicode, or UTF-8 encoding.

Solution

Create a new *System.IO.FileStream* object that references the file. To write the file, wrap the *FileStream* in a *System.IO.StreamWriter* and use the overloaded

Write method. To read the file, wrap the *FileStream* in a *System.IO.Stream-Reader* and use the *Read* or *ReadLine* method.

Discussion

.NET allows you to write or read text with any stream by using the *Stream-Writer* and *StreamReader* classes. When writing data with the *StreamWriter*, you use the *StreamWriter.Write* method. This method is overloaded to support all the common C# .NET data types, including strings, chars, integers, floating point numbers, decimals, and so on. However, the *Write* method always converts the supplied data to text. If you want to be able to convert the text back to its original data type, you should use the *WriteLine* method to make sure each value is placed on a separate line.

There is more than one way to represent a string in binary form, depending on the encoding you use. The most common encodings include:

■ ASCII, which encodes each character in a string using 7 bits. ASCII-encoded data can't contain extended Unicode characters. When using ASCII encoding in .NET, the bits will be padded and the resulting byte array will have 1 byte for each character.

■ Full Unicode (or UTF-16), which represents each character in a string using 16 bits. The resulting byte array will have 2 bytes for each character.

■ UTF-7 Unicode, which uses 7 bits for ordinary ASCII characters and multiple 7-bit pairs for extended characters. This encoding is primarily for use with 7-bit protocols such as mail, and it isn't regularly used.

■ UTF-8 Unicode, which uses 8 bits for ordinary ASCII characters and multiple 8-bit pairs for extended characters. The resulting byte array will have 1 byte for each character (provided there are no extended characters).

.NET provides a class for each type of encoding in the *System.Text* namespace. When using the *StreamReader* and *StreamWriter*, you can specify the encoding you want to use or simply use the default UTF-8 encoding.

When reading information, you use the *Read* or *ReadLine* method of the *StreamReader*. The *Read* method reads a single character, or the number of characters you specify, and returns the data as a char or char array. The *Read-Line* method returns a string with the content of an entire line.

The following Console application shows a simple demonstration that writes and then reads a text file:

```csharp
using System;
using System.IO;
using System.Text;

public class TextFileTest {

    private static void Main() {

        // Create a new file.
        FileStream fs = new FileStream("test.txt", FileMode.Create);

        // Create a writer and specify the encoding.
        // The default (UTF-8) supports special Unicode characters,
        // but encodes all standard characters in the same way as
        // ASCII encoding.
        StreamWriter w = new StreamWriter(fs, Encoding.UTF8);

        // Write a decimal, string, and char.
        w.WriteLine(124.23M);
        w.WriteLine("Test string");
        w.WriteLine('!');

        // Make sure all data is written from the internal buffer.
        w.Flush();

        // Close the file.
        w.Close();
        fs.Close();

        Console.WriteLine("Press Enter to read the information.");
        Console.ReadLine();

        // Open the file in read-only mode.
        fs = new FileStream("test.txt", FileMode.Open);
        StreamReader r = new StreamReader(fs, Encoding.UTF8);

        // Read the data and convert it to the appropriate data type.
        Console.WriteLine(Decimal.Parse(r.ReadLine()));
        Console.WriteLine(r.ReadLine());
        Console.WriteLine(Char.Parse(r.ReadLine()));

        r.Close();
        fs.Close();

        Console.ReadLine();
    }
}
```

9.8 Read and Write a Binary File

Problem

You need to write data to a binary file, with strong data typing.

Solution

Create a new *System.IO.FileStream* object that references the file. To write the file, wrap the *FileStream* in a *System.IO.BinaryWriter* and use the overloaded *Write* method. To read the file, wrap the *FileStream* in a *System.IO.Binary-Reader* and use the *Read* method that corresponds to the expected data type.

Discussion

.NET allows you to write or read binary data with any stream by using the *Binary-Writer* and *BinaryReader* classes. When writing data with the *BinaryWriter*, you use the *BinaryWriter.Write* method. This method is overloaded to support all the common C# .NET data types, including strings, chars, integers, floating point numbers, decimals, and so on. The information will then be encoded as a series of bytes and written to the file. You can configure the encoding used for strings by using an overloaded constructor that accepts a *System.Text.Encoding* object, as described in recipe 9.7.

You must be particularly fastidious with data types when using binary files. This is because when you retrieve the information, you must use one of the strongly typed *Read* methods from the *BinaryReader*. For example, to retrieve *decimal* data, you use *ReadDecimal*. To read a *string*, you use *Read-String*. (The *BinaryWriter* always records the length of a string when it writes it to a binary file to prevent any possibility of error.)

The following Console application shows a simple demonstration that writes and then reads a binary file:

```
using System;
using System.IO;

public class BinaryFileTest {

    private static void Main() {

        // Create a new file and writer.
        FileStream fs = new FileStream("test.txt", FileMode.Create);
        BinaryWriter w = new BinaryWriter(fs);
```

```
// Write a decimal, two strings, and a char.
w.Write(124.23M);
w.Write("Test string");
w.Write("Test string 2");
w.Write('!');

// Make sure all data is written from the internal buffer.
w.Flush();

// Close the file.
w.Close();
fs.Close();

Console.WriteLine("Press Enter to read the information.");
Console.ReadLine();

// Open the file in read-only mode.
fs = new FileStream("test.txt", FileMode.Open);

// Display the raw information in the file.
StreamReader sr = new StreamReader(fs);
Console.WriteLine(sr.ReadToEnd());
Console.WriteLine();

// Read the data and convert it to the appropriate data type.
fs.Position = 0;
BinaryReader br = new BinaryReader(fs);
Console.WriteLine(br.ReadDecimal());
Console.WriteLine(br.ReadString());
Console.WriteLine(br.ReadString());
Console.WriteLine(br.ReadChar());

fs.Close();

Console.ReadLine();
    }
}
```

9.9 Read a File Asynchronously

Problem

You need to read data from a file without blocking the execution of your code. This technique is commonly used if the file is stored on a slow backing store (such as a networked drive in a wide area network).

Solution

Create a separate class that will read the file asynchronously. Start reading a block of data using the *FileStream.BeginRead* method, and supply a callback method. When the callback is triggered, retrieve the data by calling *FileStream.EndRead*, process it, and read the next block asynchronously with *BeginRead*.

Discussion

The *FileStream* includes basic support for asynchronous use through the *BeginRead* and *EndRead* methods. Using these methods, you can read a block of data on one of the threads provided by the .NET thread pool, without needing to directly use the threading classes in the *System.Threading* namespace.

When reading a file asynchronously, you choose the amount of data that you want to read at a time. Depending on the situation, you might want to read a very small amount of data at a time (for example, if you are copying it block by block to another file) or a relatively large amount of data (for example, if you need a certain amount of information before your processing logic can start). You specify the block size when calling *BeginRead*, and you pass a buffer where the data will be placed. Because the *BeginRead* and the *EndRead* methods need to be able to access many of the same pieces of information, such as the *FileStream*, the buffer, the block size, and so on, it's usually easiest to encapsulate your asynchronous file reading code in a single class.

For example, consider the *AsyncProcessor* class shown in the following code. It provides a *public StartProcess* method, which starts an asynchronous read. Every time the read operation finishes, the *OnCompletedRead* callback is triggered and the block of data is processed. If there is more data in the file, a new asynchronous read operation is started. The *AsyncProcessor* reads 2 kilobytes (2048 bytes) at a time.

```
using System;
using System.IO;
using System.Threading;

public class AsyncProcessor {

    private Stream inputStream;

    // The amount that will be read in one block (2 KB).
    private int bufferSize = 2048;

    public int BufferSize {
        get {return bufferSize;}
        set {bufferSize = value;}
    }
```

```csharp
// The buffer that will hold the retrieved data.
private byte[] buffer;

public AsyncProcessor(string  file name) {

    buffer = new byte[bufferSize];

    // Open the file, specifying true for asynchronous support.
    inputStream = new FileStream( file name, FileMode.Open,
      FileAccess.Read, FileShare.Read, bufferSize, true);
}

public void StartProcess() {

    // Start the asynchronous read, which will fill the butter.
    inputStream.BeginRead(buffer, 0, buffer.Length,
      new AsyncCallback(OnCompletedRead), null);
}

private void OnCompletedRead(IAsyncResult asyncResult) {

    // One block has been read asynchronously.
    // Retrieve the data.
    int bytesRead = inputStream.EndRead(asyncResult);

    // If no bytes are read, the stream is at the end of the file.
    if (bytesRead > 0) {

        // Pause to simulate processing this block of data.
        Console.WriteLine("\t[ASYNC READER]: Read one block.");
        Thread.Sleep(TimeSpan.FromMilliseconds(20));

        // Begin to read the next block asynchronously.
        inputStream.BeginRead(
        buffer, 0, buffer.Length, new AsyncCallback(OnCompletedRead),
          null);

    }else {

        // End the operation.
        Console.WriteLine("\t[ASYNC READER]: Complete.");
        inputStream.Close();
    }
}
}
```

The following example shows a Console application that uses the *Async-Processor* to read a 2-megabyte file.

```
public class AsynchronousIO {

    public static void Main() {

        // Create a 1 MB test file.
        FileStream fs = new FileStream("test.txt", FileMode.Create);
        fs.SetLength(1000000);
        fs.Close();

        // Start the asynchronous file processor on another thread.
        AsyncProcessor asyncIO = new AsyncProcessor("test.txt");
        asyncIO.StartProcess();

        // At the same time, do some other work.
        // In this example, we simply loop for 10 seconds.
        DateTime startTime = DateTime.Now;
        while (DateTime.Now.Subtract(startTime).TotalSeconds < 10) {

            Console.WriteLine("[MAIN THREAD]: Doing some work.");

            // Pause to simulate a time-consuming operation.
            Thread.Sleep(TimeSpan.FromMilliseconds(100));
        }

        Console.WriteLine("[MAIN THREAD]: Complete.");
        Console.ReadLine();

        // Remove the test file.
        File.Delete("test.txt");
    }
}
```

This is an example of the output you'll see when you run this test:

```
[MAIN THREAD]: Doing some work.
        [ASYNC READER]: Read one block.
        [ASYNC READER]: Read one block.
[MAIN THREAD]: Doing some work.
        [ASYNC READER]: Read one block.
        [ASYNC READER]: Read one block.
        [ASYNC READER]: Read one block.
        [ASYNC READER]: Read one block.
[MAIN THREAD]: Doing some work.
        [ASYNC READER]: Read one block.
        [ASYNC READER]: Read one block.
        [ASYNC READER]: Read one block.
        . . .
```

9.10 Find Files That Match a Wildcard Expression

Problem

You need to process multiple files based on a filter expression (such as *.dll or mysheet20??.xls).

Solution

Use the overloaded version of the *System.IO.DirectoryInfo.GetFiles* method that accepts a filter expression and returns an array of *FileInfo* objects.

Discussion

The *DirectoryInfo* and *Directory* objects both provide a way to search the current directories for files that match a specific filter expression. These search expressions can use the standard ? and * wildcards. You can use a similar technique to retrieve directories that match a specified search pattern by using the overloaded *DirectoryInfo.GetDirectories* method.

For example, the following code retrieves the names of all the files in a specified directory that match a specified filter string. The directory and filter expression are submitted as command-line arguments. The code then iterates through the retrieved *FileInfo* collection of matching files and displays the name and size of each one.

```
using System;
using System.IO;

public class WildcardTest {

    private static void Main(string[] args) {

        if (args.Length != 2) {
            Console.WriteLine(
              "USAGE:  WildcardTest [directory] [filterExpression]");
            return;
        }

        DirectoryInfo dir = new DirectoryInfo(args[0]);
        FileInfo[] files = dir.GetFiles(args[1]);

        // Display the name of all the files.
        foreach (FileInfo file in files) {
            Console.Write("Name: " + file.Name + "  ");
            Console.WriteLine("Size: " + file.Length.ToString());
        }
```

```
        Console.ReadLine();
    }
}
```

If you want to search subdirectories, you'll need to add your own recursion. Several of the recipes in this chapter demonstrate recursive file processing logic, including recipes 9.3 and 9.4.

9.11 Test Two Files for Equality

Problem

You need to quickly compare the content of two files, and determine if it matches exactly.

Solution

Calculate the hash code of each file using the *System.Security.Cryptography.HashAlgorithm* class, and compare the hash codes.

Discussion

There are a number of ways you might want to compare more than one file. For example, you could examine a portion of the file for similar data, or you could read through each file byte by byte, comparing each byte as you go. Both of these approaches are valid, but in some cases it's more convenient to use a *hash code* algorithm.

A hash code algorithm generates a small (typically about 20 bytes) binary fingerprint for a file. While it's *possible* for different files to generate the same hash codes, that's statistically unlikely to occur. In fact, even a minor change (for example, modifying a single bit in the source file) has an approximately 50 percent chance of independently changing each bit in the hash code. For this reason, hash codes are often used in security code to detect data tampering. (Hash codes are discussed in more detail in Chapter 14.)

To create a hash code, you must first create a *HashAlgorithm* object, typically by calling the *static HashAlgorithm.Create* method. You can then call *HashAlgorithm.ComputeHash*, which returns a byte array with the hash data.

The following code demonstrates a simple Console application that reads two file names that are supplied as arguments and tests the files for equality.

```
using System;
using System.IO;
using System.Security.Cryptography;

public class CompareFiles {

    private static void Main(string[] args) {

        if (args.Length != 2) {
            Console.WriteLine("USAGE:  CompareFiles [ file name] [ file
name]");
            return;
        }

        Console.WriteLine("Comparing " + args[0] + " and " + args[1]);

        // Create the hashing object.
        HashAlgorithm hashAlg = HashAlgorithm.Create();

        // Calculate the hash for the first file.
        FileStream fsA = new FileStream(args[0], FileMode.Open);
        byte[] hashBytesA = hashAlg.ComputeHash(fsA);
        fsA.Close();

        // Calculate the hash for the second file.
        FileStream fsB = new FileStream(args[1], FileMode.Open);
        byte[] hashBytesB = hashAlg.ComputeHash(fsB);
        fsB.Close();

        // Compare the hashes.
        if (BitConverter.ToString(hashBytesA) ==
            BitConverter.ToString(hashBytesB)) {

            Console.WriteLine("Files match.");

        }else {

            Console.WriteLine("No match.");
        }

        Console.ReadLine();
    }
}
```

The hashes are compared by converting them into strings. Alternatively, you could compare them by iterating over the byte array and comparing each value. This approach would be slightly faster, but because the overhead of converting 20 bytes into a string is minimal, it's not required.

9.12 Manipulate Strings Representing file names

Problem

You want to retrieve a portion of a path or verify that a file path is in a normal (standardized) form.

Solution

Process the path using the *System.IO.Path* class. You can use *Path.GetFileName* to retrieve a file name from a path, *Path.ChangeExtension* to modify the extension portion of a path string, and *Path.Combine* to create a fully qualified path without worrying about whether or not your directory includes a trailing directory separation (\) character.

Discussion

File paths are often difficult to work with in code because there is an essentially unlimited number of ways to represent the same directory. For example, you might use an absolute path (c:\temp), a UNC path (\\MyServer\\MyShare\temp), or one of many possible relative paths (c:\temp\MyFiles\..\ or c:\temp\MyFiles\..\..\temp).

The easiest way to handle file system paths is to use the *static* methods of the *Path* class to make sure you have the information you expect. For example, here's how you take a file name that might include a qualified path and extract just the file name:

```
string  file name = @"..\System\MyFile.txt";
file name = Path.GetFileName(file name);

// Now file name = "MyFile.txt"
```

And here's how you might append the file name to a directory path using the *Path.Combine* method:

```
string filename = @"..\..\myfile.txt";
string fullPath = @"c:\Temp";

file name = Path.GetFileName(file name);
fullPath = Path.Combine(fullPath, filename);

// (fullPath is now "c:\Temp\myfile.txt")
```

The advantage of this approach is that a trailing backslash (\\) is automatically added to the path name if required. The *Path* class also provides the following useful methods for manipulating path information:

- *ChangeExtension* modifies the current extension of the file in a string. If no extension is specified, the current extension will be removed.

- *GetDirectoryName* returns all the directory information, which is the text between the first and last directory separators (\\).

- *GetFileNameWithoutExtension* is similar to *GetFileName*, but it omits the extension.

- *GetFullPath* has no effect on an absolute path, and it changes a relative path into an absolute path using the current directory. For example, if c:\\Temp\\ is the current directory, calling *GetFullPath* on a file name such as test.txt returns c:\\Temp\\test.txt.

- *GetPathRoot* retrieves a string with the root (for example, "C:\\"), provided that information is in the string. For a relative path, it returns a null reference.

- *HasExtension* returns *true* if the path ends with an extension.

- *IsPathRooted* returns *true* if the path is an absolute path and *false* if it's a relative path.

> **Note**   In most cases, an exception will be thrown if you try to supply an invalid path to one of these methods (for example, paths that include illegal characters). However, pathnames that are invalid because they contain a wildcard character (* or ?) will not cause the methods to throw an exception.

9.13 Determine if a Path Is a Directory or a File

Problem

You have a path (in the form of a string), and you want to determine whether it corresponds to a directory or a file.

Solution

Test the path with the *Directory.Exists* and the *File.Exists* methods.

Discussion

The *System.IO.Directory* and *System.IO.File* classes both provide an *Exists* method. The *Directory.Exists* method returns *true* if a supplied relative or absolute path corresponds to an existing directory. *File.Exists* returns *true* if the path corresponds to an existing file.

Using these two methods, you can quickly determine if a path corresponds to a file or directory, as shown here:

```
using System;
using System.IO;

public class FileOrPath {

    private static void Main(string[] args) {

        foreach (string arg in args) {

            Console.Write(arg);

            if (Directory.Exists(arg)) {
                Console.WriteLine(" is a directory");
            }
            else if (File.Exists(arg)) {
                Console.WriteLine(" is a file");
            }
            else {
                Console.WriteLine(" does not exist");
            }
        }
        Console.ReadLine();
    }
}
```

9.14 Work with Relative Paths

Problem

You want to set the current working directory so that you can use relative paths in your code.

Solution

Use the *static GetCurrentDirectory* and *SetCurrentDirectory* methods of the *System.IO.Directory* class.

Discussion

Relative paths are automatically interpreted in relation to the current working directory. You can retrieve the current working directory by calling *Directory.GetCurrentDirectory* or change it using *Directory.SetCurrentDirectory*. In addition, you can use the *static GetFullPath* method of the *System.IO.Path* class to convert a relative path into an absolute path using the current working directory.

Here's a simple example that demonstrates these concepts:

```
using System;
using System.IO;

public class RelativeDirTest {

    private static void Main() {

        Console.WriteLine("Using: " + Directory.GetCurrentDirectory());
        Console.WriteLine("The relative path 'file.txt' " +
          "will automatically become: '" +
          Path.GetFullPath("file.txt") + "'");

        Console.WriteLine();

        Console.WriteLine("Changing current directory to c:\\");
        Directory.SetCurrentDirectory("c:\\");

        Console.WriteLine("Now the relative path 'file.txt' " +
          "will automatically become '" +
          Path.GetFullPath("file.txt") + "'");

        Console.ReadLine();
    }
}
```

The output for this example might be the following (if you run the application in the directory c:\temp):

```
Using: c:\temp
The relative path 'file.txt' will automatically become 'c:\temp\file.txt'

Changing current directory to c:\
The relative path 'file.txt' will automatically become 'c:\file.txt'
```

> **Note**   If you use relative paths, it's recommended that you set the
> working path at the start of each file interaction. Otherwise, you could
> introduce unnoticed security vulnerabilities that could allow a mali-
> cious user to force your application into accessing or overwriting sys-
> tem files by tricking it into using a different working directory.

9.15 Create a Temporary File

Problem

You need to create a file that will be placed in the user-specific temporary directory and will have a unique name so that it won't collide with temporary files
generated by other programs.

Solution

Use the *static GetTempFileName* method of the *System.IO.Path* class, which
returns a path made up of the user's temporary directory and a randomly generated file name.

Discussion

There are a number of approaches to generating temporary files. In simple
cases, you might just create a file in the application directory, possibly using a
GUID or a timestamp in conjunction with a random value as the file name.
However, the *Path* class provides a helper method that can save you some
work. It creates a file with a unique file name in the current user's temporary
directory. This might be a path like c:\documents and settings\username\local
settings\temp\tmpac9.tmp.

```
using System;
using System.IO;

public class TemporaryFile {

    private static void Main() {

        string tempFile = Path.GetTempFileName();

        Console.WriteLine("Using " + tempFile);
        FileStream fs = new FileStream(tempFile, FileMode.Open);
```

```
        // (Write some data.)

        fs.Close();

        // Now delete the file.
        File.Delete(tempFile);

        Console.ReadLine();
    }
}
```

9.16 Get the Total Free Space on a Drive

Problem

You need to examine a drive and determine how many bytes of free space are available.

Solution

Use the unmanaged Win32 API function *GetDiskFreeSpaceEx*, which is declared in kernel32.dll.

Discussion

None of the .NET file system classes allow you to determine the amount of free space that's available. However, this information can easily be retrieved using the Win32 API function *GetDiskFreeSpaceEx*, which returns the amount of used space, the amount of free space, and the amount of available free space as output arguments.

The following Console application uses this technique:

```
using System;
using System.Runtime.InteropServices;

public class GetFreeSpace {

    [DllImport("kernel32.dll", EntryPoint="GetDiskFreeSpaceExA" )]
    private static extern long GetDiskFreeSpaceEx(
      string lpDirectoryName, out long lpFreeBytesAvailableToCaller,
      out long lpTotalNumberOfBytes, out long lpTotalNumberOfFreeBytes);

    private static void Main() {

        long result, total, free, available;
        result = GetDiskFreeSpaceEx("c:", out available, out total, out free);
```

```
        if (result != 0) {

            Console.WriteLine("Total Bytes: {0:N}", total);
            Console.WriteLine("Free Bytes: {0:N}", free);
            Console.WriteLine("Available Bytes: {0:N}", available);
        }
        Console.ReadLine();
    }
}
```

9.17 Show the Common File Dialogs

Problem

You need to show the standard Windows dialog boxes for opening and saving files and for selecting a folder.

Solution

Use the *OpenFileDialog*, *SaveFileDialog*, and *FolderBrowserDialog* classes in the *System.Windows.Forms* namespace. Call the *ShowDialog* method to display the dialog, examine the return value to determine whether the user clicked OK or Cancel, and retrieve the selection from the *FileName* or *SelectedPath* property.

Discussion

.NET provides objects that wrap many of the standard Windows dialog boxes, including those used for saving and selecting files and directories. These classes all inherit from *System.Windows.Forms.CommonDialog* and include the following:

- *OpenFileDialog*, which allows the user to select a file. The file name and path is provided to your code through the *FileName* property (or the *FileNames* collection, if you have enabled multiple file select by setting *Multiselect* to *true*). Additionally, you can use the Filter property to set the file format choices and set *CheckFileExists* to enforce validation. (See Figure 9-2.)

- *SaveFileDialog*, which allows the user to specify a new file. The file name and path is provided to your code through the *FileName* property. You can also use the *Filter* property to set the file format choices and set the *CreatePrompt* and *OverwritePrompt* Boolean properties to instruct .NET to display a confirmation if the user selects a new file or an existing file, respectively.

- *FolderBrowser*, which allows the user to select (and optionally create) a directory. The selected path is provided through the *Selected-Path* property, and you can specify whether or not a Create New button should appear. (See Figure 9-3.)

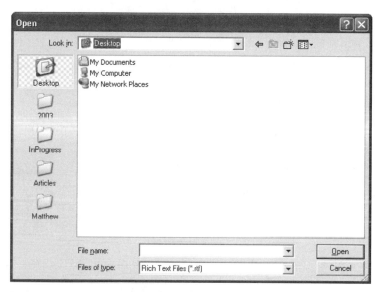

Figure 9-2 The *OpenFileDialog*.

Figure 9-3 The *FolderBrowserDialog*.

When using *OpenFileDialog* or *SaveFileDialog*, you need to set the filter string, which specifies the allowed file extensions. The filter string is separated with the pipe character (|) in this format: "[Text label] | [Extension list separated by semicolons] | [Text label] | [Extension list separated by semicolons] | . . ." You can also set the *Title* (form caption) and the *IntialDirectory*.

The following code shows a Windows-based application that allows the user to load documents into a *RichTextBox*, edit the content, and then save the modified document. When opening and saving a document, the *OpenFileDialog* and *SaveFileDialog* classes are used.

```csharp
using System;
using System.Drawing;
using System.Windows.Forms;

public class SimpleEditForm : System.Windows.Forms.Form {

    private System.Windows.Forms.MenuItem mnuFile;
    private System.Windows.Forms.MenuItem mnuOpen;
    private System.Windows.Forms.MenuItem mnuSave;
    private System.Windows.Forms.MenuItem mnuExit;
    private System.Windows.Forms.RichTextBox rtDoc;

    // (Designer code omitted.)

    private void mnuOpen_Click(object sender, System.EventArgs e) {

        OpenFileDialog dlg = new OpenFileDialog();
        dlg.Filter = "Rich Text Files (*.rtf)|*.RTF|" +
          "All files (*.*)|*.*";
        dlg.CheckFileExists = true;
        dlg.InitialDirectory = Application.StartupPath;

        if (dlg.ShowDialog() == DialogResult.OK) {
            rtDoc.LoadFile(dlg.FileName);
            rtDoc.Enabled = true;
        }
    }

    private void mnuSave_Click(object sender, System.EventArgs e) {

        SaveFileDialog dlg = new SaveFileDialog();
        dlg.Filter = "RichText Files (*.rtf)|*.RTF|Text Files (*.txt)|*.TXT" +
          "|All files (*.*)|*.*";
        dlg.CheckFileExists = true;
        dlg.InitialDirectory = Application.StartupPath;

        if (dlg.ShowDialog() == DialogResult.OK) {
            rtDoc.SaveFile(dlg.FileName);
        }
    }

    private void mnuExit_Click(object sender, System.EventArgs e) {
```

```
            this.Close();
        }
    }
}
```

9.18 Use an Isolated Store

Problem

You need to store data in a file, but your application doesn't have the required *FileIOPermission* for the local hard drive.

Solution

Use the *IsolatedStorageFile* and *IsolatedStorageFileStream* classes from the *System.IO.IsolatedStorage* namespace. These classes allow your application to write data to a file in a user-specific directory without needing permission to access the local hard drive directly.

Discussion

The .NET Framework includes support for isolated storage, which allows you to read and write to a user-specific virtual file system that the common language runtime (CLR) manages. When you create isolated storage files, the data is automatically serialized to a unique location in the user profile path (typically a path like c:\documents and settings\[username]\local settings\application data\isolated storage\[guid_identifier]).

One reason you might use isolated storage is to give a partially trusted application limited ability to store data. (See recipe 13.1 for more information on partially trusted code.) For example, the default CLR security policy gives local code unrestricted *FileIOPermission*, which allows it to open or write to any file. Code that you run from a remote server on the local Intranet is automatically assigned less permission—it lacks the *FileIOPermission*, but it has the *IsolatedStoragePermission*, giving it the ability to use isolated stores. (The security policy also limits the maximum amount of space that can be used in an isolated store.) Another reason you might use an isolated store is to better secure data. For example, data in one user's isolated store will be restricted from another nonadministrative user.

The following example shows how you can access isolated storage:

```
using System;
using System.IO;
using System.IO.IsolatedStorage;
```

```
public class IsolatedStoreTest {

    private static void Main() {

        // Create the store for the current user.
        IsolatedStorageFile store =
            IsolatedStorageFile.GetUserStoreForAssembly();

        // Create a folder in the root of the isolated store.
        store.CreateDirectory("MyFolder");

        // Create a file in the isolated store.
        Stream fs = new IsolatedStorageFileStream(
          "MyFile.txt", FileMode.Create, store);

        StreamWriter w = new StreamWriter(fs);

        // You can now write to the file as normal.
        w.WriteLine("Test");
        w.Flush();
        fs.Close();

        Console.WriteLine("Current size: " + store.CurrentSize.ToString());
        Console.WriteLine("Scope: " + store.Scope.ToString());

        Console.WriteLine("Contained files include:");
        string [] files = store.GetFileNames("*.*");
        foreach (string file in files) {
            Console.WriteLine(file);
        }

        Console.ReadLine();
    }
}
```

By default, each isolated store is segregated by user and assembly. That means that when the same user runs the same application, the application will access the data in the same isolated store. However, you can choose to segregate it further by application domain so that multiple instances of the same application receive different isolated stores, as shown here:

```
// Access isolated storage for the current user and assembly
// (which is equivalent to the first example).
store = IsolatedStorageFile.GetStore(IsolatedStorageScope.User |
  IsolatedStorageScope.Assembly, null, null);

// Access isolated storage for the current user, assembly,
// and application domain. In other words, this data is only
```

```
// accessible by the current application instance.
store = IsolatedStorageFile.GetStore(IsolatedStorageScope.User |
  IsolatedStorageScope.Assembly | IsolatedStorageScope.Domain,
  null, null);
```

The files are stored as part of a user's profile, so users can access their isolated storage files on any workstation they log on to if roaming profiles are configured on your LAN. (In this case, the store must be specifically designated as a roaming store by applying the *IsolatedStorageFile.Roaming* flag when it's created.) By letting the .NET Framework and the CLR provide these levels of isolation, you can relinquish responsibility for maintaining separation between files, and you don't have to worry that programming oversights or misunderstandings will cause loss of critical data.

9.19 Monitor the File System for Changes

Problem

You need to react when a file system change is detected in a specific path (such as a file modification or creation).

Solution

Use the *System.IO.FileSystemWatcher* component, specify the path or file you want to monitor, and handle the *Created*, *Deleted*, *Renamed*, and *Changed* events.

Discussion

When linking together multiple applications and business processes, it's often necessary to create a program that waits idly and becomes active only when a new file is received or changed. You can create this type of program by scanning a directory periodically, but you face a key tradeoff. The more often you scan, the more system resources you waste. The less often you scan, the longer it will take to detect a change. The solution is to use the *FileSystemWatcher* class to react directly to Windows file events.

To use *FileSystemWatcher*, you must create an instance and set the following properties:

■ *Path* indicates the directory you want to monitor.

■ *Filter* indicates the types of files you are monitoring.

■ *NotifyFilter* indicates the type of changes you are monitoring.

The *FileSystemWatcher* raises four key events: *Created*, *Deleted*, *Renamed*, and *Changed*. All of these events provide information through their *FileSystem-EventArgs* parameter, including the name of the file (*Name*), the full path (*Full-Path*), and the type of change (*ChangeType*). The *Renamed* event provides a *RenamedEventArgs* instance that derives from *FileSystemEventArgs*, and it adds information about the original file name (*OldName* and *OldFullPath*). If you need to, you can disable these events by setting the *FileSystemWatcher.Enable-RaisingEvents* property to *false*. The *Created*, *Deleted*, and *Renamed* events are easy to handle. However, if you want to use the *Changed* event, you need to use the *NotifyFilter* property to indicate the types of changes you are looking for. Otherwise, your program might be swamped by an unceasing series of events as files are modified.

The *NotifyFilter* property can be set using any combination of the following values from the *System.IO.NotifyFilters* enumeration:

- *Attributes*

- *CreationTime*

- *DirectoryName*

- *FileName*

- *LastAccess*

- *LastWrite*

- *Security*

- *Size*

The following example shows a Console application that handles *Created* and *Deleted* events and tests these events by creating a test file.

```
using System;
using System.IO;
using System.Windows.Forms;

public class FileWatcherTest {

    private static void Main() {

        // Configure the FileSystemWatcher.
        FileSystemWatcher watch = new FileSystemWatcher();
        watch.Path = Application.StartupPath;
        watch.Filter = "*.*";
        watch.IncludeSubdirectories = true;
```

```
        // Attach the event handler.
        watch.Created += new FileSystemEventHandler(OnCreatedOrDeleted);
        watch.Deleted += new FileSystemEventHandler(OnCreatedOrDeleted);
        watch.EnableRaisingEvents = true;

        Console.WriteLine("Press Enter to create a file.");
        Console.ReadLine();

        if (File.Exists("test.bin")) {
            File.Delete("test.bin");
        }

        FileStream fs = new FileStream("test.bin", FileMode.Create);
        fs.Close();

        Console.WriteLine("Press Enter to terminate the application.");
        Console.WriteLine();
        Console.ReadLine();
    }

    // Fires when a new file is created in the directory being monitored.
    private static void OnCreatedOrDeleted(object sender,
      FileSystemEventArgs e) {

        // Display the notification information.
        Console.WriteLine("\tNOTIFICATION: " + e.FullPath +
          "' was " + e.ChangeType.ToString());
          Console.WriteLine();
    }
}
```

9.20 Access a COM Port

Problem

You need to send data directly to a serial port.

Solution

The Win32 API provides unmanaged methods in the kernel32.dll library for directly reading and writing bytes to and from a serial port. You can import these functions into your C# application or use the higher-level Microsoft Communications ActiveX control (MSComm.ocx), which is a licensed control included with Microsoft Visual Studio 6.

Discussion

Unfortunately, .NET does not provide any managed interface for dealing with serial ports. As a result, developers who need this functionality will probably need to dive into some relatively complex interop coding.

One solution is to generate a .NET wrapper for the Microsoft Communications Control (MSComm.ocx). It provides a higher-level object model for working with serial ports. However, you must obtain this control through Visual Studio 6 to develop with it because it's a licensed control. (You can do a custom install of Visual Studio 6 and install only the ActiveX components, which require approximately 5 MB of disk space.) For more information, refer to the Visual Studio 6 documentation.

Another option is to import the API functions from kernel32.dll. This method requires some additional care because you must be careful to use the correct C# data types and preserve the layout of the memory structures. Fortunately, Justin Harrell (jharrell@aciss.com) has provided a solution to this problem with a custom C# class named *ComPort* that exposes this functionality. The full code for this class is fairly long and is available with the sample code for this recipe.

You can add this class to your applications and use the following code to interact with a COM port:

```csharp
ComPort port = new ComPort();

try {

    // Configure baud rate, parity, etc.
    port.BaudRate = 9600;
    port.Parity = 0;
    port.PortNum = 1;
    port.ReadTimeout = 10;
    port.StopBits = 1;
    port.ByteSize = 1;

    // Open the port.
    port.Open();

    // Write some data.
    port.Write(new byte[1]);

    // Close the port.
    port.Close();

}catch (ApplicationException err) {

    Console.WriteLine(err.Message);

}
```

10

Database Access

In the Microsoft .NET Framework, access to a wide variety of data sources is enabled through a group of classes collectively named Microsoft ADO.NET. Each type of data source is supported through the provision of a data provider. Each data provider contains a set of classes that not only implement a standard set of interfaces, but also provide functionality unique to the data source they support. These classes include representations of connections, commands, properties, data adapters, and data readers through which you interact with a data source. Table 10-1 lists the data providers included as standard with the .NET Framework.

Table 10-1   .NET Framework Data Provider Implementations

Data Provider	Description
.NET Framework Data Provider for ODBC	Provides connectivity to any data source that implements an ODBC interface; this includes Microsoft SQL Server, Oracle, and Microsoft Access databases. Data provider classes are contained in the *System.Data.Odbc* namespace and have the prefix *Odbc*.
.NET Framework Data Provider for OLE DB	Provides connectivity to any data source that implements an OLE DB interface; this includes Microsoft SQL Server, MSDE, Oracle, and Jet databases. Data provider classes are contained in the *System.Data.OleDb* namespace and have the prefix *OleDb*.
.NET Framework Data Provider for Oracle	Provides optimized connectivity to Oracle databases. Data provider classes are contained in the *System.Data.OracleClient* namespace and have the prefix *Oracle*.

Table 10-1 .NET Framework Data Provider Implementations *(continued)*

Data Provider	Description
.NET Framework Data Provider for SQL Server	Provides optimized connectivity to Microsoft SQL Server version 7 and later (including MSDE) by communicating directly with the SQL Server without the need to use ODBC or OLE DB. Data provider classes are contained in the *System.Data.SqlClient* namespace and have the prefix *Sql*.
.NET Compact Framework Data Provider for SQL Server CE	Provides connectivity to Microsoft SQL Server CE. Data provider classes are contained in the *System.Data.SqlServerCe* namespace and have the prefix *SqlCe*.

This chapter describes some of the most commonly used aspects of ADO.NET. However, ADO.NET is an extensive subsection of the .NET Framework class library and includes a great deal of advanced functionality. For a comprehensive coverage of ADO.NET, you should read David Sceppa's excellent book *Microsoft ADO.NET Core Reference* (Microsoft Press, 2002). The recipes in this chapter describe the following:

■ How to create, configure, open, and close database connections (recipe 10.1)

■ How to use connection pooling to improve the performance and scalability of applications that use database connections (recipe 10.2)

■ How to execute SQL commands and stored procedures and how to use parameters to improve their flexibility (recipes 10.3 and 10.4)

■ How to process the results returned by database queries (recipes 10.5 and 10.6)

■ How to discover all instances of SQL Server available on a network (recipe 10.7)

> **Note** The recipes in this chapter use the Northwind sample database provided by Microsoft to demonstrate the techniques discussed.

10.1 Connect to a Database

Problem

You need to open a connection to a database.

Solution

Create a connection object appropriate to the type of database to which you need to connect; all connection objects implement the *System.Data.IDbConnection* interface. Configure the connection object by setting its *ConnectionString* property. Open the connection by calling the connection object's *Open* method.

Discussion

The first step in database access is to open a connection to the database. The *IDbConnection* interface represents a database connection, and each data provider includes a unique implementation. Here is the list of *IDbConnection* implementations for the five standard data providers.

- *System.Data.Odbc.OdbcConnection*

- *System.Data.OleDb.OleDbConnection*

- *System.Data.OracleClient.OracleConnection*

- *System.Data.SqlServerCe.SqlCeConnection*

- *System.Data.SqlClient.SqlConnection*

You configure a connection object using a connection string. A connection string is a set of semicolon-separated name value pairs. You can supply a connection string either as a constructor argument or by setting a connection object's *ConnectionString* property before opening the connection. Each connection class implementation requires that you provide different information in the connection string. Refer to the *ConnectionString* property documentation for each implementation to see the values you can specify. Possible settings include the following:

- The name of the target database server

- The name of the database to open initially

- Connection timeout values

- Connection-pooling behavior (see recipe 10.2.)

- Authentication mechanisms to use when connecting to secured databases, including provision of user names and passwords

Once configured, call the connection object's *Open* method to open the connection to the database. You can then use the connection object to execute commands against the data source (discussed in recipe 10.3). The properties of a connection object also allow you to retrieve information about the state of a connection and the settings used to open the connection. When you're finished with a connection, you should always call its *Close* method to free up the underlying database connection and system resources. *IDbConnection* extends *System.IDisposable*, meaning that each connection class implements the *Dispose* method. *Dispose* automatically calls *Close*, making the *using* statement a very clean and efficient way of using connection objects in your code.

You achieve optimum scalability by opening your database connection as late as possible and closing it again as soon as you have finished. This ensures that you don't tie up database connections for long periods and give all code the maximum opportunity to obtain a connection. This is especially important if you are using connection pooling.

The code shown here demonstrates how to use the *SqlConnection* class to open a connection to a SQL Server database running on the local machine that uses integrated Windows security. To access a remote machine, simply change the data source name from *localhost* to the name of your database instance.

```
// Create an empty SqlConnection object.
using (SqlConnection con = new SqlConnection()) {

    // Configure the SqlConnection object's connection string.
    con.ConnectionString =
        "Data Source = localhost;"+ // local SQL Server instance
        "Database = Northwind;" +   // the sample Northwind DB
        "Integrated Security=SSPI"; // integrated Windows security

    // Open the Database connection.
    con.Open();

    // Display information about the connection.
    if (con.State == ConnectionState.Open) {
        Console.WriteLine("SqlConnection Information:");
        Console.WriteLine(" Connection State = " + con.State);
        Console.WriteLine(" Connection String = " +
            con.ConnectionString);
        Console.WriteLine(" Database Source = " + con.DataSource);
        Console.WriteLine(" Database = " + con.Database);
        Console.WriteLine(" Server Version = " + con.ServerVersion);
        Console.WriteLine(" Workstation Id = " + con.WorkstationId);
        Console.WriteLine(" Timeout = " + con.ConnectionTimeout);
        Console.WriteLine(" Packet Size = " + con.PacketSize);
    } else {
        Console.WriteLine("SqlConnection failed to open.");
        Console.WriteLine(" Connection State = " + con.State);
    }
    // At the end of the using block Dispose() calls Close().
}
```

As another example, the following excerpt from the sample code for this recipe shows the connection string used to open a connection to the same database if you were using the OLE DB data provider to provide connectivity.

```
// Create an empty OleDbConnection object.
using (OleDbConnection con = new OleDbConnection()) {

    // Configure the OleDbConnection object's connection string.
    con.ConnectionString =
        "Provider = SQLOLEDB;" +        // OLE DB Provider for SQL Server
        "Data Source = localhost;" +    // local SQL Server instance
        "Initial Catalog = Northwind;" + // the sample Northwind DB
        "Integrated Security=SSPI";      // integrated Windows security

    // Open the Database connection.
    con.Open();

    ⋮
}
```

10.2 Use Connection Pooling

Problem

You need to use a pool of database connections to improve application performance and scalability.

Solution

Configure the connection pool using settings in the connection string of a connection object.

Discussion

Connection pooling significantly reduces the overhead associated with creating and destroying database connections. Connection pooling also improves the scalability of solutions by reducing the number of concurrent connections a database must maintain—many of which sit idle for a significant portion of their lifetimes. With connection pooling, instead of creating and opening a new connection object whenever you need one, you take an already open connection from the connection pool. When you have finished using the connection, instead of closing it, you return it to the pool and allow other code to use it.

The SQL Server and Oracle data providers encapsulate connection-pooling functionality that they enable by default. One connection pool exists for each unique connection string you specify when you open a new connection. Each time you open a new connection with a connection string that you have used previously, the connection is taken from the existing pool. Only if you specify a different connection string will the data provider create a new connection pool. You can control some characteristics of your pool using the connection string settings described in Table 10-2.

Important   Once created, a pool exists until your process terminates.

Table 10-2   Connection String Settings That Control Connection Pooling

Setting	Description
Connection Lifetime	Specifies the maximum time in seconds that a connection is allowed to live in the pool before it's closed. The age of a connection is tested only when the connection is returned to the pool. This setting is useful for minimizing pool size if the pool isn't heavily used and also ensures optimal load balancing is achieved in clustered database environments. The default value is 0, which means connections exist for the life of the current process.
Connection Reset	Supported only by the SQL Server data provider. Specifies whether connections are reset as they are taken from the pool. A value of "True" ensures a connection's state is reset but requires an additional communication with the database. The default value is "True".
Max Pool Size	Specifies the maximum number of connections that should be in the pool. Connections are created and added to the pool as required until this figure is reached. If a request for a connection is made but there are no free connections, the caller will block until a connection becomes available. The default value is 100.
Min Pool Size	Specifies the minimum number of connections that should be in the pool. On pool creation, this number of connections are created and added to the pool. During periodic maintenance, or when a connection is requested, connections are added to the pool to ensure the minimum number of connections is available. The default value is 0.
Pooling	Set to "False" to obtain a non-pooled connection. The default value is "True".

This code excerpt from the sample code for this recipe demonstrates the configuration of a connection pool that contains a minimum of 5 and a maximum of 15 connections. Connections expire after 10 minutes (600 seconds) and are reset each time a connection is obtained from the pool.

```
// Obtain a pooled connection.
using (SqlConnection con = new SqlConnection()) {

    // Configure the SqlConnection object's connection string.
    con.ConnectionString =
        "Data Source = localhost;" +      // local SQL Server instance
        "Database = Northwind;" +         // the sample Northwind DB
        "Integrated Security = SSPI;" +   // integrated Windows security
        "Min Pool Size = 5;" +            // configure minimum pool size
        "Max Pool Size = 15;" +           // configure maximum pool size
        "Connection Reset = True;" +      // reset connections each use
        "Connection Lifetime = 600";      // set maximum connection lifetime

    // Open the Database connection.
    con.Open();

    // Access the database...
    :

    // At the end of the using block, the Dispose calls Close, which
    // returns the connection to the pool for reuse.
}
```

This code excerpt demonstrates how to use the *Pooling* setting to obtain a connection object that isn't from a pool. This is useful if your application uses a single long-lived connection to a database.

```
// Obtain a non-pooled connection.
using (SqlConnection con = new SqlConnection()) {

    // Configure the SqlConnection object's connection string.
    con.ConnectionString =
        "Data Source = localhost;" +      // local SQL Server instance
        "Database = Northwind;" +         // the sample Northwind DB
        "Integrated Security = SSPI;" +   // integrated Windows security
        "Pooling = False";                // specify non-pooled connection

    // Open the Database connection.
    con.Open();

    // Access the database...
    :

    // At the end of the using block, the Dispose calls Close, which
    // closes the non-pooled connection.
}
```

The ODBC and OLE DB data providers also support connection pooling, but they don't implement connection pooling within managed .NET classes and you don't configure the pool in the same way as for the SQL Server or Oracle data providers. ODBC connection pooling is managed by the ODBC Driver Manager and configured using the ODBC Data Source Administrator tool in the Control Panel. OLE DB connection pooling is managed by the native OLE DB implementation; the most you can do is disable pooling by including the setting `"OLE DB Services=-4;"` in your connection string. The SQL Server CE data provider doesn't support connection pooling because SQL Server CE supports only a single concurrent connection.

10.3 Execute a SQL Command or Stored Procedure

Problem

You need to execute a SQL command or stored procedure on a database.

Solution

Create a command object appropriate to the type of database you intend to use; all command objects implement the *System.Data.IDbCommand* interface. Configure the command object by setting its *CommandType* and *CommandText* properties. Execute the command using one of the *ExecuteNonQuery*, *ExecuteReader*, or *ExecuteScalar* methods depending on the type of command and its expected results.

Discussion

The *IDbCommand* interface represents a database command, and each data provider includes a unique implementation. Here is the list of *IDbCommand* implementations for the five standard data providers.

- *System.Data.Odbc.OdbcCommand*

- *System.Data.OleDb.OleDbCommand*

- *System.Data.OracleClient.OracleCommand*

- *System.Data.SqlServerCe.SqlCeCommand*

- *System.Data.SqlClient.SqlCommand*

To execute a command against a database you must have an open connection (discussed in recipe 10.1) and a properly configured command object appropriate to the type of database you are accessing. You can create command objects directly using a constructor, but a simpler approach is to use the *Create-Command* factory method of a connection object. The *CreateCommand* method returns a command object of the correct type for the data provider and configures it with basic information obtained from the connection you used to create the command. Before executing the command, you must configure the properties described in Table 10-3, which are common to all command implementations.

Table 10-3   Common Command Object Properties

Property	Description
CommandText	A *string* containing the text of the SQL command to execute or the name of a stored procedure. The content of the *CommandText* property must be compatible with the value you specify in the *CommandType* property.
CommandTimeout	An *int* that specifies the number of seconds to wait for the command to return before timing out and raising an exception. Defaults to 30 seconds.
CommandType	A value of the *System.Data.CommandType* enumeration that specifies the type of command represented by the command object. For most data providers, valid values are *StoredProcedure*, when you want to execute a stored procedure, and *Text*, when you want to execute a SQL text command. If you are using the OLE DB Data Provider, you can specify *TableDirect* when you want to return the entire contents of one or more tables; refer to the .NET Framework SDK documentation for more details. Defaults to *Text*.
Connection	An *IDbConnection* instance that provides the connection to the database on which you will execute the command. If you create the command using the *IDbConnection.CreateCommand* method, this property will be automatically set to the *IDbConnection* instance from which you created the command.
Parameters	A *System.Data.IDataParameterCollection* instance containing the set of parameters to substitute into the command. (See recipe 10.4 for details on how to use parameters.)
Transaction	A *System.Data.IDbTransaction* instance representing the transaction into which to enlist the command. (See the .NET Framework SDK documentation for details about transactions.)

Once you have configured your command object, there are a number of ways to execute it depending on the nature of the command, the type of data returned by the command, and the format in which you want to process the data.

To execute a command, such as **INSERT**, **DELETE**, or **CREATE TABLE**, that doesn't return database data, call *ExecuteNonQuery*. For the **UPDATE**, **INSERT**, and **DELETE** commands, *ExecuteNonQuery* method returns an *int* that specifies the number of rows affected by the command. For other commands, such as **CREATE TABLE**, *ExecuteNonQuery* returns the value -1. Here is an example that uses **UPDATE** to modify a record.

```
public static void ExecuteNonQueryExample(IDbConnection con) {

    // Create and configure a new command.
    IDbCommand com = con.CreateCommand();
    com.CommandType = CommandType.Text;
    com.CommandText = "UPDATE Employees SET Title = 'Sales Director'" +
        " WHERE EmployeeId = '5'";

    // Execute the command and process the result.
    int result = com.ExecuteNonQuery();

    if (result == 1) {
        Console.WriteLine("Employee title updated.");
    } else {
        Console.WriteLine("Employee title not updated.");
    }
}
```

To execute a command that returns a result set, such as a **SELECT** statement or stored procedure, use the *ExecuteReader* method. *ExecuteReader* returns an *IDataReader* instance (discussed in recipe 10.5) through which you have access to the result data. Most data providers also allow you to execute multiple SQL commands in a single call to the *ExecuteReader* method; the example in recipe 10.5 demonstrates this and shows how to access each result set. This code excerpt uses the *ExecuteReader* method to execute the Ten Most Expensive Products stored procedure from the Northwind database and display the results to the console.

```
public static void ExecuteReaderExample(IDbConnection con) {

    // Create and configure a new command.
    IDbCommand com = con.CreateCommand();
    com.CommandType = CommandType.StoredProcedure;
    com.CommandText = "Ten Most Expensive Products";

    // Execute the command and process the results
    using (IDataReader reader = com.ExecuteReader()) {

        Console.WriteLine("Price of the Ten Most Expensive Products.");
```

```
        while (reader.Read()) {

            // Display the product details.
            Console.WriteLine("  {0} = {1}",
                reader["TenMostExpensiveProducts"],
                reader["UnitPrice"]);
        }
    }
}
```

If you want to execute a query but only need the value from the first column of the first row of result data, use the *ExecuteScalar* method. The value is returned as an *object* reference that you must cast to the correct type. Here is an example.

```
public static void ExecuteScalarExample(IDbConnection con) {

    // Create and configure a new command.
    IDbCommand com = con.CreateCommand();
    com.CommandType = CommandType.Text;
    com.CommandText = "SELECT COUNT(*) FROM Employees";

    // Execute the command and cast the result.
    int result = (int)com.ExecuteScalar();

    Console.WriteLine("Employee count = " + result);
}
```

> **Note**   The *IDbCommand* implementations included in the Oracle and SQL data providers implement additional command execution methods. Recipe 10.6 describes how to use the *ExecuteXmlReader* method provided by the *SqlCommand* class. Refer to the .NET Frameworks SDK documentation for details on the additional *ExecuteOracleNonQuery* and *ExecuteOracleScalar* methods provided by the *OracleCommand* class.

10.4 Use Parameters in a SQL Command or Stored Procedure

Problem

You need to set the arguments of a stored procedure or use parameters in a SQL command to improve flexibility.

Solution

Create parameter objects appropriate to the type of command object you intend to execute; all parameter objects implement the *System.Data.IDataParameter* interface. Configure the parameter objects' data types, values, and directions and add them to the command object's parameter collection using the *IDbCommand.Parameters.Add* method.

Discussion

All command objects support the use of parameters, so you can do the following:

- Set the arguments of stored procedures
- Receive stored procedure return values
- Substitute values into text commands at run time

The *IDataParameter* interface represents a parameter and each data provider includes a unique implementation. Here is the list of *IDataParameter* implementations for the five standard data providers.

- *System.Data.Odbc.OdbcParameter*
- *System.Data.OleDb.OleDbParameter*
- *System.Data.OracleClient.OracleParameter*
- *System.Data.SqlServerCe.SqlCeParameter*
- *System.Data.SqlClient.SqlParameter*

A parameter object's properties describe everything about a parameter that the command object needs to use the parameter object when executing a command against a data source. Table 10-4 describes the properties that you will use most frequently when configuring parameters.

Table 10-4   Parameter Properties

Property	Description
DbType	A value of the *System.Data.DbType* enumeration that specifies the type of data contained in the parameter. Commonly used values include *String*, *Int32*, *DateTime*, and *Currency*.
Direction	A value from the *System.Data.ParameterDirection* enumeration that indicates the direction in which the parameter is used to pass data; valid values are *Input*, *InputOutput*, *Output*, and *ReturnValue*.

Table 10-4 Parameter Properties

Property	Description
IsNullable	A *bool* that indicates whether the parameter accepts null values.
ParameterName	A *string* containing the name of the parameter.
Value	An *object* containing the value of the parameter.

To use parameters with a text command, you must identify where to substitute the parameter's value within the command. The ODBC, OLE DB, and SQL Server CE data providers support positional parameters; the location of each argument is identified by a question mark (?). For example, the following command identifies two locations to be substituted with parameter values.

```
UPDATE Employees SET Title = ? WHERE EmployeeId = ?
```

The SQL Server and Oracle data providers support named parameters, which allow you to identify each parameter location using a name preceded by the at symbol (@). Here is the equivalent command using named parameters.

```
UPDATE Employees SET Title = @title WHERE EmployeeId = @id
```

To specify the parameter values to substitute into a command, you must create parameter objects of the correct type and add them to the command object's parameter collection accessible through the *Parameters* property. You can add named parameters in any order, but you must add positional parameters in the same order they appear in the text command. When you execute your command, the value of each parameter is substituted into the command string before the command is executed against the data source.

The *ParameterizedCommandExample* method shown here demonstrates the use of parameters in a SQL Server **UPDATE** statement. The *ParameterizedCommandExample* method's arguments include an open *SqlConnection* and two strings. The values of the two strings are substituted into the **UPDATE** command using parameters. The example demonstrates two ways of creating parameter objects: the *IDbCommand.CreateParameter* method, and the *IDbCommand.Parameters.Add* method. You can also create parameter objects using constructors and configure them using constructor arguments or through setting their properties.

```
public static void ParameterizedCommandExample(SqlConnection con,
    string employeeID, string title) {

    // Create and configure a new command containing 2 named parameters.
    SqlCommand com = con.CreateCommand();
    com.CommandType = CommandType.Text;
    com.CommandText = "UPDATE Employees SET Title = @title" +
        " WHERE EmployeeId = @id";
```

```
// Create a SqlParameter object for the title parameter.
SqlParameter p1 = com.CreateParameter();
p1.ParameterName = "@title";
p1.SqlDbType = SqlDbType.VarChar;
p1.Value = title;
com.Parameters.Add(p1);

// Use a shorthand syntax to add the id parameter.
com.Parameters.Add("@id",SqlDbType.Int).Value = employeeID;

// Execute the command and process the result.
int result = com.ExecuteNonQuery();
    ⋮
}
```

When using parameters to execute stored procedures, you must provide parameter objects to satisfy each argument required by the stored procedure—including both input and output arguments. You must set the *Direction* property of each parameter as described in Table 10-4; parameters are *Input* by default. If a stored procedure has a return value, the parameter to hold the return value (with a *Direction* property equal to *ReturnValue*) must be the first parameter added to the parameter collection. Here is an example that uses parameters to execute a stored procedure.

```
public static void StoredProcedureExample(SqlConnection con,
    string category, string year) {

    // Create and configure a new command.
    SqlCommand com = con.CreateCommand();
    com.CommandType = CommandType.StoredProcedure;
    com.CommandText = "SalesByCategory";

    // Create a SqlParameter object for the category parameter.
    com.Parameters.Add("@CategoryName",SqlDbType.NVarChar).Value=category;

    // Create a SqlParameter object for the year parameter.
    com.Parameters.Add("@OrdYear",SqlDbType.NVarChar).Value = year;

    // Execute the command and process the results
    using (IDataReader reader = com.ExecuteReader()) {
        ⋮
    }
}
```

10.5 Process the Results of a SQL Query Using a Data Reader

Problem

You need to process the data contained in a *System.Data.IDataReader* instance returned when you execute the *IDbCommand.ExecuteReader* method (discussed in recipe 10.3).

Solution

Use the members of the *IDataReader* instance to move through the rows in the result set sequentially and access the individual data items contained in each row.

Discussion

The *IDataReader* interface represents a data reader, which is a forward-only, read-only mechanism for accessing the results of a SQL query. Each data provider includes a unique *IDataReader* implementation. Here is the list of *IDataReader* implementations for the five standard data providers.

- *System.Data.Odbc.OdbcDataReader*
- *System.Data.OleDb.OleDbDataReader*
- *System.Data.OracleClient.OracleDataReader*
- *System.Data.SqlServerCe.SqlCeDataReader*
- *System.Data.SqlClient.SqlDataReader*

The *IDataReader* interface extends the *System.Data.IDataRecord* interface. Together these interfaces declare the functionality that provides access to both the data and the structure of the data contained in the result set. Table 10-5 describes some of the commonly used members of the *IDataReader* and *IDataRecord* interfaces.

Table 10-5 Commonly Used Members of Data Reader Classes

Member	Comments
Property	
FieldCount	Gets the number of columns in the current row.
IsClosed	Returns *true* if the *IDataReader* is closed; *false* if it's currently open.

Table 10-5 Commonly Used Members of Data Reader Classes *(continued)*

Member	Comments
Item	Returns an *object* representing the value of the specified column in the current row. Columns can be specified using a zero-based integer index or a string containing the column name. You must cast the returned value to the appropriate type. This is the indexer for data reader classes.
Method	
GetDataTypeName	Gets the name of the data source data type for a specified column.
GetFieldType	Gets a *System.Type* instance representing the data type of the value contained in the column specified using a zero-based integer index.
GetName	Gets the name of the column specified by using a zero-based integer index.
GetOrdinal	Gets the zero-based column ordinal for the column with the specified name.
GetSchemaTable	Returns a *System.Data.DataTable* instance that contains metadata describing the columns contained in the *IDataReader*.
IsDBNull	Returns *true* if the value in the specified column contains a data source null value; otherwise it returns *false*.
NextResult	If the *IDataReader* includes multiple result sets because multiple statements were executed, *NextResult* moves to the next set of results. By default, the *IDataReader* is positioned on the first result set.
Read	Advances the reader to the next record. The reader always starts prior to the first record.

In addition to those members listed in Table 10-5, the data reader provides a set of methods for retrieving typed data from the current row. Each of the following methods takes an integer argument that identifies the zero-based index of the column from which the data should be returned: *GetBoolean*, *GetByte*, *GetBytes*, *GetChar*, *GetChars*, *GetDateTime*, *GetDecimal*, *GetDouble*, *GetFloat*, *GetGuid*, *GetInt16*, *GetInt32*, *GetInt64*, *GetString*, *GetValue*, and *GetValues*.

The SQL Server and Oracle data readers also include methods for retrieving data as data source–specific data types. For example, the *SqlDataReader* includes methods such as *GetSqlByte*, *GetSqlDecimal*, and *GetSqlMoney*, and the *OracleDataReader* includes methods such as *GetOracleLob*, *GetOracleNumber*, and *GetOracleMonthSpan*. Refer to the .NET Framework SDK documentation for more details.

When you have finished with a data reader, you should always call its *Close* method so that you can use the database connection again. *IDataReader* extends *System.IDisposable*, meaning that each data reader class implements the *Dispose* method. *Dispose* automatically calls *Close*, making the *using* statement a very clean and efficient way of using data readers.

The following example demonstrates the use of a data reader to process the contents of two results sets returned by executing a batch query containing two SELECT queries. The first result set is enumerated and displayed to the console. The second result set is inspected for metadata information, which is then displayed.

```
using System;
using System.Data;
using System.Data.SqlClient;

public class DataReaderExample {

    public static void Main() {

        // Create a new SqlConnection object.
        using (SqlConnection con = new SqlConnection()) {

            // Configure the SqlConnection object's connection string.
            con.ConnectionString = "Data Source = localhost;" +
                "Database = Northwind; Integrated Security=SSPI";

            // Create and configure a new command.
            SqlCommand com = con.CreateCommand();
            com.CommandType = CommandType.Text;
            com.CommandText = "SELECT BirthDate,FirstName,LastName FROM " +
                "Employees ORDER BY BirthDate;SELECT * FROM Employees";

            // Open the Database connection and execute the example
            // commands through the connection.
            con.Open();

            // Execute the command and obtain a SqlReader.
            using (SqlDataReader reader = com.ExecuteReader()) {

                // Process the first set of results and display the
                // content of the result set.
                Console.WriteLine("Employee Birthdays (By Age).");

                while (reader.Read()) {

                    Console.WriteLine("{0,18:D} - {1} {2}",
```

```
                               reader.GetDateTime(0),    // Retrieve typed data
                               reader["FirstName"],      // Use string index
                               reader[2]);               // Use ordinal index
                }

                // Process the second set of results and display details
                // about the columns and data types in the result set.
                reader.NextResult();
                Console.WriteLine("Employee Table Metadata.");
                for (int field = 0; field < reader.FieldCount; field++) {

                    Console.WriteLine("  Column Name:{0}  Type:{1}",
                        reader.GetName(field),
                        reader.GetDataTypeName(field));
                }

            }
        }

        // Wait to continue.
        Console.ReadLine();
    }
}
```

10.6 Obtain an XML Document from a SQL Server Query

Problem

You need to execute a query against a SQL Server 2000 or MSDE database and retrieve the results as XML.

Solution

Specify the FOR XML clause on your SQL query to return the results as XML. Execute the command using the *SqlCommand.ExecuteXmlReader* method, which returns a *System.Xml.XmlReader* object through which you can access the returned XML data.

Discussion

SQL Server 2000 and MSDE provide direct support for XML. You simply need to add the clause FOR XML AUTO to the end of a SQL query to indicate that the results should be returned as XML. By default, the XML representation is not a full XML document. Instead, it simply returns the result of each record in a separate element, with all the fields as attributes. For example, the query

```
SELECT CustomerID, CompanyName FROM Customers FOR XML AUTO
```

returns XML with the following structure:

```
<Customers CustomerID="ALFKI" CompanyName="Alfreds Futterkiste"/>
<Customers CustomerID="ANTON" CompanyName="Antonio Moreno Taquería"/>
<Customers CustomerID="GOURL" CompanyName="Gourmet Lanchonetes"/>
⋮
```

Alternatively, you can add the *ELEMENTS* keyword to the end of a query to structure the results using nested elements rather than attributes. For example, the query

```
SELECT CustomerID, CompanyName FROM Customers FOR XML AUTO, ELEMENTS
```

returns XML with the following structure:

```
<Customers>
  <CustomerID>ALFKI</CustomerID>
  <CompanyName>Alfreds Futterkiste</CompanyName>
</Customers>
<Customers>
  <CustomerID>ANTON</CustomerID>
  <CompanyName>Antonio Moreno Taqueria</CompanyName>
</Customers>
<Customers>
  <CustomerID>GOURL</CustomerID>
  <CompanyName>Gourmet Lanchonetes</CompanyName>
</Customers>
⋮
```

> **Note**   You can also fine-tune the format in more detail using the *FOR XML EXPLICIT* syntax. For example, this allows you to convert some fields to attributes and others to elements. Refer to the SQL Server Books Online for more information.

The following example demonstrates how to retrieve results as XML using the *FOR XML* clause and the *ExecuteXmlReader* method. Notice that the connection can't be used for any other commands while the *XmlReader* is open. You should process the results as quickly as possible and must always close the *XmlReader*. (Chapter 5 contains more detailed examples of how to use the *XmlReader* class.)

```csharp
using System;
using System.Xml;
using System.Data;
using System.Data.SqlClient;

public class XmlQueryExample {

    public static void Main() {

        // Create a new SqlConnection object.
        using (SqlConnection con = new SqlConnection()) {

            // Configure the SqlConnection object's connection string.
            con.ConnectionString = "Data Source = localhost;" +
                "Database = Northwind; Integrated Security=SSPI";

            // Create and configure a new command that includes the
            // FOR XML AUTO clause.
            SqlCommand com = con.CreateCommand();
            com.CommandType = CommandType.Text;
            com.CommandText = "SELECT CustomerID, CompanyName" +
                " FROM Customers FOR XML AUTO";

            // Declare an XmlReader so that it can be referenced in the
            // finally clause to ensure it is closed after use.
            XmlReader reader = null;

            try {
                // Open the database connection.
                con.Open();

                // Execute the command and retrieve an XmlReader to access
                // the results.
                reader = com.ExecuteXmlReader();

                while (reader.Read()) {

                    Console.Write("Element: " + reader.Name);
                    if (reader.HasAttributes) {
                        for (int i = 0; i < reader.AttributeCount; i++) {

                            reader.MoveToAttribute(i);
                            Console.Write("  {0}: {1}",
                                reader.Name, reader.Value);
                        }

                        // Move the XmlReader back to the element node.
                        reader.MoveToElement();
```

```
                    Console.WriteLine();
                }
            }
        } catch (Exception ex) {

            Console.WriteLine(ex.ToString());
        } finally {

            // Ensure the reader is closed.
            if (reader != null) reader.Close();
        }
    }

    // Wait to continue.
    Console.ReadLine();
    }
}
```

Some of the output from this test application is shown here:

```
Element: Customers   CustomerID: ALFKI   CompanyName: Alfreds Futterkiste
Element: Customers   CustomerID: ANTON   CompanyName: Antonio Moreno Taquería
Element: Customers   CustomerID: GOURL   CompanyName: Gourmet Lanchonetes
...
```

Instead of working with the *XmlReader* and accessing the data sequentially, you can read the XML data into a *System.Xml.XmlDocument*. This way, all the data is retrieved into memory, and the database connection can be closed. You can then continue to interact with the XML document. (Chapter 5 contains numerous examples of how to use the *XmlDocument* class.) Here's the code you would need.

```
XmlDocument doc = new XmlDocument();

// Create a new SqlConnection object.
using (SqlConnection con = new SqlConnection()) {

    // Configure the SqlConnection object's connection string.
    con.ConnectionString = "Data Source = localhost;" +
        "Database = Northwind; Integrated Security=SSPI";

    // Create and configure a new command that includes the
    // FOR XML AUTO clause.
    SqlCommand com = con.CreateCommand();
    com.CommandType = CommandType.Text;
    com.CommandText =
        "SELECT CustomerID, CompanyName FROM Customers FOR XML AUTO";
```

```
        // Open the database connection.
        con.Open();

        // Load the XML data into the XmlDocument. Must first create a
        // root element into which to place each result row element.
        XmlReader reader = com.ExecuteXmlReader();
        doc.LoadXml("<results></results>");

        // Create an XmlNode from the next XML element read from the
        // reader.
        XmlNode newNode = doc.ReadNode(reader);

        while (newNode != null) {

            doc.DocumentElement.AppendChild(newNode);
            newNode = doc.ReadNode(reader);
        }
    }

    // Process the disconnected XmlDocument.
    Console.WriteLine(doc.OuterXml);
    ⋮
```

10.7 Discover All Instances of SQL Server 2000 on Your Network

Problem

You need to obtain a list of all instances of SQL Server 2000 that are accessible on the network.

Solution

Use COM interop to access the functionality of the Microsoft SQLDMO Object Library. Create an *Application* object, and call its *ListAvailableSQLServers* method. *ListAvailableSQLServers* returns a *NameList* object, which is an enumerable *string* collection containing the name of each SQL Server 2000 instance discovered on the network.

Discussion

The .NET Framework class library doesn't include the functionality to find unknown SQL Servers; however, this task is straightforward using the Microsoft SQLDMO Object Library accessed through COM interop. Recipe 15.6 details how to create an interop assembly that provides access to a COM component.

If using Microsoft Visual Studio .NET, add a reference to the Microsoft SQLDMO Object Library listed in the COM tab of the Add Reference dialog box. If you don't have Visual Studio .NET, use the Type Library Importer (Tlbimp.exe) to create an interop assembly for the sqldmo.dll file, which is usually located in the Tools\Binn folder below your SQL Server installation.

> **Note**   There is a known problem with the original SQLDMO Object Library that will cause the sample project in this recipe to fail. To run the project, you need to have installed SQL Server Service Pack 2 or higher.

Assuming you use default settings when generating your intcrop assembly, you first need to import the *SQLDMO* namespace. To obtain the list of available SQL Servers, instantiate a *SQLDMO.Application* object and call its *ListAvailableSQLServers* method. Each string in the returned *SQLDMO.NameList* object is the name of an accessible SQL Server. You can use the names in connection strings or display them in a list for a user to select. Here is an example that displays the names of all accessible SQL Servers to the console.

```
using System;
using SQLDMO;

public class SQLDMOExample {

    public static void Main() {

        // Obtain a list of all available SQL Servers.
        SQLDMO.Application app = new SQLDMO.Application();
        SQLDMO.NameList names = app.ListAvailableSQLServers();

        // Process the NameList collection.
        if (names.Count == 0) {

            Console.WriteLine("No SQL Servers visible on the network.");

        } else {

            // Display a list of available SQL Servers.
            Console.WriteLine("SQL Servers visible : " + names.Count);
```

```csharp
        foreach (string name in names) {

            Console.WriteLine("  Name : " + name);
        }
    }

    // Wait to continue.
    Console.ReadLine();
    }
}
```

11

Networking and Internetworking

The Microsoft .NET Framework includes a full set of classes for networking programming in two namespaces: *System.Net* and *System.Net.Sockets*. These classes support everything from socket-based programming with TCP/IP to downloading files and HTML pages from the Web over HTTP. The networking namespaces are also the foundation on which two higher-level networking platforms—Remoting and XML Web services—are built. This chapter won't tackle either of these platforms. Instead, they're covered in detail in Chapter 12.

This chapter presents recipes that show the following concepts:

- How to retrieve resources from the Web over HTTP (recipes 11.1, 11.2, and 11.3).

- How to display a Web page in a Microsoft Windows–based application using the Web Browser control (recipe 11.4).

- How to get IP address and DNS information about the current computer and other domains on the World Wide Web (recipes 11.5 and 11.6).

- How to send ping messages (recipe 11.7) and communicate using the TCP and UDP protocols (recipes 11.8 through 11.13).

- How to send and retrieve e-mail messages (recipes 11.14 and 11.15).

11.1 Download a File over HTTP

Problem

You need a quick, simple way to download a file from a Web site over HTTP.

Solution

Use the *static DownloadFile* method of *System.Net.WebClient* class.

Discussion

The .NET Framework provides several mechanisms for sending data over HTTP. One of the easiest approaches is to use the *System.Net.WebClient* helper class. It provides higher-level methods like *DownloadFile* and *UploadFile*. These methods don't have any built-in support for asynchronous communications or authentication. If you need these features, you can use the more sophisticated functionality provided in the *WebRequest* and *WebResponse* classes, as described in recipes 11.2 and 11.3.

The following application downloads a graphic named banner.gif from a Microsoft Web site and stores it locally.

```
using System;
using System.Net;
using System.IO;

public class Download {

    private static void Main() {

        string remoteUri =
          "http://www.microsoft.com/mspress/images/banner.gif";
        string localFileName = "banner.gif";

        WebClient client = new WebClient();
        Console.WriteLine("Downloading file " +
        remoteUri + " to " + Path.GetFullPath(localFileName));

        // Perform the download.
        client.DownloadFile(remoteUri, localFileName);
        Console.WriteLine("Download complete.");

        Console.ReadLine();
    }
}
```

11.2 Download a File and Process It Using a Stream

Problem

You need to retrieve a file from a Web site, but you don't want to save it directly to the hard drive. Instead, you want to process the data in your application.

Solution

Use the *WebRequest* class to create your request, the *WebResponse* class to retrieve the response from the Web server, and some form of reader (typically a *StreamReader* for HTML or text data or a *BinaryReader* for a binary file) to parse the response data.

Discussion

Downloading a file from the Web takes the following four basic steps:

1. Use the *static Create* method of the *System.Net.WebRequest* class to specify the page you want. This method returns a *WebRequest*-derived object, depending on the type of Uniform Resource Identifier (URI) you use. For example, if you use an HTTP URI (with the scheme http://), it will create an *HttpWebRequest* instance. If you use a file system URI (with the scheme file://), it will create a *FileWebRequest* instance. You can set the timeout through the *WebRequest.Timeout* property.

2. Use the *GetResponse* method of the *WebRequest* object to return a *WebResponse* object for the page. If the request times out, a *WebException* will be thrown.

3. Create a *StreamReader* or a *BinaryReader* for the *WebResponse* stream.

4. Perform any steps you need to with the stream, such as writing it to a file, displaying it in your application, and so on.

The following code retrieves and displays a graphic and the HTML content of a Web page. It's shown in Figure 11-1.

```
using System;
using System.Net;
using System.IO;
using System.Drawing;
using System.Windows.Forms;
```

```csharp
public class DownloadForm : System.Windows.Forms.Form {

    private System.Windows.Forms.PictureBox picBox;
    private System.Windows.Forms.TextBox textBox;

    // (Designer code omitted.)

    private void DownloadForm_Load(object sender, System.EventArgs e) {

        string picUri =
          "http://www.microsoft.com/mspress/images/banner.gif";
        string htmlUri =
          "http://www.microsoft.com/default.asp";

        // Create the requests.
        WebRequest requestPic = WebRequest.Create(picUri);
        WebRequest requestHtml = WebRequest.Create(htmlUri);

        // Get the responses.
        // This takes the most significant amount of time, particularly
        // if the file is large, because the whole response is retrieved.
        WebResponse responsePic = requestPic.GetResponse();
        WebResponse responseHtml = requestHtml.GetResponse();

        // Read the response streams.
        Image downloadedImage =
          Image.FromStream(responsePic.GetResponseStream());
        StreamReader r = new StreamReader(responseHtml.GetResponseStream());
        string htmlContent = r.ReadToEnd();
        r.Close();

        // Display the image.
        picBox.Image = downloadedImage;

        // Show the text content.
        textBox.Text = htmlContent;
    }
}
```

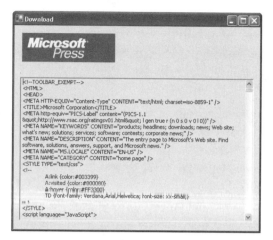

Figure 11-1   Downloading content from the Web.

To deal efficiently with large files that need to be downloaded from the Web, you might want to use asynchronous techniques, as described in Chapter 4. You can also use the *WebRequest.BeginGetResponse*, which doesn't block your code and calls a callback procedure when the response has been retrieved.

11.3 Get an HTML Page from a Site That Requires Authentication

Problem

You need to retrieve a file from a Web site, but the Web site requires some sort of authentication credentials.

Solution

Use the *WebRequest* and *WebResponse* classes as described in recipe 11.2. However, before using the request, configure the *WebRequest.Credentials* property with the authentication information.

Discussion

Some Web sites require user authentication information. When connecting through a browser, this information might be submitted transparently (for example, on a local intranet site that uses Windows integrated authentication), or the browser might request this information with a login dialog box. When accessing a Web page programmatically, your code needs to manually submit this information.

The approach you use depends on the type of authentication used by the Web site.

■ If the Web site is using basic or digest authentication, you can transmit a user name and password combination by manually creating a new *System.Net.NetworkCredential* object and assigning it to the *WebRequest.Credentials* property. With digest authentication, you may also supply a domain name.

■ If the Web site is using Windows integrated authentication, you can take the same approach and manually create a new *System.Net.NetworkCredential* object. Alternatively, you can retrieve the current user login information from the *System.Net.CredentialCache* object.

■ If the Web site requires a client-certificate, you can load the certificate from a file using the *System.Security.Cryptography.X509Certificates.X509Certificate* class, and add that to the *HttpWebRequest.ClientCertificates* collection.

Here's a code example that shows all three of these basic approaches:

```
using System;
using System.Net;
using System.Security.Cryptography.X509Certificates;

public class DownloadWithAuthentication {

    private static void Main() {

        string uriBasic, uriIntegrated, uriCertificate;
        // (Assign these three URIs.)

        // Authenticate the user with a user name and password combination
        // over Basic authentication.
        WebRequest requestA = WebRequest.Create(uriBasic);
        requestA.Credentials = CredentialCache.DefaultCredentials;
        requestA.PreAuthenticate = true;

        // Log the current user in with Windows integrated authentication.
        WebRequest requestB = WebRequest.Create(uriIntegrated);
        requestB.Credentials = new NetworkCredential("userName", "password");
        requestB.PreAuthenticate = true;
```

```
        // Authenticate the user by adding a client certificate.
        HttpWebRequest requestC = (HttpWebRequest)
          WebRequest.Create(uriCertificate);
        X509Certificate cert =
          X509Certificate.CreateFromCertFile(@"c:\user.cer");
        requestC.ClientCertificates.Add(cert);

        // (Now get and process the responses.)
    }
}
```

> **Note**   Remember that if you wish to use certificate authentication, you must load the certificate from a file. There is no way to create an *X509Certificate* object from a certificate in the computer's certificate store.

11.4 Display a Web Page in a Windows-Based Application

Problem

You need to display an HTML page (or another type of document supported by Microsoft Internet Explorer) in a Windows-based application.

Solution

Use the Web browser ActiveX control included with Internet Explorer, using a runtime callable wrapper (RCW).

Discussion

The .NET Framework doesn't include any controls for rendering HTML content. However, this functionality would be useful, either to display some local HTML content (such as a rich help document) or some information from the Web (for example, a Web page that lists downloads a user might use to update an application).

To show an HTML page, you can add an Internet Explorer window to your Windows-based applications. This window not only supports HTML, but it also supports JavaScript and Microsoft Visual Basic Scripting Edition (VBScript) code, ActiveX controls, and various plug-ins depending on your system configuration (possibilities include Microsoft Word, Microsoft Excel, and Adobe Acrobat

Reader). You can even use the Web browser control to browse the folders on a local drive or show the files on a File Transfer Protocol (FTP) site.

To add the Web browser to a project in Microsoft Visual Studio .NET, right-click the Toolbox and choose Add/Remove Items. Then select the COM Components tab, and check the Microsoft Web Browser control (shdocvw.dll). This will add the Microsoft Web Browser control to your Toolbox. When you drop this control onto a form, the necessary interop assemblies will be generated and added to your project. If you aren't using Visual Studio .NET, you can generate a wrapper using the Type Library Importer (Tlbimp.exe), as explained in recipe 15.6.

When using the Web browser control, you'll commonly use the following methods:

- *Navigate* (and *Navigate2*) redirects the page to the URL you specify.

- *GoBack* and *GoForward* navigate to pages in the history list.

- *GoHome* navigates to the home page set on the current computer, and *GoSearch* shows the search page.

In addition, the user will be able to trigger page navigation by clicking page links (if they exist). You can retrieve the current URL from the *Location-URL* property and determine if the control is still rendering the page by examining the *Busy* property. In addition, you can react to a variety of events, including ones that fire when navigation starts and stops.

Figure 11-2 shows an application that allows the user to visit two pages (and follow any links they provide).

Figure 11-2 Using the Web browser control.

```
using System;
using System.Drawing;
using System.Windows.Forms;

public class WebBrowser : System.Windows.Forms.Form {

    private AxSHDocVw.AxWebBrowser explorer;
    private System.Windows.Forms.Button cmdBack;
    private System.Windows.Forms.Button cmdHome;
    private System.Windows.Forms.Button cmdForward;

    // (Designer code omitted.)

    private void WebBrowser_Load(object sender, System.EventArgs e) {

        object nullObject = null;
        object uri = "http://www.microsoft.com";
        explorer.Navigate2(ref uri, ref nullObject, ref nullObject,
          ref nullObject, ref nullObject);
    }

    private void cmdHome_Click(object sender, System.EventArgs e) {

        explorer.GoHome();
    }

    private void cmdForward_Click(object sender, System.EventArgs e) {

        try {
            explorer.GoForward();
        } catch {
            MessageBox.Show("Already on last page.");
        }
    }

    private void cmdBack_Click(object sender, System.EventArgs e) {

        try {
            explorer.GoBack();
        } catch {
            MessageBox.Show("Already on first page.");
        }
    }
}
```

Most of the Web browser control methods require several parameters.
Because these methods aren't overloaded, and because C# doesn't support
optional parameters, you must supply a value for every parameter. You can't

simply use a *null* reference, however, because they are *ref* parameters. Instead, it's usually easiest to create an object variable that contains a *null* reference and supply it for parameters you don't need to use. This technique is demonstrated in more detail in recipe 15.8.

11.5 Get the IP Address of the Current Computer

Problem

You need to retrieve the IP address of the current computer, perhaps to use later in networking code.

Solution

Use the *System.Net.Dns* class, which provides *static GetHostName* and *GetHost-ByName* methods.

Discussion

The *Dns* class provides domain name resolution services. You can invoke its *GetHostName* to retrieve the host name for the current computer. You can then translate the host name into an IP address using *GetHostByName*. Here's an example:

```
using System;
using System.Net;

public class GetIPAddress {

    private static void Main() {

        // Look up the host name and IP address.
        string hostName = Dns.GetHostName();

        // Get the first matching IP address.
        string ipAddress =
          Dns.GetHostByName(hostName).AddressList[0].ToString();

        Console.WriteLine("Host name: " + hostName);
        Console.WriteLine("IP address: " + ipAddress);

        Console.ReadLine();
    }
}
```

Be aware that the *GetHostByName* method returns a list of usable IP addresses. In many cases, this address list will contain only one entry.

If you run this code, you'll see something like this

```
Host name: fariamat
IP address: 24.114.131.70
```

> **Note**   When using IP addresses in network communication, you can always use the loopback address 127.0.0.1 to refer to the current computer, instead of its machine-specific IP address.

11.6 Resolve a Host Name to an IP Address

Problem

You want to determine the IP address for a computer based on its domain name by performing a Domain Name System (DNS) query.

Solution

Use *GetHostByName* method of the *System.Net.Dns* class, and pass the domain name as a string parameter.

Discussion

On the Web, publicly accessible IP addresses are often mapped to host names that are easier to remember. For example, the IP address 207.171.185.16 might be mapped to the domain name www.amazon.com. To determine the IP address for a given name, the computer contacts a DNS server.

The entire process of name resolution is transparent if you use the *System.Net.Dns* class, which allows you to retrieve the IP address for a host name by calling *GetHostByName*. Here's how you might retrieve the list of IP addresses mapped to www.microsoft.com:

```
using System;
using System.Net;

public class ResolveIP {

    private static void Main() {
```

```
        foreach (IPAddress ip in
          Dns.GetHostByName("www.microsoft.com").AddressList) {

            Console.Write(ip.AddressFamily.ToString() + ": ");
            Console.WriteLine(ip.ToString());
        }

        Console.ReadLine();
    }
}
```

This test produces output similar to the following:

```
InterNetwork: 207.46.249.222
InterNetwork: 207.46.134.222
InterNetwork: 207.46.249.27
InterNetwork: 207.46.134.155
InterNetwork: 207.46.249.190
```

11.7 Ping an IP Address

Problem

You want to check to see if a computer is online and gauge its response time.

Solution

Send a ping message. This message is sent using the Internet Control Message Protocol (ICMP) protocol with a raw socket.

Discussion

A *ping message* contacts a device at a specific IP address, sends a test message, and requests that the remote device respond by echoing back the packet. To gauge the connection latency between two computers, you can measure the time taken for a ping response to be received.

Despite the simplicity of ping messages compared to other types of network communication, implementing a ping utility in .NET requires a significant amount of complex, low-level networking code. The .NET class library doesn't have a prebuilt solution—instead, you must use raw sockets and some exceedingly lengthy code.

However, at least one developer has solved the ping problem. Lance Olson, a developer at Microsoft, has provided C# code that allows you to ping a host by name or IP address and measure the milliseconds taken for a response. This code has been adapted into the following *Pinger* class (shown below with some details and error-handling code omitted). The complete code is available with this book's sample files.

```
using System;
using System.Net;
using System.Net.Sockets;

public class Pinger {

    public static int GetPingTime(string host) {

        int dwStart = 0, dwStop = 0;

        // Create a raw socket.
        Socket socket = new Socket(AddressFamily.InterNetwork,
          SocketType.Raw, ProtocolType.Icmp);

        // Get the server IPEndPoint, and convert it to an EndPoint.
        IPHostEntry serverHE = Dns.GetHostByName(host);
        IPEndPoint ipepServer = new IPEndPoint(serverHE.AddressList[0], 0);
        EndPoint epServer = (ipepServer);

        // Set the receiving endpoint to the client machine.
        IPHostEntry fromHE = Dns.GetHostByName(Dns.GetHostName());
        IPEndPoint ipEndPointFrom = new IPEndPoint(fromHE.AddressList[0], 0);

        EndPoint EndPointFrom = (ipEndPointFrom);

        // Construct the packet to send.
        int PacketSize = 0;
        IcmpPacket packet = new IcmpPacket();
        for (int j = 0; j < 1; j++) {
            packet.Type = ICMP_ECHO;
            packet.SubCode = 0;
            packet.CheckSum = UInt16.Parse("0");
            packet.Identifier   = UInt16.Parse("45");
            packet.SequenceNumber = UInt16.Parse("0");

            int PingData = 32;
            packet.Data = new Byte[PingData];

            for (int i = 0; i < PingData; i++)
                packet.Data[i] = (byte)'#';

            PacketSize = PingData + 8;
```

```
            Byte [] icmp_pkt_buffer = new Byte [PacketSize];
            int index = 0;
            index = Serialize(packet, icmp_pkt_buffer, PacketSize, PingData);

            // Calculate the checksum for the packet.
            double double_length = Convert.ToDouble(index);
            double dtemp = Math.Ceiling(double_length / 2);
            int cksum_buffer_length = Convert.ToInt32(dtemp);
            UInt16[] cksum_buffer = new UInt16[cksum_buffer_length];
            int icmp_header_buffer_index = 0;

            for (int i = 0; i < cksum_buffer_length; i++) {
                cksum_buffer[i] = BitConverter.ToUInt16(icmp_pkt_buffer,
                  icmp_header_buffer_index);
                icmp_header_buffer_index += 2;
            }

            UInt16 u_cksum = checksum(cksum_buffer, cksum_buffer_length);
            packet.CheckSum  = u_cksum;

            // Now that we have the checksum, serialize the packet again.
            byte[] sendbuf = new byte[PacketSize];
            index = Serialize(packet, sendbuf, PacketSize, PingData);

            // Start timing.
            dwStart = System.Environment.TickCount;
            socket.SendTo(sendbuf, PacketSize, 0, epServer);

            // Receive the response, and then stop timing.
            byte[] ReceiveBuffer = new byte[256];
            socket.ReceiveFrom(ReceiveBuffer, 256, 0, ref EndPointFrom);
            dwStop = System.Environment.TickCount - dwStart;
        }

        // Clean up and return the calculated ping time in seconds
        socket.Close();
        return (int)dwStop;
    }

    private static int Serialize(IcmpPacket packet, byte[] buffer,
      int packetSize, int pingData) {

        // (Private method for serializing the packet omitted.)
    }

    private static UInt16 checksum(UInt16[] buffer, int size) {

        // (Private method for calculating the checksum omitted.)
    }
}
```

```
public class IcmpPacket {
    public byte Type; // type of message
    public byte SubCode; // type of sub code
    public UInt16 CheckSum; // ones complement checksum of struct
    public UInt16 Identifier; // identifier
    public UInt16 SequenceNumber; // sequence number
    public byte[] Data;
}
```

You can use the *static Pinger.GetPingTime* method with an IP address or a domain name. The *GetPingTime* method returns the number of milliseconds that elapse before a response is received. Here's the code that tests three Web sites:

```
public class PingTest {

    private static void Main() {

        Console.WriteLine("Milliseconds to contact www.yahoo.com: " +
            Pinger.GetPingTime("www.yahoo.com").ToString());
        Console.WriteLine("Milliseconds to contact www.seti.org: " +
            Pinger.GetPingTime("www.seti.org").ToString());
        Console.WriteLine("Milliseconds to contact the local computer: " +
            Pinger.GetPingTime("127.0.0.1").ToString());

        Console.ReadLine();
    }
}
```

The ping test allows you to verify that other computers are online. It can also be useful if your application needs to evaluate several different remote computers that provide the same content and determine which one will offer the lowest network latency for communication.

Note   A ping attempt might not succeed if a firewall forbids it. For example, many heavily trafficked sites ignore ping requests because they're wary of being swamped by a flood of simultaneous pings that will tie up the server (in essence, a denial of service attack).

11.8 Communicate Using TCP

Problem

You need to send data between two computers on a network using a TCP/IP connection.

Solution

One computer (the server) must begin listening using the *System.Net.Sockets.TcpListener* class. Once a connection is established, both computers can communicate using the *System.Net.Sockets.TcpListener* class.

Discussion

TCP is a reliable, connection-based protocol that allows two computers to communicate over a network. It provides built-in flow-control, sequencing, and error handling, which makes it very reliable and easy to program with.

To create a TCP connection, one computer must act as the server and start listening on a specific *endpoint*. (An endpoint is defined as an IP address, which identifies the computer and port number.) The other computer must act as a client and send a connection request to the endpoint on which the first computer is listening. Once the connection is established, the two computers can take turns exchanging messages. .NET makes this process easy through its stream abstraction. Both computers simply write to and read from a *System.Net.Sockets.NetworkStream* to transmit data.

> **Note**   Even though a TCP connection always requires a server and a client, there's no reason an individual application can't be both. For example, in a peer-to-peer application, one thread is dedicated to listening for incoming requests (acting as a server) while another thread is dedicated to initiate outgoing connections (acting as a client). In the examples provided with this chapter, the client and server are provided as separate applications and are placed in separate subdirectories. See the readme.txt included with the code for more information.

Once a TCP connection is established, the two computers can send any type of data by writing it to the *NetworkStream*. However, it's a good idea to begin designing a networked application by defining the application-level protocol that clients and servers will use to communicate. This protocol includes constants that represent the allowable commands, ensuring that your application code doesn't include hard-coded communication strings.

```
namespace SharedComponent {

    public class ServerMessages {
        public const string AcknowledgeOK = "OK";
        public const string AcknowledgeCancel = "Cancel";
        public const string Disconnect = "Bye";
    }

    public class ClientMessages {
        public const string RequestConnect = "Hello";
        public const string Disconnect = "Bye";
    }
}
```

In this example, the defined vocabulary is basic. You would add more constants depending on the type of application. For example, in a file transfer application, you might include a client message for requesting a file. The server might then respond with an acknowledgment and return file details such as the file size. These constants should be compiled into a separate class library assembly, which must be referenced by both the client and server.

The following code is a template for a basic TCP server. It listens on a fixed port, accepts the first incoming connection, and then waits for the client to request a disconnect. At this point, the server could call the *TcpListener.AcceptTcpClient* method again to wait for the next client, but instead, it simply shuts down.

```
using System;
using System.Net;
using System.Net.Sockets;
using System.IO;
using SharedComponent;

public class TcpServerTest {

    private static void Main() {

        // Create a new listener on port 8000.
        TcpListener listener = new TcpListener(IPAddress.Parse("127.0.0.1"),
          8000);

        Console.WriteLine("About to initialize port.");
        listener.Start();
        Console.WriteLine("Listening for a connection...");
```

```csharp
        try {

            // Wait for a connection request,
            // and return a TcpClient initialized for communication.
            TcpClient client = listener.AcceptTcpClient();
            Console.WriteLine("Connection accepted.");

            // Retrieve the network stream.
            NetworkStream stream = client.GetStream();

            // Create a BinaryWriter for writing to the stream.
            BinaryWriter w = new BinaryWriter(stream);

            // Create a BinaryReader for reading from the stream.
            BinaryReader r = new BinaryReader(stream);

            if (r.ReadString() == ClientMessages.RequestConnect) {

                w.Write(ServerMessages.AcknowledgeOK);
                Console.WriteLine("Connection completed.");

                while (r.ReadString() != ClientMessages.Disconnect)
                {}

                Console.WriteLine();
                Console.WriteLine("Disconnect request received.");
                w.Write(ServerMessages.Disconnect);
            } else {
                Console.WriteLine("Could not complete connection.");
            }

            // Close the connection socket.
            client.Close();
            Console.WriteLine("Connection closed.");

            // Close the underlying socket (stop listening for new requests).
            listener.Stop();
            Console.WriteLine("Listener stopped.");
        } catch (Exception err) {
            Console.WriteLine(err.ToString());
        }

        Console.ReadLine();
    }
}
```

The following code is a template for a basic TCP client. It contacts the server at the specified IP address and port. In this example, the loopback address (127.0.0.1) is used, which always points to the current computer. Keep in mind that a TCP connection requires two ports: one at the server end and one at the client end. However, only the server port needs to be specified. The client port can be chosen dynamically at run time from the available ports, which is what the *TcpClient* class will do by default.

```
using System;
using System.Net;
using System.Net.Sockets;
using System.IO;
using SharedComponent;

public class TcpClientTest {

    private static void Main() {

        TcpClient client = new TcpClient();

        try {

            Console.WriteLine("Attempting to connect to the server " +
              "on port 8000.");
            client.Connect(IPAddress.Parse("127.0.0.1"), 8000);
            Console.WriteLine("Connection established.");

            // Retrieve the network stream.
            NetworkStream stream = client.GetStream();

            // Create a BinaryWriter for writing to the stream.
            BinaryWriter w = new BinaryWriter(stream);

            // Create a BinaryReader for reading from the stream.
            BinaryReader r = new BinaryReader(stream);

            // Start a dialogue.
            w.Write(ClientMessages.RequestConnect);

            if (r.ReadString() == ServerMessages.AcknowledgeOK) {

                Console.WriteLine("Connected.");
                Console.WriteLine("Press Enter to disconnect.");
                Console.ReadLine();
                Console.WriteLine("Disconnecting...");
                w.Write(ClientMessages.Disconnect);
            } else {
```

```
                    Console.WriteLine("Connection not completed.");
            }

            // Close the connection socket.
            client.Close();
            Console.WriteLine("Port closed.");
        } catch (Exception err) {
            Console.WriteLine(err.ToString());
        }

        Console.ReadLine();
    }
}
```

Here's a sample connection transcript on the server side:

```
About to initialize port.
Listening for a connection...
Connection accepted.
Connection completed.

Disconnect request received.
Connection closed.
Listener stopped.
```

And here's a sample connection transcript on the client side:

```
Attempting to connect to the server on port 8000.
Connection established.
Connected.
Press Enter to disconnect.

Disconnecting...
Port closed.
```

11.9 Get the Client IP Address from a Socket Connection

Problem

The server application needs to determine the client IP address after it accepts a connection.

Solution

Use the *AcceptSocket* method of the *TcpListener* class to get a lower-level *System.Net.Sockets.Socket* class instead of a *TcpClient*. Use the *Socket.RemoteEndPoint* property to get the client's IP address.

Discussion

The *TcpClient* class doesn't allow you to retrieve the underlying socket or any information about the client's port and IP address. The *TcpClient* does provide a *Socket* property, but this property is *protected* and therefore not accessible from nonderived classes. To access the underlying socket, you have two options.

■   Create a custom class that derives from *TcpClient*. This class can access the *protected Socket* property and expose it through a new property. You must then use this custom class instead of the *TcpClient*.

■   Bypass the *TcpClient* class by using the *TcpListener.AcceptSocket* method. You can still use the higher-level *BinaryWriter* and *Binary-Reader* classes to write and read data, but you'll need to create the *NetworkStream* first, using the socket.

This recipe uses the second approach. Following is a revised version of the server code from recipe 11.8, with the changed code emphasized.

```
using System;
using System.Net;
using System.Net.Sockets;
using System.IO;
using SharedComponent;

public class TcpServerTest {

    private static void Main() {

        // Create a new listener on port 8000.
        TcpListener listener = new TcpListener(IPAddress.Parse("127.0.0.1"),
            8000);

        Console.WriteLine("About to initialize port.");
        listener.Start();
        Console.WriteLine("Listening for a connection...");

        try {

            // Wait for a connection request,
            // and return a Socket initialized for communication.
            Socket socket = listener.AcceptSocket();

            Console.WriteLine("Connection accepted.");
```

```csharp
        // Create the network stream.
        NetworkStream stream = new NetworkStream(socket);

        // Create a BinaryWriter for writing to the stream.
        BinaryWriter w = new BinaryWriter(stream);

        // Create a BinaryReader for reading from the stream.
        BinaryReader r = new BinaryReader(stream);

        if (r.ReadString() == ClientMessages.RequestConnect) {

            w.Write(ServerMessages.AcknowledgeOK);
            Console.WriteLine("Connection completed.");

            // Get the client IP.
            Console.WriteLine("The client is from IP address: " +
              ((IPEndPoint)socket.RemoteEndPoint).Address.ToString());
            Console.Write("The client uses local port: " +
              ((IPEndPoint)socket.RemoteEndPoint).Port.ToString());

            while (r.ReadString() != ClientMessages.Disconnect)
            {}

            Console.WriteLine();
            Console.WriteLine("Disconnect request received.");
            w.Write(ServerMessages.Disconnect);
        } else {
            Console.WriteLine("Could not complete connection.");
        }

        // Close the connection socket.
        socket.Close();
        Console.WriteLine("Connection closed.");

        // Close the underlying socket (stop listening for new requests).
        listener.Stop();
        Console.WriteLine("Listener stopped.");
    } catch (Exception err) {
        Console.WriteLine(err.ToString());
    }

    Console.ReadLine();
  }
}
```

11.10 Set Socket Options

Problem

You need to set low-level socket options, such as those that specify send and receive timeouts.

Solution

Use the *Socket.SetSocketOption* method. You can set the properties of the socket that is used to listen for requests or those of the socket used for a specific client session.

Discussion

You can use the *Socket.SetSocketOption* method to set a number of low-level socket properties. When calling this method, you supply the following three parameters:

- A value from the *SocketOptionLevel* enumeration, which indicates the type of socket that the setting applies to (for example, TCP, UDP, and so on).

- A value from the *SocketOptionName* enumeration, which specifies the actual socket setting you are changing. Refer to the .NET Framework documentation for a full list of socket *SocketOptionName* values.

- A value that represents the new setting. This is usually an integer, but it can also be a byte array or an object type.

Here's an example that sets the send timeout of a socket:

```
// Send operations will time out if confirmation is not received within 1000
// milliseconds.
socket.SetSocketOption(SocketOptionLevel.Socket,
  SocketOptionName.SendTimeout, 1000);
```

Notice that in order to access the socket that represents a client/server connection, you must use the *TcpListener.AcceptSocket* method instead of *TcpListener.AcceptTcpClient*, as discussed in recipe 11.9.

You can also set the socket options for the socket that is used by the *TcpListener* to monitor for connection requests. However, you must take a few additional steps. The *TcpListener* provides a *Socket* property, but its accessibility is *protected*, which means you can't access it directly. Instead, you must derive a new class from *TcpListener*, as shown on the following page.

```
public class CustomTcpListener : TcpListener {

    public Socket Socket {
        get {return base.Server;}
    }

    public CustomTcpListener(IPAddress ip, int port) : base(ip, port) {}
}
```

You can now use this class when creating a *TcpListener*. Here's an example that uses this approach to set a socket option:

```
CustomTcpListener listener = new CustomTcpListener(IPAddress.Parse(
    "127.0.0.1"), 8000);

listener.Socket.SetSocketOption(SocketOptionLevel.Socket,
  SocketOptionName.ReceiveTimeout, 1000);

// (Now use CustomTcpListener in the same way you would use TcpListener.)
```

11.11 Create a Multithreaded TCP Server

Problem

You want to create a TCP server that can simultaneously handle multiple TCP clients.

Solution

Use the *AcceptTcpClient* method of the *TcpListener* class. Every time a new client connects, start a new thread to handle the request and call *TcpListener.AcceptTcpClient* again.

Discussion

A single TCP endpoint (IP address and port) can serve multiple connections. In fact, the operating system takes care of most of the work for you. All you need to do is create a worker object on the server that will handle each connection on a separate thread.

For example, consider the basic TCP client and server classes shown in recipe 11.8. You can easily convert the server into a multithreaded server that supports multiple simultaneous connections. First create a class that will interact with an individual client, as shown in the following code:

```csharp
using System;
using System.Net;
using System.Net.Sockets;
using System.IO;
using System.Threading;
using SharedComponent;

public class ClientHandler {

    private TcpClient client;
    private string ID;

    public ClientHandler(TcpClient client, string ID) {

        this.client = client;
        this.ID = ID;
    }

    public void Start() {

        // Retrieve the network stream.
        NetworkStream stream = client.GetStream();

        // Create a BinaryWriter for writing to the stream.
        BinaryWriter w = new BinaryWriter(stream);

        // Create a BinaryReader for reading from the stream.
        BinaryReader r = new BinaryReader(stream);

        if (r.ReadString() == ClientMessages.RequestConnect) {

            w.Write(ServerMessages.AcknowledgeOK);
            Console.WriteLine(ID + ": Connection completed.");
            while (r.ReadString() != ClientMessages.Disconnect) {}

            Console.WriteLine(ID + ": Disconnect request received.");
            w.Write(ServerMessages.Disconnect);

        }else {
            Console.WriteLine(ID + ": Could not complete connection.");
        }

        // Close the connection socket.
        client.Close();
        Console.WriteLine(ID + ": Client connection closed.");

        Console.ReadLine();
    }
}
```

Next modify the server code so that it loops continuously, creating new *ClientHandler* instances as required and launching them on new threads. Here's the revised code:

```
public class TcpServerTest {

    private static void Main() {

        TcpListener listener = new TcpListener(IPAddress.Parse("127.0.0.1"),
            8000);
        Console.WriteLine("Server: About to initialize port.");
        listener.Start();
        Console.WriteLine("Server: Listening for a connection...");

        int clientNum = 0;
        while (true) {

            try {

                // Wait for a connection request,
                // and return a TcpClient initialized for communication.
                TcpClient client = listener.AcceptTcpClient();
                Console.WriteLine("Server: Connection accepted.");

                // Create a new object to handle this connection.
                clientNum++;
                ClientHandler handler = new ClientHandler(client, "Client " +
                    clientNum.ToString());

                // Start this object working on another thread.
                Thread handlerThread =
                    new Thread(new ThreadStart(handler.Start));
                handlerThread.IsBackground = true;
                handlerThread.Start();

                // (You could also add the Handler and HandlerThread to
                // a collection to track client sessions.)

            }catch (Exception err) {
                Console.WriteLine(err.ToString());
            }
        }
    }
}
```

The following code shows the server-side transcript of a session with two clients:

```
Server: About to initialize port.
Server: Listening for a connection...
Server: Connection accepted.
Client 1: Connection completed.
Server: Connection accepted.
Client 2: Connection completed.
Client 2: Disconnect request received.
Client 2: Client connection closed.
Client 1: Disconnect request received.
Client 1: Client connection closed.
```

You might want to add additional code to the network server so that it tracks the current worker objects in a collection. Doing so would allow the server to abort these tasks if it needs to shut down and enforce a maximum number of simultaneous clients.

11.12 Use TCP Asynchronously

Problem

You need to write data to the network stream one "chunk" at a time, without blocking the rest of your code. This technique might be used if you wanted to stream a large file over the network.

Solution

Create a separate class that will handle the asynchronous streaming of the data. You can start streaming a block of data using the *NetworkStream.BeginWrite* method and supply a callback method. When the callback is triggered, send the next block.

Discussion

The *NetworkStream* includes basic support for asynchronous use through the *BeginRead* and *BeginWrite* methods. Using these methods, you can send or receive a block of data on one of the threads provided by the .NET runtime's thread pool, without blocking your code. This recipe demonstrates the technique with asynchronous writing.

When sending data asynchronously, you must send raw binary data (an array of bytes). It's up to you to choose the amount that you want to send or receive at a time. The following example rewrites the threaded server from recipe 11.11 so that each *ClientHandler* class sends a large amount of data read from a file. This data is sent asynchronously, which means that *ClientHandler* could continue to perform other tasks. (In this example, it simply polls the network stream for messages sent from the client.)

One advantage of the approach used in this recipe is that the entire content from the file is never held in memory at once. Instead, it is retrieved just before a new block is sent. Another advantage is that the server can abort the operation at any time. In this example, the client reads only a third of the data before disconnecting. The server then sets a Boolean member variable named *fileStop* to indicate to the callback that no more data should be sent.

Here's the revised *ClientHandler* class. Notice that *NetworkStream* and *FileStream* are now tracked as member variables, so the callback method can access them. The *TcpServerTest* class doesn't need any changes.

```csharp
using System;
using System.Net;
using System.Net.Sockets;
using System.IO;
using SharedComponent;

public class ClientHandler {

    private TcpClient client;
    private string ID;

    // The amount that will be written in one block (2 KB).
    private int bufferSize = 2048;
    // The buffer that holds the data to write.
    private byte[] buffer;

    // Used to read data from a file.
    private FileStream fileStream;
    // Used to communicate with the client.
    private NetworkStream networkStream;

    // A signal to stop sending data.
    private bool fileStop = false;

    public ClientHandler(TcpClient client, string ID) {

        this.buffer = new byte[bufferSize];
        this.client = client;
        this.ID = ID;
    }

    public void Start() {

        // Retrieve the network stream.
```

```
networkStream = client.GetStream();

// Create objects for sending and receiving text.
BinaryWriter w = new BinaryWriter(networkStream);
BinaryReader r = new BinaryReader(networkStream);

if (r.ReadString() == ClientMessages.RequestConnect) {

    w.Write(ServerMessages.AcknowledgeOK);
    Console.WriteLine(ID + ": Connection completed.");

    string message = "";
    while (message != ClientMessages.Disconnect) {

        message = r.ReadString();
        if (message == ClientMessages.RequestData) {

            // The filename could be supplied by the client,
            // but in this example a test file is hard coded.
            fileStream = new FileStream("test.bin", FileMode.Open);

            // Send the file size (this is how the client knows
            // how much to read).
            w.Write(fileStream.Length.ToString());

            // This method will start an asynchronous operation.
            StreamData(null);
        }
    }
    fileStop = true;
    Console.WriteLine(ID + ": Disconnect request received.");
} else {
    Console.WriteLine(ID + ": Could not complete connection.");
}

// Clean up.
client.Close();
Console.WriteLine(ID + ": Client connection closed.");
Console.ReadLine();
}

private void StreamData(IAsyncResult asyncResult) {

    // Abort if the client has disconnected.
    if (fileStop == true) {
        fileStop = false;
        return;
    }
```

```
        if (asyncResult != null) {
            // One block has been written asynchronously.
            networkStream.EndWrite(asyncResult);
        }

        // Get the next block from the file.
        int bytesRead = fileStream.Read(buffer, 0, buffer.Length);

        // If no bytes are read, the stream is at the end of the file.
        if (bytesRead > 0) {

            Console.WriteLine("Streaming new block.");

            // Write the next block to the network stream.
            networkStream.BeginWrite(buffer, 0, buffer.Length,
              new AsyncCallback(StreamData), null);
        } else {

            // End the operation.
            Console.WriteLine("File streaming complete.");
            fileStream.Close();
        }
    }
}
```

You could use a similar pattern to *read* the data asynchronously on the client side.

11.13 Communicate Using UDP

Problem

You need to send data between two computers on a network using a User Datagram Protocol (UDP) stream.

Solution

Use the *System.Net.Sockets.UdpClient* class, and use two threads: one to send data and the other to receive it.

Discussion

UDP is a connectionless protocol that doesn't include any flow control or error checking. Unlike TCP, UDP shouldn't be used where reliable communication is required. However, because of its lower overhead, UDP is often used for "chatty" applications where it's acceptable to lose some messages. For example, imagine you want to create a network in which individual clients send information about the current temperature at their locations to a server every few minutes. You might use UDP in this case because the communication frequency is high and the damage caused by losing a packet is trivial (because the server can just continue to use the last received temperature reading).

The application shown in the following code uses two threads: one to receive messages and one to send them. To test this application, load two instances at the same time. On computer A, specify the IP address for computer B. On computer B, specify the address for computer A. You can then send text messages back and forth at will. (You can simulate a test on a single computer by using two different ports and the loopback IP address 127.0.0.1.)

```
using System;
using System.Text;
using System.Net;
using System.Net.Sockets;
using System.Threading;

public class UdpTest {

    private static int localPort;

    private static void Main() {

        // Define endpoint where messages are sent.
        Console.Write("Connect to IP: ");
        string IP = Console.ReadLine();
        Console.Write("Connect to port: ");
        int port = Int32.Parse(Console.ReadLine());

        IPEndPoint remoteEndPoint = new IPEndPoint(IPAddress.Parse(IP),
          port);

        // Define local endpoint (where messages are received).
        Console.Write("Local port for listening: ");
        localPort = Int32.Parse(Console.ReadLine());

        Console.WriteLine();

        // Create a new thread for receiving incoming messages.
        Thread receiveThread = new Thread(
          new ThreadStart(ReceiveData));
        receiveThread.IsBackground = true;
        receiveThread.Start();

        UdpClient client = new UdpClient();
```

```
            try {
                string text;
                do {
                    text = Console.ReadLine();

                    // Send the text to the remote client.
                    if (text != "") {

                        // Encode the data to binary using UTF8 encoding.
                        byte[] data = Encoding.UTF8.GetBytes(text);

                        // Send the text to the remote client.
                        client.Send(data, data.Length, remoteEndPoint);
                    }
                } while (text != "");
            } catch (Exception err) {
                Console.WriteLine(err.ToString());
            }

            Console.ReadLine();
        }

        private static void ReceiveData() {

            UdpClient client = new UdpClient(localPort);
            while (true) {

                try {
                    // Receive bytes.
                    IPEndPoint anyIP = new IPEndPoint(IPAddress.Any, 0);
                    byte[] data = client.Receive(ref anyIP);

                    // Convert bytes to text using UTF8 encoding.
                    string text = Encoding.UTF8.GetString(data);

                    // Display the retrieved text.
                    Console.WriteLine(">> " + text);
                } catch (Exception err) {
                    Console.WriteLine(err.ToString());
                }
            }
        }
    }
```

Notice that UDP applications can't use the *NetworkStream* abstraction that TCP applications can. Instead, they must convert all data to a stream of bytes using an encoding class, as described in recipe 2.2.

You can test this application with clients on the local computer using the loopback alias 127.0.0.1, provided you use different listening ports. For example, imagine a situation with two UDP clients, client A and client B. Here's a sample transcript for client A:

```
Connect to IP: 127.0.0.1
Connect to port: 8001
Local port for listening: 8080

Hi there!
```

And here's the corresponding transcript for client B (with the received message):

```
Connect to IP: 127.0.0.1
Connect to port: 8080
Local port for listening: 8001

>> Hi there!
```

11.14 Send E-Mail Through SMTP

Problem

You need to send e-mail to an e-mail address using a Simple Mail Transfer Protocol (SMTP) server.

Solution

Use the *SmtpMail* and *MailMessage* classes in the *System.Web.Mail* namespace.

Discussion

The classes in the *System.Web.Mail* namespace provide a bare-bones wrapper for the Collaboration Data Objects for Windows 2000 (CDOSYS) component. They allow you to compose and send formatted e-mail messages using SMTP.

Using these types is easy. You simply create a *MailMessage* object, specify the sender and recipient e-mail address, and place the message content in the *Body* property.

```
MailMessage myMessage = new MailMessage();
myMessage.To = "someone@somewhere.com";
myMessage.From = "me@somewhere.com";
myMessage.Subject = "Hello";
myMessage.Priority = MailPriority.High;
```

```
myMessage.Body = "This is the message!";
```

If you want, you can send an HTML message by changing the message format and using HTML tags.

```
myMessage.BodyFormat = MailFormat.Html;
myMessage.Body = @"<HTML><HEAD></HEAD>" +
  @"<BODY>This is the message!</BODY></HTML>";
```

You can even add file attachments using the *MailMessage.Attachments* collection and the *MailAttachment* class.

```
MailAttachment myAttachment = new MailAttachment("c:\\mypic.gif");
myMessage.Attachments.Add(myAttachment);
```

To send the message, you simply specify the SMTP server name and call the *SmptMail.Send* method.

```
SmtpMail.SmtpServer = "test.mailserver.com";
SmtpMail.Send(myMessage);
```

However, there is a significant catch to using the *SmtpMail* class to send an e-mail message. This class requires a local SMTP server or relay server on your network. In addition, the *SmtpMail* class doesn't support authentication, so if your SMTP server requires a username and password, you won't be able to send any mail. To overcome these problems, you can use the CDOSYS component directly through COM interop (assuming you have a server version of Windows or Microsoft Exchange).

> **Note**   Remember that the SMTP protocol can't be used to retrieve e-mail. For this task, you need the POP3 or IMAP protocol, neither of which is exposed natively in the .NET Framework.

For more information about using and configuring your own SMTP server, consult a dedicated book on IIS.

11.15 Send and Retrieve E-Mail with MAPI

Problem

You want to send an e-mail message, but you don't have a Simple Mail Transfer Protocol (SMTP) mail server configured for the computer.

Solution

Use Simple MAPI (Messaging Application Programming Interface) by importing the required function from the unmanaged system library Mapi32.dll.

Discussion

MAPI is an interface that allows you to interact with the mailing features that are integrated into the Windows operating system. You can use MAPI (either through its unmanaged API, or through the MAPI COM component included with Visual Studio 6) to interact with the default mail client (usually Microsoft Outlook or Outlook Express). Tasks include retrieving contact information from the address book, retrieving the messages in the Inbox, and programmatically composing and sending messages. Unfortunately, there are no classes for using MAPI in the .NET Framework. However, you can use the unmanaged Mapi32.dll.

The main challenge to using Simple MAPI in .NET is marshalling the structures that are used in .NET over to structures that Simple MAPI expects and then marshalling the structures returned by Simple MAPI back to the .NET application. This isn't a trivial task. However, Microsoft provides a full solution in a generic C# component that's freely downloadable. The following two projects are available:

- A class library component that wraps Simple MAPI functions and makes them available through class methods (downloadable at *http://support.microsoft.com/?kbid=315653*).

- A test program that works with the component to log on, log off, read mail, send mail, and so on (*http://support.microsoft.com/?kbid =315367*).

The full code for both of these components is straightforward, but too lengthy to list here. It's also provided with the downloadable code for this chapter.

> **Note**   For a more sophisticated example that builds on Microsoft's Simple MAPI library to create a rich Windows Forms application, a freely downloadable (although unsupported) sample C# project is provided by Thomas Scheidegger at *http://www.codeproject.com/csharp /simplemapidotnet.asp.*

12

XML Web Services and Remoting

The Microsoft .NET Framework supports two high-level distributed programming models: Remoting and XML Web services. Although these two technologies share many similarities (for example, both abstract cross-process and cross-machine calls as method invocations on a remote objects), they also have fundamental differences.

XML Web services are built using cross-platform standards and are based on the concept of XML messaging. XML Web services are executed by the ASP.NET runtime, which means that they gain ASP.NET features such as output caching. It also means that XML Web services are always stateless. Overall, XML Web services are best suited when you need to cross platform boundaries (for example, with a Java client calling an ASP.NET Web service) or trust boundaries (for example, in business-to-business transactions). The XML Web service-related recipes in this chapter discuss how to:

■ Improve the flexibility of a proxy class by not hard coding its XML Web service address (recipe 12.1)

■ Use caching to improve the performance and scalability of XML Web services (recipes 12.2 and 12.3)

■ Create a transactional XML Web service method (recipe 12.4)

■ Pass authentication credentials to an XML Web service using a proxy (recipe 12.5)

■ Call an XML Web service method asynchronously (recipes 12.6 and 12.6)

Remoting is a .NET-specific technology for distributed objects and is the successor to DCOM. It's ideal for in-house systems in which all applications are built on the .NET platform, such as the backbone of an internal order-processing system. Remoting allows for different types of communication, including leaner binary messages and more efficient TCP/IP connections, which aren't supported by XML Web services. In addition, Remoting is the only technology that supports stateful objects and bidirectional communication through callbacks. It's also the only technology that allows you to send custom .NET objects over the wire. The Remoting-related recipes in this chapter discuss how to:

■ Make objects remotable, register them, and host them on an IIS server (recipes 12.7, 12.8, and 12.9)

■ Fire events over remoting channels (recipe 12.10)

■ Control the lifetime and versioning of remotable objects (recipes 12.11 and 12.12)

■ Implement one-way methods in remotable objects (recipe 12.13)

> **Note** This chapter points out some useful techniques with XML Web services and Remoting, but it's worth consulting a dedicated book for more detailed information. For XML Web services, you can consider *Microsoft .NET XML Web Services Step by Step* by Adam Freeman and Allan Jones (Microsoft Press, 2002), and for Remoting consider *Advanced .NET Remoting* by Ingo Rammer (Apress, 2002).

12.1 Avoid Hard-Coding the XML Web Service URL

Problem

You need to use an XML Web service located at a URL that might change after you deploy the client application.

Solution

Use a dynamic URL, which will be retrieved automatically from the client application's configuration file. You can configure a dynamic URL in the URL Behavior section of a Web Reference's Properties in Microsoft Visual Studio .NET, or by using the /*appsettingurlkey* parameter with the Web Services Description Language tool (Wsdl.exe).

Discussion

By default, when you create a proxy class, the XML Web service URL is hard-coded in the constructor of the proxy class. You can override this setting in your code by manually modifying the *Url* property of the proxy class after you instantiate it. However, there's another option: configure the proxy class to use a dynamic URL endpoint.

In Visual Studio .NET, you can make this change by selecting the Web reference in the Visual Studio .NET Solution Explorer and changing the URL Behavior option in the Properties window, as shown in Figure 12-1.

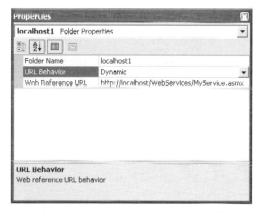

Figure 12-1   Configuring a dynamic XML Web service URL.

After you make this change, the XML Web service URL will be automatically added to the client application's configuration file. The configuration file is Web.config for all Web applications and [AppName].exe.config for all other applications, in which case the source appears in the design environment as simply App.config (and is renamed automatically by Visual Studio .NET). An example of the automatically generated configuration file setting is shown here:

```
<?xml version="1.0" encoding="utf-8"?>
<configuration>

  <appSettings>
    <add key="AppName.ServerName.ServiceName"
    value="http://localhost/WebServices/MyService.asmx"/>
  </appSettings>

</configuration>
```

You can also use a dynamic URL with a proxy class generated by Wsdl.exe. In this case, you use the */appsettingurlkey* parameter to identify the name of the configuration setting where the URL will be stored. You must create the configuration file manually.

```
wsdl /out:Proxy.cs http://localhost/WebServices/MyService.asmx?WSDL
/appsettingurlkey:AppName.ServerName.ServiceName
```

In either case, the code in the proxy class is modified so that it attempts to read the URL from the configuration file. If it doesn't find the required value, it defaults to the URL that was used during development. This approach allows you to modify the XML Web service URL after compiling and deploying the application, simply by editing the configuration file.

12.2 Use Response Caching in an XML Web Service

Problem

You want to improve XML Web service performance by caching the return value of a Web method.

Solution

Use response caching by setting the *CacheDuration* property of the *System.Web.Services.WebMethod* attribute.

Discussion

In ASP.NET, XML Web services support response caching in much the same way as ASP.NET Web pages. When response caching is enabled, your code runs only once, and the return value of the Web method is stored and returned on subsequent method invocations. With Web forms, caching is performed on a per-form basis. With XML Web services, caching is enabled and configured distinctly for each Web method.

For example, the following Web method returns the current date and time on the server. This information is cached for one minute, meaning that subsequent requests within this timeframe will receive the previously recorded date information.

```
using System;
using System.Web.Services;

public class ResponseCaching {
```

```
[WebMethod(CacheDuration=60)]
public string GetDate() {

    return DateTime.Now.ToString();
}
}
```

If your Web method accepts parameters, ASP.NET will reuse the cached method result only if it receives a request with the same parameter values. If you have a method that accepts a wide range of values, caching might be ineffective or even wasteful because a great deal of information might be stored in the cache but rarely reused. For example, a Web method that performs a mathematical calculation based on numeric input is rarely a good choice for response caching. On the other hand, a Web method that accepts an ID referencing one of a dozen different product items probably is. As always, response caching bypasses your code, making it unsuitable if your Web method needs to perform other actions (such as logging activity) or if your Web method depends on information that's not supplied through method parameters (such as user authentication information or session data).

> **Note**   One limitation of response caching with Web methods is that it allows you to reuse data only within the bounds of a single method. If you want to reuse specific data in different Web methods, data caching (described in the following recipe) will be more effective.

12.3 Use Data Caching in an XML Web Service

Problem

You need to run your Web method code but still use some cached information. Or, you want to improve XML Web service performance by caching some data, but you need to reuse cached data among several methods.

Solution

You can store any object in the cache using the *Insert* method of the *System.Web.Caching.Cache* object. You can access the cache through the *static HttpContext.Current* property.

Discussion

Data caching works almost the same with an XML Web service as it does with a Web page. (You can even store data in the cache using Web page code and retrieve it in an XML Web service, or vice versa.) For more information about data caching and the different types of expiration policies it supports, refer to recipe 7.15.

The only difference between caching in an XML Web service and caching in a Web page is that in the former case, you can't retrieve the *Cache* object as a built-in property. Instead, you need to access the cache through the *static Http-Context.Current* property.

The following example shows an XML Web service with two Web methods. *GetProductCatalog* returns a *DataSet* with a table of product information. This *DataSet* is either retrieved from the cache or generated automatically (if required) using the *private GetProductDataSet* function. The second Web method, *GetProductList*, also uses the customer *DataSet* and the *GetProductDataSet* function. However, it retrieves a subset of the available information—just the product names—and returns it as an array of strings. The end result is that both Web methods can use the same cached data, reducing the burden that is placed on the database.

The full XML Web service code is shown here:

```
using System;
using System.Data;
using System.Data.SqlClient;
using System.Web.Services;
using System.Web;

public class DataCachingTest {

    private static string connectionString = "Data Source=localhost;" +
      "Initial Catalog=Northwind;user ID=sa";

    [WebMethod()]
    public DataSet GetProductCatalog() {

        // Return the complete DataSet (from the cache, if possible).
        return GetCustomerDataSet();
    }

    [WebMethod()]
    public string[] GetProductList() {

        // Get the customer table (from the cache if possible).
        DataTable dt = GetCustomerDataSet().Tables[0];
```

```
        // Create an array that will hold the name of each customer.
        string[] names = new string[dt.Rows.Count];

        // Fill the array.
        int i = 0;
        foreach (DataRow row in dt.Rows) {
            names[i] = row["ProductName"].ToString();
            i += 1;
        }

        return names;
    }

    private DataSet GetCustomerDataSet() {

        // Check for cached item.
        DataSet ds = HttpContext.Current.Cache["Products"] as DataSet;

        if (ds == null) {

            // Recreate the item.
            string SQL = "SELECT * FROM Products";

            // Create ADO.NET objects.
            SqlConnection con = new SqlConnection(connectionString);
            SqlCommand com = new SqlCommand(SQL, con);
            SqlDataAdapter adapter = new SqlDataAdapter(com);
            ds = new DataSet();

            // Execute the command.
            try {

                con.Open();
                adapter.Fill(ds, "Products");

                // Store the item in the cache (for 60 seconds).
                HttpContext.Current.Cache.Insert("Products", ds, null,
                    DateTime.Now.AddSeconds(60), TimeSpan.Zero);
            } catch (Exception err) {
                System.Diagnostics.Debug.WriteLine(err.ToString());
            } finally {
                con.Close();
            }
        }
        return ds;
    }
}
```

You can test this example, and examine how often the cache is being used, by setting breakpoints with the Visual Studio .NET debugger. You'll also need to be running SQL Server or MSDE.

12.4 Create a Transactional Web Method

Problem

You need to execute all the actions in a Web method within the context of a single COM+ transaction so that they all either fail or succeed as a unit.

Solution

Enable an automatic transaction by choosing a value from the *System.Enterprise-Services.TransactionOption* enumeration and applying it to the *TransactionOption* property of the *WebMethod* attribute.

Discussion

In ASP.NET, XML Web services include support for automatic transactions that can be enabled on a per-method basis. When enabled, any data source that supports COM+ transactions (which includes most databases) is automatically enlisted in the current transaction when it's used in your code. The transaction is automatically committed when the Web method completes. The transaction is rolled back if any unhandled exception occurs or if you explicitly call the *Set-Abort* method of the *System.EnterpriseServices.ContextUtil* class.

To enable transaction support for a Web method, set the *TransactionOption* property of the *WebMethod* attribute to *RequiresNew*. For example, the transactional Web method shown in the following code deletes records in a database and then explicitly resets the transaction. To use this code, you must add a reference to the System.EnterpriseServices.dll assembly.

```
using System;
using System.Data.SqlClient;
using System.Web.Services;
using System.EnterpriseServices;

public class TransactionTest {

    private static string connectionString = "Data Source=localhost;" +
      "Initial Catalog=Northwind;user ID=sa";

    [WebMethod(TransactionOption=TransactionOption.RequiresNew)]
```

```
public void FailedTransaction() {

    // Create the connection.
    SqlConnection con = new SqlConnection(connectionString);

    // Create the command for filling the DataSet.
    SqlCommand cmd = new SqlCommand("DELETE * FROM Customers", con);

    // Apply the update.
    // This will be automatically registered as part of the transaction.
    con.Open();
    cmd.ExecuteNonQuery();
    con.Close();

    // Call another method.
    DoSomething();

    // (If no errors have occurred, the database changes
    // are committed here when the method ends).
}

private void DoSomething() {

    // Vote to abort the message.
    ContextUtil.SetAbort();
}
}
```

You can use the Component Services console to monitor this transaction. You can start the Component Services utility by selecting Component Services from the Administrative Tools section of the Control Panel. In the Component Services utility, select the Distributed Transaction Coordinator for the current computer and view the Transaction Statistics. Figure 12-2 shows how the display will look after running this code, which produces one failed transaction.

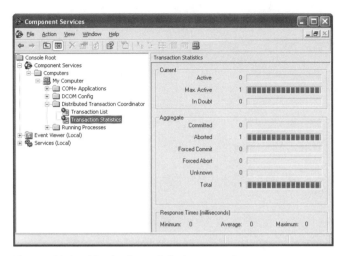

Figure 12-2   Monitoring a failed transaction.

Because of the stateless nature of the HTTP protocol, an XML Web service method can participate only as the root of a transaction, which means that you can't enlist more than one Web method in a single transaction. Although the *TransactionOption* property accepts all the standard *TransactionOption* values, the values don't have the expected meanings. For example, *Disabled*, *NotSupported*, and *Supported* all have the same effect: they disable transaction support. Similarly, *Required* and *RequiresNew* both enable transaction support and start a new transaction. I recommend that you use *RequiresNew* in your Web methods because its name most clearly matches the actual behavior.

> **Note**   COM+ transactions work seamlessly with most data sources because they provide compatible resource managers. But always remember, if you interact with a nontransactional resource, your code won't be rolled back. Some examples of actions that aren't transactional include writing a file, placing information into session state, and accessing a hardware device (such as a printer). On the other hand, data operations with most enterprise database systems (including Microsoft SQL Server and Oracle) are COM+ compatible.

12.5 Set Authentication Credentials for an XML Web Service

Problem

You want an XML Web service client to submit logon credentials for IIS authentication.

Solution

Use the *Credentials* property of the proxy class. You can create a new *NetworkCredential* object by specifying a password and username, or use the *CredentialCache* to retrieve the credentials for the current user.

Discussion

XML Web services, like Web pages, can be used in conjunction with IIS authentication. All you need to do is place your XML Web services in a virtual directory that restricts anonymous access. Unauthenticated calls to any XML Web services in this directory will fail. However, if the user can submit credentials that map to a valid user account, the user will be authenticated and you'll be able to retrieve the authentication information through the built-in *WebService.User* object.

Unlike Web pages, XML Web services have no built-in method for retrieving authentication information from the client because XML Web services are executed by other applications, not directly by the user. Thus, the application that's interacting with the XML Web service bears the responsibility for submitting any required authentication information.

The following XML Web service provides a simple user authentication test. *GetIISUser* returns the user that was authenticated by IIS. If anonymous access is allowed, the result will be an empty string because no authentication will be performed. If anonymous access is denied, the result will be a string in the form [DomainName]\[UserName] or [ComputerName]\[UserName].

```
public class AuthenticationTest : System.Web.Services.WebService {

    // Retrieves the authenticated IIS user.
    [WebMethod()]
    public string GetIISUser() {
        return User.Identity.Name;
    }
}
```

The final step is to create a client that can submit the authentication information. The credentials are submitted through the *Credentials* property of the proxy object. You set this *Credentials* property in the same way that you set the *WebRequest.Credentials* property when retrieving a Web page. See recipe 11.3 for a full discussion.

The following code snippet shows how a client can access an XML Web service that uses basic authentication by creating a new *System.Net.NetworkCredential* object that specifies the user name and password information.

```
// Create the proxy.
localhost.AuthenticationTest proxy = new localhost.AuthenticationTest();

// Create the credentials.
proxy.Credentials = new System.Net.NetworkCredential(
  "myUserName", "myPassword");

Console.WriteLine(proxy.GetIISUser());
```

Here's how you would use similar code to call an XML Web service that uses Microsoft Windows integrated authentication with the credentials from the currently logged on user:

```
// Create the proxy.
localhost.AuthenticationTest proxy = new localhost.AuthenticationTest();

// Assign the current user's credentials to the proxy class.
proxy.Credentials = System.Net.CredentialCache.DefaultCredentials;

Console.WriteLine(proxy.GetIISUser());
```

12.6 Call a Web Method Asynchronously

Problem

You need to invoke a Web method on another thread so that your program can continue with other tasks while waiting for the response.

Solution

Use the proxy class's built-in asynchronous methods, which are provided for every Web method supported by the XML Web service. The methods are named *BeginXXX* and *EndXXX*, where XXX is the name of the original, synchronous method.

Discussion

The automatically generated proxy class has the basic features that you need to call any Web method asynchronously. For example, consider the *Wait* Web method shown in the following code, which pauses for a random number of seconds (10 to 19).

```
using System;
using System.Web.Services;

public class Wait : System.Web.Services.WebService {

    [WebMethod]
    public int Wait() {

        DateTime start = DateTime.Now;
        Random rand = new Random();
        TimeSpan delay = new TimeSpan(0, 0, rand.Next(10, 20));
        while (DateTime.Now < start.Add(delay)) {}
        return delay.Seconds;
    }
}
```

The automatically generated proxy class will include three methods: *Wait*, *BeginWait*, and *EndWait*. *Wait* calls the Web method synchronously. *BeginWait* starts the method on a separate thread and returns immediately. The *BeginXXX* method always takes two parameters more than the original method and returns an *IAsyncState* object. The last two parameters are used to submit state information and a callback. The *IAsyncState* object allows you to determine when the call has completed. For example, you can periodically check the *IAsync-State.IsComplete* property to determine if the method call has finished. When it's finished, you submit the *IAsyncState* object to the *EndWait* method, which completes the call and returns the expected Web method return value. If you call *EndWait* before the method is completed, your code will then wait for it to complete.

There are two common asynchronous patterns with XML Web services. One is calling several asynchronous Web methods at once, and then waiting for them to complete. This approach allows you to collapse the total waiting time, and it works best with a *System.Threading.WaitHandle* object. Here's an example that calls the same *Wait* method three times:

```
using System;
using System.Threading;

public class WaitClient {
```

```
[MTAThread]
private static void Main() {

    localhost.WaitService proxy = new localhost.WaitService();

    // Keep track of the elapsed time.
    DateTime startDate = DateTime.Now;

    // Call three methods asynchronously.
    IAsyncResult handle1 = proxy.BeginWait(null, null);
    IAsyncResult handle2 = proxy.BeginWait(null, null);
    IAsyncResult handle3 = proxy.BeginWait(null, null);

    WaitHandle[] waitHandle = {handle1.AsyncWaitHandle,
        handle2.AsyncWaitHandle, handle3.AsyncWaitHandle};

    // Wait for all the calls to finish.
    WaitHandle.WaitAll(waitHandle);

    int totalDelay = proxy.EndWait(handle1) + proxy.EndWait(handle2) +
        proxy.EndWait(handle3);
    TimeSpan elapsedTime = DateTime.Now - startDate;

    Console.WriteLine("Completed after " + elapsedTime.ToString());
    Console.WriteLine("Total delay time: " + totalDelay.ToString());
    }
}
```

In this case, you'll see that the elapsed time is less than the total delay time:

```
Completed after 00:00:20.2591312
Total delay time: 47
```

Another common technique with asynchronous Web methods is to use a callback. With callbacks, you submit a delegate that identifies a specific method in your code. When the Web method is complete, this delegate is invoked and passed the appropriate *IAsyncResult* object.

Here's a code snippet that calls the *BeginWait* method with a callback:

```
AsyncCallback callback = new AsyncCallback(Callback);

// Start the method asynchronously, with the callback.
proxy.BeginWait(callback, proxy);
```

And here's the callback that will be triggered when the operation is complete:

```
public static void Callback(IAsyncResult handle) {
```

```
        localhost.WaitService proxy = (localhost.WaitService)handle.AsyncState;
        int result = proxy.EndWait(handle);
        Console.WriteLine("Waited " + result.ToString());
}
```

12.7 Make an Object Remotable

Problem

You need to create a class that can be accessed from another application or another computer on the network. However, you don't need cross-platform compatibility, and you want optimum performance.

Solution

Make the class remotable by deriving from *System.MarshalByRefObject*, and create a component host that registers the class with the .NET Remoting infrastructure.

Discussion

Remoting allows you to make an object accessible across process and machine boundaries. While XML Web services are ideal when you need to share functionality across platforms or trust boundaries, Remoting is the best performing choice for a closed system in which all components are built on .NET and the Windows operating system

To use .NET Remoting, you need the following ingredients, each of which must reside in a separate assembly:

- **A remotable object**   This object can be accessed from other applications and computers and must derive from the *System.MarshalByRefObject*.

- **A component host**   This application registers the remotable type with the .NET Remoting infrastructure using the *RemotingConfiguration* class from the *System.Runtime.Remoting* namespace. As long as the component host is running, remote clients can create instances of the remotable object.

- **A client application**   This application can create instances of the remotable class in the component host process and interact with them. The client uses the *RemotingConfiguration* class to register the types it wants to access remotely.

Figure 12-3 shows how these three parts interact. In this example, there's only one client. However, it's also possible for multiple clients to create instances of the remotable class at the same time. In this case, each client will have its own remotable object instance, and all the objects will reside in the application domain of the component host.

Figure 12-3   Using a remotable class.

The first step is to create the remotable class. A simple example is shown here, with a remotable class that returns a *DataSet*. This approach allows a remote client to retrieve database information without needing to connect directly to the server-side database. The remotable class gains the ability to be invoked remotely because it derives from *MarshalByRefObject*.

```csharp
using System;
using System.Data;
using System.Data.SqlClient;

public class ProductsDB : MarshalByRefObject {

    private static string connectionString = "Data Source=localhost;" +
        "Initial Catalog=Northwind;Integrated Security=SSPI";

    public DataTable GetProducts() {

        string SQL = "SELECT * FROM Products";

        // Create ADO.NET objects.
        SqlConnection con = new SqlConnection(connectionString);
        SqlCommand com = new SqlCommand(SQL, con);
        SqlDataAdapter adapter = new SqlDataAdapter(com);
        DataSet ds = new DataSet();

        // Execute the command.
        try {
            con.Open();
            adapter.Fill(ds, "Products");
        } catch (Exception err) {
            Console.WriteLine(err.ToString());
        } finally {
            con.Close();
        }
```

```
        return ds.Tables[0];
    }

    // This method allows you to verify that the object is running remotely.
    public string GetHostLocation() {
        return AppDomain.CurrentDomain.FriendlyName;
    }
}
```

This class is defined in a class library assembly named RemoteObject.dll.

> **Note**   Ideally, the remote object won't retain any state. This characteristic allows you to use *single-call activation*, in which object instances are created at the beginning of each method call and released at the end, much like an XML Web service. This ensures that your objects consume the fewest possible server resources and saves you from the added complexity of implementing a lease policy to configure object lifetime.

Next you must create the component host—the server-side application that hosts all instances of the remote class. You can use any type of long-running .NET Framework application for a component host (including Windows-based applications, Windows services, and Console applications). Here is the code for a simple console component host.

```
using System;
using System.Runtime.Remoting;

public class Server {

    private static void Main() {

        // Register the remotable classes.
        RemotingConfiguration.Configure("Server.exe.config");

        // As long as this application is running, the remote objects
        // will be accessible.
        Console.WriteLine("Press a key to shut down the server.");
        Console.ReadLine();
    }
}
```

The component host uses a configuration file (app.config) to configure the classes it will support, the ports it will support for network communication, and the Uniform Resource Identifier (URI) that the client will use to access the object. Following is a simple configuration file that registers the *RemoteObjects.RemoteObject* class from the RemoteObject.dll assembly and provides network access through TCP/IP on the port 9080. This assembly must be in the global assembly cache (GAC) or in the same directory as the server application. The configuration file also configures the remote object to use single-call activation.

```
<configuration>
  <system.runtime.remoting>
    <application>

      <!-- Define the remotable object. -->
      <service>
        <wellknown
            mode = "SingleCall"
            type="RemoteObject.ProductsDB, RemoteObject"
            objectUri="RemoteObject" />
      </service>

      <!-- Define the protocol used for network access.
          You can use tcp or http channels. -->
      <channels>
        <channel ref="tcp" port="9080" />
      </channels>

    </application>
  </system.runtime.remoting>
</configuration>
```

The component host never interacts with the remotable objects directly. All it does is register the appropriate types with the .NET Remoting infrastructure. After this point, clients can create object instances, and the server application can continue with other tasks. However, when the component host is closed, any remotable objects will be destroyed, and no more objects can be created.

The client application uses a similar configuration file that indicates the URL of the remote object and its type. The URL takes this form:

```
[Protocol]://[Server]:[PortNumber]/[ObjectURI]
```

Here is the complete client configuration file:

```
<configuration>
  <system.runtime.remoting>
    <application>

      <!-- Define the object this application will access remotely. -->
```

```
<client>
  <wellknown type="RemoteObject.ProductsDB, RemoteObject"
      url="tcp://localhost:9080/RemoteObject" />
</client>

<!-- Define the protocol used for network access.
     The protocol must match the component host, but any port is valid.
     A port of 0 means "dynamically choose an available port." -->
<channels>
  <channel ref="tcp" port="0" />
</channels>

  </application>
 </system.runtime.remoting>
</configuration>
```

The client application uses the *RemotingConfiguration.Configure* method to register the objects it wants to call. Once this step is taken, the client can create the object exactly as it would create a local object. However, the object will actually be created in the component host application domain. You can verify this with the simple console client shown here:

```
using System;
using System.Runtime.Remoting;
using System.Data;
using RemoteObject;

public class Client {

    private static void Main() {

        // Register the classes that will be accessed remotely.
        RemotingConfiguration.Configure("Client.exe.config");

        // (Now any attempts to instantiate the RemoteObjects.ProductsDB
        // class will actually create a proxy to a remote instance.)

        // Interact with the remote object through a proxy.
        ProductsDB proxy = new ProductsDB();

        // Display the name of the component host application domain
        // where the object executes.
        Console.WriteLine("Object executing in: " + proxy.GetHostLocation());

        // Get the DataSet and display its contents.
        DataTable dt = proxy.GetProducts();

        foreach (DataRow row in dt.Rows) {
```

```
            Console.WriteLine(row[1]);
        }

        Console.ReadLine();
    }
}
```

To instantiate a remote object, the client needs to have a reference to the assembly where the class is defined. This presents an additional deployment step, which you can avoid by using an interface that defines the supported functionality.

> **Note** To transmit data to and from a remote object, the types you use for parameters and return values must be serializable. All basic types (such as strings, numbers, and so on) are serializable. If you want to use custom classes to transmit data to or from a remote object, you must make sure these classes are also serializable using the *Serializable* attribute. (See recipe 16.1.)

12.8 Register All the Remotable Classes in an Assembly

Problem

You want to register all the remotable classes that are defined in an assembly without having to specify them in a configuration file.

Solution

Load the assembly with the remotable classes using reflection. Loop through all its types, and use the *RemotingConfiguration.RegisterWellKnownServiceType* method to register every remotable class.

Discussion

.NET makes it equally easy to register remotable classes through a configuration file or programmatically with code. Consider the example from recipe 12.7. To use programmatic registration, you would first remove the class declarations from the server configuration file and leave it as shown here:

```
<configuration>
```

```
<system.runtime.remoting>
  <application>

    <channels>
      <channel ref="tcp" port="9080" />
    </channels>

  </application>
 </system.runtime.remoting>
</configuration>
```

Now you can combine reflection with the *RegisterWellKnownServiceType* method to programmatically register all remotable types. However, first you'll need to add a reference to the System.Runtime.Remoting.dll assembly, which contains additional Remoting types.

The following server searches for remotable classes in the RemoteObject.dll assembly, registers each one, and then displays the channel where it's available.

```
using System;
using System.Runtime.Remoting;
using System.Runtime.Remoting.Channels;
using System.Runtime.Remoting.Channels.Tcp;
using System.Reflection;

public class Server {

    private static void Main() {

        // Use the configuration file to define networking options.
        RemotingConfiguration.Configure("Server.exe.config");

        // Get the registered Remoting channel.
        TcpChannel channel =
          (TcpChannel)ChannelServices.RegisteredChannels[0];

        // Create an Assembly object representing the assembly
        // where remotable classes are defined.
        Assembly assembly = Assembly.LoadFrom("RemoteObject.dll");

        // Process all the types in this assembly.
        foreach (Type type in assembly.GetTypes()) {

            // Check if the type is remotable.
            if (type.IsSubclassOf(typeof(MarshalByRefObject))) {

                // Register each type using the type name as the URI
```

```
                        // (like ProductsDB).
                        Console.WriteLine("Registering " + type.Name);
                        RemotingConfiguration.RegisterWellKnownServiceType(
                          type, type.Name, WellKnownObjectMode.SingleCall);

                        // Determine the URL where this type is published.
                        string[] urls = channel.GetUrlsForUri(type.Name);
                        Console.WriteLine(urls[0]);
                    }
                }

                Console.WriteLine("Press a key to shut down the server.");
                Console.ReadLine();
            }
        }
```

> **Note**   The preceding code determines whether or not a class is remotable by examining whether it derives from *MarshalByRefObject*. This approach always works, but it could lead you to expose some types that you don't want to make remotable. For example, the *System.Windows.Forms.Form* object derives indirectly from *MarshalByRefObject*. That means that if your remote object library contains any forms, they will be exposed remotely.
>
> To avoid this problem, don't include remotable types in your assembly unless you want to make them publicly available. Or, identify the types you want to register with a custom attribute. You could then check for this attribute before registering a type.

12.9 Host a Remote Object in IIS

Problem

You want to create a remotable object in IIS (perhaps so that you can use SSL or IIS authentication) instead of a dedicated component host.

Solution

Place the configuration file and assembly in a virtual directory, and modify the object URI so that it ends in .rem or .soap.

Discussion

Instead of creating a dedicated component host, you can host a remotable class in Internet Information Services (IIS). This allows you to ensure that the remotable classes will always be available, and it allows you to use IIS features such as SSL encryption and Integrated Windows authentication.

To host a remotable class in IIS, you must first create a virtual directory. The virtual directory will contain two things: a configuration file that registers the remotable classes and a bin directory where you must place the corresponding class library assembly (or install the assembly in the GAC).

The configuration file for hosting in IIS is quite similar to the configuration file you use with a custom component host. However, you must follow several additional rules:

- You must use the HTTP channel (although you can use the binary formatter for smaller message sizes).

- You can't specify a specific port number for listening. IIS listens on all the ports you have configured in the IIS manager. Typically, this will be ports 80 and 443 (for secure SSL communication).

- The object URI must end with .rem or .soap.

- The configuration file must be named Web.config, or it will be ignored.

Here's an example Web.config file that registers the remote class shown in recipe 12.7.

```
<configuration>
  <system.runtime.remoting>
    <application>
      <service>
        <wellknown mode="SingleCall"
            type="RemoteObject.ProductsDB, RemoteObject"
            objectUri="RemoteObject.rem" />
      </service>

      <channels>
        <channel ref="http">

          <!-- Uncomment the following tags to use the binary formatter
              (instead of the default SOAP formatter). -->
          <!--
            <serverProviders>
              <formatter ref="binary"/>
            </serverProviders>
            -->
```

```
        </channel>
      </channels>

    </application>
  </system.runtime.remoting>
</configuration>
```

A client can use an object hosted in IIS in the same way as an object hosted in a custom component host. However, the virtual directory name will become part of the object URI. For example, if the Web.config file shown in the preceding code is hosted in the virtual directory *http://localhost/RemoteObjects*, the full URL will be *http://localhost/RemoteObjects/RemoteObject.rem*.

> **Note**   When hosting an object with IIS, the account used to execute the object is the ASP.NET account defined in the machine.config file. If this account doesn't have the rights to access the database (which is the default situation), you will receive an error when you try this example. To solve the problem, refer to recipe 7.17.

12.10 Fire an Event Over a Remoting Channel

Problem

You need to create a client that can receive an event fired by a remote object.

Solution

Make sure you are using bidirectional channels. Create a remotable object on the client-side that can receive the event from the server.

Discussion

Although the event-handling syntax doesn't change when you use .NET Remoting, it takes additional steps to create a client that can handle an event from a remote object. Here are the key requirements:

■   The remotable class must use client-activated or singleton activation mode (not single-call). This ensures that the object remains alive in between method calls, allowing it to fire an event to the client.

- The client must use a bidirectional channel so that it can receive connections initiated by the server.

- The *EventArgs* object for the event must be serializable so that it can be transmitted across application domain boundaries.

- The client must use a remotable "listener" object to receive the event. This listener will then raise a local event that can be handled by the client. The remote object can't fire the event directly to an ordinary class because ordinary classes aren't accessible from other application domains.

- You must modify the client and server configuration files to explicitly allow full serialization. (This isn't required with .NET 1.0.)

Here's a sample remotable class that you might use to fire an event to the client. It provides a single *public* method—*StartTask*. This method starts a timer, which fires after a short delay (about 10 seconds). When the timer fires, the remotable object raises a *TaskComplete* event.

```
using System;
using System.Timers;

public delegate void TaskCompleted(object sender,
  TaskCompleteEventArgs e);

public class RemoteObject : MarshalByRefObject {

    public event TaskCompleted TaskComplete;
    private Timer tmr = new Timer();

    public void StartTask() {

        tmr.Interval = 10000;
        tmr.Elapsed += new ElapsedEventHandler(tmrCallback);
        tmr.Start();
    }

    private void tmrCallback(object sender, ElapsedEventArgs e) {

        tmr.Enabled = false;
        if (TaskComplete != null) {
            TaskComplete(this,
              new TaskCompleteEventArgs("Task completed on server"));
        }
    }
}
```

```
        public override object InitializeLifetimeService() {
            return null;
        }
}

[Serializable()]
public class TaskCompleteEventArgs : EventArgs {

    public string Result;

    public TaskCompleteEventArgs(string result) {
        this.Result = result;
    }
}
```

The next step is to define a remotable class that runs on the client and can receive this event. This class can then contact the client. The *EventListener* class shown in the following code provides one such example—it simply raises a second event, which the client can handle directly. As with all remotable objects, it will only be accessible remotely for five minutes, unless you explicitly modify the lifetime lease policy (as described in recipe 12.11). One approach is to simply override the *InitializeLifetimeService* method to allow the object to live forever, as shown here:

```
public class EventListener : MarshalByRefObject {

    public event RemoteObject.TaskCompleted TaskComplete;

    // Handle the remote event.
    public void OnTaskComplete(object sender,
      RemoteObject.TaskCompleteEventArgs e) {
        // Now raise the event to a local listener.
        TaskComplete(sender, e);
    }

    public override object InitializeLifetimeService() {
        return null;
    }
}
```

The event listener must be defined in a separate assembly so that it can be referenced by the client application and the remotable class, which both need to interact with it.

Now the client application can start the asynchronous task through the *RemoteObject* class and handle the event through the *EventListener*. The following form code shows a simple client that displays a message box when the event is received.

```
using System;
using System.Windows.Forms;
using System.Runtime.Remoting;

public class ClientForm : System.Windows.Forms.Form {

    private System.Windows.Forms.Button cmdStart;

    // (Designer code omitted.)

    RemoteObject.RemoteObject remoteObj;
    EventListener.EventListener listener;

    private void ClientForm_Load(object sender, System.EventArgs e) {

        // Create the remote object and remotable listener.
        RemotingConfiguration.Configure("Client.exe.config");
        remoteObj = new RemoteObject.RemoteObject();
        listener = new EventListener.EventListener();
    }

    private void cmdStart_Click(object sender, System.EventArgs e) {

        // Connect the remotable event handler.
        remoteObj.TaskComplete += new
          RemoteObject.TaskCompleted(listener.OnTaskComplete);

        // Connect the local event handler.
        listener.TaskComplete += new RemoteObject.TaskCompleted(TaskComplete);

        remoteObj.StartTask();
        MessageBox.Show("Task has been started.");
    }

    // Define the local event handler.
    private void TaskComplete(object sender,
      RemoteObject.TaskCompleteEventArgs e) {

        // This event fires on one of the Remoting listener threads.
        MessageBox.Show("Event received: " + e.Result);
    }
}
```

For this to work, you must make sure that the client is using bidirectional channels. Thus, the channel tag in the configuration files should look like this:

```
<channel ref="tcp" port="0" />
```

And *not* like either of these examples:

```
<channel ref="tcp server" port="0" />
<channel ref="tcp client" port="0" />
```

In addition, you must explicitly enable support for full serialization. Otherwise, the server will not be allowed to receive a delegate for the *Listener.TaskCompleted* method, and it won't be able to connect the remote event handler. To enable full serialization support on the server, you need to modify the component host configuration file as shown here:

```
<configuration>
  <system.runtime.remoting>
    <application>

      <client url="tcp://localhost:9080/Server">
        <activated type="RemoteObject.RemoteObject, RemoteObject"/>
      </client>

      <channels>
        <channel ref="tcp" port="0">
          <serverProviders>
            <formatter ref="binary" typeFilterLevel="Full" />
          </serverProviders>
        </channel>
      </channels>

    </application>
  </system.runtime.remoting>
</configuration>
```

To enable full serialization support on the client, you need to modify the client configuration file, as shown in the following code:

```
<configuration>
  <system.runtime.remoting>
    <application name="SimpleServer" >

      <service>
        <activated type="RemoteObject.RemoteObject, RemoteObject"/>
      </service>

      <channels>
        <channel ref="tcp" port="9080">
          <serverProviders>
            <formatter ref="binary" typeFilterLevel="Full" />
          </serverProviders>
        </channel>
      </channels>
```

```
      </application>
    </system.runtime.remoting>
  </configuration>
```

12.11 Control the Lifetime of a Remote Object

Problem

You want to configure how long a singleton or client-activated object lives while not in use.

Solution

Configure a lease policy by using configuration file settings, override the *MarshalByRefObject.InitializeLifetimeService* method, or implement a custom lease provider.

Discussion

If a remotable object uses single-call activation, it will be automatically destroyed at the end of each method call. This behavior changes with client-activated and singleton objects, which are given a longer lifetime dictated by a *lifetime lease*. With the default settings, a remote object will be automatically destroyed if it's inactive for two minutes, provided it has been in existence for at least five minutes.

The component host, remote object, and client each have the opportunity to change lifetime settings.

- The component host can specify different lease lifetime defaults in the configuration file. These settings will apply to all the remotable objects it hosts.

- The remote class can override its *GetLifetimeService* method to modify its initial lease settings using the provided *ILease* object.

- The client can call the *MarshalByRefObject.GetLifetimeService* method with a specific remote object to retrieve an *ILease* instance. The client can then call the *ILease.Renew* method to specify a minimum amount of time the object should be kept alive.

Here's an example that uses the first approach: a component host configuration file using the *<lifetime>* tag. These lease settings apply to all the remote objects created by the component host. Use a trailing *M* for minutes or an *S* to indicate seconds. It gives remote objects an initial lifetime of 10 minutes. When a client accesses the object, its lifetime is automatically renewed to at least three minutes.

```
<configuration>
  <system.runtime.remoting>
    <application>

      <service>
        <wellknown
            mode = "Singleton"
            type="RemoteObjects.RemoteObject, RemoteObjects"
            objectUri="RemoteObject" />
      </service>

      <channels>
        <channel ref="tcp" port="9080" />
      </channels>

      <lifetime leaseTime = "10M"
                renewOnCallTime = "3M" />

    </application>
  </system.runtime.remoting>
</configuration>
```

Another common approach is to override the *InitializeLifetimeService* method so a remote object takes control of its own lifetime. The following code shows the code you could add to a remote class to give it a default 10-minute lifetime and 5-minute renewal time.

```
public override object InitializeLifetimeService() {
    ILease lease = MyBase.InitializeLifetimeService();

    // Lease can only be configured if it is in an initial state.
    if (lease.CurrentState == LeaseState.Initial) {
        lease.InitialLeaseTime = TimeSpan.FromMinutes(10);
        lease.RenewOnCallTime = TimeSpan.FromMinutes(5);
    }

    return lease;
}
```

If you wanted the object to have an unlimited lifetime, simply return a *null* reference instead of an *ILease* object. This is most commonly the case if you are creating a singleton object that needs to run independently (and permanently), even if clients aren't currently using it.

12.12 Control Versioning for Remote Objects

Problem

You want to create a component host that can host more than one version of the same object.

Solution

Install all versions of the object into the GAC, and explicitly register each version at a different URI endpoint.

Discussion

.NET Remoting doesn't include any intrinsic support for versioning. When a client creates a remote object, the component host automatically uses the version in the local directory or, in the case of a shared assembly, the latest version from the GAC. To support multiple versions, you have three choices:

- Create separate component host applications. Each component host will have a different version of the remote object assembly and will register its version with a different URI. This approach forces you to run multiple component host applications at once and is most practical if you are using IIS hosting (as described in recipe 12.9).

- Create an entirely new remote object assembly (instead of simply changing the version). You can then register the classes from both assemblies at different URIs, using the same component host.

- Install all versions of the remote object assembly in the GAC. You can now create a component host that maps different URIs to specific versions of the remote object assembly.

The last option is the most flexible in cases where you need to support multiple versions. For example, consider the following configuration file, which registers two versions of the *RemoteObjects* assembly at two different endpoints. Notice that you need to include the exact version number and public key token when using assemblies from the GAC. You can find this information by viewing the assembly in the Windows Explorer GAC plug-in (browse to C:\[WindowsDir]\Assembly).

```
<configuration>
  <system.runtime.remoting>
    <application>
```

```
<service>
  <!-- The type information is split over two lines to accommodate the
       bounds of the page. In the configuration file, this information
       must all be placed on a single line. -->

  <wellknown mode="SingleCall"
    type="RemoteObjects.RemoteObject, RemoteObjects, Version 1.0.0.1,
        Culture=neutral, PublicKeyToken=8b5ed84fd25209e1"
    objectUri="RemoteObj" />

  <wellknown mode="SingleCall"
    type="RemoteObjects.RemoteObject, RemoteObjects, Version 2.0.0.1,
        Culture=neutral, PublicKeyToken=8b5ed84fd25209e1"
    objectUri="RemoteObj_2.0" />
</service>
<channels>
  <channel ref="tcp server" port="9080" />
</channels>
      </application>
    </system.runtime.remoting>
</configuration>
```

The client configuration file won't change at all (aside from updating the URI, if required). The client "chooses" the version it wants to use by using the corresponding URI.

12.13 Create a One-Way Method with XML Web Services or Remoting

Problem

You want a Web method or remote component to perform a long task, and you don't want to force the client to wait while the code executes.

Solution

Create a one-way Web method by applying the *SoapDocumentMethod* or the *SoapRpcMethod* attribute and setting the attribute's *OneWay* property to *true*. Create a one-way Remoting method by applying the *OneWay* attribute from the *System.Runtime.Remoting.Messaging* namespace.

Discussion

With one-way methods, the client sends a request message, and the server responds immediately to indicate that the method began processing. This behavior has the following consequences:

■ The client doesn't need to wait while the server code executes.

■ The method can't return any information to the client, either through a return value or a *ByRef* parameter.

■ If the method throws an unhandled exception, it won't be propagated back to the client.

Clearly, one-way methods aren't suitable if the client needs to receive some information from the server. However, they are ideal for simply starting some sort of server-side task (for example, beginning a batch-processing job).

To create a one-way Web method, you need to apply a *SoapDocumentMethod* attribute (from the *System.Web.Services.Protocols* namespace) to the appropriate method and set the *OneWay* property to *true*. Here's an example XML Web service that provides two methods, each of which causes a 10-second delay. One of the two methods uses the *OneWay* attribute, so the client won't experience the 10-second wait.

```
using System;
using System.Web.Services;
using System.Web.Services.Protocols;

public class OneWayTestWebService {

    [WebMethod()]
    public void DoLongTaskWithWait() {
        // (Start a long task and make the client wait.)
        Delay(10);
    }

    [WebMethod, SoapDocumentMethod(OneWay=true)]
    public void DoLongTaskWithoutWait() {
        // (Start a long task but don't make the client wait.)
        Delay(10);
    }

    private void Delay(int seconds) {
        DateTime currentTime = DateTime.Now;
        while (DateTime.Now.Subtract(currentTime).TotalSeconds < seconds) {}
    }
}
```

This example assumes that your XML Web service and client are using SOAP document encoding (the default). If you're using remote procedure call (RPC) encoding, use the corresponding *SoapRpcMethod* attribute to mark a one-way method.

To create a one-way method in a component exposed over Remoting, you need to apply a *OneWay* attribute (from the *System.Runtime.Remoting.Messaging* namespace) to the appropriate method. The following code shows the same example with a remote component:

```
using System;
using System.Runtime.Remoting.Messaging;

public class OneWayTestRemoting : MarshalByRefObject {

    public void DoLongTaskWithWait() {
        // (Start a long task and make the client wait.)
        Delay(10);
    }

    [OneWay()]
    public void DoLongTaskWithoutWait() {
        // (Start a long task but don't make the client wait.)
        Delay(10);
    }

    private void Delay(int seconds) {
        DateTime currentTime = DateTime.Now;
        while (DateTime.Now.Subtract(currentTime).TotalSeconds < seconds) {}
    }
}
```

> **Note** One-way methods aren't the only way to remove client delays. You can also modify the client to call any Web method asynchronously. In this case, the client will wait for the XML Web service to complete, but it will wait on another thread, so the client application can continue with other work. Asynchronous method calls are described in recipe 12.6.

13

Runtime Security

A principal goal of the Microsoft .NET Framework is to make computing more secure—especially with respect to the use of mobile code and distributed systems. Most modern operating systems (including Microsoft Windows) support user-based security, allowing you to control the actions and resources to which a user has access. However, in the highly connected world resulting from the proliferation of computer networks—in particular the Internet—it's insufficient to base security solely on the identity of a system's user. In the interest of security, code should not automatically receive the same level of trust that you assign to the person running the code.

The .NET Framework incorporates the following two complementary security models that address many of the issues associated with user and code security:

- Code access security (CAS)

- Role-based security (RBS)

CAS and RBS do not replace or duplicate the security facilities provided by the underlying operating system. They are platform-independent mechanisms that provide additional security capabilities to augment and enhance the overall security of your managed solutions.

CAS uses information about the source and origin of an assembly (*evidence*) gathered at run time to determine which actions and resources that code from the assembly can access (*permissions*). The .NET Framework *security policy*—a hierarchical set of configurable rules—defines the mapping between evidence and permissions. The .NET Framework class library uses permission *demands* to protect its most important functionality from unauthorized access. A demand forces the common language runtime to ensure that code calling a protected method has a specific permission. CAS ensures that the runtime capabilities of code depend on the level of trust you place in the creator and source of the code, not the level of trust you place in the user running the code. The CAS-related recipes in this chapter discuss the following topics:

- Allowing partially trusted code to access your strong-named assemblies (recipe 13.1)

- Disabling CAS altogether (recipe 13.2) or disabling only execution permission checks (recipe 13.3)

- Requesting specific code access permissions and determining which permissions the runtime has granted to your code (recipes 13.4, 13.5, 13.6, and 13.7)

- Controlling inheritance and member overrides using CAS (recipe 13.8)

- Inspecting and manipulating assembly evidence (recipes 13.9 and 13.10)

- Manipulating runtime security using application domains (recipes 13.11 and 13.12)

Following a more traditional security model, RBS allows you to make runtime decisions based on the identity and roles of the user on whose behalf an application is running. On the Windows operating system, this equates to making decisions based on the Windows user name and the Windows groups to which that user belongs. However, RBS provides a generic security mechanism that is independent of the underlying operating system, allowing you (with some development) to integrate with any user account system. The recipes in this chapter discuss the following aspects of .NET RBS:

- Integrating RBS with Windows user accounts and determining if a user is a member of a specific Windows group (recipe 13.13)

- Controlling access to application functionality based on the current user and the roles of which the user is a member (recipe 13.14)

- Impersonating Windows users to perform operating system tasks on behalf of that user (recipe 13.15)

Both the RBS and CAS related recipes in this chapter represent some of the more common actions you will need to perform in your applications, but they represent only a small portion of the security capabilities of the .NET Framework. For a more comprehensive coverage of .NET Framework security, I suggest you read *Programming .NET Security* (O'Reilly and Associates, 2003), which I wrote with Adam Freeman. *Programming .NET Security* provides in-depth coverage of all aspects of .NET Framework security and demonstrates how to extend and enhance many of the runtime's security framework capabilities.

13.1 Allow Partially Trusted Code to Use Your Strong-Named Assembly

Problem

You need to write a shared assembly that is accessible to partially trusted code. (By default, the runtime does not allow partially trusted code to access the types and members contained in a strongly-named assembly.).

Solution

Apply the assembly-level attribute *System.Security.AllowPartiallyTrusted-CallersAttribute* to your shared assembly.

Discussion

To minimize the security risks posed by malicious code, the runtime doesn't allow assemblies granted only partial trust to access strong-named assemblies. This restriction dramatically reduces the opportunity for malicious code to attack your system, but the reasoning behind such a heavy-handed approach requires some explanation.

As a rule, strong-named assemblies are installed in the global assembly cache (GAC) and contain important functionality that is shared between multiple applications. This is particularly true of the assemblies that constitute the .NET Framework class library. Other strong-named assemblies from well-known and widely distributed products will also be in the GAC and accessible to managed applications. The high chance that certain assemblies will be present in the GAC, their easy accessibility, and their importance to many different applications makes strong-named assemblies the most likely target for any type of subversive activity by malicious managed code.

Generally, the code most likely to be malicious is that which is loaded from remote locations—such as the Internet—over which you have little or no control. Under the default security policy, all code run from the local machine has full trust, whereas code loaded from remote locations has only partial trust. Stopping partially trusted code from accessing strong-named assemblies means that partially trusted code has no opportunity to use the features of the assembly for malicious purposes and can't probe and explore the assembly to find exploitable holes. Of course, this theory hinges on the assumption that you correctly administer your security policy. If you simply assign all code full trust, not only will any assembly be able to access your strong-named assembly, the code will also be able to access all of the functionality of the .NET Framework. This would be a security disaster!

> **Note** If you design, implement, and test your shared assembly correctly using code access security to restrict access to important members, there is no need to impose a blanket restriction to stop partially trusted code using your assembly. However, for an assembly of any significance, it's impossible to prove there are no security holes that malicious code can exploit. Therefore, you should carefully consider the need to allow partially trusted code to access your strong-named assembly before applying *AllowPartiallyTrustedCallersAttribute*.

The runtime stops partially trusted code from accessing strong-named assemblies by placing an implicit *LinkDemand* for the *FullTrust* permission set on every *public* and *protected* member of every publicly accessible type defined in the assembly. This means that only assemblies granted the permissions equivalent to the *FullTrust* permission set are able to access the types and members from the strong-named assembly. Applying *AllowPartiallyTrustedCallers-Attribute* to your strong-named assembly signals the runtime not to enforce the *LinkDemand* on the contained types and members.

> **Note** The runtime is responsible for enforcing the implicit *LinkDemand* security actions required to protect strong-named assemblies; the C# assembler doesn't generate declarative *LinkDemand* statements at compile time.

The following code fragment shows the application of the attribute *AllowPartiallyTrustedCallersAttribute*. Notice that you must prefix the attribute with *assembly:* to signal to the compiler that the target of the attribute is the assembly (also called a *global attribute*). In addition, there is no need to include the *Attribute* part of the attribute name—although you can if you want to. Because you target the assembly, the attribute must be positioned after any top level *using* statements, but before any namespace or type declarations.

```
using System.Security;

[assembly:AllowPartiallyTrustedCallers]

public class AllowPartiallyTrustedCallersExample {
    ⋮
}
```

> **Tip**   It's common practice to contain all global attributes in a file separate from the rest of your application code. Microsoft Visual Studio .NET uses this approach, creating a file named AssemblyInfo.cs to contain all global attributes.

If, after applying *AllowPartiallyTrustedCallersAttribute* to your assembly, you want to restrict partially trusted code from calling only specific members, you should implement a *LinkDemand* for the *FullTrust* permission set on the necessary members, as shown in the following code fragment:

```
[System.Security.Permissions.PermissionSetAttribute
    (System.Security.Permissions.SecurityAction.LinkDemand,
    Name="FullTrust")]
public void SomeMethod() {
    ⋮
}
```

13.2 Disable Code Access Security

Problem

You need to turn off all CAS checking.

Solution

From code, set the property *SecurityEnabled* of the class *System.Security.SecurityManager* to *false* and persist the change by calling *SecurityManager.SavePolicy*. Alternatively, use the Code Access Security Policy tool (Caspol.exe) and execute the command **caspol –s off** from the command line.

Discussion

CAS is a key element of the .NET runtime's security model, and one that sets it apart from many other computing platforms. Although CAS was implemented with performance in mind and has been used prudently throughout the .NET class library, there is still an overhead associated with each security demand and resulting stack walk that the runtime must execute.

In rare cases, code-level security might not be of interest to you, or the need for performance might outweigh the need for CAS. In these situations, you can completely disable CAS and remove the overhead of code-level security checks. Turning off CAS has the effect of giving all code the ability to perform any action supported by the .NET Framework (equivalent to the *FullTrust* permission set). This includes the ability to load other code, call native libraries, and use pointers to access memory directly.

> **Warning**   You should only disable CAS for performance reasons after you have exhausted all other possible measure to achieve the performance characteristics your application requires. Profiling your code will usually identify areas where you can improve performance significantly without the need to disable CAS. In addition, you should ensure that your system resources have appropriate protection using operating system security mechanisms such as Windows ACLs before disabling CAS.

Caspol.exe is a utility provided with the .NET Framework that allows you to configure all aspects of your code access security policy from the command line. When you enter the command **caspol –s off** or its counterpart **caspol –s on** from the command line, the Caspol.exe utility actually sets the *SecurityEnabled* property of the *SecurityManager* class. The *SecurityManager* class contains a set of *static* methods that provide access to critical security functionality and data. This code demonstrates the use of the *SecurityEnabled* property to disable and enable CAS.

```
// Turn off CAS security checks.
System.Security.SecurityManager.SecurityEnabled = false;

// Persist the configuration change.
System.Security.SecurityManager.SavePolicy();
```

To enable CAS, use the following statements.

```
// Turn on CAS security checks.
System.Security.SecurityManager.SecurityEnabled = true;

// Persist the configuration change.
System.Security.SecurityManager.SavePolicy();
```

To disable CAS, your code must have the *ControlPolicy* element of the permission *System.Security.Permissions.SecurityPermission*. Naturally, you need no specific permission to enable CAS.

Changing *SecurityEnabled* won't affect the enforcement of CAS in existing processes, nor will it affect new processes until you call the *SavePolicy* method, which saves the state of *SecurityEnabled* to the Windows registry. Unfortunately, the .NET Framework doesn't guarantee that changes to *SecurityEnabled* will correctly affect the operation of CAS in the current process, so you must change *SecurityEnabled* and then launch a new process to achieve reliable and expected operation.

> **Note**   The current on/off state of CAS is stored in the Windows registry in the key HKEY_LOCAL_MACHINE\SOFTWARE\Microsoft\.NET-Framework\Security\Policy as part of a set of flags contained in the Global Settings value. If the key does not exist, CAS defaults to on.

13.3 Disable Execution Permission Checks

Problem

You need to stop the runtime checking that each assembly it loads has execution permission.

Solution

In code, set the property *CheckExecutionRights* of the class *System.Security.SecurityManager* to *false* and persist the change by calling *SecurityManager.SavePolicy*. Alternatively, use the Code Access Security Policy tool (Caspol.exe), and execute the command **caspol –e off** from the command line.

Discussion

As the runtime loads each assembly, it ensures that the assembly's grant set includes the *Execution* element of *SecurityPermission*. The runtime implements a lazy policy resolution process, meaning that the grant set of an assembly is not calculated until the first time a security demand is made against the assembly. Not only does execution permission checking force the runtime to check that every assembly has the execution permission, but it also indirectly causes policy resolution for every assembly loaded, effectively negating the benefits of lazy policy resolution. These factors can introduce a noticeable delay as assemblies are loaded, especially when the runtime loads a number of assemblies together, as it does at application startup.

In many situations, simply allowing code to load and run is not a significant risk as long as all other important operation and resources are correctly secured using CAS and operating system security. The .NET runtime allows you to turn off the automatic checks for execution permissions from within code, or by using Caspol.exe.

When you enter the command **caspol –e off** or its counterpart **caspol –e on** from the command line, the Caspol.exe utility actually sets the *CheckExecutionRights* property of the *SecurityManager* class. This is shown in the following code fragments, which you can use from within your own code:

```
// Turn off Execution rights checks.
System.Security.SecurityManager.CheckExecutionRights = false;

// Persist the configuration change.
System.Security.SecurityManager.SavePolicy();
```

To enable execution permission checks, use the following statements:

```
// Turn on Execution rights checks.
System.Security.SecurityManager.CheckExecutionRights = true;

// Persist the configuration change.
System.Security.SecurityManager.SavePolicy();
```

To modify the value of *CheckExecutionRights*, your code must have the *ControlPolicy* element of *SecurityPermission*. The change will affect the current process immediately, allowing you to load assemblies at run time without the runtime checking them for execution permission. However, the change will not affect other existing processes. You must call the *SavePolicy* method to persist the change to the Windows registry for it to affect new processes.

13.4 Ensure the Runtime Grants Specific Permissions to Your Assembly

Problem

You need to ensure that the runtime grants your assembly those code access permissions that are critical to the successful operation of your application.

Solution

In your assembly, use permission requests to specify the code access permissions that your assembly must have. You declare permission requests using assembly-level code access permission attributes.

Discussion

The name *permission request* is a little misleading given that the runtime will never grant permissions to an assembly unless security policy dictates that the assembly should have those permissions. However, naming aside, permission requests serve an essential purpose, and although the way the runtime handles permission requests might initially seem strange, the nature of CAS doesn't allow for any obvious alternative.

Permission requests identify permissions that your code *must* have to function. For example, if you wrote a movie player that your customers could use to download and view movies from your Web server, it would be disastrous if the user's security policy did not allow your player to open a network connection to your media server. Your player would load and run, but as soon as the user tried to connect to your server to play a movie, the application would crash with the exception *System.Security.SecurityException*. The solution to this problem is to include in your assembly a permission request for the code access permission required to open a network connection to your server (*System.Net.WebPermission* or *System.Net.SocketPermission*, depending on the type of connection you need to open).

The runtime honors permission requests using the premise that it's better that your code never load, than load and fail sometime later when it tries to perform an action that it doesn't have permission to perform. Therefore, if after security policy resolution the runtime determines that the grant set of your assembly doesn't satisfy the assembly's permission requests, the runtime will fail to load the assembly and will instead throw the exception *System.Security.Policy.PolicyException*.

To declare a permission request, you must use the attribute counterpart of the code access permission that you need to request. All code access permissions have an attribute counterpart that you use to construct declarative security statements—including permission requests. For example, the attribute counterpart of *SocketPermission* is *SocketPermissionAttribute*, and the attribute counterpart of *WebPermission* is *WebPermissionAttribute*—all permissions and their attribute counterparts follow the same naming convention and are members of the same namespace.

The following code shows a console application named PermissionRequestExample that includes two permission requests: one for *SocketPermission* and the other for *SecurityPermission*. It's important to remember the following:

■ You must declare the permission request after any top level *using* statements but before any namespace or type declarations.

■ The attribute must target the assembly and so you must prefix the attribute name with *assembly:*.

■ There is no need to include the *Attribute* portion of an attribute's name—although you can if you want.

■ You must specify *SecurityAction.RequestMinimum* as the first positional argument of the attribute—this value identifies the statement as a permission request.

■ You must configure the attribute to represent the code access permission you want to request using the attribute's properties. Refer to the .NET Framework SDK documentation for details of the properties implemented by each code access security attribute.

■ The permission request statements do not end with a semicolon (;).

■ To make more than one permission request, simply include multiple permission request statements as shown in the following example:

```
using System.Net;
using System.Security.Permissions;

// Permission request for a SocketPermission that allows the code to open
// a TCP connection to the specified host and port.
[assembly:SocketPermission(SecurityAction.RequestMinimum,
    Access = "Connect", Host = "www.fabrikam.com",
    Port = "3538", Transport = "Tcp")]
```

```
// Permission request for the UnmanagedCode element of SecurityPermission,
// which controls the code's ability to execute unmanaged code.
[assembly:SecurityPermission(SecurityAction.RequestMinimum,
    UnmanagedCode = true)]

public class PermissionRequestExample {
    public static void Main() {
        // Do something...
    }
}
```

If you try to execute the *PermissionRequestExample* application and your security policy doesn't grant the assembly the requested permissions, you will get the *PolicyException* shown here and the application won't execute. Using the default security policy, this will happen if you run the assembly from a network share because assemblies loaded from the Intranet zone are not granted *SocketPermission*.

```
Unhandled Exception: System.Security.Policy.PolicyException: Required permis-
sion cannot be acquired.
```

When you try to load an assembly from within code (either automatically or manually), and the loaded assembly contains permission requests that security policy doesn't satisfy, the method you use to load the assembly will throw a *PolicyException*, which you must handle appropriately.

13.5 Limit the Permissions Granted to Your Assembly

Problem

You need to restrict the code access permissions granted to your assembly, ensuring that people and other software can never use your code as a mechanism through which to perform undesirable or malicious actions.

Solution

Use declarative security statements to specify optional permission requests and permission refusal requests in your assembly. Optional permission requests define the maximum set of permissions that the runtime will grant to your assembly. Permission refusal requests specify particular permissions that the runtime should not grant to your assembly.

Discussion

In the interest of security, it's ideal if your code has only those code access permissions required to perform its function. This minimizes the opportunities for people and other code to use your code to carry out malicious or undesirable actions. The problem is, the runtime resolves an assembly's permissions using security policy, which a user or administrator configures. Security policy could be different in every location where your application is run, and you have no control over what permissions the security policy assigns to your code.

Although you can't control security policy in all locations where your code runs, the .NET Framework provides two mechanisms through which you can reject permissions granted to your assembly: refuse requests and optional requests. Refuse requests allow you to identify specific permissions that you do not want the runtime to grant to your assembly. After policy resolution, if the final grant set of an assembly contains any permission specified in a refuse request, the runtime removes that permission. Optional permission requests define the maximum set of permissions that the runtime can grant to your assembly. If the final grant set of an assembly contains any permission other than those specified in the optional permission request, the runtime removes those permissions. Unlike a minimum permission request (discussed in recipe 13.4) the runtime won't refuse to load your assembly if it can't grant all of the permissions specified in the optional request.

You can think of a refuse request and an optional request as alternative ways to achieve the same result; the approach you use depends on how many permissions you want to reject. If you only want to reject a handful of permissions, a refuse request is easier to code. However, if you want to reject a large number of permissions, it's easier to code an optional request for the few permissions you want, which will automatically reject the rest.

You include optional and refuse requests in your code using declarative security statements with the same syntax as the minimum permission requests discussed in recipe 13.4. The only difference is the value of the *System.Security.Permissions.SecurityAction* that you pass to the permission attribute's constructor. Use *SecurityAction.RequestOptional* to declare an optional permission request and *SecurityAction.RequestRefuse* to declare a refuse request. As with minimal permission requests, you must declare optional and refuse requests as global attributes by beginning the permission attribute name with the prefix *assembly:*. In addition, all requests must appear after any top level *using* statements but before any namespace or type declarations.

The OptionalRequestExample sample shown here demonstrates an optional permission request for the Internet permission set. The Internet permission set is a named permission set defined by the default security policy.

When the runtime loads the *OptionalRequestExample* assembly, it won't grant the assembly any permission that is not included within the Internet permission set. (Consult the .NET Framework SDK documentation for details of the permissions contained in the Internet permission set.)

```
using System.Security.Permissions;

[assembly:PermissionSet(SecurityAction.RequestOptional, Name = "Internet")]

public class OptionalRequestExample {

    public static void Main() {

        // Do something...
    }
}
```

In contrast to OptionalRequestExample, the sample RefuseRequestExample shown here uses a refuse request to single out the permission *System. Security.Permissions.FileIOPermission*—representing write access to the C: drive—for refusal.

```
using System.Security.Permissions;

[assembly:FileIOPermission(SecurityAction.RequestRefuse, Write = @"C:\")]

public class RefuseRequestExample {

    public static void Main() {

        // Do something...
    }
}
```

13.6 View the Permission Requests Made by an Assembly

Problem

You need to view the declarative permission requests and refusals made within an assembly to correctly configure security policy or understand the limitations of a library you intend to call from your code.

Solution

Use the Permissions View tool (Permview.exe) that is supplied with the .NET Framework SDK.

Discussion

To configure security policy correctly, you need to know the code access permission requirements of the assemblies you intend to run. This is true of both executable assemblies and libraries that you access from your own applications. With libraries, it's also important to know which permissions the assembly refuses so that you don't try to use the library to perform a restricted action, which would result in a *System.Security.SecurityException*.

The Permview.exe utility provides a simple mechanism through which you can view the declarative permission requests made within an assembly—this includes minimum, optional, and refusal requests. The following code shows a class that declares a minimum, optional, and refusal request:

```
using System.Net;
using System.Security.Permissions;

// Minimum permission request for SocketPermission.
[assembly:SocketPermission(SecurityAction.RequestMinimum,
    Unrestricted = true)]

// Optional permission request for SecurityPermission.
[assembly:SecurityPermission(SecurityAction.RequestOptional,
    Unrestricted = true)]

// Refuse request for FileIOPermission.
[assembly:SecurityPermission(SecurityAction.RequestRefuse,
    Unrestricted = true)]

public class PermissionViewExample {
    public static void Main() {
        // Do something...
    }
}
```

Executing the command **permview PermissionViewExample.exe** will generate the following output. Although not particularly user friendly, you can decipher the output to determine the permission requests made by an assembly. Each of the three types of permission request—minimum, optional, and refused—is listed under a separate heading and is structured as the XML representation of a *System.Security.PermissionSet* object.

```
Microsoft (R) .NET Framework Permission Request Viewer.
Version 1.1.4322.510
Copyright (C) Microsoft Corporation 1998-2002. All rights reserved.

minimal permission set:
<PermissionSet class="System.Security.PermissionSet" version="1">
  <IPermission class="System.Net.SocketPermission, System, Version=1.
0.5000.0, Culture=neutral, PublicKeyToken=b77a5c561934e089" version="
1" Unrestricted="true"/>
</PermissionSet>

optional permission set:
<PermissionSet class="System.Security.PermissionSet" version="1">
  <IPermission class="System.Security.Permissions.SecurityPermission,
mscorlib, Version=1.0.5000.0, Culture=neutral, PublicKeyToken=b77a5c5
61934e089" version="1" Unrestricted="true"/>
</PermissionSet>

refused permission set:
<PermissionSet class="System.Security.PermissionSet" version="1">
  <IPermission class="System.Security.Permissions.SecurityPermission,
mscorlib, Version=1.0.5000.0, Culture=neutral, PublicKeyToken=b77a5c5
61934e089" version="1" Unrestricted="true"/>
</PermissionSet>
```

> **Tip**   By specifying the /decl switch when running the Permview.exe utility, you can view all of the declarative security statements contained in an assembly, including declarative demands and asserts. This can give a good insight into what the assembly is trying to do and allow you to configure security policy appropriately. However, be aware that Permview.exe doesn't show the imperative security operations contained within the assembly. There is currently no way to extract and summarize the imperative security operations executed within an assembly.

13.7 Determine at Run Time if Your Code Has a Specific Permission

Problem

You need to determine at run time if your assembly has a specific permission.

Solution

Instantiate and configure the permission you want to test for and then pass it as an argument to the *static* method *IsGranted* of the class *System.Security.Security-Manager.*

Discussion

Using minimum permission requests, you can ensure that the runtime grants your assembly a specified set of permissions; if your code is running, you can safely assume that it has the requested minimum permissions. However, you might want to implement opportunistic functionality that your application offers only if the runtime grants your assembly appropriate permissions. This approach is partially formalized using optional permission requests, which allow you to define a set of permissions that your code could make use of if security policy granted them, but which are not essential for the successful operation of your code. (Recipe 13.5 provides more detail on using optional permission requests.)

The problem with optional permission requests is that the runtime has no ability to communicate to your assembly which of the requested optional permissions it has granted. You can try to use a protected operation and fail gracefully if the call results in the exception *System.Security.SecurityException*. However, it's more efficient to determine in advance if you have the necessary permissions. You can then build logic into your code to avoid invoking protected members that will cause stack walks and raise security exceptions. The following code fragment shows how to use the *IsGranted* method to determine if the current assembly has write permission to the directory C:\Data. You could make such a call each time you needed to test for the permission, but it's more efficient to use the returned Boolean value to set a configuration flag indicating whether to allow users to save files.

```
// Define a variable to indicate whether the assembly has write access
// to the C:\Data folder.
bool canWrite = false;

// Create and configure a FileIOPermission object that represents write
// access to the C:\Data folder.
System.Security.Permissions.FileIOPermission fileIOPerm =
    new System.Security.Permissions.FileIOPermission(
    System.Security.Permissions.FileIOPermissionAccess.Write, @"C:\Data");

// Test if the current assembly has the specified permission.
canWrite = System.Security.SecurityManager.IsGranted(fileIOPerm);
```

13.8 Restrict Who Can Extend Your Classes and Override Class Members

Problem

You need to control who can extend your classes through inheritance and which class members a derived class can override.

Solution

Use declarative security statements to apply the *SecurityAction.InheritanceDemand* member to the declarations of the classes and members that you need to protect.

Discussion

Language modifiers such as *sealed*, *public*, *private*, and *virtual* give you a level of control over the ability of classes to inherit from your class and override its members. However, these modifiers are inflexible, providing no selectivity in restricting which code can extend a class or override its members. For example, you might want to allow only code written by your company or department to extend business-critical classes, or perhaps you want to allow only code loaded from the local machine to extend certain methods. By applying an *Inheritance-Demand* to your class or member declaration, you can specify runtime permissions that a class must have to extend your class or override particular members. Remember that the permissions of a class are the permissions of the assembly in which the class is declared.

Although you can demand any permission or permission set in your *InheritanceDemand*, it's more common to demand *identity permissions*. Identity permissions represent evidence presented to the runtime by an assembly. If an assembly presents certain types of evidence at load time, the runtime will automatically assign the assembly the appropriate identity permission. Identity permissions allow you to use regular imperative and declarative security statements to base security decisions directly on code identity without the need to evaluate evidence objects directly. Table 13-1 lists the type of identity permission generated for each type of evidence. (Evidence types are members of the *System.Security.Policy* namespace, and identity permission types are members of the *System.Security.Permissions* namespace.)

Table 13-1 *Evidence* **Classes That Generate Identity Permissions**

Evidence Class	Identity Permission
ApplicationDirectory	None
Hash	None
Publisher	*PublisherIdentityPermission*
Site	*SiteIdentityPermission*
StrongName	*StrongNameIdentityPermission*
Url	*UrlIdentityPermission*
Zone	*ZoneIdentityPermission*

> **Note**   The runtime assigns identity permissions to an assembly based on the evidence presented by the assembly. You can't assign additional identity permissions to an assembly through the configuration of security policy.

You must use declarative security syntax to implement an *Inheritance-Demand*, and so you must use the attribute counterpart of the permission class that you want to demand. All permission classes have an attribute counterpart that you use to construct declarative security statements—including *Inheritance-Demand*. For example, the attribute counterpart of *PublisherIdentityPermission* is *PublisherIdentityPermissionAttribute*, and the attribute counterpart of *StrongNameIdentityPermission* is *StrongNameIdentityPermissionAttribute*—all permissions and their attribute counterparts follow the same naming convention and are members of the same namespace.

To control which code can extend your class, apply the *Inheritance-Demand* to the class declaration. This code fragment shows a class protected with an *InheritanceDemand*. Only classes in assemblies signed by the publisher certificate contained in the pubcert.cer file can derive from the *Inheritance-DemandExample* class. The contents of the pubcert.cer file are read at compile time, and the necessary certificate information is built into the assembly.

```
[PublisherIdentityPermission(SecurityAction.InheritanceDemand,
    CertFile = @"C:\CSharpCookbook\13 - Runtime Security\pubcert.cer")]
public class InheritanceDemandExample {
    ⋮
}
```

To control which code can override specific members, apply the *InheritanceDemand* to the member declaration. The *InheritanceDemand* on the following method allows only classes granted the *FullTrust* permission set to override the method *SomeProtectedMethod*.

```
[PermissionSet(SecurityAction.InheritanceDemand, Name="FullTrust")]
public void SomeProtectedMethod () {
    ⋮
}
```

13.9 Inspect an Assembly's Evidence

Problem

You need to inspect the evidence that the runtime assigned to an assembly.

Solution

Obtain a *System.Reflection.Assembly* object that represents the assembly in which you are interested. Get the *System.Security.Policy.Evidence* collection from the *Evidence* property of the *Assembly* object, and access the contained evidence objects using the *GetEnumerator*, *GetHostEnumerator*, or *GetAssemblyEnumerator* methods of the *Evidence* class.

Discussion

The *Evidence* class represents a collection of evidence objects. The read-only *Evidence* property of the *Assembly* class returns an *Evidence* collection object that contains all of the evidence objects that the runtime assigned to the assembly as the assembly was loaded.

The *Evidence* class actually contains two collections, representing different types of evidence: host evidence and assembly evidence. *Host evidence* includes those evidence objects assigned to the assembly by the runtime or the trusted code that loaded the assembly. *Assembly evidence* represents custom evidence objects embedded into the assembly at build time. The *Evidence* class implements the following three methods for enumerating the evidence objects it contains:

■   *GetEnumerator*

■   *GetHostEnumerator*

■   *GetAssemblyEnumerator*

The *GetEnumerator* method returns a *System.Collections.IEnumerator* that enumerates *all* of the evidence objects contained in the *Evidence* collection. The *GetHostEnumerator* and *GetAssemblyEnumerator* methods return an *IEnumerator* instance that enumerates only those evidence objects from the appropriate collection.

The *ViewEvidenceExample* listed here demonstrates how to display the host and assembly evidence of an assembly to the console. The example relies on the fact that all standard evidence classes override the *Object.ToString* method to display a useful representation of the evidence object's state. Although interesting, this example doesn't always show the evidence that an assembly would have when loaded from within your program. The runtime host (such as the Microsoft ASP.NET or Microsoft Internet Explorer runtime hosts) is free to assign additional host evidence as it loads an assembly.

```csharp
using System;
using System.Reflection;
using System.Collections;
using System.Security.Policy;

public class ViewEvidenceExample {

    public static void Main(string[] args) {

        // Load the specified assembly.
        Assembly a = Assembly.LoadFrom(args[0]);

        // Get the Evidence collection from the
        // loaded assembly.
        Evidence e = a.Evidence;

        // Display the Host Evidence.
        IEnumerator x = e.GetHostEnumerator();
        Console.WriteLine("HOST EVIDENCE COLLECTION:");
        while(x.MoveNext()) {
            Console.WriteLine(x.Current.ToString());
        }

        // Display the Assembly Evidence.
        x = e.GetAssemblyEnumerator();
        Console.WriteLine("ASSEMBLY EVIDENCE COLLECTION:");
        while(x.MoveNext()) {
            Console.WriteLine(x.Current.ToString());
        }
    }
}
```

All of the standard evidence classes provided by the .NET Framework are immutable, ensuring that you can't change their values after the runtime has created them and assigned them to the assembly. In addition, you can't add or remove items while you are enumerating across the contents of a collection using an *IEnumerator*, otherwise, the *MoveNext* method throws a *System.Invalid-OperationException*.

13.10 Manipulate Evidence as You Load an Assembly

Problem

You need to manipulate evidence as you load an assembly to affect the permissions granted to the assembly by the runtime.

Solution

Create the evidence objects that you want to assign to the assembly, add them to an instance of the class *System.Security.Policy.Evidence*, and then pass the *Evidence* collection as an argument to the method you use to load the assembly.

Discussion

The evidence possessed by an assembly defines the assembly's identity and determines which permissions the runtime grants to the assembly. The assembly loader is primarily responsible for determining what evidence to assign to an assembly, but a trusted host (such as the ASP.NET or Internet Explorer runtime hosts) can also assign evidence to an assembly. Your code can assign evidence as you load an assembly if your code has the *ControlEvidence* element of *SecurityPermission*.

> **Warning**   If you try to load an assembly twice into a single application domain but assign different evidence to the assembly each time, the runtime will throw the exception *System.IO.FileLoadException*.

Many methods make provision for assigning evidence as you load an assembly; some are methods that load assemblies directly, whereas others instantiate types—indirectly causing the assembly containing the requested type to load. One trait all of these methods have in common is that they each take an *Evidence* collection as an argument—the *Evidence* class is a container for evidence objects. You must place the individual evidence objects you want to assign to the assembly in an *Evidence* collection and pass it to the method that loads the assembly. If you assign new evidence that conflicts with that assigned by the runtime's assembly loader, the new evidence replaces the old. Table 13-2 lists the classes and their methods that directly or indirectly load an assembly. Each method provides one or more overloads that accept an *Evidence* collection.

Table 13-2   Classes and Their Methods That Allow You to Assign Evidence to an Assembly

Class/Method	Description
System.Activator class	These methods affect the current application domain.
CreateInstance *CreateInstanceFrom*	Instantiate a type in the current application domain from a specified assembly.
System.AppDomain class	These methods affect the application domain represented by the *AppDomain* object on which the method is invoked.
CreateInstance *CreateInstanceAndUnwrap* *CreateInstanceFrom* *CreateInstanceFromAndUnwrap*	Instantiate a type from a specified assembly.
DefineDynamicAssembly	Creates a *System.Reflection.Emit.AssemblyBuilder* object that you can use to create an assembly dynamically in memory.
ExecuteAssembly	Loads and executes an assembly that has a defined entry point (*Main* method).
Load	Loads the specified assembly.
System.Reflection.Assembly class	These methods affect the current application domain.
Load *LoadFile* *LoadFrom* *LoadWithPartialName*	Load the specified assembly.

The following code fragment demonstrates the use of the *Assembly.Load* method to load an assembly into the current application domain. Before calling *Load*, the code creates an *Evidence* collection and uses its *AddHost* method to add *Site* and *Zone* evidence objects (members of the *System.Security.Policy* namespace).

```
// Create new Site and Zone evidence objects.
System.Security.Policy.Site siteEvidence =
    new System.Security.Policy.Site("www.microsoft.com");
System.Security.Policy.Zone zoneEvidence =
    new System.Security.Policy.Zone(System.Security.SecurityZone.Trusted);

// Create a new Evidence collection.
System.Security.Policy.Evidence evidence =
    new System.Security.Policy.Evidence();

// Add the Site and Zone evidence objects to the Evidence collection
// using the AddHost method.
evidence.AddHost(siteEvidence);
evidence.AddHost(zoneEvidence);

// Load the assembly named "SomeAssembly" and assign the new Site and
// Zone evidence objects to it. These override the Site and Zone evidence
// objects assigned by the assembly loader.
System.Reflection.Assembly assembly =
    System.Reflection.Assembly.Load("SomeAssembly", evidence);
```

13.11 Manipulate Runtime Security Using Application Domain Evidence

Problem

You need to enforce an upper limit on the permissions available to all assemblies loaded into a particular application domain.

Solution

Configure security policy to grant the appropriate permissions based on the evidence you plan to assign to the application domain. As you create the application domain using the *static* method *CreateDomain* of the class *System.AppDomain*, provide a *System.Security.Policy.Evidence* collection containing the application domain's evidence objects. Load the assemblies whose permissions you want to limit into the application domain for execution.

Discussion

Just as the runtime assigns permissions to assemblies based on the evidence the assemblies present at load time, the runtime also assigns permissions to application domains based on their evidence. The runtime doesn't assign evidence to application domains the same way it assigns evidence to assemblies because there is nothing to base that evidence on. Instead, the code creating an application domain must assign evidence if required.

> **Note**   The runtime only uses the enterprise, machine, and user policy levels to calculate the permissions of an application domain; the security policies of existing application domains play no part. Recipe 13.12 discusses application domain security policy.

Application domains with no evidence are transparent to the runtime's code access security mechanisms. Those application domains assigned evidence have a grant set based on security policy and play an important role in the resolution of CAS security demands. When application execution crosses an application domain boundary, the runtime records the transition on the call stack. When a security demand causes a stack walk, the application domain transition records are processed the same as other stack records—the runtime evaluates the grant set associated with the stack record to ensure it contains the demanded permissions. This means that the permissions of an application domain affect all code loaded into the application domain. In effect, the application domain establishes an upper limit on the capabilities of all code loaded into it.

An important example of using application domain evidence is Microsoft Internet Explorer. Internet Explorer creates an application domain for each site from which it downloads managed controls. All controls downloaded from a given site—as well as the assemblies they load—run in the same application domain. When Internet Explorer creates the application domain for a site, it assigns *System.Security.Policy.Site* evidence to the application domain. This ensures that if downloaded controls load an assembly (even from the local disk), the actions of the assembly are constrained by the permissions granted to the application domain based on the *Site* evidence and security policy.

> **Note**   Unless you explicitly assign evidence to an application domain as you create it, the application domain has no effect on security demands.

To assign evidence to an application domain, create an *Evidence* collection and add the required evidence objects to it using the *Evidence.AddHost* method. When you create the new application domain, pass the *Evidence* collection to one of the overloads of the *static* method *CreateDomain*. The runtime's usual policy resolution process will determine the grant set of the application domain.

The AppDomainEvidenceExample application shown here demonstrates how to assign evidence to an application domain. The example represents a scenario where the application loads code from a particular publisher into a publisher specific application domain. By assigning the application domain *System.Security.Policy.Publisher* evidence that represents the software publisher, the example limits the capabilities of the code loaded into the application domain. Using security policy, you can assign the publisher's code a maximum permission set commensurate with the level of trust you place in the publisher.

```
using System;
using System.Security.Policy;
using System.Security.Cryptography.X509Certificates;

public class AppDomainEvidenceExample {

    public static void Main() {

        // Create a new application domain for each publisher whose
        // code the application will load. Pass the CreateAppDomain
        // method the name of the company, and the name of a file
        // containing the company's X.509v3 certificate.
        AppDomain appDom1 = CreateAppDomain("Litware", "litware.cer");
        AppDomain appDom2 = CreateAppDomain("Fabrikam", "fabrikam.cer");

        // Load code from the various publishers into the appropriate
        // application domain for execution.
        :
    }

    // A method to create a new application domain in which to load and run
    // code from a specific publisher. The name argument specifies the name
    // of the application domain. The certFile argument specifies the name
    // of a file that contains an X.509v3 certificate for the software
    // publisher whose code will be run in the new application domain.
    private static AppDomain CreateAppDomain(string name, string certFile){

        // Create a new X509Certificate object from the X.509v3 certificate
        // contained in the specified file.
        X509Certificate cert =
            X509Certificate.CreateFromCertFile(certFile);
```

```
                // Create new Publisher evidence from the X509Certificate object.
                Publisher publisherEvidence = new Publisher(cert);

                // Create a new Evidence collection.
                Evidence evidence = new Evidence();

                // Add the Publisher evidence to the Evidence collection.
                evidence.AddHost(publisherEvidence);

                // Create a new application domain with the Evidence
                // collection containing the Publisher evidence
                // and return the newly created application domain.
                return AppDomain.CreateDomain(name, evidence);
        }
    }
```

13.12 Manipulate Runtime Security Using Application Domain Security Policy

Problem

You need programmatic control over the permissions granted to assemblies.

Solution

Programmatically configure the security policy of the application domain into which you load the assemblies.

Discussion

Security policy consists of four policy levels: enterprise, machine, user, and application domain. The runtime resolves which permissions to grant to an assembly by determining the permission set granted by each policy level and then calculating the intersection (logical AND) of the four permissions sets. The permissions within this intersection are the assembly's final grant set.

> **Important**   Even if the enterprise, machine, or user policy levels specify a *LevelFinal* code group, which instructs the runtime not to evaluate lower policy levels, the runtime always uses the policy level of the containing application domain to calculate an assembly's grant set.

Only the enterprise, machine, and user policy levels are statically configured using administrative tools. Because application domains do not exist outside the context of the runtime, it's not possible to configure application domain policy statically. To configure the security policy of an application domain, you must create a policy level programmatically and then assign the policy level to the application domain.

Constructing a policy level in code can be a lengthy coding exercise depending on the complexity of the security policy you need to express. The *System.Security.Policy.PolicyLevel* class represents a security policy level. Within a *PolicyLevel* object, you must build a hierarchy of code groups, defining the membership conditions, permission sets, and attributes of each code group. There are many different types used to build the policy level, and a discussion of these types is beyond the scope of this book. *Programming .NET Security*, mentioned earlier, provides detailed coverage of each of these classes and demonstrates how to construct a policy level programmatically.

Tip Most commonly, you would develop a tool to assist in the creation of a policy level and write the policy level definition to a file, you can then load this definition from disk as required. The *PolicyLevel* class includes two methods to simplify this process: *ToXml* renders a *PolicyLevel* object to a form that is easy to store, and *FromXml* reconstructs a *PolicyLevel* object from its stored form.

Once you have a *PolicyLevel* object that expresses the desired security policy, you can assign it to an application domain. Obtain a *System.AppDomain* reference to the application domain you want to configure, and pass the *PolicyLevel* object to the *AppDomain.SetAppDomainPolicy* method. Your code must have the *ControlDomainPolicy* element of *SecurityPermission* to call *SetAppDomainPolicy*. You can call *SetAppDomainPolicy* only once on each application domain; if you call *SetAppDomainPolicy* a second time, it throws the exception *System.Security.Policy.PolicyException*.

You do not have to assign the *PolicyLevel* object to an application domain before loading assemblies into the application domain. Assemblies loaded before you set the application domain security policy have grant sets based only on the enterprise, machine, and user policy levels. The application domain policy applies only to those assemblies loaded after it's configured. Commonly, you use this capability to load trusted shared assemblies into the application domain that should not be constrained by application domain policy.

The application AppDomainPolicyExample listed here demonstrates the process of creating a policy level and assigning it to an application domain. The example creates a policy level that grants permissions based on the publisher of an assembly—expressed in terms of *System.Security.Policy.Publisher* evidence.

```csharp
using System;
using System.Security;
using System.Security.Policy;
using System.Security.Cryptography.X509Certificates;

public class AppDomainPolicyExample {

    public static void Main() {

        // Create a new application domain in which to load the downloaded
        // assemblies.
        AppDomain domain = AppDomain.CreateDomain("modules");

        // Load assemblies into the application domain that you do not want
        // constrained by the application domain security policy.
        ⋮

        // Configure the security policy for the new AppDomain object.
        SetDomainPolicy(domain);

        // Load downloaded assemblies into secured application domain
        // for execution.
        ⋮
    }

    // A method that configures the security policy of the AppDomain
    // object passed to it. The security policy will assign different
    // permissions to each assembly based on the publisher of the
    // assembly. Assemblies from unknown publishers are assigned no
    // permissions.
    private static void SetDomainPolicy(AppDomain domain) {

        // Create a new empty PolicyLevel for the application domain.
        PolicyLevel policy = PolicyLevel.CreateAppDomainLevel();

        // Create a new FirstMatchCodeGroup to use as the root node of
        // the code group hierarchy. Configure this group to match all code
        // by using the membership condition AllMembershipCondition and
        // grant members the named permission set Nothing. This means
        // all assemblies start with an empty grant set for the application
        // domain policy level.
        policy.RootCodeGroup = new FirstMatchCodeGroup(
```

```
        new AllMembershipCondition(),
        new PolicyStatement(policy.GetNamedPermissionSet("Nothing"))
);


// Create the set of code groups that determine which permissions
// to assign an assembly created by a particular publisher. Because
// the root code group is a FirstMatchCodeGroup, policy resolution
// only matches the assembly against these child groups until it
// finds the first match. Each code group is created with the
// Exclusive attribute to ensure that the assembly does not pick
// up any additional permissions from other code groups.

// Create the code group that grants the FullTrust permission set
// to assemblies published by Microsoft.
X509Certificate microsoftCert =
    X509Certificate.CreateFromCertFile("microsoft.cer");

policy.RootCodeGroup.AddChild(new UnionCodeGroup(
    new PublisherMembershipCondition(microsoftCert),
    new PolicyStatement(policy.GetNamedPermissionSet("FullTrust"),
    PolicyStatementAttribute.Exclusive)
));

// Create the code group that grants the Internet permission set
// to assemblies published by Litware, Inc.
X509Certificate litwareCert =
    X509Certificate.CreateFromCertFile("litware.cer");

policy.RootCodeGroup.AddChild(new UnionCodeGroup(
    new PublisherMembershipCondition(litwareCert),
    new PolicyStatement(policy.GetNamedPermissionSet("Internet"),
    PolicyStatementAttribute.Exclusive)
));

// Create the code group that grants the Execution permission set
// to assemblies published by Fabrikam, Inc.
X509Certificate fabrikamCert =
    X509Certificate.CreateFromCertFile("fabrikam.cer");

policy.RootCodeGroup.AddChild(new UnionCodeGroup(
    new PublisherMembershipCondition(fabrikamCert),
    new PolicyStatement(policy.GetNamedPermissionSet("Execution"),
    PolicyStatementAttribute.Exclusive)
));

// Add a final code group to catch all assemblies that are not
// matched by one of the publisher specific groups. Assign this
// group the permission set Nothing. Because the group is Exclusive
```

```
                    // the assembly will get no permissions from any other group, even
                    // from higher policy levels (enterprise, machine, and user).
                    policy.RootCodeGroup.AddChild(new UnionCodeGroup(
                        new AllMembershipCondition(),
                        new PolicyStatement(policy.GetNamedPermissionSet("Nothing"),
                        PolicyStatementAttribute.Exclusive)
                    ));

                    // Assign the policy to the provided application domain.
                    domain.SetAppDomainPolicy(policy);
                }
            }
```

13.13 Determine if the Current User Is a Member of a Specific Windows Group

Problem

You need to determine if the current user of your application is a member of a specific Windows user group.

Solution

Obtain a *System.Security.Principal.WindowsIdentity* object representing the current Windows user by calling the *static* method *WindowsIdentity.GetCurrent*. Then pass the returned *WindowsIdentity* object to the constructor of the *System.Security.Principal.WindowsPrincipal* class to obtain a *WindowsPrincipal* object. Finally, call the method *IsInRole* of the *WindowsPrincipal* object to determine if the user is in a specific Windows group.

Discussion

The RBS mechanism of the .NET Framework abstracts the user-based security features of the underlying operating system through the following two key interfaces:

■   *System.Security.Principal.IIdentity*

■   *System.Security.Principal.IPrincipal*

The *IIdentity* interface represents the entity on whose behalf code is running, for example a user or service account. The *IPrincipal* interface represents the entity's *IIdentity* and the set of roles to which the entity belongs. A *role* is simply a categorization used to group entities with similar security capabilities, such as a Windows user group.

To integrate RBS with Windows user security, the .NET Framework provides the following two Windows-specific classes that implement the *IIdentity* and *IPrincipal* interfaces:

- *System.Security.Principal.WindowsIdentity*

- *System.Security.Principal.WindowsPrincipal*

The *WindowsIdentity* class implements the *IIdentity* interface and represents a Windows user. The *WindowsPrincipal* class implements *IPrincipal* and represents the set of Windows groups to which the user belongs. Because .NET RBS is a generic solution designed to be platform independent, you have no access to the features and capabilities of the Windows user account through the *IIdentity* and *IPrincipal* interfaces, and you must frequently use the *WindowsIdentity* and *WindowsPrincipal* objects directly.

To determine if the current user is a member of a specific Windows group, you must first call the *static* method *WindowsIdentity.GetCurrent*. The *GetCurrent* method returns a *WindowsIdentity* object that represents the Windows user on whose behalf the current thread is running. Next instantiate a new *WindowsPrincipal* object and pass the *WindowsIdentity* object as an argument to the constructor. Finally, call the *IsInRole* method of the *WindowsPrincipal* object to test if the user is in a specific group (role). *IsInRole* returns *true* if the user is a member of the specified group, otherwise *false*.

> **Note**   You might be able to obtain an *IPrincipal* reference to a *WindowsPrincipal* object that represents the current user by getting the *static* property *CurrentPrincipal* of the class *System.Threading.Thread*. However, this technique depends on the principal policy configuration of the current application domain; recipe 13.14 discusses this in more detail.

The *IsInRole* method provides three overloads. The first overload takes a *string* containing the name of the group for which you want to test. The group name must be of the form [DomainName]\[GroupName] for domain-based groups and [MachineName]\[GroupName] for locally defined groups. If you want to test for membership of a standard Windows group, use the form BUILTIN\[GroupName]. *IsInRole* performs a case-insensitive test for the specified group name.

The second *IsInRole* overload accepts an *int*, which specifies a Windows Role Identifier (RID). RIDs provide a mechanism to identify groups that is independent of language and localization. The third *IsInRole* overload accepts a member of the *System.Security.Principal.WindowsBuiltInRole* enumeration. The *WindowsBuiltInRole* enumeration defines a set of members that represent each of the built-in Windows groups. Table 13-3 lists the name, RID, and *WindowsBuiltInRole* value for each of the standard Windows groups.

Table 13-3   Windows Built-In Account Names and Identifiers

Account Name	RID (Hex)	*WindowsBuiltInRole* Value
BUILTIN\Account Operators	0x224	*AccountOperator*
BUILTIN\Administrators	0x220	*Administrator*
BUILTIN\Backup Operators	0x227	*BackupOperator*
BUILTIN\Guests	0x222	*Guest*
BUILTIN\Power Users	0x223	*PowerUser*
BUILTIN\Print Operators	0x226	*PrintOperator*
BUILTIN\Replicators	0x228	*Replicator*
BUILTIN\Server Operators	0x225	*SystemOperator*
BUILTIN\Users	0x221	*User*

> **Note**   The *WindowsIdentity* class provides overloaded constructors that when running on Microsoft Windows Server 2003 or later platforms allow you to obtain a *WindowsIdentity* object representing a named user. You can use this *WindowsIdentity* object and the process described in this recipe to determine if that user is a member of a specific Windows group.
>
> If you try to use one of these constructors when running on an earlier version of Windows, the *WindowsIdentity* constructor will throw the exception *System.ArgumentException*. On Windows platforms preceding Windows Server 2003, you must use native code to obtain a Windows access token representing the desired user. You can then use this access token to instantiate a *WindowsIdentity* object; recipe 13.15 explains how to obtain Windows access tokens for specific users.

The WindowsGroupExample application shown here demonstrates how to test whether the current user is a member of a set of named Windows groups. You specify the groups that you want to test for as command-line arguments; remember to prefix the group name with the machine or domain name, or BUILTIN for standard Windows groups.

```
using System;
using System.Security.Principal;

public class WindowsGroupExample {

    public static void Main (string[] args) {

        // Obtain a WindowsIdentity object representing the currently
        // logged on Windows user.
        WindowsIdentity identity = WindowsIdentity.GetCurrent();

        // Create a WindowsPrincipal object that represents the security
        // capabilities of the specified WindowsIdentity, in this case
        // the Windows groups to which the current user belongs.
        WindowsPrincipal principal = new WindowsPrincipal(identity);

        // Iterate through the group names specified as command-line
        // arguments and test to see if the current user is a member of
        // each one.
        foreach (string role in args) {

            Console.WriteLine("Is {0} a member of {1}? = {2}",
                identity.Name, role, principal.IsInRole(role));
        }
    }
}
```

If you run this example as a user named Darryl on a computer named MACHINE using the command **WindowsGroupExample BUILTIN\Administrators BUILTIN\Users MACHINE\Accountants**, you will see console output similar to the following.

```
Is MACHINE\Darryl a member of BUILTIN\Administrators? = False
Is MACHINE\Darryl a member of BUILTIN\Users? = True
Is MACHINE\Darryl a member of MACHINE\Accountants? = True
```

13.14 Restrict Which Users Can Execute Your Code

Problem

You need to restrict which users can execute elements of your code based on the user's name or the roles of which the user is a member.

Solution

Use the permission class *System.Security.Permissions.PrincipalPermission* and its attribute counterpart *System.Security.Permissions.PrincipalPermissionAttribute* to protect your program elements with RBS demands.

Discussion

The .NET Framework supports both imperative and declarative RBS demands. The class *PrincipalPermission* provides support for imperative security statements, and its attribute counterpart *PrincipalPermissionAttribute* provides support for declarative security statements. RBS demands use the same syntax as CAS demands, but RBS demands specify the name the current user must have, or more commonly the roles of which the user must be a member. An RBS demand instructs the runtime to look at the name and roles of the current user, and if they do not meet the requirements of the demand, the runtime throws a *System.Security.SecurityException*.

This code fragment shows the syntax of an imperative security demand.

```
// Imperative role-based security demand syntax.
public static void SomeMethod() {
    ⋮
    PrincipalPermission perm =
        new PrincipalPermission("UserName", "RoleName");

    perm.Demand();
    ⋮
}
```

You must first create a *PrincipalPermission* object specifying the user name and role name you want to demand, and then you must call its *Demand* method. You can specify only a single user and role name per demand. If either the user or the role name is *null*, any value will satisfy the demand. Unlike with code access permissions, an RBS demand doesn't result in a stack walk; the runtime evaluates only the user name and roles of the current user.

This code fragment shows the syntax of a declarative security demand.

```
// Declarative role-based security demand syntax.
[PrincipalPermission(SecurityAction.Demand, Name = "UserName",
    Role = "RoleName")]
public static void SomeMethod() { /*...*/}
```

You can place declarative RBS demands at the class or member level. Class-level demands apply to all members of the class unless a member-specific demand overrides the class demand.

Generally, you are free to choose whether to implement imperative or declarative RBS demands. However, imperative security demands allow you to integrate RBS demands with code logic to achieve sophisticated RBS demand behavior. In addition, if you do not know the role or user names to demand at compile time, you must use imperative demands. Declarative RBS demands have the advantage that they are separate from code logic and easier to identify. In addition, you can view declarative RBS demands using the tool Permview.exe (discussed in recipe 13.6). Whether you implement imperative or declarative RBS demands, you must ensure that the runtime has access to the name and roles for the current user to evaluate the demand correctly.

The *System.Threading.Thread* class represents an operating system thread running managed code. The *static* property *CurrentPrincipal* of the *Thread* class contains an *IPrincipal* instance representing the user on whose behalf the managed thread is running. At the operating system level, each thread also has an associated Windows access token, which represents the Windows account on whose behalf the thread is running. It's important you understand that the *IPrincipal* instance and the Windows access token are two separate entities. Windows uses its access token to enforce operating system security, whereas the .NET runtime uses its *IPrincipal* instance to evaluate application level RBS demands. Although they may, and often do, represent the same user, this is by no means always the case.

By default, the *Thread.CurrentPrincipal* property is undefined. Because obtaining user-related information can be time consuming and only a minority of applications use this information, the .NET designers opted for lazy initialization of the *CurrentPrincipal* property. The first time code gets the *Thread.CurrentPrincipal* property, the runtime assigns an *IPrincipal* instance to the property using the following logic:

1. If the application domain in which the current thread is executing has a default principal, the runtime assigns this principal to the *Thread.CurrentPrincipal* property.

    By default, application domains do not have default principals. You can set the default principal of an application domain by calling the method *SetThreadPrincipal* on a *System.AppDomain* object that represents the application domain you want to configure. Code must have the *ControlPrincipal* element of *SecurityPermission* to call *SetThreadPrincipal*. You can only set the default principal once for each application domain; a second call to *SetThreadPrincipal* results in the exception *System.Security.Policy.PolicyException*.

2. If the application domain doesn't have a default principal, the application domain's principal policy determines which *IPrincipal* implementation to create and assign to *Thread.CurrentPrincipal*.

    To configure principal policy for an application domain, obtain an *AppDomain* object that represents the application domain and call the object's *SetPrincipalPolicy* method. The *SetPrincipalPolicy* method accepts a member of the enumeration *System.Security.Principal.PrincipalPolicy*, which specifies the type of *IPrincipal* object to assign to *Thread.CurrentPrincipal*. Code must have the *ControlPrincipal* element of *SecurityPermission* to call *SetPrincipalPolicy*. Table 13-4 lists the available *PrincipalPolicy* values; the default value is *UnauthenticatedPrincipal*.

3. If your code has the *ControlPrincipal* element of *SecurityPermission*, you can instantiate your own *IPrincipal* object and assign it to the *Thread.CurrentPrincipal* property directly. This will stop the runtime assigning default *IPrincipal* objects or creating new ones based on principal policy.

Table 13-4 Members of the *PrincipalPolicy* Enumeration

Member Name	Description
NoPrincipal	No *IPrincipal* object is created, *Thread.CurrentPrincipal* returns a *null* reference.
UnauthenticatedPrincipal	An empty *System.Security.Principal.GenericPrincipal* object is created and assigned to *Thread.CurrentPrincipal*.
WindowsPrincipal	A *WindowsPrincipal* object representing the currently logged-on Windows user is created and assigned to *Thread.CurrentPrincipal*.

Whatever method you use to establish the *IPrincipal* for the current thread, you must do so before you use RBS security demands, or the correct user (*IPrincipal*) information won't be available for the runtime to process the demand. Normally, when running on the Windows platform, you would set the principal policy of an application domain to *PrincipalPolicy.WindowsPrincipal* (as shown here) to obtain Windows user information.

```
// Obtain a reference to the current application domain.
AppDomain appDomain = System.AppDomain.CurrentDomain;

// Configure the current application domain to use Windows-based principals.
appDomain.SetPrincipalPolicy(
    System.Security.Principal.PrincipalPolicy.WindowsPrincipal);
```

The RoleBasedSecurityExample.cs file in the sample code for this chapter demonstrates the use of imperative and declarative RBS demands. The first excerpt included here shows three methods protected using imperative RBS demands. If the *Thread.CurrentPrincipal* object doesn't meet the demanded user name and role membership requirements, the demand will throw a *SecurityException*, which the method must handle or pass up for a method higher on the call stack to process.

```
public static void ProtectedMethod1() {

    // An imperative role-based security demand for the current principal
    // to represent an identity with the name "Anya", the roles of the
    // principal are irrelevant.
    System.Security.Permissions.PrincipalPermission perm =
        new System.Security.Permissions.PrincipalPermission
        (@"MACHINE\Anya", null);

    perm.Demand();
}


public static void ProtectedMethod2() {

    // An imperative role-based security demand for the current principal
    // to be a member of the roles "Managers" OR "Developers". If the
    // principal is a member of either role, access is granted. Using the
    // PrincipalPermission you can only express an OR type relationship.
    // This is because the PrincipalPolicy.Intersect method always
    // returns an empty permission unless the two inputs are the same.
    // However, you can use code logic to implement more complex
    // conditions. In this case, the name of the identity is irrelevant.
    System.Security.Permissions.PrincipalPermission perm1 =
        new System.Security.Permissions.PrincipalPermission
        (null, @"MACHINE\Managers");

    System.Security.Permissions.PrincipalPermission perm2 =
        new System.Security.Permissions.PrincipalPermission
        (null, @"MACHINE\Developers");

    perm1.Union(perm2).Demand();
}
```

```
public static void ProtectedMethod3() {

    // An imperative role-based security demand for the current principal
    // to represent an identity with the name "Anya" AND be a member of the
    // "Managers" role.
    System.Security.Permissions.PrincipalPermission perm =
        new System.Security.Permissions.PrincipalPermission
        (@"MACHINE\Anya", @"MACHINE\Managers");

    perm.Demand();
}
```

The second excerpt shows three methods protected using declarative RBS demands, equivalent to the imperative demands just shown.

```
// A declarative role-based security demand for the current principal
// to represent an identity with the name "Anya", the roles of the
// principal are irrelevant.
[PrincipalPermission(SecurityAction.Demand, Name = @"MACHINE\Anya")]
public static void ProtectedMethod1() { /*...*/}

// A declarative role-based security demand for the current principal
// to be a member of the roles "Managers" OR "Developers". If the
// principal is a member of either role, access is granted. You
// can only express an OR type relationship, not an AND relationship.
// The name of the identity is irrelevant.
[PrincipalPermission(SecurityAction.Demand, Role = @"MACHINE\Managers")]
[PrincipalPermission(SecurityAction.Demand, Role = @"MACHINE\Developers")]
public static void ProtectedMethod2() { /*...*/}

// A declarative role-based security demand for the current principal
// to represent an identity with the name "Anya" AND be a member of the
// "Managers" role.
[PrincipalPermission(SecurityAction.Demand, Name = @"MACHINE\Anya",
    Role = @"MACHINE\Managers")]
public static void ProtectedMethod3() { /*...*/}
```

13.15 Impersonate a Windows User

Problem

You need your code to run in the context of a Windows user other than the currently active user account.

Solution

Obtain a *System.Security.Principal.WindowsIdentity* object representing the Windows user you need to impersonate, and then call the *Impersonate* method of the *WindowsIdentity* object.

Discussion

Every Windows thread has an associated *access token*, which represents the Windows account on whose behalf the thread is running. The Windows operating system uses the access token to determine whether a thread has the appropriate permissions to perform protected operations on behalf of the account, such as read and write files, reboot the system, and change the system time.

By default, a managed application runs in the context of the Windows account that executed the application. This is normally desirable behavior, but sometimes you will want to run an application in the context of a different Windows account. This is particularly true in the case of server-side applications that process transaction on behalf of the users remotely connected to the server. It's common for a server application to run in the context of a Windows account created specifically for the application—a service account. This service account will have minimal permissions to access system resources. Enabling the application to operate as though it were the connected user permits the application to access the operations and resources appropriate to that user's security clearance. When an application assumes the identity of another user, it's known as *impersonation*. Correctly implemented, impersonation simplifies security administration and application design, while maintaining user accountability.

> **Important**   As discussed in recipe 13.14, a thread's Windows access token and its .NET principal are separate entities and can represent different users. The impersonation technique described in this recipe changes only the Windows access token of the current thread; it doesn't change the thread's principal. To change the thread's principal, code must have the *ControlPrincipal* element of *SecurityPermission* and assign a new *System.Security.Principal.IPrincipal* object to the *CurrentPrincipal* property of the current *System.Threading.Thread*.

The *System.Security.Principal.WindowsIdentity* class provides the functionality through which you invoke impersonation. However, the exact process depends on which version of Windows your application is running on. If running on Windows Server 2003 or later, the *WindowsIdentity* class supports constructor overloads that create *WindowsIdentity* objects based on the account name of the user you want to impersonate. On all previous versions of Windows, you must first obtain a *System.IntPtr* containing a reference to a Windows access token that represents the user to impersonate. To obtain the access token reference, you must use a native method such as the function *LogonUser* from the Win32 API.

> **Note** A major issue with performing impersonation on Windows 2000 and Microsoft Windows NT is that an account must have the Windows privilege SE_TCB_NAME to execute *LogonUser*. This requires you to configure Windows security policy and grant the account the right to "Act as part of operating system". This grants the account a very high level of trust. You should never grant the privilege SE_TCB_NAME directly to user accounts.

Once you have a *WindowsIdentity* object representing the user you want to impersonate, call its *Impersonate* method. From that point on, all actions your code performs occur in the context of the impersonated Windows account. The *Impersonate* method returns a *System.Security.Principal.WindowsSecurityContext* object, which represents the active account prior to impersonation. To revert to the original account, call the *Undo* method of this *WindowsSecurityContext* object.

The console application ImpersonationExample shown here demonstrates impersonation of a Windows user. The example expects two command-line arguments: the account name of the user to impersonate and the account's password. The example uses the *LogonUser* function of the Win32 API to obtain a Windows access token for the specified user, impersonates the user, and then reverts to the original user context. For example, the command **ImpersonationExample Bob password** would impersonate the user Bob as long as that user existed in the local accounts database.

```
using System;
using System.IO;
using System.Security.Principal;
using System.Security.Permissions;
```

```csharp
using System.Runtime.InteropServices;

// Ensure the assembly has permission to execute unmanaged code
// and control the thread principal.
[assembly:SecurityPermission(SecurityAction.RequestMinimum,
    UnmanagedCode=true, ControlPrincipal=true)]

public class ImpersonationExample {

    // Define some constants for use with the LogonUser function.
    const int LOGON32_PROVIDER_DEFAULT = 0;
    const int LOGON32_LOGON_INTERACTIVE = 2;

    // Import the Win32 LogonUser function from advapi32.dll. Specify
    // "SetLastError = true" to correctly support access to Win32 error
    // codes.
    [DllImport("advapi32.dll", SetLastError=true)]
    static extern int LogonUser(string userName, string domain,
        string password, int logonType, int logonProvider,
        ref IntPtr accessToken);

    public static void Main(string[] args) {

        // Create a new IntPtr to hold the access token returned by the
        // LogonUser function.
        IntPtr accessToken = IntPtr.Zero;

        // Call LogonUser to obtain an access token for the specified user.
        // The accessToken variable is passed to LogonUser by reference and
        // will contain a reference to the Windows access token if
        // LogonUser is successful.
        int result = LogonUser(
            args[0],                        // user name to log on.
            ".",                            // use the local account database.
            args[1],                        // user's password.
            LOGON32_LOGON_INTERACTIVE,      // create an interactive login.
            LOGON32_PROVIDER_DEFAULT,       // use the default logon provider.
            ref accessToken                 // receives access token handle.
        );

        // If the LogonUser return code is zero an error has occurred.
        // Display the error and exit.
        if (result == 0)  {

            Console.WriteLine("LogonUser returned error {0}",
                Marshal.GetLastWin32Error());

        } else {
```

```csharp
            // Create a new WindowsIdentity from the Windows access token.
            WindowsIdentity identity = new WindowsIdentity(accessToken);

            // Display the active identity.
            Console.WriteLine("Identity before impersonation = {0}",
                WindowsIdentity.GetCurrent().Name);

            // Impersonate the specified user, saving a reference to the
            // returned WindowsImpersonationContext, which contains the
            // information necessary to revert to the original user
            // context.
            WindowsImpersonationContext impContext =
                identity.Impersonate();

            // Display the active identity.
            Console.WriteLine("Identity during impersonation = {0}",
                WindowsIdentity.GetCurrent().Name);

            // ****************************************
            // Perform actions as the impersonated user.
            // ****************************************

            // Revert to the original Windows user using the
            // WindowsImpersonationContext object.
            impContext.Undo();

            // Display the active identity.
            Console.WriteLine("Identity after impersonation  = {0}",
                WindowsIdentity.GetCurrent().Name);
        }
    }
}
```

14

Cryptography

Cryptography is one of the most complex aspects of software development that any developer will use. The theory of modern cryptographic techniques is extremely difficult to understand and requires a level of mathematical knowledge that relatively few people have—or, for that matter, want to have. Fortunately, the Microsoft .NET Framework class library provides easy-to-use implementations of the most commonly used cryptographic techniques and support for the most popular and well-understood algorithms. The recipes in this chapter discuss the following:

- Generating cryptographically random numbers (recipe 14.1)

- Generating and verifying cryptographic hash codes and keyed hash codes (recipes 14.2, 14.3, 14.4, and 14.5)

- Using symmetric and asymmetric algorithms to encrypt and decrypt data (recipes 14.6 and 14.8)

- Deriving, storing, and exchanging cryptographic keys (recipes 14.7, 14.9, and 14.10)

As you read the recipes in this chapter and think about how to apply the techniques to your own code, keep in mind that cryptography is never something you should implement in isolation. Cryptography does not equal security; the use of cryptography is merely one small element of creating a secure solution. For a broader explanation of secure programming and where cryptography fits in the overall security landscape, you should read *Writing Secure Code, Second Edition*, by Michael Howard and David LeBlanc (Microsoft Press, 2003), a modern classic of computer literature that contains a wealth of practical field-tested information. For a more comprehensive coverage of the .NET cryptography classes than I provide here, I shamelessly recommend the book I cowrote with Adam Freeman, *Programming .NET Security* (O'Reilly and Associates, 2003). *Programming .NET Security* provides easily understood descriptions of cryptography fundamentals, covers all the .NET cryptography classes in detail, and demonstrates how to extend most aspects of the cryptographic framework.

For those not familiar with cryptography, here are the definitions of a few important words that you will need to know to understand this chapter. The definitions are excerpts from the *Microsoft Computer Dictionary, Fifth Edition* (Microsoft Press, 2002).

- **Ciphertext** is the scrambled or otherwise encoded text of an encrypted message.

- **Encrypt** means to encode (scramble) information in such a way that it's unreadable to all but those individuals possessing the key to the code.

- **Key** is a string of bits used for encrypting and decrypting information to be transmitted.

- **Plaintext** is nonencrypted or decrypted text.

14.1 Create a Cryptographically Random Number

Problem

You need to create a random number that's suitable for use in cryptographic and security applications.

Solution

Use a cryptographic random number generator such as the *System.Security.Cryptography.RNGCryptoServiceProvider* class.

Discussion

The *System.Random* class is a pseudorandom number generator that uses a mathematical algorithm to simulate the generation of random numbers. In fact, the algorithm it uses is deterministic, meaning that you can always calculate what the next number will be based on the previously generated number. This means that numbers generated by the *Random* class are unsuitable for use in situations in which security is a priority, such as generating encryption keys and passwords.

When you need a nondeterministic random number for use in cryptographic or security-related applications, you must use a random number generator derived from the class *System.Security.Cryptography.RandomNumberGenerator*. The *RandomNumberGenerator* class is an *abstract* class from which all concrete .NET random number generator classes should inherit. Currently, the *RNGCryptoServiceProvider* class is the only concrete implementation provided. The *RNGCryptoServiceProvider* class provides a managed wrapper around the *CryptGenRandom* function of the Win32 CryptoAPI, and you can use it to fill *byte* arrays with cryptographically random *byte* values.

> **Important**   The numbers produced by the *RNGCryptoServiceProvider* class aren't truly random. However, they are sufficiently random to meet the requirements of cryptography and security applications in most commercial and government environments.

As is the case with many of the .NET cryptography classes, the *RandomNumberGenerator* base class is a factory for the concrete implementation classes that derive from it. Calling *RandomNumberGenerator.Create("System.Security.Cryptography.RNGCryptoServiceProvider")* will return an instance of *RNGCryptoServiceProvider* that you can use to generate random numbers. In addition, because *RNGCryptoServiceProvider* is the only concrete implementation provided, it's the default class created if you call the *Create* method without arguments, for example, *RandomNumberGenerator.Create()*.

The following example instantiates an *RNGCryptoServiceProvider* object and uses it to generate random values. The method *GetBytes* fills a *byte* array with random *byte* values. As an alternative, you can use the *GetNonZeroBytes* method if you need random data that contains no zero values.

```
using System;
using System.Security.Cryptography;

public class SecureRandomNumberExample {

    public static void Main() {

        // Create a byte array to hold the random data.
```

```
        byte[] number = new byte[32];

        // Instantiate the default random number generator.
        RandomNumberGenerator rng = RandomNumberGenerator.Create();

        // Generate 32 bytes of random data.
        rng.GetBytes(number);

        // Display the random number.
        Console.WriteLine(BitConverter.ToString(number));
    }
}
```

> **Warning**   The computational effort required to generate a random number with *RNGCryptoServiceProvider* is significantly greater than that required by *Random*. For everyday purposes, the use of *RNGCryptoServiceProvider* is overkill. You should consider the quantity of random numbers you need to generate and the purpose of the numbers before deciding to use *RNGCryptoServiceProvider*. Excessive and unnecessary use of the *RNGCryptoServiceProvider* class could have a noticeable effect on application performance.

14.2 Calculate the Hash Code of a Password

Problem

You need to store a user's password securely so that you can use it to authenticate the user in the future.

Solution

Do not store the user's plaintext password; storing plaintext passwords is a major security risk and one that most users would not appreciate given that many of them will use the same password to access multiple systems. Instead, create and store a cryptographic hash code of the password using a hashing algorithm class derived from the *System.Security.Cryptography.HashAlgorithm* class. On future authentication attempts, generate the hash of the provided password and compare it to the stored hash code.

Discussion

Hashing algorithms are one-way cryptographic functions that take plaintext of variable length and generate a fixed-size numeric value. They are *one-way* because it's nearly impossible to derive the original plaintext from the hash code. Hashing algorithms are deterministic; applying the same hashing algorithm to a specific piece of plaintext always generates the same hash code. This makes hash codes useful for determining if two blocks of plaintext (passwords in this case) are the same. The design of hashing algorithms ensures that—although not impossible—the chance of two different pieces of plaintext generating the same hash code is extremely small. In addition, there is no correlation between the similarity of two pieces of plaintext and their hash codes; minor differences in the plaintext cause significant differences in the resulting hash codes.

When using passwords to authenticate a user, you aren't concerned with the content of the password that the user enters. You need only to know that the entered password matches the password that you have recorded for that user in your accounts database. The nature of hashing algorithms makes them ideal for storing passwords securely. When the user provides a new password, you must create the hash code of the password and store it, and then discard the clear text password. Each time the user tries to authenticate with your application, calculate the hash code of the password he or she provides and compare it with the hash code you have stored.

> **Note**   People regularly ask how to obtain a password from a hash code. The simple answer is that you can't. The whole purpose of a hash code is to act as a token that you can freely store without creating security holes. If a user forgets a password, you can't derive it from the stored hash code; you must either reset the account to some default value, or generate a new password for the user.

Generating hash codes is quick and simple in the .NET Framework. The *abstract* class *HashAlgorithm* provides a base from which all concrete hashing algorithm implementations should derive. The .NET Framework class library includes the six hashing algorithm implementations listed in Table 14-1; each implementation class is a member of the *System.Security.Cryptography* namespace. The classes with names ending in *CryptoServiceProvider* wrap functionality provided by the native Win32 CryptoAPI, whereas those with names ending in *Managed* are fully implemented in managed code.

Table 14-1 **Hashing Algorithm Implementations**

Algorithm Name	Class Name	Hash Code Size (in Bits)
MD5	*MD5CryptoServiceProvider*	128
SHA or SHA1	*SHA1CryptoServiceProvider*	160
SHA1Managed	*SHA1Managed*	160
SHA256 or SHA-256	*SHA256Managed*	256
SHA384 or SHA-384	*SHA384Managed*	384
SHA512 or SHA-512	*SHA512Managed*	512

Although you can create instances of the hashing algorithm classes directly, the *HashAlgorithm* base class is a factory for the concrete implementation classes that derive from it. Calling the *static* method *HashAlgorithm.Create* and passing the algorithm name as an argument will return an object of the specified type. Using the factory approach allows you to write generic code that can work with any hashing algorithm implementation.

Once you have a *HashAlgorithm* object, its *ComputeHash* method accepts a *byte* array argument containing plaintext and returns a new *byte* array containing the generated hash code. Table 14-1 shows the size of hash code (in bits) generated by each hashing algorithm class.

The *HashPasswordExample* class shown here demonstrates the creation of a hash code from a string, such as a password. The application expects two command-line arguments: the name of the hashing algorithm to use and the string from which to generate the hash. Because the *HashAlgorithm.Compute-Hash* method requires a *byte* array, you must first byte encode the input string using the class *System.Text.Encoding*, which provides mechanisms for converting strings to and from various character encoding formats.

```
using System;
using System.Text;
using System.Security.Cryptography;

public class HashPasswordExample {

    public static void Main(string[] args) {
```

```
    // Create a HashAlgorithm of the type specified by the first
    // command line argument.
    using (HashAlgorithm hashAlg = HashAlgorithm.Create(args[0])) {

        // Convert the password string, provided as the second command
        // line argument, to an array of bytes.
        byte[] pwordData = Encoding.Default.GetBytes(args[1]);

        // Generate the hash code of the password.
        byte[] hash = hashAlg.ComputeHash(pwordData);

        // Display the hash code of the password to the console.
        Console.WriteLine(BitConverter.ToString(hash));
    }
  }
}
```

Running the command **HashPasswordExample SHA1 ThisIsMyPassword** will display the following hash code to the console:

```
80-36-31-2F-EA-D9-93-45-79-34-C9-FD-21-EE-8D-05-16-DC-A1-E2
```

14.3 Calculate the Hash Code of a File

Problem

You need to determine if the contents of a file have changed over time.

Solution

Create a cryptographic hash code of the file's contents using the *ComputeHash* method of the *System.Security.Cryptography.HashAlgorithm* class. Store the hash code for future comparison against newly generated hash codes.

Discussion

As well as allowing you to store passwords securely (discussed in recipe 14.2), hash codes provide an excellent means of determining if a file has changed. By calculating and storing the cryptographic hash of a file, you can later recalculate the hash of the file to determine if the file has changed in the interim. A hashing algorithm will produce a very different hash code even if there is a very small change to the file, and the chances of two different files resulting in the same hash code are extremely small.

> **Warning**   Standard hash codes aren't suitable for sending with a file to ensure the integrity of the file's contents. If someone intercepts the file in transit, that person can easily change the file and recalculate the hash code, leaving the recipient none the wiser. We discuss a variant of the hash code—a keyed hash code—in recipe 14.5 that's suitable for ensuring the integrity of a file in transit.

The *HashAlgorithm* class makes it easy to generate the hash code of a file. Firstly, instantiate one of the concrete hashing algorithm implementations derived from the *HashAlgorithm* class. To instantiate the desired hashing algorithm class, pass the name of the hashing algorithm to the *HashAlgorithm.Create* method. See Table 14-1 for a list of valid hashing algorithm names. Then, instead of passing a *byte* array to the *ComputeHash* method, you pass a *System.IO.Stream* object representing the file from which you want to generate the hash code. The *HashAlgorithm* object handles the process of reading data from the *Stream* and returns a *byte* array containing the hash code for the file.

The *HashStreamExample* class listed here demonstrates the generation of a hash code from a file. You must specify the name of the hashing algorithm and the name of the file as command line arguments, for example **HashStreamExample SHA1 HashStreamExample.cs**. The example displays the generated hash code to the console.

```
using System;
using System.IO;
using System.Security.Cryptography;

public class HashStreamExample {

    public static void Main(string[] args) {

        // Create a HashAlgorithm of the type specified by the first
        // command line argument.
        using (HashAlgorithm hashAlg = HashAlgorithm.Create(args[0])) {

            // Open a FileStream to the file specified by the second
            // command line argument.
            using (Stream file = new FileStream(args[1], FileMode.Open)) {

                // Generate the hash code of the file's contents.
                byte[] hash = hashAlg.ComputeHash(file);
```

```
                    // Display the hash code of the file to the console.
                    Console.WriteLine(BitConverter.ToString(hash));
                }
            }
        }
    }
```

14.4 Verify a Hash Code

Problem

You need to verify a password or confirm that a file remains unchanged by comparing two hash codes.

Solution

Convert both the old and the new hash codes to hexadecimal code strings, Base64 strings, or *byte* arrays and compare them.

Discussion

You can use hash codes to determine if two pieces of data (such as passwords or files) are the same, without the need to store, or even maintain access to, the original data. To determine if data changes over time, you must generate and store the original data's hash code. Later, you can generate another hash code for the data and compare the old and new hash codes, which will show if any change has occurred. The format in which you store the original hash code will determine the most appropriate way to verify a newly generated hash code against the stored one.

> **Note**   Many recipes in this chapter use the *ToString* method of the class *System.BitConverter* to convert byte arrays to hexadecimal string values for display. Although easy to use and appropriate for display purposes, you might find this approach inappropriate for use when storing hash codes because it places a hyphen (-) between each byte value (for example, 4D-79-3A-C9-...). In addition, the *BitConverter* class doesn't provide a method to parse such a string representation back into a *byte* array.

Hash codes are often stored in text files, either as hexadecimal strings (for example, *89D2221370A9CFF09A392F00E2C6C4EDC1B0EF9*), or as Base64-encoded strings (for example, *idIiExcKnP8Jo5LwDixsTtwbDvk=*). Alternatively, hash codes may be stored in databases as raw byte values. Regardless of how you store your hash code, the first step in comparing old and new hash codes is to get them both into a common form.

This first example converts a new hash code (a *byte* array) to a hexadecimal string for comparison to an old hash code. Other than the *BitConverter.ToString* method we discussed earlier, the .NET Framework class library doesn't provide an easy method to convert a *byte* array to a hexadecimal string. You must program a loop to step through the elements of the byte array, convert each individual byte to a string, and append the string to the hexadecimal string representation of the hash code. The use of a *System.Text.StringBuilder* avoids the unnecessary creation of new strings each time the loop appends the next byte value to the result string. (See recipe 2.1 for more details.)

```csharp
// A method to compare a newly generated hash code with an
// existing hash code that's represented by a hex code string
private static bool VerifyHexHash(byte[] hash, string oldHashString) {

    // Create a string representation of the hash code bytes.
    System.Text.StringBuilder newHashString =
        new System.Text.StringBuilder(hash.Length);

    // Append each byte as a 2 character upper case hex string.
    foreach (byte b in hash) {
        newHashString.AppendFormat("{0:X2}", b);
    }

    // Compare the string representations of the old and new hash
    // codes and return the result.
    return (oldHashString == newHashString.ToString());
}
```

In this second example, the new hash code is a *byte* array and the old hash code is a Base64 encoded string. The code very neatly encodes the new hash code as a Base64 string and performs a straightforward string comparison of the two values.

```csharp
// A method to compare a newly generated hash code with an
// existing hash code that's represented by a Base64 encoded string.
private static bool VerifyB64Hash(byte[] hash, string oldHashString) {

    // Create a Base64 representation of the hash code bytes.
    string newHashString = System.Convert.ToBase64String(hash);
```

```
// Compare the string representations of the old and new hash
// codes and return the result.
return (oldHashString == newHashString);
}
```

This final example compares two hash codes represented as *byte* arrays. The .NET Framework class library doesn't include a method that performs this type of comparison, and so you must program a loop to compare the elements of the two arrays. This code uses a few time-saving techniques, namely ensuring that the *byte* arrays are the same length before starting to compare them, and returning *false* on the first difference found.

```
// A method to compare a newly generated hash code with an
// existing hash code represented by a byte array.
private static bool VerifyByteHash(byte[] hash, byte[] oldHash) {

    // If either array is null, or the arrays are different lengths
    // then they are not equal.
    if (hash == null || oldHash == null || hash.Length != oldHash.Length)
        return false;

    // Step through the byte arrays and compare each byte value.
    for (int count = 0; count < hash.Length; count++) {
        if (hash[count] != oldHash[count]) return false;
    }

    // Hash codes are equal.
    return true;
}
```

14.5 Ensure Data Integrity Using a Keyed Hash Code

Problem

You need to transmit a file to somebody and provide the recipient with a means to verify the integrity of the file and its source.

Solution

Share a secret key with the intended recipient. This key would ideally be a randomly generated number, but it could also be a phrase that you and the recipient agree to use. Use the key with one of the keyed hashing algorithm classes derived from the *System.Security.Cryptography.KeyedHashAlgorithm* class to create a keyed hash code. Send the hash code with the file. On receipt of the file, the recipient will generate the keyed hash code of the file using the shared secret key. If the hash codes are equal, the recipient knows that the file is from you and that it hasn't changed in transit.

Discussion

Hash codes are useful for comparing two pieces of data to determine if they are the same, even if you no longer have access to the original data. However, you can't use a hash code to reassure the recipient of data as to the data's integrity. If somebody could intercept the data, they could replace the data and generate a new hash code. When the recipient verifies the hash code, it will seem correct, when in fact the data is nothing like what you sent to them originally.

A simple and efficient solution to the problem of data integrity is a *keyed hash code*. A keyed hash code is similar to a normal hash code (discussed in recipes 14.2 and 14.3); however, the keyed hash code incorporates an element of secret data—a key—known only to the sender and the receiver. Without the key, a person can't generate the correct hash code from a given set of data. When you successfully verify a keyed hash code, you can be certain that only somebody who knows the secret key could generate the hash code.

> **Important**   The secret key must remain secret. Anybody who knows the secret key can generate valid keyed hash codes, meaning that you would be unable to determine if they had changed the content of a document. For this reason, you shouldn't transmit or store the secret key with the document whose integrity you are trying to protect. Recipe 14.10 provides one mechanism you can use to exchange secret keys securely.

Generating keyed hash codes is similar to generating normal hash codes; the *abstract* class *System.Security.Cryptography.KeyedHashAlgorithm* extends the class *System.Security.Cryptography.HashAlgorithm. KeyedHashAlgorithm* provides a base class from which all concrete keyed hashing algorithm implementations must derive. The .NET Framework class library includes the two keyed hashing algorithm implementations listed in Table 14-2; each implementation is a member of the namespace *System.Security.Cryptography*.

Table 14-2   Keyed Hashing Algorithm Implementations

Algorithm/Class Name	Key Size (in Bits)	Hash Code Size (in Bits)
HMACSHA1	Any	160
MACTripleDES	64, 128, 192	64

As with the standard hashing algorithms, you can either create keyed hashing algorithm objects directly, or you can use the *static* factory method *KeyedHashAlgorithm.Create* and pass the algorithm name as an argument. Using the factory approach allows you to write generic code that can work with any keyed hashing algorithm implementation, but as shown in Table 14-2, each class supports different key lengths that you must cater for in generic code.

If you use constructors to instantiate a keyed hashing object, you can pass the secret key to the constructor. Using the factory approach, you must set the key using the *Key* property inherited from the *KeyedHashAlgorithm* class. Once configured with a key, call the *ComputeHash* method and pass either a *byte* array or a *System.IO.Stream* object. The keyed hashing algorithm will process the input data and return a *byte* array containing the keyed hash code. Table 14-2 shows the size of hash code generated by each keyed hashing algorithm.

The *KeyedHashStreamExample* class listed here demonstrates the generation of a keyed hash code from a file. You must specify the name of the input file and a key as command-line arguments. The application uses the *HMACSHA1* class to generate the keyed hash code and then displays it to the console.

```
using System;
using System.IO;
using System.Text;
using System.Security.Cryptography;

public class KeyedHashStreamExample {

    public static void Main(string[] args) {

        // Create a byte array from the key string, which is the
        // second command line argument.
        byte[] key = Encoding.Unicode.GetBytes(args[1]);

        // Create a HMACSHA1 object to generate the keyed hash code for
        // the input file. Pass the byte array representing the key to
        // the constructor.
        using (HMACSHA1 hashAlg = new HMACSHA1(key)) {
```

```
            // Open a FileStream to read the input file; the file name is
            // specified by the first command line argument.
            using (Stream file = new FileStream(args[0], FileMode.Open)) {

                // Generate the keyed hash code of the file's contents.
                byte[] hash = hashAlg.ComputeHash(file);

                // Display the keyed hash code to the console.
                Console.WriteLine(BitConverter.ToString(hash));
            }
        }
    }
}
```

Executing the command **KeyedHashStreamExample KeyedHash-StreamExample.cs secretKey** will display the following hash code to the console:

```
95-95-2A-8E-44-D4-3C-55-6F-DA-06-44-27-79-29-81-15-C7-2A-48
```

The sample code for this chapter also contains an application named KeyedHashMessageExample.cs, which demonstrates the generation of a keyed hash code from a *string*. This application expects two command-line arguments: a message and a key. The KeyedHashMessageExample application generates the keyed hash code of the message string using the specified key. For example, entering the command **KeyedHashMessageExample "Two hundred dollars is my final offer" secretKey** will generate the following hash code:

```
83-43-0D-9D-07-6F-AA-B7-BC-79-CD-6F-AD-7B-FA-EA-19-D1-24-44
```

14.6 Protect a File Using Symmetric Encryption

Problem

You need to encrypt a file using symmetric encryption.

Solution

First you must instantiate one of the concrete symmetric algorithm classes that extend the *System.Security.Cryptography.SymmetricAlgorithm* class. Then call the *CreateEncryptor* or *CreateDecryptor* method of the *SymmetricAlgorithm* object to obtain an object that implements the *System.Security.Cryptography.ICryptoTransform* interface. Use this *ICryptoTransform* object in conjunction with a *System.Security.Cryptography.CryptoStream* object to encrypt or decrypt data as you read it from a file—accessed using a *System.IO.FileStream* object.

Discussion

The *abstract* class *SymmetricAlgorithm* provides a base class from which all concrete symmetric algorithm implementations should derive. The .NET Framework class library includes the four symmetric algorithm implementations listed in Table 14-3; each class is a member of the *System.Security.Cryptography* namespace. The algorithms with class names ending in *CryptoServiceProvider* wrap functionality provided by the native Win32 CryptoAPI, whereas those classes whose names end in *Managed* (currently only *RijndaelManaged*) are fully implemented in managed code. The table also shows the encryption key lengths supported by each algorithm; the default key length is in bold. Generally, the longer the encryption key, the harder it is to decrypt ciphertext without the key, but there are also many other factors to consider.

Table 14-3   Symmetric Algorithm Implementations

Algorithm Name	Class Name	Key Lengths (in Bits)
DES	*DESCryptoServiceProvider*	**64**
TripleDES or 3DES	*TripleDESCryptoServiceProvider*	128, **192**
RC2	*RC2CryptoServiceProvider*	40, 48 56, 64, 72, 80, 88, 96, 104, 112, 120, **128**
Rijndael	*RijndaelManaged*	128, 192, **256**

Although you can create instances of the symmetric algorithm classes directly, the *SymmetricAlgorithm* base class is a factory for the concrete implementation classes that derive from it. Calling the *static* method *SymmetricAlgorithm.Create* and passing the name of the algorithm that you want will return an object of the specified type. Using this factory approach allows you to write generic code that can work with any symmetric algorithm implementation, as in the following example:

```
string algName = "3DES";
SymmetricAlgorithm alg = SymmetricAlgorithm.Create(algName);
```

> **Note**   If you call *SymmetricAlgorithm.Create* and don't specify an algorithm name, *SymmetricAlgorithm* will return a *RijndaelManaged* object. If you specify an invalid value, *SymmetricAlgorithm* will return *null*. You can configure new name/class mappings using .NET configuration files. (See the .NET Framework SDK documentation for further details.)

Before you can encrypt data with one of the symmetric algorithm classes, you need a key and an *initialization vector*. The key is the secret information used to encrypt and decrypt the data. The initialization vector is random data used to seed the encryption algorithm to protect your encrypted data against certain types of cryptographic attack. You must use the same key and initialization vector to both encrypt and decrypt your data—hence the name *symmetric encryption*. However, only the key must remain secret; you can store or send the initialization vector with the encrypted data.

The key for each of the *SymmetricAlgorithm* derived classes is accessible through the *Key* property, and the initialization vector is accessible through the *IV* property. The simplest and least error-prone way to generate new keys and initialization vectors is to allow the class to create them for you. After you instantiate a symmetric algorithm object, if you don't explicitly set its *Key* and *IV* properties, the object will generate new values automatically the first time you invoke a member that uses the *Key* and *IV* values. Once set, the symmetric algorithm object will continue to use the same *Key* and *IV* values. To change the values of *Key* and *IV*, you can either assign new values directly or call the *GenerateKey* and *GenerateIV* methods, which force the symmetric algorithm object to generate new random values.

You can't perform encryption and decryption directly with a symmetric algorithm object. Once you have created and configured the symmetric algorithm object, you must call its *CreateEncryptor* or *CreateDecryptor* methods to obtain an object that implements the *System.Security.Cryptography.ICryptoTransform* interface. You can then use the methods of this *ICryptoTransform* object to encrypt or decrypt data. However, the *ICryptoTransform* object requires you to pass data in fixed block sizes and to manually pad the last data block, which will rarely be the correct size.

Although not overly difficult to use, the *ICryptoTransform* interface isn't particularly friendly, so the .NET Framework includes the *System.Security.Cryptography.CryptoStream* class. The *CryptoStream* class, derived from *System.IO.Stream*, simplifies the encryption and decryption of data read from other *Stream* objects. This class allows you to encrypt and decrypt data from files and network connections easily using a familiar processing model, and it provides you with all the familiar benefits of *Stream*-based data access.

The *CryptoStream* constructor requires three things: an underlying *Stream*, an *ICryptoTransform* instance, and a value from the *System.Security.Cryptography.CryptoStreamMode* enumeration. The *CryptoStreamMode* value specifies the mode of the new *CryptoStream* object; valid values are *Read* and *Write*. As you call the *Read* or *Write* methods of the *CryptoStream*, the *CryptoStream* uses the *ICryptoTransform* instance to encrypt or decrypt the data passing through the *CryptoStream*. The *CryptoStream* object ensures the correct block sizes are used for the *ICryptoTransform* instance.

The configuration of a *CryptoStream* object provides great flexibility, but it can be a little confusing. Table 14-4 describes the operation of a *CryptoStream* object based on the *CryptoStream* mode and the type of *ICryptoTransform* instance used in the construction of the *CryptoStream* object.

Table 14-4   Operation of a *CryptoStream* Object

CryptoStream Mode	*ICryptoTransform* Direction	Description
Read	Encrypt	The underlying *Stream* contains the source plaintext. Each call to *CryptoStream.Read* writes ciphertext to an output buffer.
Read	Decrypt	The underlying *Stream* contains the source ciphertext. Each call to *CryptoStream.Read* writes plaintext to an output buffer.
Write	Encrypt	Each call to *CryptoStream.Write* provides plaintext to encrypt. The underlying *Stream* receives new ciphertext.
Write	Decrypt	Each call to *CryptoStream.Write* provides ciphertext to decrypt. The underlying *Stream* receives decrypted plaintext.

The example *SymmetricEncryptionExample* class shown here demonstrates the use of a *SymmetricAlgorithm* to Triple DES encrypt a specified file and then decrypt it. The example's *Main* method (not shown here but available in the accompanying sample code) takes the name of the file to encrypt as a command-line argument. First the *Main* method generates a Triple DES key and initialization vector to use for encryption and decryption. Then the *Main* method calls the *EncryptFile* method, followed by the *DecryptFile* method, producing two files in the process. The first file has the same name as the source file, but with the prefix *encrypted*; this file contains the Triple DES encrypted version of the source file. The second file also has the same name as the source file, but this time with the prefix *decrypted*; this file contains a decrypted version of the encrypted file, which should be the same as the source file.

```
using System;
using System.IO;
using System.Security.Cryptography;

public class SymmetricEncryptionExample {

    // Main method not shown, see sample code.
    ⋮
```

```csharp
// A method to Triple DES encrypt a specified file using the key and iv
// provided.
private static void EncryptFile(string srcFileName,
    string destFileName, byte[] key, byte[] iv) {

    // Create streams to access the source and destination files.
    Stream srcFile =
      new FileStream(srcFileName, FileMode.Open, FileAccess.Read);
    Stream destFile =
      new FileStream(destFileName, FileMode.Create, FileAccess.Write);

    // Create a new Triple DES algorithm to encrypt the file.
    using(SymmetricAlgorithm alg = SymmetricAlgorithm.Create("3DES")){

        // Configure the Key and IV properties of the symmetric
        // algorithm based on the values provided.
        alg.Key = key;
        alg.IV = iv;

        // Create a CryptoStream to encrypt the contents of the source
        // Stream as it is read. Call the CreateEncryptor method of
        // the SymmetricAlgorithm to return an encrypting ICryptoTransform
        // instance and pass it to the CryptoStream.
        CryptoStream cryptoStream = new CryptoStream(srcFile,
                                      alg.CreateEncryptor(),
                                      CryptoStreamMode.Read);

        // Declare a buffer to use for reading data from the source
        // file via the CryptoStream and writing to the encrypted file.
        int bufferLength;
        byte[] buffer = new byte[1024];

        // Read the source file in blocks of 1024 bytes and write the
        // encrypted version to the destination file.
        do {
            bufferLength = cryptoStream.Read(buffer, 0, 1024);
            destFile.Write(buffer, 0, bufferLength);
        } while (bufferLength > 0);

        // Close the Stream resources and clear secret data from
        // objects to which we are about to lose reference.
        destFile.Flush();
        Array.Clear(key,0,key.Length);
        Array.Clear(iv,0,iv.Length);
        cryptoStream.Clear();
        cryptoStream.Close();
        srcFile.Close();
```

```
                destFile.Close();
        }
}


// A method to decrypt a specified Triple DES encrypted file using the
// key and iv provided.
private static void DecryptFile(string srcFileName,
    string destFileName, byte[] key, byte[] iv) {

    // Create streams to access the source and destination files.
    Stream srcFile =
      new FileStream(srcFileName, FileMode.Open, FileAccess.Read);
    Stream destFile =
      new FileStream(destFileName, FileMode.Create, FileAccess.Write);

    // Create a new Triple DES algorithm to decrypt the file.
    using(SymmetricAlgorithm alg = SymmetricAlgorithm.Create("3DES")){

        // Configure the Key and IV properties of the symmetric
        // algorithm based on the values provided.
        alg.Key = key;
        alg.IV = iv;

        // Create a CryptoStream to decrypt the contents of the
        // encrypted data as it is written. Call the CreateDecryptor
        // method of the SymmetricAlgorithm to return a decrypting
        // ICryptoTransform instance and pass it to the CryptoStream.
        CryptoStream cryptoStream = new CryptoStream(destFile,
                                    alg.CreateDecryptor(),
                                    CryptoStreamMode.Write);

        // Declare a buffer to use for reading data from the encrypted
        // file and writing to the decrypted file via the CryptoStream.
        int bufferLength;
        byte[] buffer = new byte[1024];

        // Read the encrypted file in blocks of 1024 bytes and write
        // the plaintext version to the destination file via the
        // CryptoStream.
        do {
            bufferLength = srcFile.Read(buffer, 0, 1024);
            cryptoStream.Write(buffer, 0, bufferLength);
        } while (bufferLength > 0);

        // Close the Stream resources and clear secret data from
        // objects to which we are about to lose reference.
        cryptoStream.FlushFinalBlock();
        Array.Clear(key,0,key.Length);
```

```
                    Array.Clear(iv,0,iv.Length);
                    cryptoStream.Clear();
                    cryptoStream.Close();
                    srcFile.Close();
                    destFile.Close();
                }
            }
        }
```

14.7 Derive a Symmetric Encryption Key from a Password

Problem

You need to generate a symmetric encryption key from a password so that users can easily remember their keys and don't need to store them.

Solution

Use the class *System.Security.Cryptography.PasswordDeriveBytes* to create a symmetric encryption key from a string.

Discussion

It's impossible for all but the most exceptional of people to remember the value of a symmetric key, and it's impractical to expect users to enter such lengthy numbers manually. This means that keys must be stored in a secure form that's accessible to applications. Usually this means storing keys on a smart card, floppy disk, or in a database or file. The problem associated with assigning, distributing, accessing, and storing keys is one of the most difficult aspects of implementing any cryptographic solution—a problem collectively referred to as *key management*. As soon as you need to record a secret (the key), you have to concern yourself with not only protecting your data, but also protecting the secrets used to protect the data!

One alternative to storing a key is to assign the user a more easily remembered password (or pass phrase) and use a key derivation protocol to create a symmetric key from the password. Then, whenever the user needs to encrypt or decrypt data, the user simply enters the password and the computer generates the correct key. As long as the user enters the same password, the key derivation protocol will generate the same key.

Important   Deriving keys from memorable words and phrases significantly reduces the randomness of the keys, which in turn reduces the security provided by any cryptographic function that uses those keys. This is the tradeoff you must make for simplicity. In the worst-case scenario, it's feasible that a hacker could guess a poorly chosen password, saving them the time and effort of cracking your data through cryptanalysis.

The .NET Framework class library includes one symmetric key derivation implementation: *PasswordDeriveBytes*. The *PasswordDeriveBytes* class uses a hashing algorithm applied repeatedly to a password to generate a key of the desired length. When configuring a *PasswordDeriveBytes* object, you can specify which of the .NET hashing algorithms to use as well as the number of repetitions to perform—the default is SHA-1 applied 100 times. In addition, you should provide something called *salt*. Salt is random data that the key derivation process uses to make the derived key more resilient to certain forms of cryptographic attack. You don't need to keep the salt value secret; you must store it and use it when deriving the key from the password in the future. Without the correct salt value, you won't be able to derive the correct key and you won't be able to decrypt your encrypted data.

Note   You can't create asymmetric encryption keys using a key derivation protocol. Asymmetric encryption algorithms rely on specific mathematical relationships between their public and private key components. As such, each asymmetric encryption algorithm requires you to follow a specific process to generate new keys.

The following example demonstrates the use of the *PasswordDeriveBytes* class to generate a 64-bit symmetric key from a password string. The example requires two command-line arguments. The first is the name of the hashing algorithm to use when generating the key, and the second is the password to use as input to the key derivation process. The supported hashing algorithm names are listed in Table 14-1.

```csharp
using System;
using System;
using System.Security.Cryptography;

public class DerivedKeyExample {

    public static void Main(string[] args) {

        // Use a cryptographic random number generator to create
        // the salt used to seed the derivation algorithm.
        byte[] salt = new byte[8];
        RandomNumberGenerator.Create().GetBytes(salt);

        // Create a PasswordDeriveBytes object to generate the
        // key from the password. Supply the source password, which
        // is the second command line argument, and the salt.
        PasswordDeriveBytes pdb =
            new PasswordDeriveBytes(args[1], salt);

        // Set the hashing algorithm used to generate the key, the
        // algorithm name is specified by the first command line argument.
        // The default algorithm used is SHA-1.
        pdb.HashName = args[0];

        // Set the number of iterations to 200. This controls the number
        // of times the hashing algorithm is applied to the password in
        // order to generate the key. The default is 100.
        pdb.IterationCount = 200;

        // Generate an 8 byte (64 bit) key from the password
        // The strength of the key is limited by the length
        // of the hash code - 160 bits for SHA-1.
        byte[] key = pdb.GetBytes(8);

        // Display the key and salt to the console.
        Console.WriteLine("Key  = {0}", BitConverter.ToString(key));
        Console.WriteLine("Salt = {0}", BitConverter.ToString(salt));
    }
}
```

Running the command **DerivedKeyExample SHA1 S0meVereeStr@ngeP@$$w0rd** uses the SHA-1 hashing algorithm to derive an 8-byte (64-bit) key from the string "S0meVereeStr@ngeP@$$w0rd". The output will look similar to this:

```
Key  = 53-72-74-5B-A4-88-A4-80
Salt = 70-82-79-F4-3B-F9-DF-D2
```

Notice that each time you run the same command, DerivedKeyExample produces a different key; this is the effect of the salt. If you comment out the code that assigns a random value to the *salt* array (in boldface in the code listing), and then recompile and run DerivedKeyExample, you will find that the example always generates the same key for a given password.

14.8 Send a Secret Securely Using Asymmetric Encryption

Problem

You need to use asymmetric encryption to send a secret.

Solution

Instantiate the asymmetric algorithm class *System.Security.Cryptography.RSACryptoServiceProvider*. Use the *RSACryptoServiceProvider.Encrypt* method and the intended recipient's *public* key to encrypt the message. Later the recipient will use the *RSACryptoServiceProvider.Decrypt* method and the *private* key to decrypt the encrypted secret.

Discussion

The .NET Framework defines a class hierarchy for asymmetric algorithms similar to that defined for symmetric algorithms (discussed in recipe 14.6). All asymmetric algorithms must extend a common *abstract* base class named *System.Security.Cryptography.AsymmetricAlgorithm*. There are two concrete asymmetric algorithm implementations:

■   *System.Security.Cryptography.RSACryptoServiceProvider*

■   *System.Security.Cryptography.DSACryptoServiceProvider*

As the class name suffix *CryptoServiceProvider* implies, both classes wrap functionality provided by the native Win32 CryptoAPI. However, only the *RSACryptoServiceProvider* class supports data encryption. The *DSACryptoServiceProvider* class implements the Digital Signature Algorithm (DSA), which you can use only to create digital signatures. (See the Federal Information Processing Standard [FIPS] 186-2 available at *http://www.itl.nist.gov/fipspubs/* for details of the DSA.)

Although you can instantiate an asymmetric algorithm object using the *static* factory method *Create* of the *AsymmetricAlgorithm* base class, there is little value in doing so. The *AsymmetricAlgorithm* class does not declare the methods used by the *RSACryptoServiceProvider* class to encrypt and decrypt data. Instead, you should instantiate the *RSACryptoServiceProvider* class directly using one of its constructors.

Before you can encrypt or decrypt data with an *RSACryptoServiceProvider* object, you need access to the appropriate keys. Asymmetric algorithm keys are very different from those of symmetric algorithms. First, there are two components: a public key and a private key. Together these keys are referred to as a *key pair*. Second, instead of simply being a series of randomly generated bytes, asymmetric keys are created according to a special formula. There is a special mathematical relationship between the public and private keys; this special relationship enables the asymmetric algorithm to encrypt data with one key and decrypt the data only with the other key. Each asymmetric algorithm uses its own key generation formula, and the concrete implementation classes encapsulate the functionality necessary to generate new keys correctly.

As the name suggests, the public key isn't secret and the owner can freely send it to you via an e-mail message, or even post it up on a Web site or key distribution server for the world to see. People wanting to send secrets use the public key to encrypt the secret. The recipient then uses the private key to decrypt the secret. The private key must remain secret; anybody who possesses the private key can decrypt data encrypted using the public key counterpart.

To create an asymmetrically encrypted secret, you must have the intended recipient's public key and load it into an *RSACryptoServiceProvider* object. There are two ways to load the public key:

- Use the *RSACryptoServiceProvider.ImportParameters* method to import a *System.Security.Cryptography.RSAParameters* structure, which contains the recipient's public key information. The key owner would normally generate the *RSAParameters* structure using the *RSACryptoServiceProvider.ExportParameters* method and send it to you. However, they might send you the public key byte values, which you must load manually into an *RSAParameters* structure.

- Use the *RSACryptoServiceProvider.FromXmlString* method to load the public key data from an XML string encoding of the public key. The owner would normally generate the XML key data using the *RSACryptoServiceProvider.ToXmlString* method and send it to you.

> **Important**   Both the *ExportParameters* and *ToXmlString* methods of the *RSACryptoServiceProvider* class take a single Boolean argument, which if *true*, causes an *RSACryptoServiceProvider* object to export both its public and private keys. It's important that you specify *false* when exporting keys for distribution or storage.

Once you have loaded the recipient's public key into the *RSACryptoServiceProvider* object, you are ready to encrypt the data. Asymmetric algorithms are much slower than symmetric algorithms when encrypting and decrypting data. Because of this, you will rarely use an asymmetric algorithm to encrypt large quantities of data. Usually, if encrypting large amounts of data, you will use a symmetric algorithm and then encrypt the symmetric keys using an asymmetric algorithm so that you can safely send the symmetric keys with the data. Recipe 14.10 contains a complete discussion of just such a scenario. In keeping with this usage pattern, the *RSACryptoServiceProvider* class does not support a *System.IO.Stream*-based encryption and decryption model, which was used in recipe 14.6.

To encrypt data with an *RSACryptoServiceProvider* object, call the *Encrypt* method, passing it a *byte* array containing the plaintext you want to encrypt; *Encrypt* will return a *byte* array containing the ciphertext. The *Encrypt* method also takes a second Boolean argument that specifies the type of *padding* the *RSACryptoServiceProvider* object should use. Padding specifies how the asymmetric algorithm object should process the plaintext data before encryption. Padding both ensures that the asymmetric algorithm does not need to process partial blocks of data, and protects ciphertext against certain forms of cryptographic attack. A description of the available padding schemes is beyond the scope of this book. Generally, if you are running Microsoft Windows XP or a later operating system, you should specify *true* for the padding argument; otherwise, you must specify *false* or *Encrypt* will throw the exception *System.Security.Cryptography.CryptographicException*.

Decryption of the message is as simple as encryption. The recipient creates an *RSACryptoServiceProvider* object and loads it with their private key. Usually, this key will be stored in a CryptoAPI managed key container (discussed further in recipe 14.9). The recipient calls *RSACryptoServiceProvider.Decrypt* and passes in the ciphertext you sent them. Again, they must specify the padding mechanism to use, and it must be the same as that used to encrypt the data. The *Decrypt* method returns a *byte* array containing the decrypted plaintext. If this represents a string, the recipient must convert the *byte* array to its appropriate string value using the *System.Text.Encoding* class.

Note The *RSACryptoServiceProvider* class inherits the methods named *EncryptValue* and *DecryptValue* from its parent class *System.Security.Cryptography.RSA*. The *RSACryptoServiceProvider* class does not implement these methods and throws the exception *System.NotSupportedException* if you call them.

The example *AsymmetricEncryptionExample* class listed here demonstrates the use of the *RSACryptoServiceProvider* class to encrypt a *string* and then decrypt it. The example's *Main* method (not shown here but available in the accompanying sample code) takes the message to encrypt as a command-line argument. The *Main* method generates a key pair and stores them to a CryptoAPI managed key container named *MyKeys*; the public key is exported to an *RSAParameters* object. This is purely to facilitate the demonstration—in the real world, the sender would have only the recipient's public key, while the recipient kept the private key secret.

The *Main* method then calls the example's *EncryptMessage* method passing a *byte* representation of the message string and the *RSAParameters* object containing the recipient's public key. The *EncryptMessage* method returns a *byte* array containing the ciphertext version of the message, which you would send to the intended recipient. Next the *Main* method calls the example's *DecryptMessage* method, passing the message ciphertext and a *CspParameters* object that contains a reference to the MyKeys key container, which contains the recipient's private key. During the process, the *Main* method displays the original message, the ciphertext, and finally the decrypted message.

```
using System;
using System.Text;
using System.Security.Cryptography;

public class AsymmetricEncryptionExample {

    // Main method not shown, see sample code
    ⋮

    // A method to RSA encrypt a message using the PUBLIC KEY
    // contained in an RSAParameters structure.
```

```
private static byte[] EncryptMessage(byte[] plaintext,
    RSAParameters rsaParams) {

    byte[] ciphertext = null;

    // create an instance of the RSA algorithm.
    using (RSACryptoServiceProvider rsaAlg =
        new RSACryptoServiceProvider()) {

        rsaAlg.ImportParameters(rsaParams);

        // encrypt the plaintext using OAEP padding, which
        // is only supported on Windows XP and later versions
        // of Windows.
        ciphertext = rsaAlg.Encrypt(plaintext, true);
    }

    // Clear the values held in the plaintext byte array. This ensures
    // that the secret data does not sit in memory after you release
    // your reference to it.
    Array.Clear(plaintext, 0, plaintext.Length);

    return ciphertext;
}

// A method to decrypt an RSA encrypted message using the PRIVATE KEY
// from the key container specified by the CspParameters object.
private static byte[] DecryptMessage(byte[] ciphertext,
    CspParameters cspParams ) {

    // Declare a byte array to hold the decrypted plaintext.
    byte[] plaintext = null;

    // create an instance of the RSA algorithm.
    using (RSACryptoServiceProvider rsaAlg =
        new RSACryptoServiceProvider(cspParams)) {

        // decrypt the plaintext using OAEP padding.
        plaintext = rsaAlg.Decrypt(ciphertext, true);
    }

    return plaintext;
}
}
```

Running the command, **AsymmetricEncryptionExample "Meet me under the clock tower at noon."** produces output similar to that shown here.

```
Original message = Meet me under the clock tower at noon.
Formatted Ciphertext = 78-16-4C-17-20-1C-F6-94-95-4A-FE-BE-2A-CF-6A-8B-2C-
D2-16-E6-BB-55-F0-DE-E1-93-F6-31-A4-05-AA-33-29-33-D9-6D-43-D2-1E-D0-10-45-
AF-34-7C-B6-FB-18-ED-D1-CF-B2-30-4E-43-85-3C-65-A5-57-B3-A2-2E-19-95-2A-0F-
11-98-71-F7-1B-57-B3-BB-5E-E3-05-A8-61-A7-FA-99-C6-4A-B5-E2-90-B1-B6-70-64-
6F-EA-45-69-4D-2B-16-27-DC-6A-2E-26-E1-9D-F7-B8-93-2A-87-3D-3C-7F-7A-DF-C5-
A0-7E-B9-9F-41-6D-95-A0-21-93-11
Decrypted message = Meet me under the clock tower at noon.
```

> **Note**   Notice that if you run the example multiple times using the same message and keys as input, the ciphertext is different. Although initially confusing, this is expected behavior. The padding mechanism used by the *RSACryptoServiceProvider* class introduces random data to thwart certain types of cryptographic attack.

14.9 Store an Asymmetric Encryption Key Securely

Problem

You need to store an asymmetric key pair in a secure location that's easily accessible from your applications.

Solution

Rely on the key persistence functionality provided by the two asymmetric algorithm classes *System.Security.Cryptography.RSACryptoServiceProvider* and *System.Security.Cryptography.DSACryptoServiceProvider*.

Discussion

Both of the concrete asymmetric algorithm classes—*RSACryptoServiceProvider* and *DSACryptoServiceProvider*—wrap functionality implemented by a native cryptographic service provider (CSP), which is a component of the Win32 CryptoAPI. In addition to the obvious cryptographic services such as encryption, decryption, and digital signatures, each CSP provides a *key container* facility.

Key containers are storage areas for cryptographic keys that the CSP manages; the CSP uses strong encryption and operating system security to protect the container's contents. Key containers provide applications easy access to keys without compromising the security of the keys. When invoking the cryptographic functions of a CSP, an application specifies the name of a key container and the CSP accesses the necessary keys as required. Because the keys don't pass from the CSP to the application, the application can't accidentally compromise the security of the keys.

The *RSACryptoServiceProvider* and *DSACryptoServiceProvider* classes allow you to configure their underlying CSP implementation using an instance of the class *System.Security.Cryptography.CspParameters*. To configure an *RSACryptoServiceProvider* or *DSACryptoServiceProvider* object to use a specific key container, you must complete the following steps:

1.   Create a new *CspParameters* object.

2.   Set the *public* field *KeyContainerName* of the *CspParameters* object to a *string* value representing the name of the key container to use; the *string* may include spaces.

3.   Create a new *RSACryptoServiceProvider* or *DSACryptoServiceProvider* object, and pass the *CspParameters* object as a constructor argument.

If the named key container exists within the scope of the CSP and contains the appropriate keys, the CSP will use these keys when performing cryptographic operations. If the key container or keys don't exist, the CSP automatically creates new keys. To force the CSP to store newly generated keys to the named key container, you must set the value of the *PersistKeyInCsp* property on the *RSACryptoServiceProvider* or *DSACryptoServiceProvider* object to *true*.

The *LoadKeys* method shown here is an excerpt from the StoreAsymmetricKeyExample.cs file provided as part of the sample code for this chapter. *LoadKeys* creates a new *RSACryptoServiceProvider* object and configures it to use a key container named *MyKeys*. By specifying *PersistKeyInCsp* = *true*, the algorithm automatically stores newly generated keys in the named key container.

```
// A method to create an RSACryptoServiceProvider and load keys from
// a named CryptoAPI key container if they exist; otherwise, the
// RSACryptoServiceProvider automatically generates new keys and
// persists them to the named key container for future use.
public static void LoadKeys(string container) {

    // Create a new CspParameters object and set its KeyContainerName
    // field to the name of the specified container.
    System.Security.Cryptography.CspParameters cspParams =
        new System.Security.Cryptography.CspParameters();
    cspParams.KeyContainerName = container;
```

```
// Create a new RSA asymmetric algorithm and pass the CspParameters
// object that specifies the key container details.
using (System.Security.Cryptography.RSACryptoServiceProvider rsaAlg =
    new System.Security.Cryptography.RSACryptoServiceProvider(cspParams)){

    // Configure the RSACryptoServiceProvider object to persist
    // keys to the key container.
    rsaAlg.PersistKeyInCsp = true;

    // Display the public keys to the console.
    System.Console.WriteLine(rsaAlg.ToXmlString(false));

    // Because the RSACryptoServiceProvider object is configured to
    // persist keys, the keys are stored in the specified key container.
}
}
```

The *RSACryptoServiceProvider* and *DSACryptoServiceProvider* classes provide no direct method of removing key containers. To delete persisted keys, set the value of *PersistKeyInCsp* to *false* and call the *Clear* or *Dispose* method of the *RSACryptoServiceProvider* or *DSACryptoServiceProvider* object. The *DeleteKeys* method shown here demonstrates this technique.

```
// A method to create an RSACryptoServiceProvider and clear existing
// keys from a named CryptoAPI key container.
public static void DeleteKeys(string container) {

    // Create a new CspParameters object and set its KeyContainerName
    // field to the name of the container to be cleared.
    System.Security.Cryptography.CspParameters cspParams =
        new System.Security.Cryptography.CspParameters();
    cspParams.KeyContainerName = container;

    // Create a new RSA asymmetric algorithm and pass the CspParameters
    // object that specifies the key container details.
    using (System.Security.Cryptography.RSACryptoServiceProvider rsaAlg =
        new System.Security.Cryptography.RSACryptoServiceProvider(cspParams)){

        // Configure the RSACryptoServiceProvider object not to persist
        // keys to the key container.
        rsaAlg.PersistKeyInCsp = false;

        // Display the public keys to the console. Because we call
        // Dispose() after this call, existing keys will not appear to
        // change until the second time the method is called.
        System.Console.WriteLine(rsaAlg.ToXmlString(false));

        // As the code leaves this "using" block, Dispose is called on
```

```
        // the RSACryptoServiceProvider object. Because the object is
        // configured NOT to persist keys, the associated key container
        // is cleared. Instead of Dispose(), calling rsaAlg.Clear() would
        // have the same effect, as it indirectly calls Dispose().
    }
}
```

The Win32 CryptoAPI supports both user key stores and machine key stores. The Windows operating system ensures that a user key store is accessible only to the user that created it, but a machine key store is accessible to any user of the machine. By default, the *RSACryptoServiceProvider* and *DSACryptoServiceProvider* classes will use a user key store. You can specify the use of the machine key store by setting the *static* property *UseMachineKeyStore* of the *RSACryptoServiceProvider* or *DSACryptoServiceProvider* class to *true*. This will affect all code running in the current application domain. For finer-grained control, you can set the *CspParameters.Flags* property to the value *System.Security.Cryptography.CspProviderFlags.UseMachineKeyStore* before you create your asymmetric encryption object.

> **Warning**   You should think about your security requirements carefully before opting to use the machine key store. The fact that any user who has access to the machine can gain access to the keys contained in the store negates most of the benefits of using asymmetric encryption.

14.10 Exchange Symmetric Session Keys Securely

Problem

You need to exchange symmetrically encrypted data with somebody, and you need a secure method of delivering the symmetric session key with the data.

Solution

Use the key exchange mechanism implemented by the *System.Security.Cryptography.RSACryptoServiceProvider* class. This will asymmetrically encrypt your symmetric key using the intended recipient's *public* key. You can then send the encrypted symmetric key along with the encrypted data to the recipient. The recipient must decrypt the symmetric key using the *private* key, and then proceed to decrypt the data.

Discussion

Each time you symmetrically encrypt data for transmission you should generate a new key, also known as a *session key*. The use of session keys provides two major benefits:

■   If an unauthorized person obtains multiple blocks of ciphertext encrypted using the same symmetric key, it increases the chance of decrypting the data using cryptanalytic techniques.

■   If a person does discover your session key, it gives them access to only a single set of encrypted data—not all of your past and future secrets as well.

The problem with session keys is an issue of key distribution and security. If you always use the same key, it's not such a problem to meet the other party or arrange a high-security courier to physically exchange keys. However, if you generate new keys for every data exchange, physical meetings are simply out of the question. One answer would be to agree upon a large number of session keys up front with those people with whom you exchange data. Unfortunately, this quickly becomes hard to administer, and the fact that all of your future keys are stored somewhere increases the chances that they will be compromised. A better approach is to send the session key in a strongly encrypted form along with the data that you encrypted with that key—a process known as *key exchange*.

Key exchange involves using asymmetric encryption to encrypt the symmetric session key. If you want to send data to somebody, you generate a symmetric session key, encrypt the data, and then encrypt the session key using the recipient's public key. When the intended recipient receives the data, they decrypt the session key using their private key, and then decrypt the data. Importantly, key exchange allows you to exchange large amounts of encrypted data with anybody, even people you have never communicated with before, as long as you have access to their asymmetric public keys.

> **Note**   Ideally, you would use an asymmetric algorithm to encrypt all data, thus avoiding the need to exchange symmetric keys. However, the speed at which asymmetric algorithms encrypt and decrypt data makes them impractical for use with large amounts of data. Using asymmetric algorithms to encrypt symmetric session keys is a solution that, although more complex, offers the best of both worlds: flexibility and speed.

The .NET Framework class library includes support for key exchange using only the RSA algorithm, but you must choose between two formatting schemes: Optimal Asymmetric Encryption Padding (OAEP) and PKCS #1 v 1.5. A discussion of these formatting schemes is beyond the scope of this book. Generally, you should use OAEP formatting unless you have a specific need to communicate with a legacy system that uses PKCS formatting. The following two classes implement the key exchange mechanism—one for each formatting scheme:

- *System.Security.Cryptography.RSAOAEPKeyExchangeFormatter*

- *System.Security.Cryptography.RSAPKCS1KeyExchangeFormatter*

To prepare a symmetric key for exchange you must create a formatter object of the desired type and then assign an asymmetric algorithm object (*RSACryptoServiceProvider*) to the formatter by calling the formatter's *SetKey* method. You must configure the asymmetric algorithm to use the recipient's public key. Once configured, call the formatter's *CreateKeyExchange* method and pass a *byte* array containing the symmetric session key that you want to format. The *CreateKeyExchange* method returns a *byte* array containing the key exchange data that you should send to the intended recipient.

Deformatting the exchanged key mirrors the formatting process. There are two deformatter classes—one for each formatting scheme.

- *System.Security.Cryptography.RSAOAEPKeyExchangeDeformatter*

- *System.Security.Cryptography.RSAPKCS1KeyExchangeDeformatter*

To deformat a formatted session key, create a deformatter object of the appropriate type and call its *SetKey* method to assign an asymmetric algorithm object. You must load your private key into the asymmetric algorithm. Finally, call the *DecryptKeyExchange* method passing in the key exchange data. The *DecryptKeyExchange* method returns a *byte* array containing the original symmetric session key.

The KeyExchangeExample.cs file contains a demonstration of key exchange. The sample's *Main* method (not shown here, but available in the sample code for this chapter) simulates the creation, formatting, exchange, and deformatting of a symmetric session key. The *Main* method generates an asymmetric key pair for use throughout the example. In a real key exchange situation, the sender who created the symmetric key would only have the recipient's public key. The recipient would have the private key, which is kept secret.

> **Note** Just as it's important that you use a symmetric key of a length appropriate to the secrecy of the data being protected, it's important that you encrypt your session key using an asymmetric algorithm and key length that's at least the equivalent of your symmetric key. If your asymmetric key is weaker than your symmetric key, an attacker will more likely attempt to break your asymmetric encryption and obtain the symmetric key instead of trying to decrypt the symmetrically encrypted data. See *http://ietf.org/internet-drafts/draft-orman-public-key-lengths-05.txt* for details on the equivalence of asymmetric and symmetric key lengths.

The *Main* method then calls the example's *FormatKeyExchange* method passing a *byte* array containing the symmetric key and an *RSAParameters* object containing the recipient's public key. The *FormatKeyExchange* method returns a *byte* array containing the encrypted and formatted symmetric key, ready to send to the intended recipient. Next the *Main* method calls the example's *DeformatKeyExchange* method passing the formatted key exchange data and a *CspParameters* object that contains a reference to the *MyKeys* key container, which contains the recipient's private key. During the process, the *Main* method displays the original session key, the formatted exchange data, and finally the deformatted session key.

```
using System;
using System.Text;
using System.Security.Cryptography;

public class KeyExchangeExample {

    // Main method not shown, see sample code for a complete listing
    ⋮

    // Method to encrypt the symmetric session key and format it for
    // key exchange. To encrypt the session key we need access to the
    // RSA public key of the intended recipient, which is passed to the
    // method contained in an RSAParameters structure. This key could have
    // been sent to us, or we could have downloaded it from a key
    // distribution service.
    private static byte[] FormatKeyExchange(byte[] sessionKey,
        RSAParameters rsaParams) {

        // Create an RSA asymmetric algorithm.
```

```
        using (RSACryptoServiceProvider asymAlg =
            new RSACryptoServiceProvider()) {

            // Import the recipient's public key to the algorithm.
            asymAlg.ImportParameters(rsaParams);

            // Create an RSA OAEP formatter to format the key
            // exchange data.
            RSAOAEPKeyExchangeFormatter formatter
                = new RSAOAEPKeyExchangeFormatter();

            // Specify the RSA algorithm as the one to use to encrypt the
            // session key.
            formatter.SetKey(asymAlg);

            // Encrypt and format the session key and return the result.
            return formatter.CreateKeyExchange(sessionKey);
        }
    }

    // Method to decrypt the key exchange data and extract the symmetric
    // session key. To decrypt the key exchange data, we need access to
    // the RSA private key, which we access from the key container
    // specified in the cspParams argument. This approach avoids the need
    // to hold secret data in memory and pass it between methods.
    private static byte[] DeformatKeyExchange(byte[] exchangeData,
        CspParameters cspParams) {

        // Create an RSA asymmetric algorithm.
        using (RSACryptoServiceProvider asymAlg =
            new RSACryptoServiceProvider(cspParams)) {

            // Create an RSA OAEP deformatter to extract the session key
            // from the key exchange data.
            RSAOAEPKeyExchangeDeformatter deformatter
                = new RSAOAEPKeyExchangeDeformatter();

            // Specify the RSA algorithm as the one to use to decrypt the
            // key exchange data.
            deformatter.SetKey(asymAlg);

            // Decrypt the key exchange data and return the session key.
            return deformatter.DecryptKeyExchange(exchangeData);
        }
    }
}
```

Running *KeyExchangeExample* will generate console output similar to that shown here.

```
Session Key at Source = EE-5B-16-5B-AC-46-3D-72-CC-73-19-D9-0B-8A-19-E2-A6-
02-13-BE-F8-CE-DF-40

Exchange Data = 60-FA-3B-63-41-25-F1-AD-08-F9-FC-67-CD-C6-FB-3E-0F-C3-62-
C6-3F-5C-C0-7E-D1-60-2D-19-58-07-EE-BB-7C-53-A5-C2-FB-CA-D7-64-FF-BA-33-77-
AC-52-87-5F-75-E7-57-99-01-90-CD-70-36-1E-53-0C-82-C6-CE-B8-BC-8B-C9-39-6F-
29-39-5F-6C-A6-43-E5-B0-A1-42-46-1C-9B-1C-72-EB-5E-67-06-44-C0-CE-AB-70-B8-
39-8E-9F-01-E8-49-51-36-D6-27-09-94-DA-42-CE-79-C2-72-88-4D-CE-63-B4-A0-AC-
07-AF-26-A7-76-DE-21-BE-A5

Session Key at Destination = EE-5B-16-5B-AC-46-3D-72-CC-73-19-D9-0B-8A-19-
E2-A6-02-13-BE-F8-CE-DF-40
```

15

Unmanaged Code Interoperability

The Microsoft .NET Framework is an extremely ambitious platform, combining a new language (C#), a managed runtime (the CLR), a platform for hosting Web applications (Microsoft ASP.NET), and an extensive class library for building all types of applications. However, as expansive as the .NET Framework is, it doesn't duplicate all the features that are available in unmanaged code. Currently, the .NET Framework doesn't include every function that's available in the Win32 API, and many businesses are using complex proprietary solutions that they've built with COM-based languages such as Microsoft Visual Basic 6 and Microsoft Visual C++ 6.

Fortunately, Microsoft doesn't intend for businesses to abandon the code base they've built up when they move to the .NET platform. Instead, the .NET Framework is equipped with interoperability features that allow you to use legacy code from .NET Framework applications and even access .NET assemblies as though they are COM components. The recipes in this chapter describe the following:

- How to call functions exposed by unmanaged DLLs (recipes 15.1 through 15.5)

- How to use COM components from .NET Framework applications (recipes 15.6 through 15.8)

- How to use ActiveX controls from .NET Framework applications (recipe 15.9)

- How to expose the functionality of a .NET assembly as a COM component (recipe 15.10)

15.1 Call a Function in an Unmanaged DLL

Problem

You need to call a C function in a DLL. This function might be a part of the Win32 API or your own legacy code.

Solution

Declare a method in your C# code that you will use to access the unmanaged function. Declare this method as both *extern* and *static*, and apply the attribute *System.Runtime.InteropServices.DllImportAttribute* to specify the DLL file and the name of the unmanaged function.

Discussion

To use a C function from an external library, all you need to do is declare it appropriately. The CLR automatically handles the rest, including loading the DLL into memory when the function is called and marshalling the parameters from .NET data types to C data types. The .NET service that supports this cross-platform execution is named *PInvoke* (Platform Invoke), and the process is usually seamless. Occasionally, you'll need to do a little more work, such as when you need to support in-memory structures, callbacks, or mutable strings.

PInvoke is often used to access functionality in the Win32 API, particularly if it includes features that are not present in the set of managed classes that make up the .NET Framework. Throughout this book are examples that use PInvoke in this way. There are three core libraries that make up the Win32 API:

- Kernel32.dll includes operating specific-functionality such as process loading, context switching, and file and memory I/O.

- User32.dll includes functionality for manipulating windows, menus, dialog boxes, icons, and so on.

- GDI32.dll includes graphical capabilities for drawing directly on windows, menus and control surfaces, as well as printing.

As an example, consider the Win32 API functions used for writing and reading INI files, such as *GetPrivateProfileString* and *WritePrivateProfileString* in Kernel32.dll. The .NET Framework doesn't include any classes that wrap this functionality. However, you can import these functions using the attribute *DllImportAttribute*, like this:

```
[DllImport("kernel32.DLL", EntryPoint="WritePrivateProfileString")]
private static extern bool WritePrivateProfileString(string lpAppName,
  string lpKeyName, string lpString, string lpFileName);
```

The arguments specified in the signature of the *WritePrivateProfileString* method must match the DLL method, or a runtime error will occur when you attempt to invoke it. Remember that you don't define any method body because the declaration refers to a method in the DLL. The *EntryPoint* portion of the attribute *DllImportAttribute* is optional in this example. There's no need to specify the *EntryPoint* when the declared function name matches the function name in the external library.

Here's an example of a custom *IniFileWrapper* class that declares these methods privately and then adds *public* methods that call them based on the current designated file:

```
using System;
using System.Text;
using System.Runtime.InteropServices;
using System.Windows.Forms;

public class IniFileWrapper {

    private string filename;

    public string Filename {
        get {return filename;}
    }

    public IniFileWrapper(string filename) {
        this.filename = filename;
    }

    [DllImport("kernel32.dll", EntryPoint="GetPrivateProfileString")]
    private static extern int GetPrivateProfileString(string lpAppName,
      string lpKeyName, string lpDefault, StringBuilder lpReturnedString,
      int nSize, string lpFileName);

    [DllImport("kernel32.dll", EntryPoint="WritePrivateProfileString")]
    private static extern bool WritePrivateProfileString(string lpAppName,
      string lpKeyName, string lpString, string lpFileName);

    public string GetIniValue(string section, string key) {

        StringBuilder buffer = new StringBuilder();
        string sDefault = "";
        if (GetPrivateProfileString(section, key, sDefault,
          buffer, buffer.Capacity, filename) != 0) {
```

```
            return buffer.ToString();
        } else {
            return null;
        }
    }

    public bool WriteIniValue(string section, string key, string value) {

        return WritePrivateProfileString(section, key, value, filename);
    }
}
```

There are several other Win32 API functions for getting INI file information, including methods that retrieve all the sections in an INI file. These aren't used in this simple example.

> **Tip** The *GetPrivateProfileString* method is declared with one *String-Builder* parameter (*lpReturnedString*). This is because this string must be mutable—when the call completes, it will contain the returned INI file information. Whenever you need a mutable string, you must substitute *StringBuilder* in place of the *String* class. Often, you will need to create the *StringBuilder* with a character buffer of a set size and then pass the size of the buffer to the function as another parameter. You can specify the number of characters in the *StringBuilder* constructor. (See recipe 2.1 for more information on using the *StringBuilder* class.)

You can test this program quite easily. First create the INI file shown in this code.

```
[SampleSection]
Key1=Value1
Key2=Value2
Key3=Value3
```

Now, execute the following code. This code demonstrates a console application that reads and writes an INI value.

```
public class IniTest {

    private static void Main() {

        IniFileWrapper ini = new IniFileWrapper(
            Application.StartupPath + "\\initest.ini");
```

```
            string val = ini.GetIniValue("SampleSection", "Key1");
            Console.WriteLine("Value of Key1 in [SampleSection] is: " + val);

            ini.WriteIniValue("SampleSection", "Key1", "New Value");
            val = ini.GetIniValue("SampleSection", "Key1");
            Console.WriteLine("Value of Key1 in [SampleSection] is now: " + val);

            ini.WriteIniValue("SampleSection", "Key1", "Value1");
            Console.ReadLine();
        }
    }
```

15.2 Get the Handle for a Control, a Window, or a File

Problem

You need to call an unmanaged function that requires the handle for a control, a window, or a file.

Solution

Many classes, including all *Control*-derived classes and the *FileStream* class, return the handle as an *IntPtr* through a property named *Handle*. Other classes also provide similar information; for example, the *System.Diagnostics.Process* class provides a *Process.MainWindowHandle* property in addition to the *Handle* property.

Discussion

The .NET Framework doesn't hide underlying details such as the operating system handles used for controls and windows. Although you usually won't use this information, you can retrieve it if you need to call an unmanaged function that requires it. Many Microsoft Windows API functions, for example, require control or window handles.

As an example, consider the Windows-based application shown in Figure 15-1. It consists of a single window that always stays on top of all other windows regardless of focus. (This behavior is enforced by setting the *Form.TopMost* property to *true*.) The form also includes a timer that periodically calls the unmanaged *GetForegroundWindow* and *GetWindowText* WinAPI functions to determine which window currently has the focus.

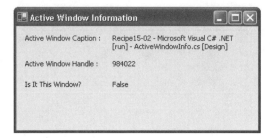

Figure 15-1   Retrieving information about the active window.

There's one additional detail in this example. The code also uses the *Form.Handle* property to get the handle of the main application form. It then compares with the handle of the active form to test if the current application has focus. Here's the complete form code:

```
using System;
using System.Windows.Forms;
using System.Runtime.InteropServices;
using System.Text;

public class ActiveWindowInfo : System.Windows.Forms.Form {

    // (Designer code omitted.)

    private System.Windows.Forms.Timer tmrRefresh;
    private System.Windows.Forms.Label lblCurrent;
    private System.Windows.Forms.Label lblHandle;
    private System.Windows.Forms.Label lblCaption;

    [DllImport("user32.dll")]
    private static extern int GetForegroundWindow();

    [DllImport("user32.dll")]
    private static extern int GetWindowText(int hWnd, StringBuilder text,
      int count);

    private void tmrRefresh_Tick(object sender, System.EventArgs e) {

        int chars = 256;
        StringBuilder buff = new StringBuilder(chars);
        int handle = GetForegroundWindow();

        if (GetWindowText(handle, buff, chars) > 0) {

            lblCaption.Text = buff.ToString();
            lblHandle.Text = handle.ToString();
```

```
        if (new IntPtr(handle) == this.Handle) {
            lblCurrent.Text = "True";
        } else {
            lblCurrent.Text = "False";
        }
    }
  }
}
```

> **Tip**   The Windows Forms infrastructure manages handles transparently. Changing some form properties can force the CLR to generate a new handle. For that reason, you should always retrieve the handle before you use it (rather than storing it in a member variable for a long period of time).

15.3 Call an Unmanaged Function That Uses a Structure

Problem

You need to call an unmanaged function that accepts a structure as a parameter.

Solution

Define the structure in your C# code. Use the attribute *System.Runtime.InteropServices.StructLayoutAttribute* to configure how the structure is allocated in memory. Use the *static SizeOf* method of the *System.Runtime.Interop.Marshal* class if you need to determine the size of the unmanaged structure in bytes.

Discussion

In pure C# code, you aren't able to directly control memory allocation. Instead, the CLR is free to move data around in memory at any time to optimize performance. This can cause problems when interacting with legacy C functions that expect structures to be laid out sequentially in memory. Fortunately, .NET allows you to solve this problem using the attribute *StructLayoutAttribute*, which allows you to specify how the members of a given class or structure should be arranged in memory.

As an example, consider the unmanaged *GetVersionEx* function provided in the Kernel32.dll file. This function accepts a pointer to an *OSVERSIONINFO* structure and uses it to return information about the current operating system version. To use the *OSVERSIONINFO* structure in C# code, you must define it with the attribute *StructLayoutAttribute*, as shown here:

```
[StructLayout(LayoutKind.Sequential)]
public class OSVersionInfo {

    public int dwOSVersionInfoSize;
    public int dwMajorVersion;
    public int dwMinorVersion;
    public int dwBuildNumber;
    public int dwPlatformId;
    [MarshalAs(UnmanagedType.ByValTStr, SizeConst=128)]
    public String szCSDVersion;
}
```

Notice that this structure also uses the attribute *System.Runtime.Interop-Services.MarshalAsAttribute*, which is required for fixed-length strings. In this example, *MarshalAsAttribute* specifies the string will be passed by value and will contain a buffer of exactly 128 characters, as specified in the *OSVERSION-INFO* structure. In this example, sequential layout is used, which means the data types in the structure are laid out in the order they are listed in the class or structure. When using sequential layout, you can also configure the packing for the structure by specifying a named *Pack* field in the *StructLayoutAttribute* constructor. The default is 8, which means the structure will be packed on 8-byte boundaries.

Instead of using sequential layout, you could use *LayoutKind.Explicit*, in which case you must define the byte offset of each field using *FieldOffset-Attribute*. This layout is useful when dealing with an irregularly packed structure or one where you want to omit some of the fields that you don't want to use. Here's an example that defines the *OSVersionInfo* class with explicit layout:

```
[StructLayout(LayoutKind.Explicit)]
public class OSVersionInfo {

    [FieldOffset(0)] public int dwOSVersionInfoSize;
    [FieldOffset(4)]public int dwMajorVersion;
    [FieldOffset(8)]public int dwMinorVersion;
    [FieldOffset(12)]public int dwBuildNumber;
    [FieldOffset(16)]public int dwPlatformId;
    [MarshalAs(UnmanagedType.ByValTStr, SizeConst=128)]
    [FieldOffset(20)]public String szCSDVersion;
}
```

Now that you've defined the structure used by the *GetVersionEx* function, you can declare the function and then use it. The following console application shows all the code you'll need. Notice that the *InAttribute* and *OutAttribute* are applied to the *OSVersionInfo* parameter to indicate that marshalling should be performed on this structure when it is passed to the function, and when it is returned from the function. In addition, the code uses the *Marshal.SizeOf* method to calculate the size the marshaled structure will occupy in memory.

```
using System;
using System.Runtime.InteropServices;

public class CallWithStructure {

    // (OSVersionInfo class omitted.)

    [DllImport("kernel32.dll")]
    public static extern bool GetVersionEx([In, Out] OSVersionInfo osvi);

    private static void Main() {

        OSVersionInfo osvi = new OSVersionInfo();
        osvi.dwOSVersionInfoSize = Marshal.SizeOf(osvi);

        GetVersionEx(osvi);

        Console.WriteLine("Class size: " + osvi.dwOSVersionInfoSize);
        Console.WriteLine("Major Version: " + osvi.dwMajorVersion);
        Console.WriteLine("Minor Version: " + osvi.dwMinorVersion);
        Console.WriteLine("Build Number: " + osvi.dwBuildNumber);
        Console.WriteLine("Platform Id: " + osvi.dwPlatformId);
        Console.WriteLine("CSD Version: " + osvi.szCSDVersion);
        Console.WriteLine("Platform: " + Environment.OSVersion.Platform);
        Console.WriteLine( "Version: " + Environment.OSVersion.Version);
        Console.ReadLine();
    }
}
```

If you run this application on a Windows XP system, you'll see information such as this:

```
Class size: 148
Major Version: 5
Minor Version: 1
Build Number: 2600
Platform Id: 2
CSD Version:
Platform: Win32NT
Version: 5.1.2600.0
```

15.4 Call an Unmanaged Function That Uses a Callback

Problem

You need to call an unmanaged function and allow it to call a method in your code.

Solution

Create a delegate that has the required signature for the callback. Use this delegate when defining and using the unmanaged function.

Discussion

Many of the Win32 API functions use callbacks. For example, if you want to retrieve the name of all the windows that are currently open, you can call the unmanaged *EnumWindows* function in the User32.dll file. When calling *Enum-Windows*, you need to supply a pointer to a function in your code. The Windows operating system will then call this function repeatedly, once for each window that it finds, and pass the window handle to your code.

The .NET Framework allows you to handle callback scenarios like this without resorting to pointers and unsafe code blocks. Instead, you can define and use a delegate that points to your callback function. When you pass the delegate to the *EnumWindows* function, for example, the CLR will automatically marshal the delegate to the expected unmanaged function pointer.

Following is a console application that uses *EnumWindows* with a callback to display the name of every open window.

```
using System;
using System.Text;
using System.Runtime.InteropServices;

public class GetWindows {

    // The signature for the callback method.
    public delegate bool CallBack(int hwnd, int lParam);

    // The unmanaged function that will trigger the callback
    // as it enumerates the open windows.
    [DllImport("user32.dll")]
    public static extern int EnumWindows(CallBack callback, int param);
```

```
[DllImport("user32.dll")]
public static extern int GetWindowText(int hWnd, StringBuilder lpString,
  int nMaxCount);

private static void Main() {

    CallBack callBack = new CallBack(DisplayWindowInfo);

    // Request that the operating system enumerate all windows,
    // and trigger your callback with the handle of each one.
    EnumWindows(callBack, 0);

    Console.ReadLine();
}

// The method that will receive the callback. The second
// parameter is not used, but is needed to match the
// callback's signature.
public static bool DisplayWindowInfo(int hWnd, int lParam) {

    int chars = 100;
    StringBuilder buf = new StringBuilder(chars);
    if (GetWindowText(hWnd, buf, chars) != 0) {
        Console.WriteLine(buf);
    }
    return true;
}
}
```

15.5 Retrieve Unmanaged Error Information

Problem

You need to retrieve error information (either an error code or a text message) explaining why a Win32 API call failed.

Solution

On the declaration of the unmanaged method, set the *SetLastError* field of the *DllImportAttribute* to *true*. If an error occurs when you execute the method, call the *static Marshal.GetLastWin32Error* method to retrieve the error code. To get a text description for a specific error code, use the unmanaged *FormatMessage* function.

Discussion

You can't retrieve error information directly using the unmanaged *GetLastError* function. The problem is that the error code returned by *GetLastError* might not reflect the error caused by the unmanaged function you are using. Instead, it might be set by other .NET Framework classes or the CLR. Instead, you can retrieve the error information safely using the *static Marshal.GetLast-Win32Error* method. This method should be called immediately after the unmanaged call, and it will return the error information only once. (Subsequent calls to *GetLastWin32Error* will simply return the error code 127.) In addition, you must specifically set the *SetLastError* field of the *DllImportAttribute* to *true* to indicate that errors from this function should be cached.

```
[DllImport("user32.dll", SetLastError=true)]
```

You can extract additional information from the Win32 error code using the unmanaged *FormatMessage* function from the Kernel32.dll file.

The following console application attempts to show a message box, but submits an invalid window handle. The error information is retrieved with *Marshal.GetLastWin32Error*, and the corresponding text information is retrieved using *FormatMessage*.

```
using System;
using System.Runtime.InteropServices;

public class TestError {

    [DllImport("kernel32.dll")]
    private unsafe static extern int FormatMessage(int dwFlags, int lpSource,
      int dwMessageId, int dwLanguageId, ref String lpBuffer, int nSize,
      int Arguments);

    [DllImport("user32.dll", SetLastError=true)]
    public static extern int MessageBox(int hWnd, string pText,
      string pCaption, int uType);

    private static void Main() {

        int badWindowHandle = 453;
        MessageBox(badWindowHandle, "Message", "Caption", 0);

        int errorCode = Marshal.GetLastWin32Error();
        Console.WriteLine(errorCode);
        Console.WriteLine(GetErrorMessage(errorCode));

        Console.ReadLine();
    }
```

```
// GetErrorMessage formats and returns an error message
// corresponding to the input errorCode.
public static string GetErrorMessage(int errorCode) {

    int FORMAT_MESSAGE_ALLOCATE_BUFFER = 0x00000100;
    int FORMAT_MESSAGE_IGNORE_INSERTS = 0x00000200;
    int FORMAT_MESSAGE_FROM_SYSTEM  = 0x00001000;

    int messageSize = 255;
    string lpMsgBuf = "";
    int dwFlags = FORMAT_MESSAGE_ALLOCATE_BUFFER |
      FORMAT_MESSAGE_FROM_SYSTEM | FORMAT_MESSAGE_IGNORE_INSERTS;

    int retVal = FormatMessage(dwFlags, 0, errorCode, 0,
      ref lpMsgBuf, messageSize, 0);

    if (0 == retVal) {
        return null;
    } else {
        return lpMsgBuf;
    }
  }
}
```

Here's the output generated by the preceding program:

```
1400
Invalid window handle.
```

15.6 Use a COM Component in a .NET Client

Problem

You need to use a COM component in a .NET client.

Solution

Use a primary interop assembly, if one is available. Otherwise, generate a run-time callable wrapper using the Type Library Importer (Tlbimp.exe), or the Add Reference feature in Visual Studio .NET.

Discussion

The .NET Framework includes extensive support for COM interoperability. To allow .NET clients to interact with a COM component, .NET uses a *runtime callable wrapper* (RCW)—a special .NET proxy class that sits between your .NET code and the COM component. The RCW handles all the details, including marshalling data types, using the traditional COM interfaces, and handling COM events.

You have the following three options for using an RCW:

- Obtain one from the author of the original COM component. In this case, the RCW is called a *primary interop assembly* (PIA).

- Generate one using the Tlbimp.exe command-line utility or Visual Studio .NET.

- Create your own using the types in the *System.Runtime.InteropServices* namespace. (This can be an extremely tedious and complicated process.)

If you want to use Visual Studio .NET to generate an RCW, you simply need to select Project | Add Reference from the menu and then select the appropriate component from the COM tab. When you click OK, you will be prompted to continue and create the RCW. The interop assembly will then be generated and added to your project references. After that, you can use the Object Browser to inspect the namespaces and classes that are available.

If you aren't using Visual Studio .NET, you can create a wrapper assembly using the Tlbimp.exe command-line utility that is included with the .NET Framework. The only mandatory piece of information is the file name that contains the COM component. For example, the following statement creates an RCW with the default file name and namespace, assuming that the MyCOMComponent.dll file is in the current directory.

```
tlbimp MyCOMComponent.dll
```

Assuming that the MyCOMComponent has a type library named MyClasses, the generated RCW file will have the name MyClasses.dll and will expose its classes through a namespace named MyClasses. You can also configure these options with command-line parameters, as described in the MSDN reference. For example, you can use /out:[Filename] to specify a different assembly file name and /namespace:[Namespace] to set a different namespace for the generated classes. You can also specify a key file using /keyfile[keyfilename] so that the component will be signed and given a strong name, allowing it to be placed in the global assembly cache (GAC). Use the /primary parameter to create a PIA.

If possible, you should always use a PIA instead of generating your own RCW. Primary interop assemblies are more likely to work as expected, because they are created by the original component publisher. They might also include additional .NET refinements or enhancements. If a PIA is registered on your system for a COM component, Visual Studio .NET will automatically use that PIA when you add a reference to the COM component. For example, the .NET Framework includes an adodb.dll assembly that allows you to use the ADO classic COM objects. If you add a reference to the Microsoft ActiveX Data Objects component, this interop assembly will be used automatically; no new RCW will be generated. Similarly, Microsoft Office XP provides a PIA that improves .NET support for Office Automation. However, you must download this assembly from the MSDN Web site (at *http://msdn.microsoft.com/downloads/list/office.asp*).

The following example shows how you can use COM interop to access the classic ADO objects from a .NET Framework application:

```csharp
using System;

public class ADOClassic {

    private static void Main() {

        ADODB.Connection con = new ADODB.Connection();
        string connectionString = "Provider=SQLOLEDB.1;" +
          "Data Source=localhost;" +
          "Initial Catalog=Northwind;Integrated Security=SSPI";
        con.Open(connectionString, null, null, 0);

        object recordsAffected;
        ADODB.Recordset rs = con.Execute("SELECT * From Customers",
          out recordsAffected, 0);

        while (rs.EOF != true) {

            Console.WriteLine(rs.Fields["CustomerID"].Value);
            rs.MoveNext();
        }

        Console.ReadLine();
    }
}
```

15.7 Release a COM Component Quickly

Problem

You need to ensure that a COM component is removed from memory immediately, without waiting for garbage collection to take place. Or, you need to make sure that COM objects are released in a specific order.

Solution

Release the reference to the underlying COM object using the *static Marshal.ReleaseComObject* method and passing the appropriate RCW.

Discussion

COM uses reference counting to determine when objects should be released. When you use an RCW, the reference will be held to the underlying COM object even when the object variable goes out of scope. The reference will be released only when the garbage collector disposes of the RCW object. As a result, you can't control when or in what order COM objects will be released from memory.

To get around this limitation, you can use the *Marshal.ReleaseComObject* method. For example, in the ADO example in recipe 15.6, you could release the underlying ADO *Recordset* and *Connection* objects by adding these two lines to the end of your code:

```
Marshal.ReleaseComObject(rs);
Marshal.ReleaseComObject(con);
```

> **Note** Technically, the *ReleaseComObject* method doesn't actually release the COM object, it just decrements the reference count. If the reference count reaches 0 (zero), the COM object will be released. However, if you have multiple pieces of code using the same instance of a COM object, they will all need to release it before it will be removed from memory.

15.8 Use Optional Parameters

Problem

You need to call a method in a COM component without supplying all the required parameters.

Solution

Use the *Type.Missing* field.

Discussion

The .NET Framework is designed with a heavy use of method overloading. Most methods are overloaded several times so that you can call the version that requires only the parameters you choose to supply. COM, on the other hand, doesn't support method overloading. Instead, COM components usually use methods with a long list of optional parameters. Unfortunately, C# doesn't support optional parameters, which means C# developers are often forced to supply numerous additional or irrelevant values when accessing a COM component. And because COM parameters are often passed by reference, your code can't simply pass a *null* reference—instead, it must declare an object variable and then pass that variable.

You can mitigate the problem to some extent by supplying the *Type.Missing* field whenever you wish to omit an optional parameter. If you need to pass a parameter by reference, you can simply declare a single object variable, set it equal to *Type.Missing*, and use it in all cases, like this:

```
private static object n = Type.Missing;
```

The following example uses the Word COM objects to programmatically create and show a document. Many of the methods the example uses require optional parameters passed by reference. You'll notice that the use of the *Type.Missing* field simplifies this code greatly. Each use is emphasized in the code listing.

```
using System;

public class OptionalParameters {

    private static object n = Type.Missing;

    private static void Main() {
```

```
// Start Word in the background.
Word.ApplicationClass app = new Word.ApplicationClass();
app.DisplayAlerts = Word.WdAlertLevel.wdAlertsNone;

// Create a new document (this is not visible to the user).
Word.Document doc = app.Documents.Add(ref n, ref n, ref n,
  ref n);

Console.WriteLine();
Console.WriteLine("Creating new document.");
Console.WriteLine();

// Add a heading and two lines of text.
Word.Range range = doc.Paragraphs.Add(ref n).Range;
range.InsertBefore("Test Document");
string style = "Heading 1";
object objStyle = style;
range.set_Style(ref objStyle);

range = doc.Paragraphs.Add(ref n).Range;
range.InsertBefore("Line one.\nLine two.");
range.Font.Bold = 1;

// Show a print preview, and make Word visible.
doc.PrintPreview();
app.Visible = true;

Console.ReadLine();
    }
}
```

15.9 Use an ActiveX Control in a .NET Client

Problem

You need to place an ActiveX control on a window in a .NET Framework application.

Solution

Use an RCW exactly as you would with an ordinary COM component. To work with the ActiveX control at design time, add it to the Visual Studio .NET Toolbox.

Discussion

The .NET Framework includes the same support for all COM components, including ActiveX controls. The key difference is that the RCW class for an ActiveX control derives from the special .NET type *System. Windows.Forms.AxHost*. Technically, you add the *AxHost* control to your form, and it communicates with the ActiveX control "behind the scenes." Because *AxHost* derives from *System.Windows.Forms.Control*, it provides the standard .NET control properties, methods, and events, such as *Location, Size, Anchor*, and so on. In the case of an auto-generated RCW, the *AxHost* classes will always begin with the letters *Ax*.

You can create an RCW for an ActiveX control as you would for any other COM component, by using Tlbimp.exe or the Add Reference feature in Visual Studio .NET, and then creating the control programmatically. However, an easier approach in Visual Studio .NET is to add the ActiveX control to the Toolbox. (See recipe 11.4 for details.)

Nothing happens to your project when you add an ActiveX control to the Toolbox. However, you can use the toolbox icon to add an instance of the control to your form. The first time you do this, Visual Studio .NET will create the interop assembly and add it to your project. For example, if you add the Microsoft Masked Edit control, which has no direct .NET equivalent, Visual Studio .NET creates an RCW assembly with a name such as AxInterop.MSMask.dll. Here's the code you might expect to see in the hidden designer region that creates the control instance and adds it to the form:

```
this.axMaskEdBox1 = new AxMSMask.AxMaskEdBox();
((System.ComponentModel.ISupportInitialize)(this.axMaskEdBox1)).BeginInit();

//
// axMaskEdBox1
//
this.axMaskEdBox1.Location = new System.Drawing.Point(16, 12);
this.axMaskEdBox1.Name = "axMaskEdBox1";
this.axMaskEdBox1.OcxState = ((System.Windows.Forms.AxHost.State)
  (resources.GetObject("axMaskEdBox1.OcxState")));

this.axMaskEdBox1.Size = new System.Drawing.Size(112, 20);
this.axMaskEdBox1.TabIndex = 0;

this.Controls.Add(this.axMaskEdBox1);
```

Notice that the custom properties for the ActiveX control are not applied directly through property set statements. Instead, they are restored as a group when the control sets its persisted *OcxState* property. However, your code can use the control's properties directly.

15.10 Expose a .NET Component Through COM

Problem

You need to create a .NET component that can be called by a COM client.

Solution

Create an assembly that follows certain restrictions identified in this recipe. Export a type library for this assembly using the Type Library Exporter (Tlbexp.exe) command-line utility.

Discussion

The .NET Framework includes support for COM clients to use .NET components. When a COM client creates a .NET object, the CLR creates the managed object and a COM callable wrapper (CCW) that wraps the object. The COM client interacts with the managed object through the CCW. The runtime creates only one CCW for a managed object, regardless of how many COM clients are using it.

Types that need to be accessed by COM clients must meet certain requirements:

- The managed type (class, interface, struct, or enum) must be *public*.

- If the COM client needs to create the object, it must have a *public* default constructor. COM doesn't support parameterized constructors.

- The members of the type that are being accessed must be *public* instance members. *Private*, *protected*, *internal*, and *static* members are not accessible to COM clients.

In addition, you should consider the following recommendations:

- It is recommended that you don't create inheritance relationships between classes, because these relationships will not be visible to COM clients (although .NET will attempt to simulate it by declaring a shared base class interface).

■ It is recommended that the classes you are exposing implement an interface. For added versioning control, you can use the attribute *System.Runtime.InteropServices.GuidAttribute* to specify the GUID that should be assigned to an interface.

■ Ideally, you should give the managed assembly a strong name so that it can be installed into the GAC and shared among multiple clients.

In order for a COM client to create the .NET object, it requires a type library (a .tlb file). The type library can be generated from an assembly using the Tlbexp.exe command-line utility. Here's an example of the syntax you use:

```
tlbexp ManagedLibrary.dll
```

Once you generate the type library, you can reference it from the unmanaged development tool. With Visual Basic 6, you reference the .tlb file from the Project/References dialog. In Visual C++ 6, you can use the *#import* statement to import the type definitions from the type library.

16

Commonly Used Interfaces and Patterns

The recipes in this chapter show you how to implement patterns you will use frequently during the development of Microsoft .NET Framework applications. Some of these patterns are formalized using interfaces defined in the .NET Framework class library. Others are less rigid, but still require you to take specific approaches to the design and implementation of your types. The recipes in this chapter describe how to

- Create serializable types that you can easily store to disk, send across the network, or pass by value across application domain boundaries (recipe 16.1).

- Provide a mechanism that creates accurate and complete copies (clones) of objects (recipe 16.2).

- Implement types that are easy to compare and sort (recipe 16.3).

- Support the enumeration of the elements contained in custom collections (recipe 16.4).

- Ensure that a type that uses unmanaged resources correctly releases those resources when they are no longer needed (recipe 16.5).

- Display string representations of objects that vary based on format specifiers (recipe 16.6).

- Correctly implement custom exception and event argument types, which you will use frequently in the development of your applications (recipes 16.7 and 16.8).

■ Implement the commonly used *Singleton* and *Observer* design patterns using the built-in features of C# and the .NET Framework class library (recipes 16.9 and 16.10).

16.1 Implement a Serializable Type

Problem

You need to implement a custom type that is serializable, allowing you to

■ Store instances of the type to persistent storage (for example, a file or a database).

■ Transmit instances of the type across a network.

■ Pass instances of the type "by value" across application domain boundaries.

Solution

For serialization of simple types, apply the attribute *System.SerializableAttribute* to the type declaration. For types that are more complex, or to control the content and structure of the serialized data, implement the interface *System.Runtime.Serialization.ISerializable*.

Discussion

Recipe 2.12 showed how to serialize and deserialize an object using the formatter classes provided with the .NET Framework class library. However, types aren't serializable by default. To implement a custom type that is serializable, you must apply the attribute *SerializableAttribute* to your type declaration. As long as all of the data fields in your type are serializable types, applying *SerializableAttribute* is all you need to do to make your custom type serializable. If you are implementing a custom class that derives from a base class, the base class must also be serializable.

Each formatter class contains the logic necessary to serialize types decorated with *SerializableAttribute* and will correctly serialize all *public*, *protected*, and *private* fields. This code excerpt shows the type and field declarations of a serializable class named *Employee*.

```
using System;

[Serializable]
public class Employee {
```

```
private string name;
private int age;
private string address;
    ⋮
}
```

> **Note**   Classes that derive from a serializable type don't inherit the attribute *SerializableAttribute*. To make derived types serializable, you must explicitly declare them as serializable by applying the *SerializableAttribute* attribute.

You can exclude specific fields from serialization by applying the attribute *System.NonSerializedAttribute* to those fields. As a rule, you should exclude the following fields from serialization:

- Fields that contain nonserializable data types

- Fields that contain values that might be invalid when the object is deserialized, for example, database connections, memory addresses, thread IDs, and unmanaged resource handles

- Fields that contain sensitive or secret information, for example, passwords, encryption keys, and the personal details of people and organizations

- Fields that contain data that is easily re-creatable or retrievable from other sources—especially if the data is large

If you exclude fields from serialization, you must implement your type to compensate for the fact that some data won't be present when an object is deserialized. Unfortunately, you can't create or retrieve the missing data fields in an instance constructor because formatters don't call constructors during the process of deserializing objects. The most common solution to this problem is to implement the "Lazy Initialization" pattern, in which your type creates or retrieves data the first time it's needed.

The following code shows a modified version of the *Employee* class with *NonSerializedAttribute* applied to the *address* field, meaning that a formatter won't serialize the value of this confidential field. The *Employee* class implements *public* properties to give access to each of the *private* data members, providing a convenient place in which to implement lazy initialization of the *address* field.

```csharp
using System;

[Serializable]
public class Employee {

    private string name;
    private int age;

    [NonSerialized]
    private string address;

    // Simple Employee constructor
    public Employee(string name, int age, string address) {

        this.name = name;
        this.age = age;
        this.address = address;
    }

    // Public property to provide access to employee's name
    public string Name {
        get { return name; }
        set { name = value; }
    }

    // Public property to provide access to employee's age
    public int Age {
        get { return age; }
        set { age = value; }
    }

    // Public property to provide access to employee's address.
    // Uses lazy initialization to establish address because
    // a deserialized object will not have an address value.
    public string Address {
        get {
            if (address == null) {
                // Load the address from persistent storage
                ;<$VE>
            }
            return address;
        }

        set {
            address = value;
        }
    }
}
```

For the majority of custom types, use of the attributes *SerializableAttribute* and *NonSerializedAttribute* will be sufficient to meet your serialization needs. If you require more control over the serialization process, you can implement the interface *ISerializable*. The formatter classes use different logic when serializing and deserializing instances of types that implement *ISerializable*. To implement *ISerializable* correctly you must

- Declare that your type implements *ISerializable*.

- Apply the attribute *SerializableAttribute* to your type declaration as just described; do not use *NonSerializedAttribute* because it will have no effect.

- Implement the *ISerializable.GetObjectData* method (used during serialization), which takes the following argument types:

    ❏   *System.Runtime.Serialization.SerializationInfo*

    ❏   *System.Runtime.Serialization.StreamingContext*

- Implement a nonpublic constructor (used during deserialization) that accepts the same arguments as the *GetObjectData* method. Remember, if you plan to derive classes from your serializable class, make the constructor *protected*.

- If creating a serializable class from a base class that also implements *ISerializable*, your type's *GetObjectData* method and deserialization constructor must call the equivalent method and constructor in the parent class.

During serialization, the formatter calls the *GetObjectData* method and passes it *SerializationInfo* and *StreamingContext* references as arguments. Your type must populate the *SerializationInfo* object with the data you want to serialize. The *SerializationInfo* class provides the *AddValue* method that you use to add each data item. With each call to *AddValue*, you must specify a name for the data item—you use this name during deserialization to retrieve each data item. The *AddValue* method has 16 overloads that allow you to add different data types to the *SerializationInfo* object.

The *StreamingContext* object provides information about the purpose and destination of the serialized data, allowing you to choose which data to serialize. For example, you might be happy to serialize secret data if it's destined for another application domain in the same process, but not if the data will be written to a file.

When a formatter deserializes an instance of your type, it calls the deserialization constructor, again passing a *SerializationInfo* and a *StreamingContext* reference as arguments. Your type must extract the serialized data from the *SerializationInfo* object using one of the *SerializationInfo.Get** methods, for example, *GetString*, *GetInt32*, or *GetBoolean*. During deserialization, the *StreamingContext* object provides information about the source of the serialized data, allowing you to mirror the logic you implemented for serialization.

> **Note**   During standard serialization operations, the formatters don't use the capabilities of the *StreamingContext* object to provide specifics about the source, destination, and purpose of serialized data. However, if you wish to perform customized serialization, your code can configure the formatter's *StreamingContext* object prior to initiating serialization and deserialization. Consult the .NET Framework SDK documentation for details of the *StreamingContext* class.

This example shows a modified version of the *Employee* class that implements the *ISerializable* interface. In this version, the *Employee* class doesn't serialize the *address* field if the provided *StreamingContext* object specifies that the destination of the serialized data is a file. The full code for this example is contained in the file SerializableExample.cs in the sample code for this chapter. The SerializableExample.cs file also includes a *Main* method that demonstrates the serialization and deserialization of an *Employee* object.

```
using System;
using System.Runtime.Serialization;

[Serializable]
public class Employee : ISerializable {

    private string name;
    private int age;
    private string address;

    // Simple Employee constructor
    public Employee(string name, int age, string address) {

        this.name = name;
        this.age = age;
        this.address = address;
    }
```

```
// Constructor required to enable a formatter to deserialize an
// Employee object. You should declare the constructor private or at
// least protected to ensure it is not called unnecessarily.
private Employee(SerializationInfo info, StreamingContext context) {

    // Extract the name and age of the Employee, which will always be
    // present in the serialized data regardless of the value of the
    // StreamingContext
    name = info.GetString("Name");
    age = info.GetInt32("Age");

    // Attempt to extract the Employee's address and fail gracefully
    // if it is not available
    try {
        address = info.GetString("Address");
    } catch (SerializationException) {
        address = null;
    }
}

// Name, Age, and Address properties not shown
  ⋮

// Declared by the ISerializable interface, the GetObjectData method
// provides the mechanism with which a formatter obtains the object
// data that it should serialize
public void GetObjectData(SerializationInfo inf, StreamingContext con){

    // Always serialize the Employee's name and age.
    inf.AddValue("Name", name);
    inf.AddValue("Age", age);

    // Don't serialize the Employee's address if the StreamingContext
    // indicates that the serialized data is to be written to a file.
    if ((con.State & StreamingContextStates.File) == 0) {

        inf.AddValue("Address", address);
    }
}
}
```

16.2 Implement a Cloneable Type

Problem

You need to create a custom type that provides a simple mechanism for programmers to create copies of type instances.

Solution

Implement the *System.ICloneable* interface.

Discussion

When you assign one value type to another, you create a copy of the value. There's no link between the two values—a change to one won't affect the other. However, when you assign one reference type to another (excluding strings, which receive special treatment by the runtime), you don't create a new copy of the reference type. Instead, both reference types refer to the same object, and changes to the value of the object are reflected in both references. To create a true copy of a reference type, you must *clone* the object to which it refers.

The *ICloneable* interface identifies a type as cloneable and declares the *Clone* method as the mechanism through which you obtain a clone of an object. The *Clone* method takes no arguments and returns a *System.Object*, regardless of the implementing type. This means that once you clone an object, you must explicitly cast the clone to the correct type.

The approach you take to implementing the *Clone* method for a custom type depends on the data members declared within the type. If the custom type contains only value-type (*int*, *byte*, and so on) and *System.String* data members, you can implement the *Clone* method by instantiating a new object and setting its data members to the same values as the current object. The *Object* class (from which all types derive) includes the *protected* method *MemberwiseClone*, which automates this process. Here is an example that shows a simple class named *Employee*, which contains only *string* members. Therefore, the *Clone* method relies on the inherited *MemberwiseClone* method to create a clone.

```
using System;

public class Employee : ICloneable {

    public string Name;
    public string Title;
```

```
    // Simple Employee constructor
    public Employee(string name, string title) {

        Name = name;
        Title = title;
    }

    // Create a clone using the Object.MemberwiseClone method because the
    // Employee class contains only string references
    public object Clone() {

        return MemberwiseClone();
    }
}
```

If your custom type contains reference-type data members, you must decide whether your *Clone* method will perform a *shallow copy* or a *deep copy*. A shallow copy means that any reference-type data members in the clone will refer to the same objects as the equivalent reference-type data members in the original object. A deep copy means that you must create clones of the entire object graph so that the reference-type data members of the clone refer to physically independent copies (clones) of the objects referenced by the original object.

A shallow copy is easy to implement using the *MemberwiseClone* method just described. However, a deep copy is often what programmers expect when they first clone an object—but it's rarely what they get. This is especially true of the collection classes in the *System.Collections* namespace, which all implement shallow copies in their *Clone* methods. Although it would often be useful if these collections implemented a deep copy, there are two key reasons why types (especially generic collection classes) do not implement deep copies:

- Creating a clone of a large object graph is processor intensive and memory intensive.

- Generic collections can contain wide and deep object graphs consisting of any type of object. Creating a deep copy implementation to cater for such variety isn't feasible because some objects in the collection might not be cloneable, and others might contain circular references, which would send the cloning process into an infinite loop.

For strongly typed collections in which the nature of the contained elements are understood and controlled, a deep copy can be a very useful feature; for example, the *System.Xml.XmlNode* implements a deep copy in its *Clone* method. This allows you to create true copies of entire XML object hierarchies with a single statement.

> **Tip**   If you need to clone an object that does not implement *IClone-able* but is serializable, you can often serialize and then deserialize the object to achieve the same result as cloning. However, be aware that the serialization process might not serialize all data members (as discussed in recipe 16.1). Likewise, if you create a custom serializable type, you can potentially use the serialization process just described to perform a deep copy within your *ICloneable.Clone* method implementation. To clone a serializable object, use the class *System.Runtime.Serialization.Formatters.Binary.BinaryFormatter* to serialize the object to, and then deserialize the object from, a *System.IO.MemoryStream* object.

The *Team* class shown in the following listing contains an implementation of the *Clone* method that performs a deep copy. The *Team* class contains a collection of *Employee* objects, representing a team of people. When you call the *Clone* method of a *Team* object, the method creates a clone of every contained *Employee* object and adds it to the cloned *Team* object. The *Team* class provides a *private* constructor to simplify the code in the *Clone* method—the use of constructors is a common approach to simplify the cloning process. The file CloneableExample.cs in the sample code for this chapter contains the *Team* and *Employee* classes. The file also provides a *Main* method that demonstrates the effect of making a deep copy.

```
using System;
using System.Collections;

public class Team : ICloneable {

    public ArrayList TeamMembers = new ArrayList();

    public Team() {
    }

    // Private constructor called by the Clone method to create a new Team
    // object and populate its ArrayList with clones of Employee
    // objects from a provided ArrayList
    private Team(ArrayList members) {

        foreach (Employee e in members) {
```

```
            TeamMembers.Add(e.Clone());
        }
    }

    // Adds an Employee object to the Team
    public void AddMember(Employee member) {

        TeamMembers.Add(member);
    }

    public object Clone() {

        // Create a deep copy of the team by calling the private Team
        // constructor and passing the ArrayList containing team members
        return new Team(this.TeamMembers);

        // The following command would create a shallow copy of the Team
        // return MemberwiseClone();
    }
}
```

16.3 Implement a Comparable Type

Problem

You need to provide a mechanism that allows you to compare custom types, enabling you to easily sort collections containing instances of those types.

Solution

To provide a standard comparison mechanism for a type, implement the *System.IComparable* interface. To support the comparison of a type based on more than one characteristic, create separate types that implement the *System.Collections.IComparer* interface.

Discussion

If you need to sort your type into only a single order, such as ascending ID number, or alphabetically based on surname, you should implement the *IComparable* interface. *IComparable* defines a single method named *CompareTo*, shown here.

```
int CompareTo(object obj);
```

The *object* (*obj*) passed to the method must be an object of the same type as that being called, or *CompareTo* must throw a *System.ArgumentException*. The value returned by *CompareTo* is calculated as follows:

- If the current object is less than *obj*, return less than zero (for example, -1).

- If the current object has the same value as *obj*, return zero.

- If the current object is greater than *obj*, return greater than zero (for example, 1).

What these comparisons mean depends on the type implementing the *IComparable* interface. For example, if you were sorting people based on their surname, you would do a *String* comparison. However, if you wanted to sort by birthday, you would need to perform a comparison of *System.DateTime* objects.

To support a variety of sort orders for a particular type, you must implement separate helper types that implement the *IComparer* interface, which defines the *Compare* method shown here.

```
int Compare(object x, object y);
```

These helper types must encapsulate the necessary logic to compare two objects and return a value based on the following logic:

- If *x* is less than *y*, return less than zero (for example, -1).

- If *x* has the same value as *y*, return zero.

- If *x* is greater than *y*, return greater than zero (for example, 1).

The *Newspaper* class listed here demonstrates the implementation of both the *IComparable* and *IComparer* interfaces. The *Newspaper.CompareTo* method performs a case-insensitive comparison of two *Newspaper* objects based on their *name* fields. A *private* nested class named *AscendingCirculationComparer* implements *IComparer* and compares two *Newspaper* objects based on their *circulation* fields. An *AscendingCirculationComparer* object is obtained using the *static Newspaper.CirculationSorter* property.

```
using System;
using System.Collections;

public class Newspaper : IComparable {

    private string name;
    private int circulation;
```

```
private class AscendingCirculationComparer : IComparer {

    int IComparer.Compare(object x, object y) {

        // Handle logic for null reference as dictated by the
        // IComparer interface. Null is considered less than
        // any other value.
        if (x == null && y == null) return 0;
        else if (x == null) return -1;
        else if (y == null) return 1;

        // Short circuit condition where x and y are references
        // to the same object
        if (x == y) return 0;

        // Ensure both x and y are Newspaper instances
        Newspaper newspaperX = x as Newspaper;
        if (newspaperX == null) {

            throw new ArgumentException("Invalid object type", "x");
        }

        Newspaper newspaperY = y as Newspaper;
        if (newspaperY == null) {

            throw new ArgumentException("Invalid object type", "y");
        }

        // Compare the circulation figures. IComparer dictates that:
        //      return less than zero if x < y
        //      return zero if x = y
        //      return greater than zero if x > y
        // This logic is easily implemented using integer arithmetic.
        return newspaperX.circulation - newspaperY.circulation;
    }
}

public Newspaper(string name, int circulation) {

    this.name = name;
    this.circulation = circulation;
}

// Declare a read-only property that returns an instance of the
// AscendingCirculationComparer.
public static IComparer CirculationSorter{
    get { return new AscendingCirculationComparer(); }
}
```

```
public override string ToString() {

    return string.Format("{0}: Circulation = {1}", name, circulation);
}

// The CompareTo method compares two Newspaper objects based on a
// case insensitive comparison of the Newspaper names.
public int CompareTo(object obj) {

    // IComparable dictates that an object is always considered greater
    // than null.
    if (obj == null) return 1;

    // Short circuit the case where the other object is a reference
    // to this object.
    if (obj == this) return 0;

    // Try to cast the other object to a Newspaper instance.
    Newspaper other = obj as Newspaper;

    // If "other" is null, it must not be a Newspaper instance.
    // IComparable dictates CompareTo must throw the exception
    // System.ArgumentException in this situation.
    if (other == null) {

        throw new ArgumentException("Invalid object type", "obj");

    } else {

        // Calculate return value by performing a case-insensitive
        // comparison of the Newspaper names.

        // Because the Newspaper name is a string, the easiest approach
        // is to rely on the comparison capabilities of the String
        // class, which perform culture-sensitive string comparisons.
        return string.Compare(this.name, other.name, true);
    }
}
}
```

The *Main* method shown here demonstrates the comparison and sorting capabilities provided by implementing the *IComparable* and *IComparer* interfaces. The method creates a *System.Collections.ArrayList* collection containing five *Newspaper* objects. *Main* then sorts the *ArrayList* twice using the *ArrayList.Sort* method. The first *Sort* operation uses the default *Newspaper* comparison mechanism provided by the *IComparable.CompareTo* method. The second

Sort operation uses an *AscendingCirculationComparer* object to perform comparisons through its implementation of the *IComparer.Compare* method.

```
public static void Main() {

    ArrayList newspapers = new ArrayList();

    newspapers.Add(new Newspaper("The Echo", 125780));
    newspapers.Add(new Newspaper("The Times", 55230));
    newspapers.Add(new Newspaper("The Gazette", 235950));
    newspapers.Add(new Newspaper("The Sun", 88760));
    newspapers.Add(new Newspaper("The Herald", 5670));

    Console.WriteLine("Unsorted newspaper list:");
    foreach (Newspaper n in newspapers) {
        Console.WriteLine(n);
    }

    Console.WriteLine(Environment.NewLine);
    Console.WriteLine("Newspaper list sorted by name (default order):");
    newspapers.Sort();
    foreach (Newspaper n in newspapers) {
        Console.WriteLine(n);
    }

    Console.WriteLine(Environment.NewLine);
    Console.WriteLine("Newspaper list sorted by circulation:");
    newspapers.Sort(Newspaper.CirculationSorter);
    foreach (Newspaper n in newspapers) {
        Console.WriteLine(n);
    }
}
```

Running the *Main* method will produce the results shown here.

```
Unsorted newspaper list:
The Echo: Circulation = 125780
The Times: Circulation = 55230
The Gazette: Circulation = 235950
The Sun: Circulation = 88760
The Herald: Circulation = 5670

Newspaper list sorted by name (default order):
The Echo: Circulation = 125780
The Gazette: Circulation = 235950
The Herald: Circulation = 5670
The Sun: Circulation = 88760
The Times: Circulation = 55230
```

```
Newspaper list sorted by circulation:
The Herald: Circulation = 5670
The Times: Circulation = 55230
The Sun: Circulation = 88760
The Echo: Circulation = 125780
The Gazette: Circulation = 235950
```

16.4 Implement an Enumerable Type

Problem

You need to create a collection type whose contents you can enumerate using a *foreach* statement.

Solution

Implement the interface *System.IEnumerable* on your collection type. The *Get-Enumerator* method of the *IEnumerable* interface returns an *enumerator*—an object that implements the interface *System.IEnumerator*. The *IEnumerator* interface defines the methods used by the *foreach* statement to enumerate the collection.

Discussion

A numerical indexer allows you to iterate through the elements of a collection using a *for* loop. However, this technique doesn't always provide an appropriate abstraction for nonlinear data structures, such as trees and multidimensional collections. The *foreach* statement provides an easy-to-use and syntactically elegant mechanism for iterating through a collection of objects regardless of their internal structures.

In order to support *foreach* semantics, the object containing the collection of objects must implement the *System.IEnumerable* interface. The *IEnumerable* interface declares a single method named *GetEnumerator*, which takes no arguments and returns an object that implements *System.IEnumerator*, as shown here.

```
IEnumerator GetEnumerator();
```

The *IEnumerator* instance returned by *GetEnumerator* is the object that actually supports enumeration of the collection's data elements. The *IEnumerator* interface provides a read-only, forward-only cursor for accessing the members of the underlying collection. Table 16-1 describes the members of the *IEnumerator* interface.

Table 16-1   Members of the *IEnumerator* Interface

Member	Description
Current	Property that returns the current data element. When the enumerator is created, *Current* refers to a position preceding the first data element. This means you must call *MoveNext* before using *Current*. If *Current* is called and the enumerator is positioned before the first element or after the last element in the data collection, *Current* must throw a *System.InvalidOperationException*.
MoveNext	Method that moves the enumerator to the next data element in the collection. Returns *true* if there are more elements; otherwise, it returns *false*. If the underlying source of data changes during the life of the enumerator, *MoveNext* must throw an *InvalidOperationException*.
Reset	Method that moves the enumerator to a position preceding the first element in the data collection. If the underlying source of data changes during the life of the enumerator, *Reset* must throw an *InvalidOperationException*.

The *TeamMember*, *Team*, and *TeamMemberEnumerator* classes demonstrate the implementation of the *IEnumerable* and *IEnumerator* interfaces. The *TeamMember* class (listed here) represents a member of a team.

```
// TeamMember class represents an individual team member.
public class TeamMember {

    public string Name;
    public string Title;

    // Simple TeamMember constructor.
    public TeamMember(string name, string title) {

        Name = name;
        Title = title;
    }

    // Returns a string representation of the TeamMember.
    public override string ToString() {

        return string.Format("{0} ({1})", Name, Title);
    }
}
```

The *Team* class, which represents a team of people, is a collection of *TeamMember* objects. *Team* implements the *IEnumerable* interface and declares a separate class, named *TeamMemberEnumerator*, to provide enumeration functionality. Often, collection classes will implement both the *IEnumer-*

able and *IEnumerator* interfaces directly. However, the use of a separate enumerator class is the simplest approach to allow multiple enumerators—and multiple threads—to enumerate the *Team* concurrently.

   Team implements the *Observer Pattern* using delegate and event members to notify all *TeamMemberEnumerator* objects if their underlying *Team* changes. (See recipe 16.10 for a detailed description of the Observer Pattern.) The *TeamMemberEnumerator* class is a *private* nested class, so you can't create instances of it other than through the *Team.GetEnumerator* method. Here is the code for the *Team* and *TeamMemberEnumerator* classes.

```
// Team class represents a collection of TeamMember objects. Implements
// the IEnumerable interface to support enumerating TeamMember objects.
public class Team : IEnumerable {

    // TeamMemberEnumerator is a private nested class that provides
    // the functionality to enumerate the TeamMembers contained in
    // a Team collection. As a nested class, TeamMemberEnumerator
    // has access to the private members of the Team class.
    private class TeamMemberEnumerator : IEnumerator {

        // The Team that this object is enumerating.
        private Team sourceTeam;

        // Boolean to indicate whether underlying Team has changed
        // and so is invalid for further enumeration.
        private bool teamInvalid = false;

        // Integer to identify the current TeamMember. Provides
        // the index of the TeamMember in the underlying ArrayList
        // used by the Team collection. Initialize to -1, which is
        // the index prior to the first element.
        private int currentMember = -1;

        // Constructor takes a reference to the Team that is the source
        // of enumerated data.
        internal TeamMemberEnumerator(Team team) {

            this.sourceTeam = team;

            // Register with sourceTeam for change notifications
            sourceTeam.TeamChange +=
                new TeamChangedEventHandler(this.TeamChange);
        }

        // Implement the IEnumerator.Current property.
        public object Current {
            get {
```

```
            // If the TeamMemberEnumerator is positioned before
            // the first element or after the last element then
            // throw an exception.
            if (currentMember == -1 ||
                currentMember > (sourceTeam.teamMembers.Count-1)) {

                throw new InvalidOperationException();
            }

            //Otherwise, return the current TeamMember
            return sourceTeam.teamMembers[currentMember];
        }
    }

    // Implement the IEnumerator.MoveNext method.
    public bool MoveNext() {

        // If underlying Team is invalid, throw exception
        if (teamInvalid) {

            throw new InvalidOperationException("Team modified");
        }

        // Otherwise, progress to the next TeamMember
        currentMember++;

        // Return false if we have moved past the last TeamMember
        if (currentMember > (sourceTeam.teamMembers.Count-1)) {
            return false;
        } else {
            return true;
        }
    }

    // Implement the IEnumerator.Reset method.
    // This method resets the position of the TeamMemberEnumerator
    // to the beginning of the Team collection.
    public void Reset() {

        // If underlying Team is invalid, throw exception
        if (teamInvalid) {

            throw new InvalidOperationException("Team modified");
        }

        // Move the currentMember pointer back to the index
        // preceding the first element.
        currentMember = -1;
    }
```

```csharp
        // An event handler to handle notifications that the underlying
        // Team collection has changed.
        internal void TeamChange(Team t, EventArgs e) {

            // Signal that the underlying Team is now invalid
            teamInvalid = true;
        }
    }

    // A delegate that specifies the signature that all team change event
    // handler methods must implement.
    public delegate void TeamChangedEventHandler(Team t, EventArgs e);

    // An ArrayList to contain the TeamMember objects
    private ArrayList teamMembers;

    // The event used to notify TeamMemberEnumerators that the Team
    // has changed.
    public event TeamChangedEventHandler TeamChange;

    // Team constructor
    public Team() {

        teamMembers = new ArrayList();
    }

    // Implement the IEnumerable.GetEnumerator method.
    public IEnumerator GetEnumerator() {
        return new TeamMemberEnumerator(this);
    }

    // Adds a TeamMember object to the Team
    public void AddMember(TeamMember member) {

        teamMembers.Add(member);

        // Notify listeners that the list has changed
        if (TeamChange != null) {

            TeamChange(this, null);
        }
    }
}
```

If your collection class contains different types of data that you want to enumerate separately, implementing the *IEnumerable* interface on the collection class is insufficient. In this case, you would implement a number of properties that returned different *IEnumerator* instances. For example, if the *Team* class represented both the team members and hardware assigned to the team, you might implement properties like those shown here.

```
// Property to enumerate team members
public IEnumerator Members {
    get {
        return new TeamMemberEnumerator(this);
    }
}


// Property to enumerate team computers
public IEnumerator Computers {
    get {
        return new TeamComputerEnumerator(this);
    }
}
```

To use these different enumerators, you would use the following code:

```
Team team = new Team();
    :
foreach(TeamMember in team.Members) {
    // Do something...
}

foreach(TeamComputer in team.Computers) {
    // Do something...
}
```

> **Note**   The *foreach* statement also supports types that implement a pattern equivalent to that defined by the *IEnumerable* and *IEnumerator* interfaces, even though the type doesn't implement the interfaces. However, your code is clearer and more easily understood if you implement the *IEnumerable* interface. See the C# Language Specification for details on the exact requirements of the *forcach* statement (*http://msdn.microsoft.com/net/ecma/*).

16.5 Implement a Disposable Class

Problem

You need to create a class that references unmanaged resources and provide a mechanism for users of the class to free those unmanaged resources deterministically.

Solution

Implement the *System.IDisposable* interface, and release the unmanaged resources when client code calls the *IDisposable.Dispose* method.

Discussion

An unreferenced object continues to exist on the heap and consume resources until the garbage collector releases the object and reclaims the resources. The garbage collector will automatically free managed resources (such as memory), but it won't free unmanaged resources (such as file handles and database connections) referenced by managed objects. If an object contains data members that reference unmanaged resources, the object must free those resources explicitly.

One solution is to declare a destructor—or finalizer—for the class; destructor is a C# term equivalent to the more general .NET term finalizer. Prior to reclaiming the memory consumed by an instance of the class, the garbage collector calls the object's finalizer. The finalizer can take the necessary steps to release any unmanaged resources. Unfortunately, because the garbage collector uses a single thread to execute all finalizers, use of finalizers can have a detrimental effect on the efficiency of the garbage collection process, which will affect the performance of your application. In addition, you can't control when the runtime frees unmanaged resources because you can't call an object's finalizer directly, and you have only limited control over the activities of the garbage collector using the *System.GC* class.

As an alternative to using finalizers, the .NET Framework defines the *Dispose pattern* as a means to provide deterministic control over when the runtime frees unmanaged resources. To implement the Dispose pattern, a class must implement the *IDisposable* interface, which declares a single method named *Dispose*. In the *Dispose* method, you must implement the code necessary to release any unmanaged resources.

Instances of classes that implement the Dispose pattern are called *disposable objects*. When code has finished with a disposable object, it calls the object's *Dispose* method to free unmanaged resources, still relying on the garbage collector to eventually release the object's managed resources. It's important to understand that the runtime doesn't enforce disposal of objects; it's the responsibility of the client to call the *Dispose* method. However, because the .NET Framework class library uses the Dispose pattern extensively, C# provides the *using* statement to simplify the correct use of disposable objects with the using statement. The following code shows the structure of a using statement:

```
using (FileStream fileStream = new FileStream("SomeFile.txt", FileMode.Open)) {
    // Do something with the fileStream object
}
```

Here are some points to consider when implementing the Dispose pattern:

- Client code should be able to call the *Dispose* method repeatedly with no adverse effects.

- In multithreaded applications, it's important that only one thread execute the *Dispose* method concurrently. It's normally the responsibility of the client code to ensure thread synchronization, although you could decide to implement synchronization within the *Dispose* method.

- The *Dispose* method should not throw exceptions.

- Because the *Dispose* method does all necessary clearing up, there's no need to call the object's finalizer. Your *Dispose* method should call the *GC.SuppressFinalize* method to ensure the finalizer isn't called during garbage collection.

- Implement a finalizer that calls the *Dispose* method as a safety mechanism in case client code doesn't call *Dispose* correctly. However, avoid referencing managed objects in finalizers because you can't be certain of the object's state.

- If a disposable class extends another disposable class, the *Dispose* method of the child must call the *Dispose* method of its base class. Wrap the child's code in a *try* block and call the parent's *Dispose* method in a *finally* clause to ensure execution.

- Other methods and properties of the class should throw a *System.ObjectDisposedException* if client code attempts to execute a method on an already disposed object.

The *DisposeExample* class contained in the following listing demonstrates a common implementation of the Dispose pattern:

```
using System;

// Implement the IDisposable interface
public class DisposeExample : IDisposable {

    // Private data member to signal if the object has already been
    // disposed
    bool isDisposed = false;

    // Private data member that holds the handle to an unmanaged resource
    private IntPtr resourceHandle;

    // Constructor
    public DisposeExample() {

        // Constructor code obtains reference to unmanaged resource.
        // resourceHandle = ...
    }

    // Destructor / Finalizer. Because Dispose calls GC.SuppressFinalize,
    // this method is only called by the garbage collection process if
    // the consumer of the object does not call Dispose as they should.
    ~DisposeExample() {

        // Call the Dispose method as opposed to duplicating the code to
        // clean up any unmanaged resources. Use the protected Dispose
        // overload and pass a value of "false" to indicate that Dispose is
        // being called during the garbage collection process, not by
        // consumer code.
        Dispose(false);
    }

    // Public implementation of the IDisposable.Dispose method, called
    // by the consumer of the object in order to free unmanaged resources
    // deterministically.
    public void Dispose() {

        // Call the protected Dispose overload and pass a value of "true"
        // to indicate that Dispose is being called by consumer code, not
        // by the garbage collector.
        Dispose(true);

        // Because the Dispose method performs all necessary clean up,
        // ensure the garbage collector does not call the class destructor.
        GC.SuppressFinalize(this);
    }
```

```
// Protected overload of the Dispose method. The disposing argument
// signals whether the method is called by consumer code (true), or by
// the garbage collector (false).
protected virtual void Dispose(bool disposing) {

    // Don't try to Dispose of the object twice
    if (!isDisposed) {

        // Determine if consumer code or the garbage collector is
        // calling. Avoid referencing other managed objects during
        // finalization.
        if (disposing) {

            // Method called by consumer code. Call the Dispose method
            // of any managed data members that implement the
            // IDisposable interface.
            // :
        }

        // Whether called by consumer code or the garbage collector,
        // free all unmanaged resources and set the value of managed
        // data members to null.
        // Close(resourceHandle);
    }

    // Signal that this object has been disposed.
    isDisposed = true;
}

// Before executing any functionality, ensure that Dispose has not
// already been executed on the object.
public void SomeMethod() {

    // Throw an exception if the object has already been disposed
    if (isDisposed) {

        throw new ObjectDisposedException("DisposeExample");
    }

    // Execute method functionality.
    // :
}

public static void Main() {

    // The using statement ensures the Dispose method is called
    // even if an exception occurs.
    using (DisposeExample d = new DisposeExample()) {
```

```
                // Do something with d
            }
        }
    }
```

16.6 Implement a Formattable Type

Problem

You need to implement a type that you can use in formatted strings, which can create different string representations of its content based on the use of format specifiers.

Solution

Implement the *System.IFormattable* interface.

Discussion

The following code fragment demonstrates the use of format specifiers in the *WriteLine* method of the *System.Console* class. The codes in the braces (emphasized in the example) are the format specifiers.

```
double a = 345678.5678;
uint b = 12000;
byte c = 254;
Console.WriteLine("a = {0}, b = {1}, and c = {2}", a, b, c);
Console.WriteLine("a = {0:c0}, b = {1:n4}, and c = {2,10:x5}", a, b, c);
```

When run on a machine configured with English (U.K.) regional settings, this code will result in the output shown here. As you can see, changing the contents of the format specifiers changes the format of the output significantly even though the data has not changed.

```
a = 345678.5678, b = 12000, and c = 254
a = £345,679, b = 12,000.0000, and c =      000fe
```

To enable support for format specifiers in your own types, you must implement the *IFormattable* interface. *IFormattable* declares a single method named *ToString* with the following signature:

```
string ToString(string format, IFormatProvider formatProvider);
```

The *format* argument is a *System.String* containing a *format string*. The format string is the portion of the format specifier that follows the colon. For example, in the format specifier {2,10:x5}, from the previous example, "x5" is the format string. The format string contains the instructions the *IFormattable* instance should use when it's generating the string representation of its content. The .NET Framework documentation for *IFormattable* states that types that implement *IFormattable* must support the "G" (general) format string, but that the other supported format strings are implementation dependent. The *format* argument will be *null* if the format specifier doesn't include a format string component, for example {0} or {1,20}.

The *formatProvider* argument is a reference to a *System.IFormatProvider* instance, which provides access to information about the cultural and regional preferences to use when generating the string representation of the *IFormatta ble* object. This information includes data such as the appropriate currency symbol to use or the number of decimal places to use. By default, *formatProvider* is *null*, which means you should use the current thread's regional and cultural settings, which are available through the *static* method *CurrentCulture* of the *System.Globalization.CultureInfo* class. Some methods that generate formatted strings, such as *String.Format*, allow you to specify an alternative *IFormat-Provider* to use.

The .NET Framework uses *IFormattable* primarily to support the formatting of value types, but it can be used to good effect with any type. The following example contains a class named *Person* that implements the *IFormattable* interface. The *Person* class contains the title and names of a person and will render the person name in different formats depending on the format strings provided. The *Person* class doesn't make use of regional and cultural settings provided by the *formatProvider* argument.

```
using System;

public class Person : IFormattable {

    // Private members to hold the person's title and name details.
    private string title;
    private string[] names;

    // Constructor used to set the person's title and names.
    public Person(string title, params string[] names) {

        this.title = title;
        this.names = names;
    }

    // Override the Object.ToString method to return the person's
    // name using the general format.
    public override string ToString() {
        return ToString("G", null);
    }
```

```
// Implementation of the IFormattable.ToString method to return the
// person's name in different forms based on the format string
// provided.
public string ToString(string format, IFormatProvider formatProvider) {

    string result = null;

    // Use the general format if none is specified
    if (format == null) format = "G";

    // The contents of the format string determine the format of the
    // name returned.
    switch (format.ToUpper()[0]) {

        case 'S':
            // Use short form - first initial and surname
            result = names[0][0] + ". " + names[names.Length-1];
            break;

        case 'P':
            // Use polite form - title, initials, and surname
            // Add the person's title to the result
            if (title != null && title.Length != 0) {
                result = title + ". ";
            }
            // Add the person's initials and surname
            for (int count = 0; count < names.Length; count++) {

                if ( count != (names.Length - 1)) {
                    result += names[count][0] + ". ";
                } else {
                    result += names[count];
                }
            }
            break;

        case 'I':
            // Use informal form - first name only
            result = names[0];
            break;

        case 'G':
        default:
            // Use general/default form - first name and surname
            result = names[0] + " " + names[names.Length-1];
            break;
```

```
        }
        return result;
    }
}
```

The following code demonstrates how to use the formatting capabilities of the *Person* class:

```
// Create a Person object representing a man with the name
// Mr. Richard Glen David Peters.
Person person =
    new Person("Mr", "Richard", "Glen", "David", "Peters");

// Display the person's name using a variety of format strings.
System.Console.WriteLine("Dear {0:G},", person);
System.Console.WriteLine("Dear {0:P},", person);
System.Console.WriteLine("Dear {0:I},", person);
System.Console.WriteLine("Dear {0},", person);
System.Console.WriteLine("Dear {0:S},", person);
```

When executed, the code produces the following output:

```
Dear Richard Peters,
Dear Mr. R. G. D. Peters,
Dear Richard,
Dear Richard Peters,
Dear R. Peters,
```

16.7 Implement a Custom Exception Class

Problem

You need to create a custom exception class so that you can use the runtime's exception-handling mechanism to handle application-specific exceptions.

Solution

Create a serializable class that extends the *System.ApplicationException* class and implements constructors with these signatures.

```
public CustomException() : base() {}
public CustomException(string message): base(message) {}
public CustomException(string message, Exception inner)
    : base(message, inner) {}
```

Add support for any custom data members required by the exception, including constructors and properties required to manipulate the data members.

Discussion

Exception classes are unique in the fact that you do not declare new classes solely to implement new or extended functionality. The runtime's exception-handling mechanism—exposed by the C# statements *try*, *catch*, and *finally*—works based on the *type* of exception thrown, not the functional or data members implemented by the thrown exception.

If you need to throw an exception, you should use an existing exception class from the .NET Framework class library, if a suitable one exists. For example, some useful exceptions include

- *System.ArgumentNullException*, when code passes a *null* argument value to your method that doesn't support null arguments.

- *System.ArgumentOutOfRangeException*, when code passes an inappropriately large or small argument value to your method.

- *System.FormatException*, when code attempts to pass your method a *String* argument containing incorrectly formatted data.

If there's no suitable exception class to meet your needs, or you feel your application would benefit from using application-specific exceptions, it's a simple matter to create your own exception class. In order to integrate your custom exception with the runtime's exception-handling mechanism and remain consistent with the pattern implemented by .NET Framework–defined exception classes, you should

- Give your exception class a meaningful name ending in the word *Exception*, for example, *TypeMismatchException* or *RecordNotFound-Exception*.

- Extend the *ApplicationException* class. Your custom exception must ultimately extend the *System.Exception* class, or the compiler will raise an error when you try to *throw* the exception; *Application-Exception* extends *Exception* and is the recommended base for all application-specific exception classes.

- Mark your exception class as *sealed* if you do not intend other exception classes to extend it.

- Implement additional data members and properties to support custom information that the exception class should provide.

- Implement three *public* constructors with the signatures shown here and ensure they call the base class constructor.

```
public CustomException() : base() {}
public CustomException(string message): base(message) {}
public CustomException(string message, Exception inner)
    : base(message, inner) {}
```

■ Make your exception class serializable so that the runtime can marshal instances of your exception across application domain and machine boundaries. Applying the attribute *System.Serializable-Attribute* is sufficient for exception classes that don't implement custom data members. However, because *Exception* implements the interface *System.Runtime.Serialization.ISerializable*, if your exception declares custom data members, you must override the *ISerializable.GetObjectData* method of the *Exception* class as well as implement a deserialization constructor with this signature. If your exception class is *sealed*, mark the deserialization constructor as *private*; otherwise mark it *protected*.

```
private CustomException(SerializationInfo info,
    StreamingContext context) {}
```

The *GetObjectData* method and deserialization constructor must call the equivalent base class method to allow the base class to serialize and deserialize its data correctly. (See recipe 16.1 for details on making classes serializable.)

The *CustomException* class shown here is a custom exception that extends *ApplicationException* and declares two custom data members: a *string* named *stringInfo* and a *bool* named *booleanInfo*.

```
using System;
using System.Runtime.Serialization;

// Mark CustomException as Serializable.
[Serializable]
public sealed class CustomException : ApplicationException {

    // Custom data members for CustomException.
    private string stringInfo;
    private bool booleanInfo;

    // Three standard constructors and simply call the base class
    // constructor (System.ApplicationException).
    public CustomException() : base() {}

    public CustomException(string message): base(message) {}

    public CustomException(string message, Exception inner)
        : base(message, inner) {}
```

```
// The deserialization constructor required by the ISerialization
// interface. Because CustomException is sealed, this constructor
// is private. If CustomException were not sealed, this constructor
// should be declared as protected so that derived classes can call
// it during deserialization.
private CustomException(SerializationInfo info,
    StreamingContext context) : base (info, context) {

    // Deserialize each custom data member.
    stringInfo = info.GetString("StringInfo");
    booleanInfo = info.GetBoolean("BooleanInfo");
}


// Additional constructors to allow code to set the custom data
// members.
public CustomException(string message, string stringInfo,
    bool booleanInfo): this(message) {

    this.stringInfo = stringInfo;
    this.booleanInfo = booleanInfo;
}


public CustomException(string message, Exception inner,
    string stringInfo, bool booleanInfo) : this(message, inner) {

    this.stringInfo = stringInfo;
    this.booleanInfo = booleanInfo;
}


// Read only properties that provide access to the custom data members.
public string StringInfo {
    get { return stringInfo; }
}


public bool BooleanInfo {
    get { return booleanInfo; }
}


// The GetObjectData method (declared in the ISerializable interface)
// is used during serialization of CustomException. Because
// CustomException declares custom data members, it must override the
// base class implementation of GetObjectData.
public override void GetObjectData(SerializationInfo info,
    StreamingContext context) {

    // Serialize the custom data members
    info.AddValue("StringInfo", stringInfo);
    info.AddValue("BooleanInfo", booleanInfo);
```

```
        // Call the base class to serialize its members
        base.GetObjectData(info, context);
    }

    // Override the base class Message property to include the custom data
    // members.
    public override string Message {
        get {
            string message = base.Message;
            if (stringInfo != null) {
                message += Environment.NewLine +
                    stringInfo + " = " + booleanInfo;
            }
            return message;
        }
    }
}
```

In large applications, you will usually implement quite a few custom exception classes. It pays to put significant thought into how you organize your custom exceptions and how code will use them. Generally, avoid creating new exception classes unless code will make specific efforts to catch that exception; use data members to achieve informational granularity, not additional exception classes. In addition, avoid deep class hierarchies when possible in favor of broad, shallow hierarchies.

16.8 Implement a Custom Event Argument

Problem

When you raise an event, you need to pass an event-specific state to the event handlers.

Solution

Create a custom event argument class derived from the *System.EventArg* class. When you raise the event, create an instance of your event argument class and pass it to the event handlers.

Discussion

When you declare your own event types, you will often want to pass event-specific state to any listening event handlers. To create a custom event argument class that complies with the *Event pattern* defined by the .NET Framework, you should

■   Derive your custom event argument class from the *EventArgs* class. The *EventArgs* class contains no data and is used with events that don't need to pass event state.

■   Give your event argument class a meaningful name ending in the word *EventArgs*, for example, *DiskFullEventArgs* or *MailReceived-EventArgs*.

■   Mark your argument class as *sealed* if you do not intend other event argument classes to extend it.

■   Implement additional data members and properties to support event state that you need to pass to event handlers. It's best to make event state immutable, so you should use *private readonly* data members and use *public* properties to provide read-only access to the data members.

■   Implement a *public* constructor that supports the initial configuration of the event state.

■   Make your event argument class serializable so that the runtime can marshal instances of it across application domain and machine boundaries. Applying the attribute *System.SerializableAttribute* is usually sufficient for event argument classes. However, if your class has special serialization requirements, you must also implement the interface *System.Runtime.Serialization.ISerializable*. (See recipe 16.1 for details on making classes serializable.)

The following listing shows the implementation of an event argument class named *MailReceivedEventArgs*. Theoretically, an e-mail server passes instances of the *MailReceivedEventArgs* class to event handlers in response to the receipt of an e-mail message. The *MailReceivedEventArgs* class contains information about the sender and subject of the received e-mail message.

```
using System;

[Serializable]
public sealed class MailReceivedEventArgs : EventArgs {

    // Private read-only members that hold the event state that is to be
    // distributed to all event handlers. The MailReceivedEventArgs class
    // will specify who sent the received mail and what the subject is.
    private readonly string from;
    private readonly string subject;
```

```
    // Constructor, initializes event state
    public MailReceivedEventArgs(string from, string subject) {

        this.from = from;
        this.subject = subject;
    }

    // Read-only properties to provide access to event state
    public string From { get { return from; } }
    public string Subject { get { return subject; } }
}
```

16.9 Implement the Singleton Pattern

Problem

You need to ensure that only a single instance of a type exists at any given time and that the single instance is accessible to all elements of your application.

Solution

Implement the type using the "Singleton Pattern" by

■   Implementing a *private static* member within the type to hold a reference to the single instance of the type.

■   Implementing a publicly accessible *static* property in the type to provide read-only access to the singleton instance.

■   Implementing a *private* constructor so that code can't create additional instances of the type.

Discussion

Of all the identified patterns, the Singleton Pattern is perhaps the most widely known and commonly used. The purpose of the Singleton Pattern is to ensure that only one instance of a type exists at a given time and to provide global access to the functionality of that single instance. The following code demonstrates an implementation of the Singleton Pattern for a class named *SingletonExample*:

```
public class SingletonExample {

    // A static member to hold a reference to the singleton instance
    private static SingletonExample instance;
```

```
    // A static constructor to create the singleton instance. Another
    // alternative is to use lazy initialization in the Instance property.
    static SingletonExample () {
        instance = new SingletonExample();
        }

    // A private constructor to stop code from creating additional
    // instances of the singleton type
    private SingletonExample () {}

    // A public property to provide access to the singleton instance
    public static SingletonExample Instance {

        get { return instance; }
    }

    // Public methods that provide singleton functionality
    public void SomeMethod1 () { /*..*/ }
    public void SomeMethod2 () { /*..*/ }
}
```

To invoke the functionality of the *SingletonExample* class, you can obtain a reference to the singleton using the *Instance* property and then call its methods. Alternatively, you can execute members of the singleton directly through the *Instance* property. The following code shows both approaches.

```
// Obtain reference to singleton and invoke methods
SingletonExample s = SingletonExample.Instance;
s.SomeMethod1();

// Execute singleton functionality without a reference
SingletonExample.Instance.SomeMethod2();
```

16.10 Implement the Observer Pattern

Problem

You need to implement an efficient mechanism for an object (the subject) to notify other objects (the observers) about changes to its state.

Solution

Implement the *Observer Pattern* using delegate types as type-safe function pointers and event types to manage and notify the set of observers.

Discussion

The traditional approach to implementing the Observer Pattern is to implement two interfaces: one to represent an observer (*IObserver*) and the other to represent the subject (*ISubject*). Objects that implement *IObserver* register with the subject, indicating that they want to be notified of important events (such as state changes) affecting the subject. The subject is responsible for managing the list of registered observers and notifying them in response to events affecting the subject. The subject usually notifies observers by calling a *Notify* method declared in the *IObserver* interface. The subject might pass data to the observer as part of the *Notify* method, or the observer might need to call a method declared in the *ISubject* interface to obtain additional details about the event.

Although you are free to implement the Observer Pattern in C# using the approach just described, the Observer Pattern is so pervasive in modern software solutions that C# and the .NET Framework include event and delegate types to simplify its implementation. The use of events and delegates means that you don't need to declare *IObserver* and *ISubject* interfaces. In addition, you don't need to implement the logic necessary to manage and notify the set of registered observers—the area where most coding errors occur.

The .NET Framework uses one particular implementation of the event-based and delegate-based Observer Pattern so frequently that it has been given its own name—the *Event pattern*. (Pattern purists might prefer the name *Event idiom*, but I will stick to the name most commonly used in Microsoft documentation.)

The ObserverExample.cs file in the sample code for this chapter contains a complete implementation of the Event pattern. The example contains the following types:

- *Thermostat* class (the subject of the example), which keeps track of the current temperature and notifies observers when a temperature change occurs.

- *TemperatureChangeEventArgs* class, which is a custom implementation of the *System.EventArgs* class used to encapsulate temperature change data for distribution during the notification of observers.

- *TemperatureEventHandler* delegate, which defines the signature of the method that all observers of a *Thermostat* object must implement, and which a *Thermostat* object will call in the event of temperature changes.

- *TemperatureChangeObserver* and *TemperatureAverageObserver* classes, which are observers of the *Thermostat* class.

The *TemperatureChangeEventArgs* class (in the following listing) derives from the class *System.EventArgs*. The custom event argument class should contain all of the data that the subject needs to pass to its observers when it notifies them of an event. If you don't need to pass data with your event notifications, you don't need to define a new argument class; simply pass a *null* argument when you raise the event. See recipe 16.8 for details on implementing custom event argument classes.

```
// An event argument class that contains information about a temperature
// change event. An instance of this class is passed with every event.
public class TemperatureChangeEventArgs : System.EventArgs {

    // Private data members contain the old and new temperature readings
    private readonly int oldTemperature, newTemperature;

    // Constructor that takes the old and new temperature values
    public TemperatureChangeEventArgs(int oldTemp, int newTemp) {

        oldTemperature = oldTemp;
        newTemperature = newTemp;
    }

    // Read-only properties provide access to the temperature values
    public int OldTemperature { get { return oldTemperature; } }
    public int NewTemperature { get { return newTemperature; } }
}
```

The following code shows the declaration of the *TemperatureEventHandler* delegate. Based on this declaration, all observers must implement a method (the name is unimportant), which returns *void* and takes two arguments: a *Thermostat* object as the first argument and a *TemperatureChangeEventArgs* object as the second. During notification, the *Thermostat* argument refers to the *Thermostat* object that raises the event, and the *TemperatureChangeEventArgs* argument contains data about the old and new temperature values.

```
// A delegate that specifies the signature that all temperature event
// handler methods must implement
public delegate void TemperatureEventHandler(Thermostat s,
    TemperatureChangeEventArgs e);
```

The *Thermostat* class is the observed object in this Observer (Event) pattern. In theory, a monitoring device sets the current temperature by calling the *Temperature* property on a *Thermostat* object. This causes the *Thermostat* object to raise its *TemperatureChange* event and send a *TemperatureChangeEventArgs* object to each observer. Here is the code for the *Thermostat* class.

```
// A class that represents a thermostat, which is the source of temperature
// change events. In the "Observer" pattern, a thermostat object is the
// "Subject" that "Observers" listen to for change notifications.
public class Thermostat {

    // Private field to hold current temperature
    private int temperature = 0;

    // The event used to maintain a list of observer delegates and raise
    // a temperature change event when a temperature change occurs
    public event TemperatureEventHandler TemperatureChange;

    // A protected method used to raise the TemperatureChange event.
    // Because events can be triggered only from within the containing
    // type, using a protected method to raise the event allows derived
    // classes to provide customized behavior and still be able to raise
    // the base class event.
    virtual protected void RaiseTemperatureEvent
        (TemperatureChangeEventArgs e) {

        // Notify all observers. A test for null indicates whether any
        // observers are registered
        if (TemperatureChange != null) {

            TemperatureChange(this, e);
        }
    }

    // Public property to get and set the current temperature. The "set"
    // side of the property is responsible for raising the temperature
    // change event to notify all observers of a change in temperature.
    public int Temperature {

        get { return temperature; }

        set {
            // Create a new event argument object containing the old and
            // new temperatures
            TemperatureChangeEventArgs e =
                new TemperatureChangeEventArgs(temperature, value);

            // Update the current tempertature
            temperature = value;

            // Raise the temperature change event
            RaiseTemperatureEvent(e);
        }
    }
}
```

For the purpose of demonstrating the Observer Pattern, the example contains two different observer types: *TemperatureAverageObserver* and *TemperatureChangeObserver*. Both classes have the same basic implementation. *TemperatureAverageObserver* keeps a count of the number of temperature change events and the sum of the temperature values and displays an average temperature when each event occurs. *TemperatureChangeObserver* displays information about the change in temperature each time a temperature change event occurs.

The following listing shows the *TemperatureChangeObserver* class. (See the sample file for *TemperatureAverageObserver* code.) Notice that the constructor takes a reference to the *Thermostat* object that the *TemperatureChangeObserver* object should observe. When you instantiate an observer, pass it a reference to the subject. The observer must create a delegate instance containing a reference to the observer's event-handler method. To register as an observer, the observer object must then add its delegate instance to the subject using the subject's *public* event member.

Once the *TemperatureChangeObserver* object has registered its delegate instance with the *Thermostat* object, you need to maintain a reference to the delegate only if you want to stop observing the subject later. In addition, there's no need to maintain a reference to the subject because a reference to the event source is included as the first argument each time the *Thermostat* object raises an event through the *TemperatureChange* method.

```
// A Thermostat observer that displays information about the change in
// temperature when a temperature change event occurs
public class TemperatureChangeObserver {

    // A constructor that takes a reference to the Thermostat object that
    // the TemperatureChangeObserver object should observe
    public TemperatureChangeObserver(Thermostat t) {

        // Create a new TemperatureEventHandler delegate instance and
        // register it with the specified Thermostat
        t.TemperatureChange +=
            new TemperatureEventHandler(this.TemperatureChange);
    }

    // The method to handle temperature change events
    public void TemperatureChange(Thermostat sender,
        TemperatureChangeEventArgs temp) {

        System.Console.WriteLine
            ("ChangeObserver: Old={0}, New={1}, Change={2}",
```

```
            temp.OldTemperature, temp.NewTemperature,
            temp.NewTemperature - temp.OldTemperature);
    }
}
```

The *Thermostat* class defines a *Main* method (shown here) that drives the example. After creating a *Thermostat* object and two different observer objects, the *Main* method repeatedly prompts you to enter a temperature. Each time you enter a new temperature, the *Thermostat* object notifies the listeners, which display information to the console.

```
public static void Main() {

    // Create a Thermostat instance
    Thermostat t = new Thermostat();

    // Create the Thermostat observers
    new TemperatureChangeObserver(t);
    new TemperatureAverageObserver(t);

    // Loop, getting temperature readings from the user.
    // Any non-integer value will terminate the loop.
    do {

        System.Console.Write("\n\rEnter current temperature: ");

        try {
            // Convert the user's input to an integer and use it to set
            // the current temperature of the thermostat
            t.Temperature =
                System.Int32.Parse(System.Console.ReadLine());

        } catch (System.Exception) {
            // Use the exception condition to trigger termination
            System.Console.WriteLine("Terminating ObserverExample.");
            return;
        }
    } while (true);
}
```

The following listing shows the kind of output you should expect if you build and run ObserverExample.cs. The bolded values show your input.

```
Enter current temperature: 50
ChangeObserver: Old=0, New=50, Change=50
AverageObserver: Average=50.00

Enter current temperature: 20
```

```
ChangeObserver: Old=50, New=20, Change=-30
AverageObserver: Average=35.00

Enter current temperature: 40
ChangeObserver: Old=20, New=40, Change=20
AverageObserver: Average=36.67
```

17

Windows Integration

The intention is for the Microsoft .NET Framework to run on a wide variety of operating systems to improve code mobility and simplify cross-platform integration. At the time this book was written, versions of the .NET Framework were available for various operating systems, including Microsoft Windows, FreeBSD, Linux, and Mac OS X. However, many of these implementations are still incomplete or yet to be widely adopted. Microsoft Windows is currently the operating system on which the .NET Framework is most commonly installed. The recipes in this chapter focus on performing the following tasks that are specific to the Windows operating system:

- Retrieving run-time environment information (recipes 17.1 and 17.2)
- Writing to the Windows event log (recipe 17.3)
- Accessing the Windows registry (recipe 17.4)
- Creating and installing Windows services (recipes 17.5 and 17.6)
- Creating a shortcut on the Windows Start menu or desktop (recipe 17.7)

> **Note** The majority of functionality discussed in this chapter is protected by code access security permissions enforced by the common language runtime (CLR). See Chapter 13 for information about code access security, and see the .NET Framework SDK documentation for the specific permissions required to execute each member.

17.1 Access Run-Time Environment Information

Problem

You need to access information about the run-time environment in which your application is running.

Solution

Use the members of the *System.Environment* class.

Discussion

The *Environment* class provides a set of *static* members that you can use to obtain (and in some cases modify) information about the environment in which an application is running. Table 17-1 describes some of the most commonly used *Environment* members.

Table 17-1 Commonly Used Members of the *Environment* Class

Member	Description
Property	
CommandLine	Gets a *string* containing the command line used to execute the current application, including the application name; see recipe 1.5 for details.
CurrentDirectory	Gets and sets a *string* containing the current application directory. Initially, this property will contain the name of the directory in which the application was started.
HasShutdownStarted	Gets a *bool* that indicates whether the CLR has started to shutdown or the current application domain has started unloading.
MachineName	Gets a *string* containing the name of the machine.
OSVersion	Gets a *System.OperatingSystem* object that contains information about the platform and version of the underlying operating system. See the paragraph following this table for more details.
SystemDirectory	Gets a *string* containing the fully qualified path of the system directory.
TickCount	Gets an *int* representing the number of milliseconds that have elapsed since the system was started.

Table 17-1   Commonly Used Members of the *Environment* Class

Member	Description
UserDomainName	Gets a *string* containing the Windows domain name to which the current user belongs. This will be the same as *MachineName* if the machine is stand-alone.
UserInteractive	Gets a *bool* indicating whether the application is running in user interactive mode. *UserInteractive* will return *false* when the application is running as a service or is a Web application.
UserName	Gets a *string* containing the name of the user that started the current thread.
Version	Gets a *System.Version* object that contains information about the version of the CLR.
Method	
ExpandEnvironmentVariables	Replaces the names of environment variables in a *string* with the value of the variable; see recipe 17.2 for details.
GetCommandLineArgs	Returns a *string* array containing all elements of the command line used to execute the current application, including the application name; see recipe 1.5 for details.
GetEnvironmentVariable	Returns a *string* containing the value of a specified environment variable; see recipe 17.2 for details.
GetEnvironmentVariables	Returns a *System.Collections.IDictionary* containing all environment variables and their values; see recipe 17.2 for details.
GetFolderPath	Returns a *string* containing the path to a special system folder specified using the *System.Environment.Special-Folder* enumeration. This includes folders for the Internet cache, cookies, history, desktop, and favorites; see the .NET framework SDK documentation for a complete list of values.
GetLogicalDrives	Returns a *string* array containing the names of all logical drives.

The *OperatingSystem* object returned by *OSVersion* contains two properties: *Platform* and *Version*. The *Platform* property returns a value of the *System.PlatformID* enumeration identifying the current operating system; valid values are *Win32NT*, *Win32S*, *Win32Windows*, and *WinCE*. The *Version* property returns a *System.Version* object that identifies the specific operating system version. To determine the operating system on which you are running, you must use both the platform and the version information as detailed in Table 17-2.

Table 17-2 **Determining the Current Operating System**

PlatformID	Major Version	Minor Version	Operating System
Win32Windows	4	10	Windows 98
Win32Windows	4	90	Windows Me
Win32NT	4	0	Windows NT 4
Win32NT	5	0	Windows 2000
Win32NT	5	1	Windows XP
Win32NT	5	2	Windows Server 2003

The *AccessEnvironmentExample* class uses the *Environment* class to display information about the current environment to the console.

```
using System;

public class AccessEnvironmentExample {

    public static void Main() {

        // Command line.
        Console.WriteLine("Command line : " + Environment.CommandLine);

        // OS and CLR version information.
        Console.WriteLine("OS PlatformID : " +
            Environment.OSVersion.Platform);
        Console.WriteLine("OS Major Version : " +
            Environment.OSVersion.Version.Major);
        Console.WriteLine("OS Minor Version : " +
            Environment.OSVersion.Version.Minor);
        Console.WriteLine("CLR Version : " + Environment.Version);

        // User, machine, and domain name information.
        Console.WriteLine("User Name : " + Environment.UserName);
        Console.WriteLine("Domain Name : " + Environment.UserDomainName);
        Console.WriteLine("Machine name : " + Environment.MachineName);

        // Other environment information.
        Console.WriteLine("Is interactive ? : "
            + Environment.UserInteractive);
        Console.WriteLine("Shutting down ? : "
            + Environment.HasShutdownStarted);
```

```
        Console.WriteLine("Ticks since startup : "
            + Environment.TickCount);

        // Display the names of all logical drives.
        foreach (string s in Environment.GetLogicalDrives()) {
            Console.WriteLine("Logical drive : " + s);
        }

        // Standard folder information.
        Console.WriteLine("Current folder : "
            + Environment.CurrentDirectory);
        Console.WriteLine("System folder : "
            + Environment.SystemDirectory);

        // Enumerate all special folders and display them.
        foreach (Environment.SpecialFolder s in
            Enum.GetValues(typeof(Environment.SpecialFolder))) {

            Console.WriteLine("{0} folder : {1}",
                s, Environment.GetFolderPath(s));
        }

        // Wait to continue.
        Console.WriteLine("Main method complete. Press Enter.");
        Console.ReadLine();
    }
}
```

17.2 Retrieve the Value of an Environment Variable

Problem

You need to retrieve the value of an environment variable for use in your application.

Solution

Use the *GetEnvironmentVariable*, *GetEnvironmentVariables*, and *ExpandEnvironmentVariables* methods of the *Environment* class.

Discussion

The *GetEnvironmentVariable* method allows you to retrieve a string containing the value of a single named environment variable, whereas the *GetEnvironmentVariables* method returns an *IDictionary* containing the names and values of all environment variables as strings. The *ExpandEnvironmentVariables* method provides a simple mechanism for substituting the value of an environment variable into a string by including the variable name enclosed in percent signs (%) within the string. Here is an example that demonstrates the use of all three methods.

```
using System;
using System.Collections;

public class VariableExample {

    public static void Main () {

        // Retrieve a named environment variable.
        Console.WriteLine("Path = " +
            Environment.GetEnvironmentVariable("Path"));
        Console.WriteLine();

        // Substitute the value of named environment variables.
        Console.WriteLine(Environment.ExpandEnvironmentVariables(
            "The Path on %computername% is %Path%"));
        Console.WriteLine();

        // Retrieve all environment variables and display the values
        // of all that begin with the letter 'P'.
        IDictionary vars = Environment.GetEnvironmentVariables();
        foreach (string s in vars.Keys) {
            if (s.ToUpper().StartsWith("P")) {
                Console.WriteLine(s + " = " + vars[s]);
            }
        }
        Console.WriteLine();

        // Wait to continue.
        Console.WriteLine("Main method complete. Press Enter.");
        Console.ReadLine();
    }
}
```

17.3 Write an Event to the Windows Event Log

Problem

You need to write an event to the Windows event log.

Solution

Use the members of the *System.Diagnostics.EventLog* class to create a log (if required), register an event source, and write events.

Discussion

You can write to the Windows event log using the *static* methods of the *EventLog* class, or you can create an *EventLog* object and use its members. Whichever approach you choose, before writing to the event log you must decide which log you will use and register an event source against that log. The event source is simply a string that uniquely identifies your application. An event source may be registered against only one log at a time.

By default, the event log contains three separate logs: Application, System, and Security. Usually, you will write to the Application log, but you might decide that your application warrants a custom log in which to write events. You do not need to explicitly create a custom log; when you register an event source against a log, if the specified log doesn't exist, it's created automatically.

Once you have decided on the destination log and registered an event source, you can start to write event log entries using the *WriteEntry* method. *WriteEntry* provides a variety of overloads that allow you to specify some or all of the following values:

- A *string* containing the event source for the log entry (*static* versions of *WriteEntry* only).

- A *string* containing the message for the log entry.

- A value from the *System.Diagnostics.EventLogEntryType* enumeration, which identifies the type of log entry. Valid values are *Error*, *FailureAlert*, *Information*, *SuccessAudit*, and *Warning*.

- An *int* that specifies an application-specific event ID for the log entry.

- A *short* that specifies an application-specific subcategory for the log entry.

- A *byte* array containing any raw data to associate with the log entry.

The *EventLog* class shown here demonstrates the use of the *static* members of *EventLog* class to write an entry to the event log of the local machine. The methods of the *EventLog* class also provide overloads that support the writing events to the event log of remote machines; see the .NET Framework SDK documentation for more information.

```
using System;
using System.Diagnostics;

public class EventLogExample {

    public static void Main () {

        // If it does not exist, register an event source for this
        // application against the Application log of the local machine.
        // Trying to register an event source that already exists on the
        // specified machine will throw a System.ArgumentException.
        if (!EventLog.SourceExists("EventLogExample")) {

            EventLog.CreateEventSource("EventLogExample","Application");
        }

        // Write an event to the event log.
        EventLog.WriteEntry(
            "EventLogExample",                  // Registered event source
            "A simple test event.",             // Event entry message
            EventLogEntryType.Information,      // Event type
            1,                                  // Application specific ID
            0,                                  // Application specific category
            new byte[] {10, 55, 200}           // Event data
        );

        // Wait to continue.
        Console.WriteLine("Main method complete. Press Enter.");
        Console.ReadLine();
    }
}
```

17.4 Access the Windows Registry

Problem

You need to read information from, or write information to, the Windows registry.

Solution

Use the *Microsoft.Win32.Registry* class to obtain a *Microsoft.Win32.RegistryKey* object that represents the root key of a registry hive. Use the members of this *RegistryKey* object to navigate through and enumerate the registry key hierarchy as well as to read, modify, and create registry keys and values.

Discussion

It isn't possible to gain direct access to keys and values contained in the registry. You must first obtain a *RegistryKey* object that represents a base-level key and navigate through the hierarchy of *RegistryKey* objects to the key you need. The *Registry* class implements a set of seven *static* fields that return *RegistryKey* objects representing base level registry keys; Table 17-3 describes the registry location to where each of these fields maps.

Table 17-3   *Static* Fields of the *Registry* Class

Field	Registry Mapping
ClassesRoot	HKEY_CLASSES_ROOT
CurrentConfig	HKEY_CURRENT_CONFIG
CurrentUser	HKEY_CURRENT_USER
DynData	HKEY_DYN_DATA
LocalMachine	HKEY_LOCAL_MACHINE
PerformanceData	HKEY_PERFORMANCE_DATA
Users	HKEY_USERS

> **Tip**   The *static* method *RegistryKey.OpenRemoteBaseKey* allows you to open a registry base key on a remote machine. See the .NET Framework SDK documentation for details of its use.

Once you have the base level *RegistryKey* object, you must navigate to the key with which you want to work. To support navigation, the *RegistryKey* class allows you to do the following:

- Get the number of immediate subkeys using the *SubKeyCount* property.

- Get a *string* array containing the names of all subkeys using the *Get-SubKeyNames* method.

- Get a *RegistryKey* reference to a subkey using the *OpenSubKey* method. The *OpenSubKey* method provides two overloads: the first opens the named key as read-only; the second accepts a *bool* argument that if *true* will open a writable *RegistryKey* object.

Once you obtain a *RegistryKey* object that represents the registry key you need, you can create, read, update, and delete subkeys and values using the methods listed in Table 17-4. Methods that modify the contents of the key require you to have a writable *RegistryKey* object.

Table 17-4 *RegistryKey* **Methods to Create, Read, Update, and Delete Registry Keys and Values**

Method	Description
CreateSubKey	Creates a new subkey with the specified name and returns a writable *RegistryKey* object. If the specified subkey already exists, *CreateSubKey* returns a writable reference to the existing subkey.
DeleteSubKey	Deletes the subkey with the specified name, which must be empty of subkeys (but not values); otherwise, a *System.InvalidOperationException* is thrown.
DeleteSubKeyTree	Deletes the subkey with the specified name along with all of its subkeys.
DeleteValue	Deletes the value with the specified name from the current key.
GetValue	Returns the value with the specified name from the current key. The value is returned as an *object*, which you must cast to the appropriate type. The simplest form of *GetValue* returns *null* if the specified value doesn't exist. An overload allows you to specify a default value to return (instead of *null*) if the named value doesn't exist.
GetValueNames	Returns a *string* array containing the names of all values in the current registry key.
SetValue	Creates (or updates) the value with the specified name. You can't specify the registry data type used to store the value; *SetValue* chooses the data type automatically based on the type of data stored.

The *RegistryKey* class implements *IDisposable*; you should call the *IDisposable.Dispose* method to free operating system resources when you have finished with the *RegistryKey* object.

The *RegistryExample* class shown here takes a single command-line argument and recursively searches the *CurrentUser* hive of the registry looking for keys with names matching the supplied argument. When *RegistryExample* finds a match, it displays all *string* type values contained in the key to the console. The *RegistryExample* class also maintains a usage count in the registry key HKEY_CURRENT_USER\RegistryExample.

```csharp
using System;
using Microsoft.Win32;

public class RegistryExample {

    public static void Main(String[] args) {

        if (args.Length > 0) {

            // Open the CurrentUser base key.
            using(RegistryKey root = Registry.CurrentUser) {

                // Update the usage counter.
                UpdateUsageCounter(root);

                // Search recursively through the registry for any keys
                // with the specified name.
                SearchSubKeys(root, args[0]);
            }
        }

        // Wait to continue.
        Console.WriteLine("Main method complete. Press Enter.");
        Console.ReadLine();
    }

    public static void UpdateUsageCounter(RegistryKey root) {

        // Create the key where the usage count is stored, or obtain a
        // reference to an existing key.
        RegistryKey countKey = root.CreateSubKey("RegistryExample");

        // Read the current usage count value and specify a default value
        // of 0 (zero). Cast the Object to Int32, and assign to an int.
        int count = (Int32)countKey.GetValue("UsageCount", 0);

        // Write the incremented usage count back to the registry, or
        // create a new value if it does not yet exist.
        countKey.SetValue("UsageCount", ++count);
    }

    public static void SearchSubKeys(RegistryKey root, String searchKey) {

        // Loop through all subkeys contained in the current key.
        foreach (string keyname in root.GetSubKeyNames()) {

            try {
                using (RegistryKey key = root.OpenSubKey(keyname)) {
```

```
                  if (keyname == searchKey) PrintKeyValues(key);
                  SearchSubKeys(key, searchKey);
               }
         } catch (System.Security.SecurityException) {
               // Ignore SecurityException for the purpose of the example.
               // Some subkeys of HKEY_CURRENT_USER are secured and will
               // throw a SecurityException when opened.
         }
      }
   }

   public static void PrintKeyValues(RegistryKey key) {

      // Display the name of the matching subkey and the number of
      // values it contains.
      Console.WriteLine("Registry key found : {0} contains {1} values",
         key.Name, key.ValueCount);

      // Loop through the values and display.
      foreach (string valuename in key.GetValueNames()) {
         if (key.GetValue(valuename) is String) {
            Console.WriteLine("  Value : {0} = {1}",
               valuename, key.GetValue(valuename));
         }
      }
   }
}
```

The example will display output similar to the following when executed using the command **RegistryExample Environment** on a machine running Windows XP.

```
Registry key found : HKEY_CURRENT_USER\Environment contains 4 values
  Value : TEMP = C:\Documents and Settings\Allen\Local Settings\Temp
  Value : TMP = C:\Documents and Settings\Allen\Local Settings\Temp
  Value : LIB = C:\Dev\Microsoft Visual Studio .NET 2003\SDK\v1.1\Lib\
  Value : INCLUDE = C:\Dev\Microsoft Visual Studio .NET 2003\SDK\v1.1\include\
```

17.5 Create a Windows Service

Problem

You need to create an application that will run as a Windows service.

Solution

Create a class that extends *System.ServiceProcess.ServiceBase*. Use the inherited properties to control the behavior of your service, and override inherited methods to implement the functionality required. Implement a *Main* method that creates an instance of your service class and passes it to the *static Service-Base.Run* method.

Discussion

If you are using Microsoft Visual C# .NET (other than the standard edition), you can use the Windows Service project template to create a Windows service. The template provides the basic code infrastructure required by a Windows service class, which you can extend with your custom functionality. To create a Windows service manually, you must implement a class derived from the *Service-Base* class. The *ServiceBase* class provides the base functionality that allows the Windows Service Control Manager (SCM) to configure the service, operate the service as a background task, and control the life cycle of the service. The SCM also controls how other applications can control the service programmatically.

> **Important**   The *ServiceBase* class is defined in the System.Service-process assembly, so you must include a reference to this assembly when you build your service class.

To control your service, the SCM uses the seven *protected* methods inherited from *ServiceBase* class described in Table 17-5. You should override these inherited methods to implement the functionality and behavior required by your service. Not all services must support all control messages. The properties inherited from the *ServiceBase* class declare to the SCM which control messages your service supports; the property that controls each message type is specified in Table 17-5.

Table 17-5   Methods That Control the Operation of a Service

Method	Description
OnStart	All services must support the *OnStart* method, which the SCM calls to start the service. The SCM passes a *string* array containing arguments specified for the service. The *OnStart* method must return within 30 seconds or the SCM will abort the service.
OnStop	Called by the SCM to stop a service—the SCM will call *OnStop* only if the *CanStop* property is *true*.
OnPause	Called by the SCM to pause a service—the SCM will call *OnPause* only if the *CanPauseAndContinue* property is *true*.
OnContinue	Called by the SCM to continue a paused service—the SCM will call *OnContinue* only if the *CanPauseAndContinue* property is *true*.
OnShutdown	Called by the SCM when the system is shutting down—the SCM will call *OnShutdown* only if the *CanShutdown* property is *true*.
OnPowerEvent	Called by the SCM when a system-level power status change occurs, such as a laptop going into suspend mode. The SCM will call *OnPowerEvent* only if the *CanHandlePowerEvent* property is *true*.
OnCustomCommand	Allows you to extend the service control mechanism with custom control messages; see the .NET Framework SDK documentation for more details.

As mentioned in Table 17-5, the *OnStart* method must return within 30 seconds, so you shouldn't use *OnStart* to perform lengthy initialization tasks. A service class should implement a constructor that performs initialization, including configuring the inherited properties of the *ServiceBase* class. In addition to the properties that declare the control messages supported by a service, the *ServiceBase* class implements three other important properties.

■   *ServiceName* is the name used internally by the SCM to identify the service and must be set before the service is run.

■   *AutoLog* controls whether the service automatically writes entries to the event log when it receives any of the *OnStart*, *OnStop*, *OnPause*, and *OnContinue* control messages from Table 17-5.

■   *EventLog* provides access to an *EventLog* object that's preconfigured with an event source name that's the same as the *ServiceName* property registered against the Application log. (See recipe 17.3 for more information about the *EventLog* class.)

The final step in creating a service is to implement a *static Main* method. The *Main* method must create an instance of your service class and pass it as an argument to the *static* method *ServiceBase.Run*. If you want to run multiple services in a single process, you must create an array of *ServiceBase* objects and pass it to the *ServiceBase.Run* method. Although service classes have a *Main* method, you can't execute service code directly; attempting to run a service class directly results in Windows displaying the Windows Service Start Failure message box shown in Figure 17-1. Recipe 17.6 describes what you must do to install your service before it will execute.

Figure 17-1   The Windows Service Start Failure message box.

The *ServiceExample* class shown here uses a configurable *System.Timers.Timer* to write an entry to the Windows event log periodically.

```
using System;
using System.Timers;
using System.ServiceProcess;

public class ServiceExample : ServiceBase {

    // A Timer that controls when ServiceExample writes to the
    // event log.
    private System.Timers.Timer timer;

    public ServiceExample() {

        // Set the ServiceBase.ServiceName property.
        ServiceName = "ServiceExample";

        // Configure the level of control available on the service.
        CanStop = true;
        CanPauseAndContinue = true;

        // Configure the service to log important events to the
        // Application event log.
        AutoLog = true;
    }

    // The method executed when the timer expires - writes an
    // entry to the Application event log.
    private void WriteLogEntry(object sender, ElapsedEventArgs e) {
```

```
        // Use the EventLog object automatically configured by the
        // ServiceBase class to write to the event log.
        EventLog.WriteEntry("ServiceExample active : " + e.SignalTime);
    }

    protected override void OnStart(string[] args) {

        // Obtain the interval between log entry writes from the first
        // argument. Use 5000 milliseconds by default and enforce a 1000
        // millisecond minimum.
        double interval;

        try {
            interval = System.Double.Parse(args[0]);
            interval = Math.Max(1000, interval);
        } catch {
            interval = 5000;
        }

        EventLog.WriteEntry(String.Format("ServiceExample starting. " +
            "Writing log entries every {0} milliseconds...", interval));

        // Create, configure, and start a System.Timers.Timer to
        // periodically call the WriteLogEntry method. The Start
        // and Stop methods of the System.Timers.Timer class
        // make starting, pausing, resuming, and stopping the
        // service straightforward.
        timer = new Timer();
        timer.Interval = interval;
        timer.AutoReset = true;
        timer.Elapsed += new ElapsedEventHandler(WriteLogEntry);
        timer.Start();
    }

    protected override void OnStop() {

        EventLog.WriteEntry("ServiceExample stopping...");
        timer.Stop();

        // Free system resources used by the Timer object.
        timer.Dispose();
        timer = null;
    }

    protected override void OnPause() {

        if (timer != null) {
            EventLog.WriteEntry("ServiceExample pausing...");
```

```
                    timer.Stop();
            }
    }

    protected override void OnContinue() {

            if (timer != null) {
                EventLog.WriteEntry("ServiceExample resuming...");
                timer.Start();
            }
    }

    public static void Main() {

            // Create an instance of the ServiceExample class that will write
            // an entry to the Application event log. Pass the object to the
            // static ServiceBase.Run method.
            ServiceBase.Run(new ServiceExample());
    }
}
```

17.6 Create a Windows Service Installer

Problem

You have created a Windows service application and need to install it.

Solution

Extend the *System.Configuration.Install.Installer* class to create an installer class that contains the information necessary to install and configure your service class. Use the Installer tool (Installutil.exe) to perform the installation.

Discussion

As recipe 17.5 points out, you can't run service classes directly. The high level of integration with the Windows operating system and the information stored about the service in the Windows registry means that services require explicit installation.

If you have Microsoft Visual Studio .NET, you can create an installation component for your service automatically by right-clicking in the design view of your service class and selecting Add Installer from the context menu. This installation component can be called by deployment projects or the Installer tool to install your service. You can also create installer components for Windows services manually by following these steps:

1. Create a class derived from the *Installer* class.

2. Apply the attribute *System.ComponentModel.RunInstallerAttribute(true)* to the installer class.

3. In the constructor of the installer class, create a single instance of the *System.ServiceProcess.ServiceProcessInstaller* class. Set the *Account*, *User*, and *Password* properties of the *ServiceProcessInstaller* to configure the account under which your service will run.

4. In the constructor of the installer class, create one instance of the *System.ServiceProcess.ServiceInstaller* class for each individual service you want to install. Use the properties of the *ServiceInstaller* objects to configure information about each service, including the following:

    ❑   *ServiceName*, which specifies the name that Windows uses internally to identify the service. This *must* be the same as the value assigned to the *ServiceBase.ServiceName* property.

    ❑   *DisplayName*, which provides a user-friendly name for the service.

    ❑   *StartType*, which uses values of the *System.ServiceProcess.ServiceStartMode* enumeration to control whether the service is started automatically or manually or is disabled.

    ❑   *ServiceDependsUpon*, which allows you to provide a *string* array containing a set of service names that must be started before this service can start.

5. Add the *ServiceProcessInstaller* object and all *ServiceInstaller* objects to the *System.Configuration.Install.InstallerCollection* object accessed through the *Installers* property, which is inherited by your installer class from the *Installer* base class.

The *ServiceInstallerExample* class shown here is an installer for the *ServiceExample* service created in recipe 17.5. The sample code project for this recipe includes both the *ServiceExample* and *ServiceInstallerExample* classes and produces a file named ServiceInstallerExample.exe.

```
using System.ServiceProcess;
using System.Configuration.Install;
using System.ComponentModel;
```

```
[RunInstaller(true)]
public class ServiceInstallerExample : Installer {

    public ServiceInstallerExample() {

        // Instantiate and configure a ServiceProcessInstaller.
        ServiceProcessInstaller ServiceExampleProcess =
            new ServiceProcessInstaller();
        ServiceExampleProcess.Account = ServiceAccount.LocalSystem;

        // Instantiate and configure a ServiceInstaller.
        ServiceInstaller ServiceExampleInstaller =
            new ServiceInstaller();
        ServiceExampleInstaller.DisplayName =
            "C# Programmers Cookbook Service Example";
        ServiceExampleInstaller.ServiceName = "ServiceExample";
        ServiceExampleInstaller.StartType = ServiceStartMode.Automatic;

        // Add both the ServiceProcessInstaller and ServiceInstaller to
        // the Installers collection, which is inherited from the
        // Installer base class.
        Installers.Add(ServiceExampleInstaller);
        Installers.Add(ServiceExampleProcess);
    }
}
```

To install the *ServiceExample* service, build the project, navigate to the directory where the ServiceInstallerExample.exe is located (bin\debug by default), and execute the command **Installutil ServiceInstallerExample.exe**. You can then see and control the *ServiceExample* service using the Windows Computer Management console. However, despite specifying a *StartType* of *Automatic*, the service is initially installed unstarted; you must start the service manually (or restart your computer) before the service will write entries to the event log. Once the service is running, you can view the entries it writes to the Application event log using the Event Viewer application. To uninstall the *ServiceExample* service, add the /u switch to the Installutil command **Installutil /u ServiceInstallerExample.exe**.

17.7 Create a Shortcut on the Desktop or Start Menu

Problem

You need to create a shortcut on the user's desktop or start menu.

Solution

Use COM interop to access the functionality of the Windows Script Host. Create and configure an *IWshShortcut* instance that represents the shortcut. The folder in which you save the shortcut determines whether it appears on the desktop or start menus.

Discussion

The .NET Framework class library doesn't include the functionality to create desktop or start menu shortcuts; however, this is relatively easy to do using the Windows Script Host component accessed through COM Interop. Recipe 15.6 details how to create an interop assembly that provides access to a COM component. If you're using Visual Studio .NET, add a reference to the Windows Script Host Object Model listed in the COM tab of the Add Reference dialog. If you don't have Visual Studio .NET, use the Type Library Importer (Tlbimp.exe) to create an interop assembly for the wshom.ocx file, which is usually located in the Windows\System32 folder. (You can obtain the latest version of the Windows Script Host from *http://msdn.microsoft.com/scripting*. At the time of this writing, the latest version was 5.6.)

Once you have generated and imported the interop assembly into your project, follow these steps to create a desktop or start menu shortcut.

1. Instantiate a *WshShell* object, which provides access to the Windows shell.

2. Use the *SpecialFolders* property of the *WshShell* object to determine the correct path of the folder where you want to put the shortcut. You must specify the name of the folder that you want as an index to the *SpecialFolders* property. For example, to create a desktop shortcut, specify the value *Desktop*, and to create a start menu shortcut, specify *StartMenu*. Using the *SpecialFolders* property, you can obtain the path to any of the special system folders; other commonly used values include *AllUsersDesktop* and *AllUsersStartMenu*.

3. Call the *CreateShortcut* method of the *WshShell* object, and provide the fully qualified file name of the shortcut file you want to create. The file should have the extension *.lnk*. *CreateShortcut* will return an *IWshShortcut* instance.

4. Use the properties of the *IWshShortcut* instance to configure the shortcut. You can configure properties such as the executable that the shortcut references, a description for the shortcut, a hotkey sequence, and the icon displayed for the shortcut.

5. Call the *Save* method of the *IWshShortcut* instance to write the shortcut to disk. The shortcut will appear either on the desktop or in the
start menu (or elsewhere) depending on the path specified when the
IWshShortcut instance was created.

The *ShortcutExample* class creates a shortcut to Notepad.exe on both the
desktop and start menu of the current user. *ShortcutExample* creates both shortcuts by calling the *CreateShortcut* method and specifying a different destination
folder for each shortcut file. This approach makes it possible to create the shortcut file in any of the special folders returned by the *WshShell.SpecialFolders*
property. Here is the *ShortcutExample* code:

```
using System;
using IWshRuntimeLibrary;

public class ShortcutExample {

    public static void Main() {

        // Create the Notepad shortcut on the Desktop.
        CreateShortcut("Desktop");

        // Create the Notepad shortcut on the Windows Start menu of
        // the current user.
        CreateShortcut("StartMenu");

        // Wait to continue.
        Console.WriteLine("Main method complete. Press Enter.");
        Console.ReadLine();
    }

    public static void CreateShortcut(string destination) {

        // Create a WshShell instance through which to access the
        // functionality of the Windows shell.
        WshShell wshShell = new WshShell();

        // Assemble a fully qualified name that places the Notepad.lnk
        // file in the specified destination folder. You could use the
        // System.Environment.GetFolderPath method to obtain a path, but
        // the WshShell.SpecialFolders method provides access to a wider
        // range of folders. You need to create a temporary object reference
        // to the destination string to satisfy the requirements of the
        // Item method.
        object destFolder = (object)destination;
        string fileName =
```

```
            (string)wshShell.SpecialFolders.Item(ref destFolder)
            + @"\Notepad.lnk";

    // Create the shortcut object. Nothing is created in the
    // destination folder until the shortcut is saved.
    IWshShortcut shortcut =
        (IWshShortcut)wshShell.CreateShortcut(fileName);

    // Configure the fully qualified name to the executable.
    // Use the Environment class for simplicity.
    shortcut.TargetPath =
        Environment.GetFolderPath(Environment.SpecialFolder.System)
        + @"\notepad.exe";

    // Set the working directory to the Personal (My Documents) folder.
    shortcut.WorkingDirectory =
        Environment.GetFolderPath(Environment.SpecialFolder.Personal);

    // Provide a description for the shortcut.
    shortcut.Description = "Notepad Text Editor";

    // Assign a hotkey to the shortcut.
    shortcut.Hotkey = "CTRL+ALT+N";

    // Configure Notepad to always start maximized.
    shortcut.WindowStyle = 3;

    // Configure the shortcut to display the first icon in notepad.exe.
    shortcut.IconLocation = "notepad.exe, 0";

    // Save the configured shortcut file.
    shortcut.Save();
    }
}
```

Index

Symbols & Numerics

A

Allen Jones

Allen Jones is coauthor of the popular *C# for Java Developers* and *Microsoft .NET XML Web Services Step by Step* (Microsoft Press). A 13-year technology veteran, he is known for the depth of his C# and .NET expertise. Allen specializes in developing and implementing enterprise solutions, including e-commerce and security systems.

Matthew MacDonald

Matthew MacDonald is an author, educator, and MCSD developer with a passion for emerging technologies. He is the author of several books about programming with .NET, including *Microsoft Visual Basic .NET Programmer's Cookbook* (Microsoft Press), *Microsoft .NET Distributed Applications: Integrating XML Web Services and .NET Remoting* (Microsoft Press), *The Book of VB .NET* (No Starch), and *Beginning ASP.NET· Novice to Pro* (Apress). Visit his home on the web at *www.prosetech.com*.

The road to .NET
starts with the
core MCAD
self-paced training kits!

?ct the training you need to build the broadest range of applications quickly—and get industry recognition, ?ccess to inside technical information, discounts on products, invitations to special events, and more—with ?he new Microsoft Certified Application Developer (MCAD) credential. MCAD candidates must pass two core ?xams and one elective exam. The best way to prepare is with the core set of MCAD/MCSD TRAINING KITS, ?ach features a comprehensive training manual, lab exercises, reusable source code, and sample exam ?uestions. Work through the system of self-paced lessons and hands-on labs to gain practical experience ?ith essential development tasks. By the end of each course, you're ready to take the corresponding exams ?r MCAD or MCSD certification for Microsoft .NET.

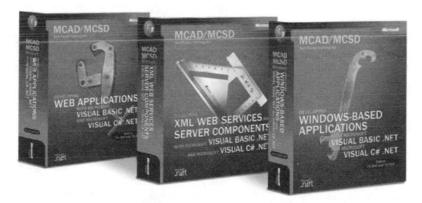

?AD/MCSD Self-Paced Training Kit: Developing
?dows®-Based Applications with Microsoft® Visual
?c® .NET and Microsoft Visual C#™ .NET
?aration for exams 70-306 and 70-316
?.A. $69.99
?ada $99.99
?N: 0-7356-1533-0

MCAD/MCSD Self-Paced Training Kit:
Developing Web Applications with Microsoft
Visual Basic .NET and Microsoft Visual C# .NET
Preparation for exams 70-305 and 70-315
U.S.A. $69.99
Canada $99.99
ISBN: 0-7356-1584-5

MCAD/MCSD Self-Paced Training Kit: Developing XML
Web Services and Server Components with Microsoft
Visual Basic .NET and Microsoft Visual C# .NET
Preparation for exams 70-310 and 70-320
U.S.A. $69.99
Canada $99.99
ISBN: 0-7356-1586-1

?rosoft Press® products are available worldwide wherever quality
?puter books are sold. For more information, contact your book or
?puter retailer, software reseller, or local Microsoft® Sales Office, or visit
?Web site at microsoft.com/mspress. To locate your nearest source for
?rosoft Press products, or to order directly, call 1-800-MSPRESS in the
?ed States (in Canada, call 1-800-268-2222).

?es and availability dates are subject to change.

Microsoft®
microsoft.com/mspress

Microsoft Press

Expert guidance for anyone who develops with
Visual Basic .NET!

Microsoft® Visual Basic® .NET Step by Step
ISBN 0-7356-1374-5

Graduate to the next generation of Visual Basic at your own pace! This primer is the fast way for any Visual Basic developer to begin creating professional applications for the Microsoft .NET platform by unleashing all the power of the .NET-ready version of Visual Basic. Learn core programming skills by selecting just the chapters you need—with code, optimization tips, advice, and samples straight from the experts. Upgrade your Visual Basic 6 applications quickly using "Upgrade Notes" sidebars, a special upgrading index, and practical advice about the Visual Basic .NET Upgrade Wizard.

Programming Microsoft Visual Basic .NET (Core reference)
ISBN 0-7356-1375-3

Accelerate your productivity with Visual Basic .NET! Building on the success of Programming Microsoft Visual Basic 6.0, this core reference equips new and veteran developers with instruction and code to get them up to speed with the Web-enabled Microsoft Visual Basic .NET environment. The book demonstrates best practices for porting and reusing existing Visual Basic code in the Microsoft .NET environment, as well as exploiting the object-oriented capabilities of the new version—complete with code samples and the book's text on CD-ROM.

Designing Enterprise Applications with Microsoft Visual Basic .NET
ISBN 0-7356-1721-X

Learn how to put the power of Visual Basic .NET to work to build enterprise applications! Most books about Microsoft Visual Basic .NET focus on the language or development environment. This book provides the detailed guidance you need to make the right design choices as you build enterprise-level applications with Visual Basic .NET. The author, who has extensive experience in designing, testing, and optimizing enterprise applications, discusses the technical and architectural tradeoffs you'll face as you develop large, multitier, distributed applications with multiple developers.

crosoft Press has many other titles to help you put the power of Visual Basic to work. To learn more about the full line of Microsoft Press® products for developers, please visit:

microsoft.com/mspress/developer